The Social Dimensions of Science

STUDIES IN SCIENCE AND THE HUMANITIES
FROM THE REILLY CENTER FOR SCIENCE,
TECHNOLOGY, AND VALUES

VOLUME III

The Social Dimensions of Science

Ernan McMullin, Editor

UNIVERSITY OF NOTRE DAME PRESS
NOTRE DAME, INDIANA 46556

Manufactured in the United States of America

Library of Congress Cataloging-in-Publication Data

The Social dimensions of science / Ernan McMullin, editor.
     p.   cm. — (Studies in science and the humanities
from the Reilly Center for Science, Technology, and
Values ; v. 3)
  Includes bibliographical references and index.
  ISBN 0-268-01741-7
  1. Science—Social aspects—History.   2. Science—
Philosophy—History. I. McMullin, Ernan, 1924– .
II. Series.
Q175.5.S589   1992
306.4'5—dc20   91–50577
                                  CIP

This volume is dedicated to Jack Reilly (Notre Dame, 1963), whose generous endowing of the Reilly Center has done much to energize the relationship of the sciences and the humanities at the University of Notre Dame.

CONTENTS

Contents

PREFACE

The development of natural science in the broadly "Galilean" style has, from the early seventeenth century onwards, furnished philosophers with a series of challenges; indeed, some would say that it has virtually dictated the agenda of philosophy since Descartes's day. Already in the Renaissance, scholars sketched the history of the oldest of the "mixed" mathematical-physical sciences, astronomy; only in the late eighteenth and early nineteenth centuries did historiography of science on a larger scale begin to come into prominence, and only in the twentieth did it take on full professional status. And only in the twentieth did the activities of scientists begin to attract the attention of sociologists, themselves exponents of a relatively new discipline. At first hesitant to turn science into an object of social inquiry like any other, with all of the implications for their own discipline that this would entail, they gradually came to recognize that the scientific community displayed a wealth of features that lent themselves particularly well to sociological inquiry. By the late 1930s, the sociology of science was launched as a new and fruitful branch of the broader discipline of sociology.

And then came the "social turn" in science studies, conventionally dated by the publication of Thomas Kuhn's *The Structure of Scientific Revolutions* in 1962. This was not, as it might at first seem, a new emphasis on sociology of science, a new directing of interest away from philosophy and history of science, on the part of those concerned to understand the complex human achievement we call "science." Rather, it was a redefining of that achievement itself, with profound and controversial consequences for the traditional disciplines of philosophy of science and history of science. If science is not just a set of propositions about the natural and social worlds but is itself *constitutively* social, then it has to be approached (it would seem) in a new way. The assumption underlying classical philosophy of science was that something like a logic could be discerned in the patterns of inference underlying scientific claims to "knowledge." How was this to be squared with the emerging emphasis on the irreducibly social character of science in all its aspects? Likewise, the older dichotomy between two approaches to the history of science, one "internalist" and the other "externalist," each entirely legitimate in its own right, came under attack. If the activities of scientists are to be understood in the last analysis by referring them to their social and political sources, then this dichotomy between "internal" and "external" fails, and neither the internalist nor the externalist enterprises can be carried on as before. What is significant about the "social turn," then, is not merely a new emphasis on "externalist" topics but a presumptive transformation in the long-established disciplines of philosophy of science and history of science.

The necessity of such a transformation is a matter of vigorous debate. Many philosophers and historians argue that the social character of science has been either overstated or misunderstood, and that it is still not just legitimate but essential to devote attention to the traditional epistemic concerns of the philosopher of science, as well as tracing in the traditional way the historical development of science as a distinctive linkage between claim and evidence. The issues themselves are at bottom philosophical, which is why the label 'sociology of science' often given them could be misleading. Like the "sociology of knowledge" earlier in the century, this new "sociology" is properly philosophical since it claims to offer a new approach to some of the traditional problems of philosophy, notable those of epistemology. And since these claims bear on the manner in which the historiography of science ought to be pursued, and also rely on historical case-studies in an essential way, the historian is equally involved.

It seems safe to say, then, that the implications of the "social turn" are likely to rate high on the discussion agenda of the 1990s both in the history and in the philosophy of science. A conference on "The Social Dimension of Science" involving philosophers, historians, and sociologists seemed an appropriate way, therefore, to greet the new decade. The conference was sponsored and entirely funded by the Reilly Center for Science, Technology, and Values at the University of Notre Dame, October 5–8, 1989. Those who presented papers at the conference were encouraged to revise their papers subsequently in the light of the often lively discussions that took place during those days. This volume gathers together most of those reworked papers, with the welcome addition of an essay by Helen Longino.

The volume is the third in the series, Studies in Science and the Humanities from the Reilly Center for Science, Technology, and Values. The earlier volumes were: *Construction and Constraint* (ed. Ernan McMullin,

1988), and *Philosophical Consequences of Quantum Theory* (ed. James T. Cushing and Ernan McMullin, 1989). The editor wishes to thank the contributors to the volume for their patience during the long process leading to publication. And a special word of appreciation goes to Mary Lister who saw the manuscript through that process.

CONTRIBUTORS

Cornelius Delaney is Professor of Philosophy at the University of Notre Dame. He specializes in the history of modern philosophy and the history of American philosophy. Among his publications are *Mind and Nature: A Study of the Naturalistic Philosophies of Cohen, Woodbridge and Sellars* (1969) and (coauthor) *The Synoptic Vision: Essays on the Philosophy of Wilfred Sellars* (1977). He is a contributing editor of the chronological edition of Peirce's works and is presently finishing a book titled *Peirce on Science, Knowledge, and Mind.*

Thomas F. Gieryn is Associate Professor in Sociology at Indiana University, and Director of its Program on Scientific Dimensions of Society. He is coeditor (with Susan E. Cozzens) of *Theories of Science in Society* (1990), and is finishing a monograph tentatively titled *Making Space for Science: Cultural Cartography Episodically Exposed.* He has recently begun an investigation of the design and construction of new laboratory buildings for biotechnological research.

Ian Hacking is Professor of Philosophy at the University of Toronto. Among his works are: *Logic of Statistical Inference* (1965), *Why Does Language Matter to Philosophy* (1975), *Representing and Intervening* (1983), *The Emergence of Probability* (1975), and *The Taming of Chance* (1990). Recent articles: "A tradition of natural kinds" (1990); "The making and molding of child abuse" (1990).

Martin Hollis is Professor of Philosophy at the University of East Anglia in England and a Fellow of the British Academy. He has written extensively on the philosophy of the social sciences. His works include: *Rational Economic Man* (with E. J. Nell, 1975), *Models of Man* (1977), *Rationality and Relativism* (edited with Steven Lukes, 1982), *The Cunning of Reason* (1988), and *Explaining and Understanding International Relations* (with S. Smith, 1990). He is currently exploring paradoxes of rationality in the theory of choice and game theory.

Philip Kitcher is Professor of Philosophy at the University of California at San Diego. He has published *The Nature of Mathematical Knowledge*

(1983), and *Essays on the History and Philosophy of Modern Mathematics* (edited with W. Aspray, 1988), *Abusing Science* (1982), *Vaulting Ambition: Sociobiology and the Quest for Human Nature* (1987), and has a book in preparation on scientific rationality.

Bruno Latour is Professor at the Centre de Sociologie de l'Innovation at the Ecole des Mines in Paris, and in the Science Studies Program at the University of California at San Diego. He has published: *Laboratory Life: The Construction of Scientific Facts* (1979); *Science in Action* (1986); *The Pasteurization of French Society* (1987). Among recent articles: "Visualization and cognition" (1986); "A relativistic account of Einstein's relativity" (1988). He is currently working on the social history of French science.

Helen Longino is Associate Professor of Philosophy at Rice University and author of *Science as Social Knowledge: Values and Objectivity in Scientific Inquiry* (1990). Her current research concerns the articulation of a social theory of knowledge, as well as the intersection between feminist and philosophical questions about knowledge, nature, and science.

Timothy Lenoir is Professor of the History of Science at Stanford University. His dissertation on *The Social and Intellectual Roots of Discovery in Seventeenth Century Mathematics* (1974), was followed by *The Strategy of Life: Teleology and Mechanism in Nineteenth Century German Biology* (1982). He is currently working on the intellectual and socio-political contexts of Helmholtz's optics.

Ernan McMullin is Director of the Program in History and Philosophy of Science at the University of Notre Dame. Author of *Newton on Matter and Activity* (1978), he has edited: *Galileo Man of Science* (1967), *The Concept of Matter in Modern Philosophy* (1979), *Evolution and Creation* (1985), *Construction and Constraint* (1988), *The Philosophical Consequences of Quantum Theory* (with J. T. Cushing, 1989). His *Rationality, Realism, and the Growth of Knowledge* will appear shortly.

Thomas Nickles is Professor of Philosophy at the University of Nevada-Reno. He edited *Scientific Discovery, Logic, and Rationality* and *Scientific Discovery: Case Studies* (1980). Among his recent essays: "From natural philosophy to metaphilosophy of science" (1987), "Reconstructing science: discovery and experiment" (1988), "Justification and experiment" (1989). He is currently working on "bootstrap" epistemology and heuristic appraisal.

Fritz Ringer is Mellon Professor of History at the University of Pittsburgh. He is the author of *The Decline of the German Mandarins: The*

German Academic Community 1890–1933 (1969), *Education and Society in Modern Europe* (1979), and essays in French and German social and intellectual history. His latest book, *Fields of Knowledge: French Academic Culture, 1890–1920, in Comparative Perspective,* is to be published in the fall of 1991.

INTRODUCTION:
THE SOCIAL DIMENSIONS OF SCIENCE

Ernan McMullin

> Everyone has a cave or den of his own which refracts and discolors the light of nature, owing either to his own proper and peculiar nature, or to his conversation with others, or to the readings of books and the authority of those whom he esteems and admires, or to the differences of impressions accordingly as they take place in a mind preoccupied and predisposed or in a mind indifferent and settled, or the like. The spirit of man . . . is in fact a thing variable and full of perturbation, and governed as it were by chance. (Francis Bacon, *The New Organon*, 1624, Book I, aphorism 42)

> It is not that science has its "social aspects," thus implying that a residual (hard core) kernel of science proceeds untainted by extraneous non-scientific (i.e. "social") factors, but that science is itself constitutively social. This means that just as we should abandon the idea of science as a privileged or even just a separate domain of activity and inquiry, similarly the notion of 'social' . . . has to be substantially modified. The potential consequence of our radical study of science is no less than to make redundant the very concepts of 'social' and 'society.' (Steve Woolgar, *Science: The Very Idea*, 1988, p. 13)

Bacon at the beginning of the seventeenth century and Woolgar at the end of the twentieth define the opposite ends of a very broad spectrum in regard to the nature of science, and in particular in regard to the implications of its "social" character. For Bacon, the experienced lawyer, the spirit of man is "a thing variable . . . governed as it were by chance." Not of itself a source of truth, then, but more likely to "discolor" the light of nature, to introduce particularity and subjectivity into what should be a search for universality and objectivity. The "idols" against which he warns are the distortive forces that tend to pull inductive inquiry out of shape. They are due in part to the contingencies of individual upbringing and individual self-interest, but even more to the involvement of the "tribe,"

1

the "marketplace," and the "theater," that is, to the social setting in which scientific inquiry must needs be carried on.

Bacon distrusts the surreptitious influence of the larger community on those who pursue the demanding task of inductive inquiry. There is no reason to suppose, indeed every reason to doubt, that the concerns and prejudices of that larger community will map neatly onto nature. We all see (he wryly reminds us) what we *want* to see, or what others have led us to expect we *should* see, rather than what is really there: "The human understanding is no dry light but receives an infusion from the will and the affections; whence proceed sciences which may be called sciences as one would."[1] The proper remedy, he urges, is to follow the path of "true induction"; only thus can the idols be cleared away. If science proper is to be attained, the sources of particularity and contingency have to be systematically eliminated. Method is the answer, a method which transcends individual and society alike:

> The course I propose for the discovery of the sciences is such that it leaves but little to the acuteness and strength of wits, but places all wits and understandings nearly on a level. For as in the drawing of a straight line or a perfect circle much depends on the steadiness and practice of the hand . . . but if it be done with the aid of rule or compass, little or nothing. So it is exactly with my plan.[2]

Steve Woolgar is an articulate contemporary spokesman for what he calls "the sociology of scientific knowledge" (SSK), one of the more radical versions of the new sociology of science. Woolgar's account of the nature of science contrasts with Bacon's on almost every major point. His view is

> that there is no essential difference between science and other forms of knowledge production, that there is nothing intrinsically special about "the scientific method"; indeed, even if there is such a thing as "the scientific method," much scientific practice proceeds in spite of [its] canons rather than because of them.[3]

So much for "true induction"! The new sociologists are brisk in their dismissal of the classical ideal of a privileged method of inquiry, one that would mark off science from other human products. More fundamentally, they would deny that there is a "light of nature," a source of objective knowledge accessible to us, provided that we limit the "discoloration" to which the social setting of scientific inquiry makes us liable. The rational and the social (they insist) cannot be separated in this way. On the contrary, science must be viewed as *constitutively* social. It is to be understood first and foremost in social terms, not in the objectivist philosophical categories that have until recently been universally accepted as its obligatory dress.

One consequence of this reductively social understanding of science is that the title chosen for this collection of essays could be disputed. Science ought not be described as having "social aspects," Woolgar remarks, for this might imply that the social is extraneous to it, that at a deeper and more properly constitutive level, it escapes from the contingencies imposed by its social origins. But the choice of "The Social Dimensions of Science" as title was meant merely to convey that each of the essayists has chosen a theme which (it is hoped) will illuminate some aspect of the current debate about the role of the social in the construction of physical science.

In this introductory essay, I will not attempt to survey the contemporary literature in the sociology of science; this has been done quite thoroughly already.[4] Nor will I try to distill the points made in the essays gathered here; they have already been capably conveyed, and need no further gloss. My goal is merely to set the stage, to try to make a little less puzzling a history that links authors as diametrically opposed as the Baconians of an earlier day and the sociologists of scientific knowledge of our own time.

1. Classical Conceptions of Science

It may be somewhat idealized to speak of "classical" conceptions of science. But for our purposes here, it will be worth noting that neither the deductivist account that dominated in a tradition stretching from Aristotle to Descartes, nor the inductivist model favored from Newton's time onwards, allowed a substantive role to the social dimensions of science, as these are now being emphasized. Let us see why.

In the deductivist model, demonstration proceeds from premise (axiom, principle) to conclusion (theorem) by means of deductive rules, in this way (ideally) giving rise to truths that are "eternal and necessary," as Aristotle put it. The necessity of the formal rules of deduction can be directly seen. The truth of the premises is grasped by an intuition (*epagógé*) of the necessary inherence of the predicate in the subject. The concepts (ideas) in which subject and predicate are expressed are derived by abstraction from the particulars of individual experience. The intellect has the capacity to abstract the form of the sensible object, that which makes it intelligible.

There is an identity of a qualified sort between the form as it exists in the object and the idea as it exists in the mind. It is this identity that allows one to suppose that the structure of property and essence laid out in demonstration corresponds to the real structures of the world of nature. The story as Aristotle tells it is a complicated one, and there are gaps in it that later generations of commentators labored to fill, ambiguities capable of alternative development.

But these gaps and ambiguities need not concern us here. The essentials of the notion of demonstration that defined science proper for nearly two thousand years are reasonably clear-cut. And they leave no room for a significant social dimension to the process. Abstraction, intuition, application of rule, all are activities of the individual knower. One has to learn how to proceed, of course, and Aristotle has much to say about the joint process of teaching and learning. And one has to rely on language, which is a communal possession. But this oblique involvement of others in the acquiring of science (*epistémé*) does not affect the basic simplicity of the individual act of grasping the necessity of a certain relationship between properties or between property and essence, faithfully conveyed by the words/ideas that signify forms.

It was an ambitious and demanding ideal of how secure knowledge might be gained. But was it really capable of being achieved? The first effective challenge came in the fourteenth century from empirically minded philosophers and theologians who maintained that demonstration started from the wrong end, from shakily grounded general principles. Instead, they proposed, one must begin from perception of particulars and work upwards by means of generalizations based on likeness. They rejected the notions of form and nature on which rested the tight relationship of language, idea, and reality presupposed by the earlier scheme. There are just singulars, with varying degrees of similarity between them. And some went on to infer that the knowledge so arrived at can never be better than probable. Generalizations from limited samples of entities lacking a common nature (they said) cannot yield the sort of necessity that demonstration had promised.

Nominalism was in the first instance a rather abstract theory of knowledge and an alternative metaphysics. Though it emphasized induction, it did not right away prompt a turn to inductive practice among natural philosophers. Much more would have to happen before the experimental orientation of a Galileo or a Boyle would be possible, and before a work like the *New Organon* could be written. Our concern here, however, is not with the difficult issues involved in reconstructing the historical antecedents of inductive science but with the matter of its implicit social dimensions. At first sight, it may seem to be as resolutely nonsocial as was the earlier method of demonstration in natural philosophy. But, in fact, there were two crucial changes in that respect.

The first was that of starting point. Instead of an intuitive insight into the necessity of a premise, the new science took observation and experiment as its basis.[5] But individual observation was not enough: induction requires generalization over many instances. And Bacon pointed to a more fundamental problem: "the dullness, incompetency and deceptions of the senses. For the sense by itself is a thing infirm and erring."[6] A simple empiricism in which "data" are taken as foundational would not be acceptable. Observational claims have to be tested, evaluated, replicated. This is the work of many, not just of an individual. There is thus the problem of testimony, just as in the law-court. For Bacon and later for Boyle, legal analogies played something of the role that analogies with mathematics had done for exponents of the earlier model of science.[7] Since natural philosophers have to rely on the testimony of others, they must develop the faculty of evaluating evidence, just as the common-law jurist does. And the evidence itself has to be acquired and recorded in such a way as to carry weight within the community of natural philosophers.

The contrast between Galileo and Boyle in that regard is quite striking. Both performed extensive experiments. Galileo, however, was cavalier in the manner in which he "certified" his experimental results. He made claims for experiments he almost certainly did not perform. He overstated the accuracy of the experiments he *did* perform. Insofar as he kept records, these were for his own use; there was no thought (it would seem) of their serving as testimony open to the inspection of others. Most striking, perhaps, was his jotting down of experimental results on a matter crucial to his mechanics (the parabolic shape of projectile trajectories) but his failure to make use of these results where they could have supported the theoretical analysis of projectile motion in the *Discorsi*.[8]

It is not easy to decide just what Galileo's own view would have been in regard to the relative epistemic weight of the two very different ways of structuring argument, one demonstrative, the other inductive.[9] But it is safe to say that the readers of the *Discorsi* would have expected some form of demonstration as the hallmark of a proper science of motion. In the infant field of telescopic astronomy there was already some sense of a community of investigators using common methods and similar instruments, and regularly exchanging results. Galileo himself had a hand in establishing this community, although he met with frequent failure in his attempts to persuade other users of the telescope of the validity of his claims. But in mechanics, matters were otherwise. Since the appropriate mode of persuasion in that domain was (and would long remain) demonstration, the role of inductive inquiry appeared less crucial, and hence there was less inducement to regard the project itself as that of a community of experimentalists, each in some sense monitoring the other.

When we come to Boyle thirty years later, the emphasis shifts sharply towards the experimental and the inductive. The shift was in large part due, not to some more general shift in the conception of how scientific knowledge should be obtained, but to the focus of Boyle's work which was not at all on mechanics but on fields where inductive investigation of particular phenomena seemed to offer the only road ahead. Unlike Galileo, Boyle was acutely sensitive to the problem of witnessing: his science was to be based not just on observations but on observations that were certified by reliable witnesses and capable of being reproduced by other observers. [10] The experimental ideal thus involved the community of observers in an essential way. For the results of experiment to be accepted as "facts," they have to be accredited by the community. The norms or means of accreditation are thus crucial to an appreciation of what this "factual" character amounts to.

Boyle himself saw these norms as warranted in a transparently rational way. The distortions due to unreliable apparatus, inaccuracy, or bias on the part of the experimenter, omission of relevant causal factors, and the rest, would gradually be eliminated by repetition, cross-check, and the careful analysis of anomaly. This is what one should *expect* these practices to accomplish. And this (Boyle would undoubtedly have added) is what the experimenter's own work-experience would show *does* occur. The convergence that is seen to occur in experimental practice over the course of time testifies to the well-foundedness of the practice itself.

Boyle would very likely not have been comfortable with the metaphor of social construction in regard to the "facts" of the experimenter. His philosophy was an objectivist one in which parameters have real values independently of the observer, and the methods of experiment properly carried out are such as to lead gradually to an establishing of what those values are. The fact that the methods are socially sanctioned and can be said to characterize a particular community (or "form of life," in the current phrase) would not, for Boyle and the experimental philosophers who came after him, in the least detract from their objectivist basis.

That basis has, of course, been challenged in recent sociology of science, and the debate will be joined in later essays in this book. Shapin and

Schaffer have argued, with a wealth of historical detail, for a very different construal of Boyle's work:

> The establishment of a set of accepted matters of fact about pneumatics required the establishment and definition of a community of experimenters who worked with shared social conventions: that is to say, the effective solution to the problem of knowledge was predicated upon a solution to the problem of social order.[11]

What kind of solution? Shapin and Schaffer leave the reader in no doubt as to the solution they have in mind. The triumph of the experimental ideal in the later seventeenth century (in England, at least) has to be understood ultimately in *political* terms: "This experimental form of life achieved local success to the extent that the Restoration was secured. Indeed, it was one of the important elements in that security."[12] In the closing lines of their book, they summarize their philosophical position, one diametrically opposite to that of Boyle:

> As we come to recognize the conventional and artifactual status of our forms of knowing, we put ourselves in a position to realize that it is ourselves and not reality that is responsible for what we know. Knowledge, as much as the state, is the product of human action. Hobbes was right.[13]

Our intention in this introductory essay is not to attempt to arbitrate the differences between objectivism of Boyle and the strong constructivism of the Shapin-Schaffer approach. We are looking here for origins only, and our point is that once science be seen as resting in some way upon experimental results, one is sooner or later going to be forced to inquire into the significance of the undoubtedly social cast that this gives to the establishing of what should count as experimental "fact."

2. Hypothesis and Retroduction

The shift away from the demonstrative to the inductive model of science involved more than acceptance of a major role for observation and experiment. A second feature of the change was the gradual (and reluctant) admission that causal explanation of the regularities revealed by systematic observation had to involve hypothesis in an essential way. Descartes drew particular attention to the tentative movement of thought from observed effect back to hypothesized cause that Peirce would later felicitously name "retroduction," distinguishing it from the simpler movement of induction where an empirical generalization (a "law") is extrapolated from a finite set of observations. In the *Discourse on Method*, Descartes remarks that even though the most general principles of mechanics may be known with certainty, "I observed hardly any particular effect such that I could not at once recognize that it might be deduced from the principles in many different ways."[14] The *Discourse* was intended to serve as an introduction to three short scientific treatises, in which he postulates all sorts of hidden structures that could be mechanically responsible for the phenomena he is surveying. The refraction of light, for example, occurs when a "subtle material" is deflected at the boundary between two media. Heat may be understood as the agitation of imperceptibly small particles. The action of salt in preserving meat is due to the rigidity of the salt particles which act like "little rods" in stiffening the meat and thus preventing corruption. And so forth.

Descartes was anxious to show that even though different underlying causes might possibly suffice to explain such effects, in the end one could always narrow the field to a single one. Thus, the apparently hypothetical status of the explanations he is offering can (he hopes) be overcome and certainty restored. The reasonings are so closely interwoven in the *Discourse*, he remarks, that taken together, they have the force of demonstration. Or, as he later put it in a letter to Morin, "it is not always so easy to adjust one single cause to many effects, if it is not the actual cause from which they proceed."[15] Descartes had caught a glimpse of the far-reaching epistemic consequences of allowing into science causal explanation of the observable by the unobserved, but he was not yet ready to accept these consequences. Once explanations are validated retroductively by the consequences drawn from them (rather than the reverse), the problem that has come to be called the underdetermination of theory by data is already implicitly present.

Boyle's response to the problem was to enumerate the qualities to be sought in an explanatory hypothesis; he lists ten of these, ranging from consistency to the making of further predictions that can be tested.[16] But he was keenly aware that this would not be sufficient to allow one to decide what were the precise causes of such phenomena as those ascribed to magnetism, electricity, and chemical reaction. According to the mechanical philosophy, the causes of all such phenomena are the "precise and determinate figures, sizes, and motions of atoms."[17] Though one might in a general way attribute the observable phenomena to atomic-level causes, there was no obvious way, Boyle realized, to link specific chemical reactions, say, with specific atomic shapes or motions.

This point was made much more forcefully by Locke; in fact, it became the central theme of Book IV of his *Essay Concerning Human Understanding*. If science requires demonstration, he says, then a science of bodies is forever out of reach. Not only can one not associate particular atomic figures and motions with observable qualities of bodies, but it seems out of the question that such associations should ever be shown to be necessary, as demonstration would require. Locke concludes, therefore, that probability is the best that can be managed; perhaps with the aid of causal analogies some explanations in terms of the primary (i.e., mechanical) qualities of constituent corpuscles might some day be devised.

Newton's response to the problem of underdetermination was quite different. It was to ban "hypothesis" from "experimental philosophy," i.e., from science proper, and to impose as a test on theory that it should be "deducible" from the phenomena directly. It is not easy to reconstruct what his *Discourse on Method*, had he written one, might have looked like. His comments on method come as asides. His negative views on hypothesis appear to harden as he grows older. His terminology is often loose, notably his use of the terms 'deduction' and 'induction'. But it is clear that, if his prescriptions are followed, the problem of underdetermination will not be allowed to arise in "experimental philosophy."

What allowed him to avoid it, in his mechanics, at least, was the ambiguous status of his principal explanatory concept, *force*. Are forces *causes* of motion, agents that *explain* the motion? Newton's language often suggests that they are: the sun is said to "attract" planets; forces "compel" bodies to change their state of motion, and so on. But elsewhere they seem to be merely propensities to move in a certain way given a particular configuration of bodies, whose own causes still have to be sought. The cause of "gravity," i.e., of the tendency of bodies to fall and of planets to move as they do in their orbits, Newton expressly sets aside in the *Principia* as a question he is not yet ready to address. This ambiguity allowed him to claim that he could determine forces directly from motions, and at the same time represent this as deducing causes from effects: "By this way of analysis we may proceed . . . from motions to the forces producing them, and in general from effects to their causes."[18] "Forces producing them"— one can observe a planet departing from a rectilinear path but one cannot observe forces *producing* this deviation, as critics of Newton, like Leibniz and Berkeley, were quick to point out. To see the deviation as the "action of force," one requires an interpretive theory, the theory embodied in the eight Definitions and three Laws that serve as preface to the *Principia*. But this theory was transparent to Newton, as indeed it was to those who came after him. He obviously did not see it as an hypothesis: as far as he was concerned, the Definitions and Laws expressed the phenomena of motion in the most capacious and exact way possible.

The significance of this for our theme is that the hypothetical character of mechanics, the possibility that another and better theory of motion might one day replace Newton's, was almost entirely hidden from view and remained so for two centuries. Kant's *Metaphysical Foundation of Natural Science* gave memorable expression to this persuasion. Kant attributes *a priori* status to the conceptual structure prescribed by the Definitions and Laws of the *Principia,* and in consequence feels justified in holding that natural science ought to have the status of necessity. Anything that falls short of this, chemistry for instance, is "merely empirical," no more than a "systematic art"; it cannot be accepted as part of "science proper."[19] Yet in the *Opticks,* Newton had introduced a whole series of theoretical entities: ethers, active principles, spirits, in an effort to explain the action of light, the operation of nerves in the animal body, and even perhaps the action of gravity itself. He carefully labels these speculations "queries"; before they may become part of science proper, these hypothetical causes will presumably have to be deducible from the phenomena, but he never really faces the question as to how such a deduction might be carried out in the case of agencies whose mode of action is postulated, not observed. His legacy was thus a divided one: an aspiration to something like *a priori* status in the foundations of mechanics, and the encouragement of the most imaginative theorizing elsewhere, though always with the proviso that this was not yet "science."

One can thus trace two very different sorts of development in the eighteenth century back to Newton's influence. One was an intolerance of "hypothesis," given most effective expression in the work of Thomas Reid. The other was the profusion of ethers in such areas as optics and the theory of heat, and a determined (but unsuccessful) effort to explain chemical reactions by means of Newtonian force-laws operating between (hypothetical) constituent particles. There was less concern than there had been earlier with articulating the appropriate criteria for the evaluation of hypothesis; the general explanatory hypotheses in optics and chemistry seemed to a Newtonian eye to be no more than "queries."

But with the work of Young and Fresnel in optics, Avogadro in theory of gases, and Dalton in chemistry, things began to change. Retroductive explanation took on a new authority, and philosophically minded scientists like William Whewell turned their attention to its logical structure.

Though Whewell used the single term 'induction' to cover what Peirce would later show to be two very different sorts of inference (induction and retroduction), he was keenly aware of the peculiar features of retroduction; in particular he noted that in every retroduction there is what he called "the invention of a new conception."[20] The designation of an unobserved cause requires a relative novelty of language, a conception that does not occur in the propositions describing the effects to be explained. Hence, the inference itself cannot possibly be deductive (or even inductive, if induction be restricted to generalization only). Can it still arrive at certainty? Must theory remain (as we would now put it) underdetermined?

Whewell was confident that over the course of time a retroductive explanation in terms of unobserved entities *could* take on the status of certainty. Phlogiston theory had allowed chemists to predict successfully, but oxygen theory greatly enlarged the scope of chemical prediction and allowed successful new predictions to be made. Even more impressive was the wave theory of light which had made a wide array of phenomena "fall together" under a single simple model:

> The evidence in favor of our induction is of a much higher and more forcible character when it enables us to explain and determine cases of a *kind different* from those which were contemplated in the formation of our hypothesis. The instances in which this has occurred, indeed, impress us with a conviction that the truth of our hypothesis is certain. No accident could give rise to such an extraordinary coincidence. No false supposition could, after being adjusted to one class of phenomena, exactly represent a different class, where the agreement was unforeseen and uncontemplated. That rules springing from remote and unconnected quarters should thus leap to the same point, can only arise from *that* being the point where truth resides.[21]

This optimistic assessment would probably have been shared by most scientists of the day. Though it was *logically* possible that many different theories might explain the same evidence, the ability of one particular theory to unify and simplify domains over time and to predict new and unexpected results, seemed sufficient to narrow the field to that theory, while allowing that it might (and probably would) require further modification. Crucial to this assessment was the role of *time* and *community*. What philosopher-scientists like Whewell found convincing as a way of overcoming the underdetermination implicit in the growing reliance on retroduction was not the saving of the phenomena at a particular instant, but the performance of a theory over a considerable period of time. And for this, a complex and continuing cooperative action on the part of many scientists was required.

In this section and the last, we have reviewed two of the characteristic features of the "new science" that developed between the seventeenth and the nineteenth centuries. Reliance on experiment and construction of theories that work backwards from observed effect to postulated cause laid the ground for a future sociology of science which has used these as its main ports of entry. If experiment *could* properly lay claim to the objectivity Boyle hoped to secure for it, if theory *could* be as definitive as Whewell believed it could, then these ports would have been sealed against the constructivist forays of the last twenty years. But, of course, there would still have been much of sociological interest to discuss in regard to the organization of science generally, including the management of experiment and the conduct of theoretical debate: sociology of science rather than sociology of scientific *knowledge,* in the current phraseology. Boyle and Whewell would have found the sociology of scientific knowledge entirely unacceptable, one supposes, but might have looked benignly on a more general sociology of science, while finding it, no doubt, a rather odd enterprise. But there was one founding father who would very likely have seen such an interest as quite in keeping with his own anticipations of the future.

3. Bacon on the Organization of Science

One of Bacon's most intriguing works was a short essay, left unfinished at his death in 1626, on how the work of natural philosophy might be organized. It is written in the form of a fable:

> This fable my Lord devised, to the end that he might exhibit therein a model or description of a college instituted for the interpreting of nature and the producing of great and marvellous works for the benefit of men, under the name of Salomon's House, or the College of the Six Days' Works. . . . Certainly the model is more vast and high than can possibly be imitated in all things; notwithstanding, most things therein are within men's power to effect.[22]

Bacon describes a large island called Bensalem in the Pacific where natural philosophy has progressed much more than it has in Europe. This progress has been in part due to the cohesive social organization given it by "Salomon's House" where all the activities of research have been concentrated. The visitor is told: "The end of our Foundation is the knowledge of causes and secret motions of things, and the enlarging of the bounds of human empire to the affecting of all things possible."[23] The "Father" of the House describes the caves where mining experiments are carried on, the high towers where meteorological phenomena are systematically observed, the mineral springs whose effects on health are studied, the gardens and farms where different strains of plants and animals are transformed by careful cross-breeding, the furnaces that produce a "diversity of heats," "perspective-houses" where experiments on optical phenomena are carried on, "sound-houses" where "we practice and demonstrate all sounds and their generation," "perfume-houses" where the objects of smell and taste are catalogued, "engine-houses" for the construction of machines, including machines of war, "houses of deceits of the senses" where illusion is studied, and a "mathematical house" for making instruments for astronomical and geometrical use.

The emphasis is clearly on technology, on transformation for practical use. It is not clear (any more than it is in the *New Organon*) how the "secret motions of things" are to be discovered. Bacon describes induction as though it were simply a matter of generalizing relationships between observables. But this technique alone could never attain to the latent processes and configurations "which for the most part escape the sense," on which he takes observable phenomena to depend.[24] The role that theory would soon take on in this regard still lies below Bacon's horizon. There is more than a hint in his prospectus of alchemy, of techniques that "endow bodies with new natures." Research is organized, oddly, to our eyes, around the distinctions between the human senses of sight, sound, and smell. The role of mathematics is minor, and typically, is tied to the construction of instruments.

One can see how all this mirrors the prescriptions scattered throughout Bacon's works and the natural histories on which the new inductive science is to be based. Even more significant is the description of how the work is to be carried on. There is a sharp division of labor. Instead of single investigators (like a Descartes or a Galileo) who carry on research, if not single-handedly, at least with only the distant assistance of collaborators and predecessors, there are "Depredators" who collect experiments from books, "Merchants of Light" who travel in secret abroad to bring back accounts of experiments performed in other parts, "Mystery Men" who study the practices of the different arts and sciences, "Pioneers" who try new experiments, "Compilers" who draw together the findings of the previous groups, "Dowry Men" who investigate practical applications of the knowledge thus far gained, "Lamps" who on the basis of all the foregoing devise further experiments "of a higher light," "Inoculators" who execute the actual experiments, and finally "Interpreters of Nature" who "raise the former discoveries by experiments into greater observations, axioms, and aphorisms."[25] And all is to be carried on in secret: "All take an oath of secrecy for the concealing of those [inventions] which we think fit to keep secret though some of those we do reveal sometimes to the state, and some not."[26]

As a lawyer, Bacon had been much concerned with the new practice of allowing "patents," open letters (*litterae patentes*) under the Royal seal, supposedly for rewarding technological innovation, but in fact much misused by both Elizabeth and James I as patronage for their favorite courtiers to whom monopolies over such common substances as lead, iron, and saltpetre had been granted. In 1615, during Bacon's tenure as Lord Chancellor, a celebrated legal judgment was handed down ("The cloth-workers of Ipwich") in which it was held that the Crown could not grant a monopoly except where technological innovation was involved. In the following year, Bacon loyally defended the King's right to award profitable monopolies to his favorites; Parliament had to be convened to deal with the consequent political unrest. The Statute of Monopolies of 1623, the basis of modern English and U.S. patent law, was its answer; by then, Bacon had been disgraced.[27]

Those were years, then, when the matter of technological innovation was in the forefront of discussion, and certainly a preoccupation on Bacon's part. This is only one of the factors that go to explain the emphasis in the organization of Salomon's House, an organization so widely at variance with the one that someone like Descartes or Galileo, working in the more theoretical traditions of natural philosophy, would have given. Bacon's experience with the crafts and his tendency to view technological change in broadly alchemical categories, gave him a perspective altogether different from that of the "mechanical philosophers" of the next generation. This perspective was one which required large-scale and costly collaborative effort, needing therefore the assistance of the Crown. Despite Bacon's best efforts, this assistance was never forthcoming. The Royal Society chartered by a later monarch was on a far less ambitious scale than Salomon's House, and fostered notions of research importantly different from those of Bacon. Not until our own century, when for the first time natural science began in a significant way to shape and to be shaped by technological change, would there be "Foundations" with the ability to accomplish the goals of Salomon's House, though with types of organization very different from the one he recommended. The giant industrial firm of today is closer in that respect, perhaps, to the model in which Bacon embodied his hopes than was the Royal Society or the later scientific academies that claimed his mantle.[28]

Salomon's House was an object of hope, a utopia in Mannheim's sense of that term: an imagined state of affairs that seeks to legitimize new beliefs and practices by projecting an order different from the existing one. The *New Atlantis* was not a work of sociology. It was a speculative construction in social terms of an institution that did not yet exist, but one that Bacon's vision of natural philosophy appeared to require and thus to legitimate. The book was also a work of propaganda, designed to influence those in the best position to ensure that such an institution would come to pass. What links it with the modern discipline of the sociology of science is that Bacon (like Robert Merton) saw natural science as an activity that could best be described in organizational terms.

Many have found utopian elements (in a different sense of 'utopian') in Merton's work also, his stress on "the purity of science," in particular:

> One sentiment which is assimilated by the scientist from the very outset of his training pertains to the purity of science. Science must not suffer itself to become the handmaiden of theology or economy or state. The function of this sentiment is likewise to preserve the autonomy of science. For if such extra-scientific criteria of the value of science as presumable consonance with religious doctrines or economic utility or political appropriateness are adopted, science becomes acceptable only in so far as it meets these criteria. In other words, as the pure science element is eliminated, science becomes subject to the direct control of other institutional agencies and its place in society becomes increasingly uncertain. The persistent repudiation by scientists of the application of utilitarian norms to their work has as its chief function the avoidance of this danger, which is particularly marked at the present time.[29]

And he goes on to characterize "the ethos of science" by a set of values that include disinterestedness, universalism, organized skepticism, and humility.[30] Merton was perfectly well aware that these values are by no means always characteristic of the way in which scientists conduct their affairs, but he clearly regarded them as norms which on the whole are observed.[31] His concern with how science *should* be carried on has been challenged by a later generation of sociologists of scientific knowledge. And his assessment of the "purity" of the motives actually animating the efforts of scientists would not be shared by many of his more skeptical successors, who would quarrel with both the language and the implications of his claim that the social processes of science act to maintain the integrity of the cognitive processes through an impersonal moral ethos and a universalistic distribution of rewards. In the *New Atlantis,* Bacon conjured up an imaginary society on the authority of his own vision of how natural philosophy and technological change might fruitfully be conjoined. Merton had a simpler task. The society that he described already existed, indeed had existed for several centuries, even if it did not always live up to the ideals he projected for it.

4. The Last Chapter

Mention of Merton returns us from our excursion in the byways of the seventeenth century to the more travelled highways of the present. In these concluding pages we shall sketch in outline some of the developments that have in a short half century created a new discipline, or rather, clusters of disciplines, focused on the study of science as a complex form of social activity. Prior to that, there had been C. S. Peirce, of course, who had already set about redefining science in partially social terms.[32] And there were the founders of modern sociology, Weber and Mannheim, in particular, who extended the concepts and techniques of the newly forming discipline of sociology to activities clustered under the loose label of 'knowledge'.[33] They tended, however, to exempt the natural sciences from the scope of their analysis. So great at that time was the authority and the cumulative weight of sciences like physics and chemistry that inquiry into the particularities of knowledge-formation in such fields seemed unlikely to yield fruit. The ascendancy of logical positivism in the thirties and forties further reinforced the classical emphasis on science as basically atemporal and asocial.

The beginnings of a specifically sociological approach to the activity of science, as we have just seen, can be traced to the work of Merton in the U.S. From the thirties onwards, Merton and his students made use of the standard tools of sociological analysis to investigate the workings of the scientific community in functionalist terms. Merton shared with the earlier sociologists of knowledge the assumption that the natural sciences are objectively certified by means of methods that are presumptively universal in scope. His goal was to understand the social dynamics that enabled such a process to operate. The "Merton school" shaped the growth of sociology of science as a discipline in the U.S. during the sixties and seventies, and remains one of the main influences in the broader "social studies of science" enterprise today.

Kuhn's challenge to the older "asocial" image of science ran deeper. He argued that science is, first and foremost, the characteristic set of activities of a particular social group. Even though it is legitimate to abstract a set of propositions of which a physics text, say, might be composed, it must be understood that these propositions cannot be understood or evaluated in isolation from the particular community producing them. A paradigm is not simply a theory. It involves its own mechanisms for training students to see the world in a particular way; it requires its own methods of assessment of the claims it makes. It cannot be understood without detailed study of the social processes sustaining it. Historical analysis does not confirm the universalistic ethos presupposed by the earlier sociologists of knowledge.

In the light of later developments, Kuhn now seems relatively conservative in intention. For example, he insisted that the "mature" sciences are relatively insulated from the larger society of which the scientists are members. The methods of training and assessment characteristic of a mature science ensure this. Thus, the content of the typical theory in fields such as mechanics or chemistry is not influenced to any appreciable degree by the values and assumptions of the larger political and social groupings to which scientists belong.

Again, though there is no logic to coerce theory-choice in science, there are "values" like empirical accuracy, consistency, and fertility, which carry over from one paradigm to the next and provide a guide to the scientist in evaluating problem-solutions of a sort that can be called "objective," provided it be kept in mind that they leave wide room for disagreement.[34] Kuhn, like Merton before him, focused attention on what was *distinctive* about the scientific community, on the ways that scientists are trained, on the manner in which they communicate, on the ways in which they formulate and solve problems, and so forth. Though the notion of paradigm might be (and was) exported to fields distant from science, the mechanics of paradigm change he described were specific to a quite definitely marked-off group, practitioners of the natural sciences.

In Europe, the growth of "science studies" was to lead in more radical directions. Though originally inspired in part by Kuhn, European sociologists of science of the seventies, especially in Britain, were not as inclined as he had been to allow any special privilege to scientific knowledge or to scientific methods. The most influential group, proponents of the "strong program" in the sociology of knowledge, many of them associated with the University of Edinburgh, argued that knowledge is to be construed, in science as elsewhere, as accepted (and not as true) belief. The form of analysis used by the sociologist of science ought not depend, then, on the truth or falsity of the scientific claim that is being investigated. Barnes and Bloor stressed the theoretical character of scientific knowledge, and argued that theories are imposed upon reality rather than deriving from it.[35] Thus, even though the natural world exerts some constraint upon scientific theory, it is the various commitments that scientists bring to their theorizing that are decisive in explaining the outcome. The truth of the outcome is not a relevant factor in that explanation. The commitments themselves can best be understood in social terms. It is through the existence of a complex web of social relationships that the scientific community is enabled to carry through an enterprise that could never be completed in terms of logic and "pure" observation alone.

Philosophers of science have always supposed that their schemes could allow one to understand the historical activity of the scientist, that they can reveal what was *really* going on as science progressed. This is just what proponents of the strong program denied. They argued that philosophy of science had to rely on a false inductivist epistemology and an untenable essentialism in order to get under way. Once these be replaced, philosophy of science is seen to be incapable of carrying through its aims. It must itself be abandoned, or at least thoroughly reconstituted within a properly sociological structure.

Barnes and Bloor saw their analysis as *causal:* ideas and reasons were taken to be causes of human behavior and were to be understood in lawlike terms, like other causes. They took the goal of sociology of science to be the discovery of general regularities and systematic social relationships, just as Ben David had earlier done, but unlike him they supposed these regularities to be constitutive even of the *content* of scientific knowledge. The implicit causal determinism of this view appeared to clash with the notion of an "interest" as an active construction of the social world. In later work, Barnes has weakened the claim to lawlikeness, allowing room for the particularities of social context and the perceptions of individual interests.

One field that has held a particular challenge for sociologists of science has been mathematics. From Plato to the present day, mathematics has seemed the paradigm of an eternal and necessary structure, the very antithesis of a contingent social product. Must it, therefore, be held exempt from sociological analysis? To allow this would be a serious limitation of scope. Building on the earlier work of Wittgenstein and Lakatos, Bloor argued that the historical development of mathematics has been influenced in quite fundamental ways by social factors, and that the appearance of objectivity and inevitability this history possesses for us is an artifact. Critics of Bloor's thesis have suggested that mathematics is more (not less) open to constructivist interpretations than are the physical sciences, since it does not have the constraint on it that empirical anomaly imposes on the latter. So that even if Bloor's reading of the history of mathematics were to be conceded, this would by no means license an *a fortiori* inference in regard to the applicability of constructivist categories to the history of the physical sciences.

So far, the emphasis has been on sociology. But much of the force of the sociological case has derived from case histories directed to specific episodes in the past history of science, particularly episodes involving controversy.[36] The more "internalist" historiography of science of earlier decades has been, if not replaced, then at the least greatly augmented by a broader sort of historiography that emphasizes social influences, and tends to see in the science of a particular place and time a reflection of the prevailing institutional structures and the popular ideologies. A typical chapter on French science in the late eighteenth century, for example, is headed: "Aristocratic science, 1789–1793," "Democratic science, 1793–1795," "Bureaucratic science, 1795–1799," "Imperial science, 1799–1815."

Likewise, a book on Newtonian science claims to find in the new mechanics an image of the political structures of the ruling establishment of early eighteenth-century England. A history of statistical theory argues that in its nineteenth-century beginnings this theory was shaped in content as well as in the sequence of its development by the social interests of the rising British middle class. The earlier schematic work of Marxist historians of science like Bernal has been succeeded by detailed studies of the role played by politics and class-interest in the shaping of the "big science" of our own century.

In the last decade, sociology of science itself has continued to diversify. One lively new direction is toward studies of "laboratory life," using the methods of the anthropologists, analogous (in the words of Latour and Woolgar) to those of the "intrepid explorer of the Ivory Coast, who having studied the belief system or material production of 'savage minds' by living with tribesmen, sharing their hardships and almost becoming one of them, eventually returns with a body of observations which he can present as as preliminary research report."[37] This trend reflects a dissatisfaction with scientists' own reports of what goes on, which are idealized in a number of ways. There is little agreement as yet among the ethnographers themselves as to what the most profitable lines of approach to scientific practice might be. In particular, how can ethnographers claim to give an objective account of science "as it happens," if they deny a similar ability to natural scientists in *their* pursuit of natural knowledge? An ethnographic study, it would appear, cannot be taken as a *report*, a way of setting straight what is *really* going on in the laboratory. Woolgar speaks of a "reflexive ethnography," one whose aim is "to gain insight into general processes of reasoning practices," rather than giving the news about what is happening in the laboratory.

Despite the fact that sociologists of science have been applying their skills to the community of scientists for more than fifty years past, no serious effort seems as yet to have been made to apply these same skills to sociologists of science themselves. There is much work to be done here, as social historians and sociologists apply themselves to the question of why the field of sociology of science has exploded in the way it has, in the last two decades especially. To what extent is the marked "social turn" in history of science journals itself to be understood in social terms, by the premium set in matters of academic advancement on novel formulations, for instance? What sorts of interest prompt the strongly critical approach to science adopted by exponents of SSK? Does it, for example, in some way reflect the anti-science sentiments characteristic of large segments of British, German, and French society since World War II? These are important questions from the perspective of the new sociology of science itself, since they bear on the status of the knowledge-claims being advanced. When Shapin and Schaffer claim to have "shown" that Boyle's science reflected certain features of the society of which he was so active a member, does their "showing" reflect, in some significant way, particular features of *their* society? If not, why not? If so, what does this do to the interest of the claim they are making? How these issues are to be dealt with has not yet been clarified satisfactorily.[38]

A development of a different sort is that of scientometrics, or the "science of science," as it is sometimes called in Europe. Already in the 1960s Derek Price was studying the growth patterns of science, using as indicators the numbers of scientists and the production of scientific articles. A topic of special interest is the research network, or the "invisible college," and a research instrument of choice is the citation index. The dominance of "elites" is easily shown by this means. In any field, a small proportion of the workers produces the bulk of the literature and monopolizes the rewards. The more eminent the scientist, the more likely he or she is to get credit for work shared with other less well-known scientists (what Merton called the "Matthew effect"). The more eminent the scientist, the more likely it is that he or she studied with another eminent scientist. And so forth. Scientometrics is often linked with policy studies, on the assumption that the development of science and technology for political ends can best be planned if some kind of quantitative instruments are available for measuring and perhaps even predicting its directions and rates of growth.

In most of these sociological studies the stress is on negotiation and compromise. But some sociologists prefer to emphasize the role of conflict, and underline the alienation and exploitation that may accompany scientific development. Though broadly Marxist in inspiration, this sort of emphasis is in a certain tension with the commitment to science that was so central to Marx's own thinking. It tends rather to be anti-science; it sees science as potentially oppressive since it is always at the service of the reigning political orthodoxy. Radical sociology of science is usually part of a larger political program; it is unashamedly ideological but in its defense argues that the supposed ideological neutrality of science is in any case an illusion.

One of the liveliest areas of discussion at present is that of feminist theories of science. Uncontroversial is the claim that research in some specific parts of science (notably primatology and brain physiology) has in the past embodied a caricature of women or of the male/female relationship. Equally uncontroversial is the assertion that women have been, until recently, largely excluded from active participation in the doing of science, and that significant barriers still exist. Debate begins to arise, however, when the claim is made that the methods and goals of science, as it is currently practiced, betray a strong masculine bias: patriarchal, authoritarian, deterministic, purportedly neutral, detached from nature, lending itself to destructive and oppressive application. Feminists divide over the preferred alternative.[39] Is it a science free of bias, or is it one where the masculine is replaced by a feminine bias? Is bias acceptable provided it is the *right* bias? Many criticize the notion of a value-free science, and advocate a science which is guided by feminist values throughout. Political commitments to a certain view of human action, for example, would be allowed to determine the choice between alternative theories in such fields as neuro-anatomy.

Some feminist theorists argue that there is a distinctively feminine worldview which is characterized by wholism, interaction, and complexity, and which derives from the female sensibility or temperament; it would support a very different sort of science. Other feminists strongly disagree, but would still want to transform science in the direction of wholism and a more interactive view of relationships, not because of a uniquely feminine form of validating insight but because the resultant science would, in their view, be better as science. Finally, since the androcentric structures of science as it is now practiced are rooted (it is claimed) in the equally androcentric structures of the larger society, some feminists conclude that the only way in which a truly feminist science can ever be achieved is to work for the radical transformation of the larger society first. All of these views are premised on a particular sociological analysis of science, as it is currently carried on. They are, in effect, radical sociologies of science, more politically radical than most versions of SSK since their primary aim is to transform entirely the way in which science is carried on. Yet they are less epistemically radical than the constructivist versions of SSK since their defenders generally believe that a "truer" science is, in fact, attainable.

And so, finally, back once again to Steve Woolgar, whose constructivism is as far from the tradition of Bacon and Whewell as the string could stretch. He is emphatic about his ontology. The discovery of pulsars at Cambridge:

> undermines the standard presumption about the existence of the object prior to its discovery. The argument is not just that social networks mediate between the object and observational work done by the participants. Rather, the social network constitutes the object (or lack of it).[40]

The problem, then, in his eyes is to try to explain how discoverers manage to convince themselves they *have* discovered something "out there". As far as he is concerned: "realist ontology is a *post hoc* justification of existing institutional arrangements."[41] He is equally explicit about his epistemology:

> The representational practices [of the scientist] constitute the objects of the world, rather than being a reflection of (or arising from) them. . . . We think the objects precede and give rise to their representation precisely because this is the way we happen to organize our perceptions of the world.[42]

Scientists, in effect, "rewrite history so as to give the discovered object its ontological foundation."[43] But no matter how hard they try, "facts and objects in the world are inescapably textual constructions." And then a final thrust: "Relativism has not yet been pushed far enough. Proponents of relativism (both within and beyond SSK) are still wedded to an objectivist ontology, albeit one slightly displaced."[44]

Not yet pushed far enough? Only *slightly* displaced? One suspects a genial attempt to *épater les philosophes*. But here a serious issue is joined, and the arguments of Bacon and Whewell and their realist descendants have to face the constructivist counterarguments head-on, without any distracting talk of the social networks that sustain each side. May the (epistemically) best side win!

* * * *

In a short fifty years, a set of interlocking (and often competing) disciplines have sprung up, each claiming to provide an insight into what scientists do, most of them challenging the older assumption that science, if properly executed, reflects the world of nature. In this rapid sketch, we have passed over developments in philosophy associated with Wittgenstein, Quine, Heidegger, and others, which have helped to accelerate the decline of the older asocial model of science. At this point, there would be little disagreement about the claim that the social dimensions of science must be taken seriously. But there would be just as little agreement as to what this advice amounts to.

NOTES

1. *New Organon,* trans. James Spedding et al. (Boston: Taggard and Thompson, 1863), Book I, aph, 49.

2. *New Organon,* Book I, aph. 61.

3. *Science: The Very Idea* (London: Tavistock, 1988), 12.

4. See, in particular, Michael Mulkay's monograph, *"Sociology of science in the West,"* which appeared in *Current Sociology 28* (3), (1982): 1–116, accompanied by an annotated bibliography of 342 items (same volume, 134–184), focusing especially on publications in English subsequent to 1970. See also Steven Shapin, "History of science and its social reconstructions," *History of Science 20* (1982): 157–211, containing a useful bibliography of 149 items; the essays in *Science Observed: Perspectives on Social Studies of Science,* ed. Karin Knorr-Cetina and Michael Mulkay (London: Sage, 1983); Steve Woolgar, "Laboratory studies: A comment on the state of the art," *Social Studies of Science 12* (1980):481–498; Randall Collins, "Development, diversity, and conflict in the sociology of science," *Sociological Quarterly 24* (1983), 185–200; the essays in *Knowledge and Reflexivity,* ed. Steve Woolgar (London: Sage, 1988).

5. This is, of course, a highly schematic claim, and needs all sorts of qualification when one attends to the detail of such complex achievements as those of Descartes and Galileo, for instance. See McMullin, "Conceptions of science in the

Scientific Revolution," in *Reappraisals of the Scientific Revolution*, ed. D. Lindberg and R. Westman (Cambridge: Cambridge University Press, 1990), 27–92.

6. *New Organon*, Book I, aph. 50.

7. See Rose-Mary Sargent, "Scientific experiment and legal expertise: The way of experience in seventeenth-century England," *Studies in the History and Philosophy of Science 20* (1989): 19–45.

8. Ronald Naylor was the first to interpret some working notes left by Galileo as indications of a series of experimental trials of the shape of the trajectory followed by a ball projected horizontally: "Galileo: Search for the parabolic trajectory," *Annals of Science 33* (1976): 153–174. Since then a considerable literature has been devoted to three manuscript pages on each of which Galileo scribbled a diagram and some figures. This literature is reviewed in David K. Hill, "Dissecting trajectories: Galileo's early experiments on projectile motion and the law of fall," *Isis 79* (1988): 646–668. Since there is no indication in Galileo's published work that he already had *experimental* proof of the parabolic trajectory curve (often said to be his most significant discovery in mechanics), the implications of these notes came as a surprise to Galileo scholars. In the Fourth Day of the *Discorsi*, the parabolic law is presented as a theoretical result based on a geometrical deduction from a composition of motions. What is equally surprising is that although these experiments were performed prior to Galileo's leaving Padua in 1610, and the *Discorsi* was not put in final form until 1636, Galileo does not seem to have communicated his (to us highly significant) experimental results to any of his many correspondents during all of this long period. Galileo was not ordinarily slow to claim credit for a discovery that would increase his renown. Hill concludes that "however useful experiment appeared to Galileo as a tool for the discovery and initial confirmation of principles (as revealed in the working notes) and as a means of shoring up soft spots in his geometrical exposition (as in the *Discorsi*), he did not regard it as a primary vehicle for justifying his final results in the eyes of his fellow natural philosophers." (*op. cit.*, p. 666).

9. On this issue, see McMullin, "The conception of science in Galileo's work," in *New Perspectives on Galileo*, ed. R. Butts and J. Pitt (Dordrecht: Reidel, 1978), 209–257.

10. Steven Shapin and Simon Schaffer in their influential *Leviathan and the Air-Pump: Hobbes, Boyle and the Experimental Life* (Princeton: Princeton University Press, 1985) have called into vigorous question the objectivity that this way of expressing Boyle's experimental ideal conveys.

11. Ibid., 282.

12. Ibid., 341.

13. Ibid., 344.

14. *Discourse on Method*, trans. E. S. Haldane and G. R. T. Ross (New York: Dover, 1955), 121.

15. *Oeuvres*, ed. C. Adam and P. Tannery (Paris: Cerf, 1897–1913), vol. 2, 199. For an extended discussion of these texts, see McMullin, "Conceptions of science," 32–44.

16. McMullin, "Conceptions of Science," 55.

17. Robert Boyle, *Works*, ed. Thomas Birch (London, 1772), vol. 2, p. 45.

18. *Opticks* (New York: Dover, 1952), 404. See McMullin, "Conceptions of science," 73.

19. Preface to the *Metaphysical Foundations of Natural Science*. See McMullin, "Philosophy of Science 1600–1900," in *Companion to the History of Modern Science*, ed. R. C. Olby *et al.* (London: Routledge, 1990), 816–837; pp. 830–831.

20. In Book II, chapter 7 of the *Novum Organum Renovatum* (London, 1858), he draws a sharp distinction between two types of "inductive truth"; one he calls "laws of phenomena" (what we would call empirical laws) and the other "theories of causes." He recognizes that causal theories postulating underlying structures and processes are much more problematic than empirical generalizations relating observables to one another. Such theories involve what we have been calling retroduction.

21. Ibid., chap. 5, par. 11.

22. William Rawley in his Introduction to the first English edition of the *New Atlantis, Francis Bacon: A Selection of His Works*, ed. S. Warhaft (New York: Odyssey, 1965), 418.

23. Ibid., 447.

24. *New Organon*, Book II, aph. 6.

25. *New Atlantis*, 456.

26. Ibid.

27. McMullin, "Openness and secrecy in science: Some notes on early history," *Science, Technology and Human Values 10* (1985): 14–23.

28. The academies *did*, of course, encourage systematic experimentation and the development of the technologies this experimentation required. The numerous affinities between them and the model sketched so imaginatively, if somewhat prematurely, by Bacon are dealt with in illuminating detail in *Salomon's House Revisited: The Organization and Institutionalization of Science*, ed. T. Frängsmyr (Canton Mass.: Science History, 1990).

29. Robert K. Merton, *Social Theory and Social Structure* (New York: Free Press, 1957), 549.

30. Ibid., 552–561.

31. "Priorities in scientific discovery," *American Sociological Review 22* (1957): 635–659.

32. See the essay on Peirce by C. F. Delaney below.

33. See the essay on the origins of the sociology of knowledge by Fritz Ringer below.

34. Thomas Kuhn, "Objectivity, value judgement, and theory choice," in *The Essential Tension* (Chicago: University of Chicago Press, 1977), 320–339.

35. Barry Barnes, *Scientific Knowledge and Sociological Theory* (London: Routledge, 1974); B. Barnes, *Interests and the Growth of Knowledge* (London: Routledge, 1977); David Bloor, *Knowledge and Social Imagery* (London: Routledge, 1976).

36. For an extensive review and bibliography, see Steven Shapin, "History of science and its social reconstructions."

37. Bruno Latour and Steve Woolgar, *Laboratory Life: The Construction of Scientific Facts* (Princeton: Princeton University Press, 1986), 28.

38. See Barry Gruenberg, "The problem of reflexivity in the sociology of science," *Philosophy of the Social Sciences* 8 (1978):321–343, and the essays in *Knowledge and Reflexivity: New Frontiers in the Sociology of Knowledge,* ed. Steve Woolgar (London: Sage, 1988).

39. See the essay by Helen Longino below, and her book, *Science as Social Knowledge* (Princeton: Princeton University Press, 1990).

40. *Science: The Very Idea,* 65.

41. Ibid., 67.

42. Ibid.

43. Ibid., 69.

44. Ibid., 98.

PEIRCE ON THE SOCIAL AND
HISTORICAL DIMENSIONS OF SCIENCE

C. F. Delaney

1. Introduction

Once we put to one side the various *abstract* conceptions of science as
'an organized body of knowledge' or as 'a rationally established set of
propositions' or as 'an empirically justified set of beliefs about the world'
(all of which Peirce has called textbook conceptions of science) and view it
concretely as a kind of cognitive activity which is both social and historical
in nature, science like all other social phenomena invites sociological analysis. Like other cultural institutions science as an interrelated set of human practices has a history, has an internal social structure, and has
external relationships to other social phenomena. The sociology of science
emerged as the project of attending to these features of science.

The first wave of the sociology of science left untouched the conception
of science as a privileged kind of cognitive activity, not only thoroughly
rational but the very paradigm of rationality. There were obviously social
and historical dimensions to the behavior of scientists and to the institutionalization of science but these did not determine its content or compromise its rationality. In the Mertonian tradition, attention was paid to
the ethos of the scientific community analyzed as a system of controlled
functional interactions governed by sets of norms and counter-norms
which guided its rational progressive development. Studies of specialization, communication, stratification, and reward systems emerged, but a
direct sociological account of scientific knowledge was avoided because the
belief persisted that to the extent that knowledge is genuinely scientific it
is determined by the physical world and not the social world. The sociology of science was exempted from the sociology of knowledge.

The next wave of the sociology of science was more thoroughgoing in its
contextualization of science. Influenced in part by post-positivist developments in the history and philosophy of science, the epistemological barriers to the sociological analysis of scientific knowledge were lifted. The

sociology of science took its place within the sociology of knowledge, and scientific knowledge was exhibited as influenced by external causal determinants much like all other systems of belief and practice. Seen as an historically contingent social enterprise driven by various human interests, it may well have no distinctive claim to rationality or objectivity. The conclusions of science are viewed as offering us an account of the physical world which is mediated by available cultural resources such that at the highest level of generality science should be seen as an interpretive enterprise in which our picture of the physical world is socially constructed.

I have rehearsed this familiar narrative to provide a context for taking another look at an important nineteenth-century thinker who was vitally concerned with many of the issues that weave their way through our current problematic. Charles Sanders Peirce, both a scientist and a philosopher, explored at length the social and historical dimensions of science in their bearing on its rationality and objectivity. I am enough of an historian of thought to hope that by taking a closer look at the ways in which the creative minds of the past have conceptualized sets of issues that are of current concern to us, we can achieve a certain distance from our familiar ways of thinking of these matters—which distance may well be a necessary condition for the emergence of those insights that will enable us to go on constructively. In any event, what I propose to do is to take a closer look at Peirce's views on the issues just mentioned and then briefly return to the contemporary discussion with some suggestions as to future reflection.

2. Peirce's Conception of Science

Peirce is very clear about the primacy of what I have called the concrete as opposed to the abstract characterization of science. For him there were two quite different perspectives on science: the first was characterization of science primarily as a systematic or organized body of knowledge; and the second was the characterization of it primarily as a method of knowing. The former he viewed as a "rather shallow cut" which was backward looking and captured only "the fossilized remains of science" (MS 614.7).[1] The latter he saw as a "deeper cut" which was, appropriately for a pragmatist, forward looking and got at the essence of science in process. He drew on his own experience as a scientist, his knowledge of the history of science, and his expertise as a methodologist of science for his project of characterizing the concrete reality that is living science in contrast to some abstract specification of some feature thereof.

He maintained that the focal meaning of the word 'science' should be to designate the concrete life of a social group of inquirers informed by a particular methodological strategy and animated by the desire to discover the truth. The socio-historical picture of science that emerges in Peirce receives its ultimate generalization in his construal of science as a "mode of life." Applauding Bacon's vision of science (while demurring at many particulars), Peirce proposes the following definition of the word 'science':

> For him man is nature's interpreter; and in spite of the crudity of some anticipations, the idea of science is in his mind inseparably bound up with that of a life devoted to single-minded inquiry. That is also the way in which every scientific man thinks of science. That is the sense in which the word is understood in this chapter. Science is to mean for us a *mode of life* whose single animating purpose is to find out the real truth, which pursues this purpose by a well-considered method, founded on a thorough acquaintance with such scientific results already ascertained by others as may be available, and which seeks co-operation in the hope that the truth may be found, if not by any of the actual inquirers, yet ultimately by those who come after them and who shall make use of their results. It makes no difference how imperfect a man's knowledge may be, how mixed with error and prejudice; from the moment he engages in an inquiry in the spirit described, that which occupies him is *science* as the word will here be used (CP 7.54, emphasis mine).

This concrete characterization he also extends to our conceptions of the particular branches of science. He views a particular science, e.g., chemistry, as "no mere word manufactured by some academic pendant but as a real object, being the very concrete life of a social group constituted by real facts of interaction" (CP 7.52). From Peirce's perspective, then, when we speak of science in general or of some particular science, what we are concretely talking about is a community of inquirers extended over time with a unity of purpose and method which enables the product to be much more than the sum of the individual contributors. It is in this spirit that Peirce returns to the question of definition and states that "if we are to define science, not in the sense of stuffing it into an artificial pigeonhole where it may be found again by some insignificant mark, but in the sense of characterizing it as a living historical entity, we must conceive of it as that about which men such as I have described busy themselves" (CP 1.44).

Science, however, is not the only model of cognitive inquiry. Peirce characterizes three others (which he calls 'tenacity', 'authority', and 'self-

evidence') that have had historical periods of dominance and which continue to vie with science for our allegiance. But, by the same token,
although there are others, science is not just one model of cognitive inquiry on the same footing with these others. For him science is clearly
privileged; it is *the* model of cognitive inquiry if we are interested in solidifying opinion, proceeding rationally and ultimately attaining the
truth. It is instructive to look at the kinds of reasons Peirce brings to bear
on this issue of the preeminence of science so understood.

In his early defense of the privileged status of scientific inquiry, the
argument for its primacy focuses on the notion of solidifying opinion and
has a socio-historical character. He views cognition in general as a kind of
adaption-oriented human activity, with 'science' being one of the competitive cognitive models. The "best" cognitive model will be the one which
enables the one who uses it most effectively to adapt to his environment
and hence survive. The considerations that Peirce brings to bear to show
that the scientific model is the best are social and developmental. The failure of the models of tenacity and authority are traceable to their insularity.
The former model would be effective at fixing belief if one were a hermit,
but Peirce's simple objection is that "the social impulse is against it" (CP
5.378). Given our social nature, it will break down in practice. The latter
model would be effective in a closed society, but gives way in the face of
"wider social feeling" (CP 5.381). The inevitable glimpses of other societies or other times, while they may have an initial hardening effect, sow
the seeds of doubt which once they take root cannot be overcome by this
model itself. The third model, the a priori or self-evidence model, reduces
cognition to a matter of taste and hence will not be effective in enabling
belief to survive and prosper in a public intersubjective domain.

The scientific model alone, according to Peirce, seems to have the resources to fix belief in such a way as to give its employer any founded hope
for effective long-run cooperative interaction with his expanding community and shrinking environment. In other words, it is the only model
which, given our world, can fix belief effectively. Such is Peirce's contention. What I am interested in doing is taking a closer look at just those
social and historical features that make science so distinctive in this regard; and, even more importantly, exploring the connection between
these features initially tied to the fixation of belief and the notions of "objectivity" and "truth" that Peirce also associates with scientific methodology. To do this I will have to take a more fine-grained look at his
conception of science in process, science as a specific model of inquiry.

Since Peirce thinks of science as the collective activity of a particular interactive and cooperative group of inquirers (MS 615.15), it is incumbent upon him to specify those features that distinguish this social group from others. He locates its distinction in certain norms, practices, and institutions which characterize its members, define its structure, and delineate its boundaries.

Starting from the bottom up, he locates the distinctiveness of science in certain virtues being embodied in the individual members of the community of investigators. Sometimes he speaks of these as "norms" or even a "code of honor" (MS 615.14) but most frequently simply as "moral factors":

> The most vital factors in the method of modern science have not been the following of this or that logical prescription—although these have had their value too—but they have been the moral factors (CP 7.87).

And the particular moral factors which he specifies are *the love of truth, the sense of community,* and *the sense of confidence.*

The first of what Peirce calls "moral factors" seems initially to be completely uncontroversial: "the first of these has been the genuine love of truth and the conviction that nothing else could long endure" (CP 7.87). This apparently straightforward claim, however, masks some complexities. Peirce is not claiming that an inquiry qua scientific is either disinterested or presuppositionless. On the contrary, he is well aware of the many interests that can motivate a given line of scientific inquiry. His claim is that for the truly scientific mind the search for truth is the dominant one. Sometimes the contrast he has in mind is between this purely cognitive motivation and other more or less noble motives such as fame, money, or social welfare (CP 8.143), but most often the contrast is between two cognitive attitudes, namely, the mind-set of the inquirer and the mind-set of the pedagogue. He sees the scientist as the one whose dominant driving interest is in the search for truth wherever it may lead, whereas he sees the pedagogue, whether teacher or preacher, as one whose dominant interest is in organizing and communicating what he already knows. At times, he characterizes the distinction as that between the laboratory mind and the seminary mind. This contrast between the quest for truth and the elaboration and dissemination of belief runs deep into the human character, and it is a contrast that Peirce sees 'writ large' in the difference between the spirit of modern science and that of the middle ages.

Nor does Peirce think that scientific inquiry is presuppositionless. Any given scientific inquiry is not only conducted against the background of the "established scientific verities" of the moment but also against the background of more general metaphysical assumptions which guide our orientation to the world (CP 7.82). It is our attitude toward these presuppositions that can be either scientific or not. If the quest for truth is dominant, these background presuppositions are never regarded as beyond question. Although, as entrenched, the presumption is in their favor, if the direction of the inquiry seems to call for their revision, then such a revision must be regarded as a real option in the interest of truth.

The second moral factor, the sense of community, is more complicated and attracts more of Peirce's attention. In addition to making the obvious points about the requirement of intersubjectivity of evidence imposed by the social character of scientific investigation, he goes on to explore the deeper commitments of self-sacrifice and self-abnegation involved in the enterprise which is science:

> The method of modern science is social in respect to the solidarity of its efforts. The scientific world is like a colony of insects in that the individual strives to produce that which he cannot himself hope to enjoy. One generation collects premises in order that a distant generation may discover what they mean. When a problem comes before the scientific world, a hundred men immediately set all their energies to work on it. One contributes this, another that. Another company, standing on the shoulders of the first, strikes a little higher until at last the parapet is attained (CP 7.87).

Mixing his metaphors between a "colony of insects" and a "company of troops," Peirce makes the point that the life of science is essentially that of an historical community that is teleological in structure. The development and continuance of this life depends on the social sense becoming supreme through the individual investigators developing those virtues that will enable them to subordinate their own satisfaction to the long range goals of the community.

For Peirce these personal virtues that constitute the sense of community are not merely an extrinsic support for the life of science but are essentially tied to the very logic of scientific method: "It can be shown that no inference of any individual can be thoroughly logical without certain determinations of his mind which do not concern any one inference immediately" (CP 5.354). And these "determinations of mind" involve the individual's viewing his particular inferences not just as part of the larger set of *his own* inferences but in terms of their role in that ongoing inquiry the proper logical subject of which is the historical community. It is with this in mind that Peirce articulates what he calls the three logical sentiments, namely, "interest in an indefinite community, recognition of the possibility of this interest being made supreme, and hope in the unlimited continuance of intellectual activity" (CP 2.655) as indispensable requirements of logic. The life of science demands the transcendence of both selfishness and skepticism through the active hope that rational cooperative effort will in the end prevail.

This leads to the third moral factor undergirding the development of science, namely, the sense of confidence. He thinks that a sense of confidence is particularly crucial in an enterprise that proceeds by the method of conjecture and refutation. With regard to our specific proposed explanations, we are clearly going to be wrong more often than we are right, so it is important that we continue to view our proximate failures in terms of their contribution to the long-range effort. He sees this confidence as characteristic of scientists: "modern science has never faltered in its confidence that it would ultimately find out the truth concerning any question to which it could apply the check of experiment" (CP 7.87). This attitude of mind implies both the correctness and completeness of science, and takes the form of the action-guiding hope that the indefinite application of scientific methodology will lead to success in the long run.

Given Peirce's pragmatism, it should not be surprising that he saw these moral factors not as private internal states but as embodied in a co-ordinated set of *practices* constitutive of the scientific community. He saw this single-minded concern for truth together with the sense of community and confidence manifested behaviorally in scientists' "unreserved discussions with one another" and their "availing themselves of their neighbor's results"—which practices developed into the constraints to make experiments replicable and evidence intersubjectively available. It is the network of these practices that is seen to constitute given science as "a real object, being the concrete life of a social group constituted by real facts of interrelation" (CP 7.52).

Moreover, the *institution* so constituted is not only the judge and repository of past results but even more importantly the locus of those criteria of evaluation of present programs and prognoses of future ones that afford dynamic continuity to the scientific enterprise and give it an identity over time that transcends any individual or group of practitioners. With regard to these matters, Peirce's involvement was not merely abstract and theoretical but concrete and practical. On the institutional level Peirce, through his father, was involved in the founding of both the American Association for the Advancement of Science and the National Academy of Sciences; and on the criteriological level his involvement was both more personal and more substantive. With regard to criteria of evaluation that could be used by the community's institutions, he was an enthusiastic although unsuccessful contributor.

Peirce saw as one of the most fundamental problems of the scientific community the rational determination of "how, with a given expenditure of money, time and energy, to obtain the most valuable addition to our knowledge" (CP 7.140). In response to this problem, he worked out specific criteria in an area he called "The Economy of Research" that would function in the rational assessment on a cost-benefit basis of proposed research programs so as to optimize the allocation of limited resources in its pursuit of long-range goals. It was his conviction that if these or criteria like them were to be adopted by the funding arm of the scientific community, judgments otherwise unprincipled would come under the purview of rational criteria designed with long-range success in mind.

It is this network of specific norms, practices, and institutions that distinguishes science as a cognitive way of life from other modes of fixing belief. Now back to the first of my two questions: what precisely is it about a cognitive process so constituted that would enable it to fix belief most effectively? For Peirce the answer is straightforward. On his account the other three cognitive models have their effectiveness undermined for the same reason; the ever-widening sphere of social interaction inevitably introduces factors of diversity which erode the insular consensus that forms their respective bases. Having no cognitive resources to deal with dissonance, confidence wanes and effective action breaks down. The scientific model, on the other hand, makes a virtue out of this vice by incorporating the social factors from the beginning and by building in mechanisms to take account of the diversity of opinion and plurality of perspectives. The data base is allowed to be as broad as it can be and is presumed to be diverse; the cognitive machinery is designed for continual adjustment to new inputs so that successive equilibrium points are found which are stable and can function as guides for action. The social factors are neutralized as threats by being incorporated as contributors. Our beliefs are guaranteed a dynamic stability.

So far, so good; but this only sets the stage for the second question, namely, what reason do we have to believe that a method effective for stabilizing belief bears any presumptive relation to the production of beliefs characterizable as "objective" and "true"?

3. Peirce on Objectivity and Truth in Science

What is it about the scientific way of proceeding that guarantees or at least renders probable its cognitive success? Since Peirce is looking at scientific inquiry as an historical process, the notion of validity *here and now* is replaced by the notion of validity *in the long run;* however, it is still far from obvious why procedures effective for belief stabilization should have anything to do with success understood as objectivity or truth. To get clear about this issue it will be essential to take an even more detailed look at Peirce's account of scientific methodology.

His general characterization of scientific method as involving abductive, deductive, and inductive phases is well-known. The abductive phase of inquiry is concerned with the original generation and recommendation of explanatory hypotheses; the deductive phase has to do with the logical elaboration of a given hypothesis; while the inductive phase has to do with the confirmation or falsification of the hypothesis by future experience. The deductive phase as "objectivity" or "truth" preserving seems relatively unproblematic, but the abductive and inductive phases seem to involve evidential gaps that call for some kind of rational bridging if our confidence in science's objectivity and truth is to be grounded. Given the number of possible explanations abstractly available for any set of phenomena, what account can be given of our ability to come up with antecedently plausible explanations of our world; and, secondly, what justification can we give for our confidence that continued application of confirmation procedures will lead to truth in the long run?

Peirce's account of the factors that cognitively ground abduction and induction falls somewhere between a likely story and a transcendental argument. He takes the history of science as the phenomenon to be explained, and he sees it as exhibiting a progressive development of empirical adequacy, predictive success, manipulative control, and explanatory power. It is to account for this multifaceted progressive development that Peirce sees fit to postulate certain special features to man's relation to the world which would render his *rate* and *degree* of the various kinds of success intelligible.

This strategy is most pronounced in his explication of the abductive or "discovery" phase of scientific inquiry, the phase which Peirce clearly thought was the most important and which most called for explanation:

> What sort of validity can be attributed to the First Stage of inquiry? Observe that neither Deduction nor Induction contributes the smallest *positive item* to the final conclusion of the inquiry. They render the

indefinite, definite; Deduction explicates; Induction evaluates; that's all. Over the chasm that yawns between the ultimate goal of science and such ideas of man's environment as those coming over him during his primeval wanderings in the forest . . . we are building a cantilever bridge of induction, held together by scientific struts and ties. Yet every plank of its advance is first laid by Retroduction [Abduction] alone . . . and neither Deduction nor Induction contributes a single new concept to the structure (CP 6.475).

It is not that deduction and induction are not crucial to scientific inquiry; it is that all the concepts that figure in the propositional content of scientific explanations—all the "positive items" as he calls them—must enter through the abductive process.[2]

The issue is the legitimacy of the inputs, the grounding of the process whereby the ideas which are to be the building blocks of explanations are initially introduced into scientific inquiry. The thought seems to be that if we cannot have confidence in the material introduced, how can we have confidence in the security of the completed building? But this very thought should set off warning bells. The building metaphor certainly suggests epistemic foundations, and is not one of the more salient features of Peirce's overall philosophical orientation his critique of foundationalism? Reflection on this point can lead us deeper into Peirce's conception of science.[3]

His pragmatism is forward-looking, not backward-looking; the engine of justification is self-correction, not foundations. In contrast to Aristotle and Descartes, his point is *not* that if there is going to be any justification at the end, then there must be solid justification at the beginning; or that the process of inquiry is at best justification-preserving and most frequently justification-diminishing. On the contrary, Peirce's own view is that whatever errors we start with or are led into at the beginning will be corrected over time by the process of inquiry itself such that the justification of the conclusion is genuinely built through the process.

Why, then, is he concerned with the grounding of the initial inputs?— for his concern with the validity of abduction *is* an epistemic concern about the initial introduction of explanatory ideas. The answer, I believe, is to be found in his reflections on this history of science. Peirce thinks that we have made genuine *progress* in scientific understanding that calls for explanation at many different levels. Moreover, he thinks that the question "How was man ever led to entertain a correct theory?" is prior to the questions having to do with "How he came to believe it" or "How is his belief justified?" Speaking of scientific theories that we acknowledge to be true, he asks:

> How was it that man was ever led to entertain that true theory? You can't say that it happened by chance because the possible theories, if not strictly innumerable, at any rate exceed a trillion . . . and therefore the chances are too overwhelmingly against the single true theory in the twenty or thirty thousand years during which man has been a thinking animal ever to have come into man's head (CP 5.591).

The point is that when one looks at the history of science and sees this history as exhibiting a multifaceted cognitive progress, one feels that this could not be explained on the basis of merely random inputs. Given the de facto time span presented us, without some special assumptions bearing on the antecedent reliability of the inputs, it would be extremely improbable that "even the greatest mind would have attained the amount of knowledge which is actually possessed by the lowest idiot" (CP 2.753). Hence the point is not that scientific explanation would be impossible without firm foundations but rather that the de facto success rate of science—its progress in the time allotted—would be unintelligible given purely random inputs or initial ideas that had no grounding in the order of things or in logical principles. Hence his speculation about the "validity of abduction."

Peirce's concern with this issue of the introduction of ideas into the inquiry process is structured by his division of the abductive phase into two different moments, each with a quite different kind of grounding or rationale. The first moment bears on discovery, properly so-called, namely, the origination of those conjectures which will make up the list of possible explanations of the phenomena under consideration. Here he ruminates about man's ability to select from the potentially infinite set of hypotheses a subset of possible explanations that will contain the ultimately adequate account. In the end, he posits a "natural instinct for guessing right" as the first part of any account of the de facto historical rate of success of science. This instinct, he says, is "strong enough not to be overwhelmingly more often wrong than right" (CP 5.173) and, given the iteration of the process, this should be enough to get the right explanation on the list to be considered.[4]

Moreover, this cognitively crucial natural instinct is not left as a bare posit but is accompanied by a likely story of its existence and functioning in creative scientific minds. His story is broadly evolutionary in nature. Given the obvious presence of survival instincts in the rest of the animal kingdom, Peirce's first thought is that it is not unreasonable to believe that we too have those instincts necessary for the effective continuance of our distinctive mode of life (CP 6.476). He sees this ability to guess right

as having obvious adaptive value and hence as a clear candidate for natural
selection. In particular, he views a rudimentary grasp of certain fundamental principles of mechanics as crucially important to certain organic
practices necessary for survival.

> The great utility and indispensability of the conceptions of time,
> space and force even to the lowest intelligence are such as to suggest
> that they are the results of natural selection. Without something like
> geometrical, kinetic and mechanical conceptions, no animal could
> seize his food or do anything which might be necessary for the pres-
> ervation of the species. . . . As that animal would have an immense
> advantage in the struggle for life whose mechanical conceptions did
> not break down in a novel situation (such as development must
> bring about), there would be a constant selection in favor of more
> and more correct ideas of these matters (CP 6.418).

It is important to note that Peirce is here talking about the ability to guess
right (the impetus toward "more and more correct ideas of these matters");
he thinks that it is only beliefs that are on the right track that will have
staying power and developmental fecundity in our ever-changing circumstances. Since it is correct beliefs that will have survival value, it should
not be at all surprising that we—the survivors—should have this ability
to guess correctly to a considerable degree.

There is another chapter to the evolutionary story, one having to do
with how we came to have this ability in the first place. If we are operating
with a Cartesian picture of man's relation to nature such that the human
mind is, as it were, outside nature looking in, trying to guess at the laws
which describe its structure, then our apparent success rate would indeed
be mysterious. But if we assume that the human mind is constituted by
nature's evolving development, its affinity with its object becomes less
mysterious:

> If the universe conforms with any approach to accuracy to certain
> highly pervasive laws, and if man's mind has been developed under
> the influence of those laws, it is to be expected that he should have
> a *natural light* or *light of nature* or *instinctive insight* or genius tending
> to make him guess those laws aright or nearly aright (CP 5.604).

Quite ironically he finds the ultimate ground for these Cartesian notions
(natural light or light of nature) in a decidedly anti-Cartesian picture of
mind: "our minds having been formed under the influence of phenomena
governed by the laws of mechanics, certain conceptions entering into these
laws become implanted in our minds so that we readily guess at what the

laws are" (CP 6.10). Being nature's products, we have ready access to her secrets.

Finally, this general story is particularized for the major players in the history of science: "Galileo appeals to *il lume naturale* at the most crucial stages of his reasoning; Kepler, Gilbert and Harvey—not to speak of Copernicus—substantially rely on an inward power, not sufficient to reach the truth by itself, but yet supplying an essential factor to the influences carrying their minds to the truth" (CP 1.80). Evolutionary speculation is tied down to the specific historical phenomenon of the occasional creative genius who is indispensable to the progress of science.

As mentioned, on Peirce's account the introduction of ideas into the inquiry process is a two-stage affair, and the second moment of abduction is quite different from the first. It is to a degree rule-governed and bears on the task of singling out from our initial list of possible explanations (generated in the first moment) those we are to take as serious candidates for investigation and the order in which we are to take them. It is with regard to this second moment of abduction that Peirce, while allowing for a continuing role for "the natural instinct for guessing right," develops methodological criteria such as "simplicity" and those bearing on "the economics of research" which rationalize the antecedent preference ordering of those hypotheses that should be taken up by our specific research programs.

The specifics of his account of the second moment of abduction will reward closer scrutiny. It is under the general rubric of *economy* that Peirce proposes to organize the regulative principles that bear on this second moment of the abductive process. He puts the point forcefully: "what really is in all cases the leading consideration in Abduction is the question of Economy—Economy of money, time, thought and energy" (CP.5.600). It is important to note the broad scope of the term 'economy' here before moving on to examine some of the concrete regulative principles in terms of which he specifies the maxim. The term ranges over the various human resources that are invested in our cognitive endeavors and suggests that our principle concern ought to be to realize the best possible cognitive return on our investment.

The various rules Peirce articulates for employment in this moment of antecedent theory-choice can be seen to emanate from the above-mentioned general statement of the principle of economy. The first rule is a straightforward application of the general maxim: "if any hypothesis can be put to the test of experiment with very little expense of any kind, that should be regarded as a recommendation for giving it precedence in the inductive procedure" (CP 7.220). In the same vein is the suggestion that that hypothesis should be preferred which "can be most readily refuted if it is false" (CP 1.120). A second rule, which could be seen as a corollary of the first, recommends that one hypothesis should be preferred over another if one could not test the latter without doing almost all the work required to test the former but not vice versa (CP 7.93). A third rule, expressed in the jargon of the game of billiards, maintains that that hypothesis should be preferred which, if found to be false, would give the best "leave," that is, whose residuals would be the most instructive with reference to the next avenue to be explored (CP 7.221). Again, in the same vein, he invokes the game of Twenty Questions and recommends the preference for that hypothesis which would halve the number of possible explanations (CP 7.220). A fourth rule that he suggests enjoins us on the basis of economy to prefer (all else being equal) the broader of two hypotheses on the grounds that the illumination that it will shed on the general inquiry will be greater whether it is true or false (CP 7.221). Taken together, these rules amount to the injunction that at the abductive stage of inquiry the investigator should do a cost-benefit analysis of the various paths along which he can proceed.

The reason for this Peirce thinks is obvious. Proposals as hypotheses can inundate us in an overwhelming flood, while the process of evaluation to which each must be subjected before it can count at all as an item even of likely knowledge is very costly in time, energy, and money (and consequently in ideas which might be had for that time, energy, and money). Thus "economy would override every other consideration even if there were any other serious considerations" (CP 5.602). The various rules provide guidelines for this cost-benefit analysis. The decision procedure is far from automatic or simple, however, because the various rules are not only difficult to apply in concrete cases but also are often in conflict with one another. In concretely deciding what line of investigation to pursue seriously, a kind of practical rationality—again a species of "natural instinct"—is involved which cannot be reduced to a mere following of rules.

The point to be emphasized is that in this account of the criteria of antecedent theory-choice, Peirce clearly construes these criteria both *historically* and *socially*. One hypothesis is to be preferred over another not in terms of *its* likelihood of being true but in terms of the role it can play in the process of inquiry which is aimed at truth in the long run. An hypothesis is recommended to the degree that its pursuance at this point in time would move the inquiry along most efficiently. His invocation of the game of Twenty Questions is instructive. In this game a line of questioning recommends itself not in terms of the likelihood it will hit upon the correct answer immediately but in terms of the role this line of questioning will play in getting the answer eventually. Secondly, the justification of these abductive rules is not in terms of the individual investigator but in terms of the community of investigators of which he is a member. The hypothesis recommended to any individual may not at all be the one most likely to enable him to attain the truth but rather the one which will most effectively ensure the eventual attainment of truth. Given the state of the inquiry, an individual investigator may be rationally constrained to spend his days eliminating some unlikely possibilities. In the cognitive order, the individual's good is embedded in the good of the community.

Accordingly, just as evolutionary factors were intrinsic to the account of the validity of the first moment of abduction, historical, social, and moral factors are intrinsic to the account of the validity of the second. So whatever the distinction between internal and external explanations of science, for Peirce there has to be considerable room for evolution, history, society, and values on the internal side of the divide.

These features are even more pronounced in his account of the inductive phase of inquiry, his "justification of induction." 'Induction', as Peirce uses the term, is to be understood not simply in terms of the relation of individual cases to a general law but in terms of the *role* such a logical relationship plays in the inquiry-process in general. And the role this relationship does play is that of confirmation or falsification. The relationship between propositions describing individual instances to the relevant laws or theories is not that of the latter being "induced" from them but rather of these instances, having been predicted by the theory, functioning either to confirm or falsify it. It is through the inductive phase that the speculative flight of scientific inquiry is continually monitored by experience. It is specifically in virtue of this view of the continual monitoring of the inquiry process at the inductive phase that Peirce sees himself able to construe science as *self-regulating* and *self-corrective*. It is because of it that Peirce is able to claim of scientific method that "if it be persisted in long enough, it will assuredly correct any error concerning future experience into which it may temporarily lead us" (CP 5.145).

Is his confidence that continued application of confirmation procedures will lead to truth in the long run merely an unfounded hope or can it be shown to have some objective foundation? What must the world be like so as to render intelligible the success of this self-monitoring feature of scientific inquiry and thereby the long-run objectivity of science as a whole? Specifically, this is a question about the alleged self-corrective dimension of science while more generally it is a question about the justification of induction. For, if the confirmation procedures of science are going to be viewed as playing this crucial role in this movement toward truth over time, then we must have reason to believe that the inductive sampling that functions in the confirmation stage is not destined to be misleading and can function as a reliable guide to the structure of the real.

That Peirce believes that inductive procedures have this feature is quite clear. He views it as a procedure which "if steadily persisted in must lead to true knowledge in the long run of cases of its application whether to the existing world or to any imaginable world whatsoever" (CP 7.207). Induction is for him self-monitoring in that its continued use will uncover the mistakes in its earlier uses such that by this process of purification truth will be eventually attained. He sees this as quite independent of any particular features of the world. In fact, he cannot even imagine a world in which such procedures would not be reliable:

> If men were not able to learn from induction it might be because, as a general rule, when they have made an induction the order of things would then undergo a revolution. . . . But this general rule would itself be capable of being discovered by induction; and so it must be a law of such a universe that when this was discovered it would cease to operate. But this second law would itself be capable of discovery. And so in such a universe there would be nothing which would not sooner or later be known; and it would have an order capable of discovery by a sufficiently long course of reasoning (CP 5.352).

If even in such a demonically contrived universe inductive procedures would be reliable, surely they would be reliable in any ordinary universe—ours in particular.

It is important to reemphasize that he is not looking at the confirmation process (the inductive phase of inquiry) in terms of the degree of warrant any specific theory has in terms of specific test results but in terms of the long-run effect of continued empirical testing. The self-correctiveness of science crucially involves the monitoring role of the inductive phase, but the inductive phase does not supply the successive hypotheses; it functions only to eliminate. Better hypotheses are generated by the whole process of inquiry over time; it is a matter of genuinely promising suggestions continually subjecting themselves to elaboration, prediction, and possible elimination. The individual scientist is viewed as a member of an historical community whose bond of unity is the employment of this self-corrective method. The logical subject of the inquiry is the *scientific community over time.* The continual monitoring at the inductive phase occasions conceptual revision through the abductive phase with the overall process of inquiry resulting over time in a more and more adequate picture of the world.

Peirce's acceptance of this picture of science is tied to his construal of the monitoring phase (induction-confirmation) specifically in terms of statistical inductions. Specific predictions as to the character of our world are derived from the hypothesis under investigation, and then our world is checked for this character. "Samples" are drawn from our world to see if it has the characteristics we suppose it to have. Obviously there is some initial evidence for this character, but if controlled sampling belies its presence, continued sampling should reveal which of the other proposed characteristics really map onto our world. Why this should be the case brings us to the heart of Peirce's pragmatic realism:

> An endless series must have some character; and it would be absurd to say that experience has a character which is never manifested. But there is no other way in which the character of that series can manifest itself than while the endless series is still incomplete. Therefore, if the character which the entire series possesses, still, as the series goes on, it must certainly tend however irregularly toward becoming so; and all the rest of the reasoner's life will be a continuation of this inferential process. This inference does not depend on any assumption that the series will be endless, that the future will be like the past, or that nature is uniform, or any other material assumption whatsoever (CP 2.784).

His idea is that inductive inference is basically an inference from part to whole and its validity depends simply on the fact that parts do make up and constitute the whole. In confirmation we are basically involved in drawing samples from a population, and if the frequency with which some relevant property is distributed over the individuals of that sample does not correspond to its frequency of distribution over the population, the discrepancy is sure to become apparent as the sampling process is extended over the long run. To resist this line of thought is to entertain a conception of the population or the whole which will never manifest itself in the samples or the parts. But to entertain this is to conceive of truth as possibly transcendent, reality as possibly incognizable; both of which Peirce thinks he has good reason to reject.

This brings us to the final chapter of the story, namely, Peirce's account of "truth" and "reality." Given the socio-historical conception of scientific inquiry he has unfolded, one might think that the natural capstone of such an account would be a consensus theory of truth and a social construction view of reality with all the contingency and relativity such views involve. There may be texts in Peirce that suggest this line, and given that there can be several quasi-natural conclusions to a story, one might make the case that this is where the story naturally leads. It is my contention, however, that while Peirce does have a view of truth and reality as tied to scientific inquiry, it is not the view suggested above but rather one importantly different from it in several crucial respects.

His conclusion of the story is as follows: "truth is that correspondence of an abstract statement with the ideal limit towards which endless investigation would tend to bring scientific belief" (CP 5.565). It is the consensus, if one insists on that notion, that *would* emerge if a properly conducted inquiry were to continue indefinitely. Truth is a property of an opinion and as such is not independent of thought, but "it is independent of all that is arbitrary and individual in thought, and is quite independent of how you or I or any number of men think" (CP 8.12). *Truth* is an objective and absolute notion as is *reality,* which is defined quite simply as that which is represented in a true opinion: "To make a distinction between the true conception of a thing and the thing itself is . . . only to regard one and the same thing from two different points of view; for the immediate object of thought in a true judgment *is* the reality" (CP 8.16). Here "truth" and "reality" are tied to inquiry but in a way that preserves the objective and absolute character of both. That this is Peirce's conclusion to the story about the validity of scientific inference is manifest in his claim that "though a synthetic inference cannot by any means be reduced to deduction, yet that the rule of induction will hold good in the long run may be deduced from the principle that reality is only the object of the final opinion to which a sufficient investigation would lead" (CP 2.693).

4. Peirce on the Social Dimensions of Science

Viewed from the perspective of the present, the account of science articulated by Peirce can be seen to embody features of the classical picture of science together with features of both the earlier and later sociological traditions. Moreover, these various features, which from our vantage point are supposed discordant, seem to fit together in something like a coherent whole.

In the classical spirit he maintains that (1) the aim of science is objectivity and truth, (2) that there is specifically characterizable scientific method, and (3) that this method defines the paradigmatic case of rational cognitive behavior. He also holds (4) that the history of science exhibits progress toward objectivity and truth, and (5) that there is a logic of scientific inquiry that provides a rationale for this progress.

But he also maintains (one must resist the temptation to say "on the other hand") that scientific inquiry is (6) informed by interests, (7) structured by norms, and (8) driven by certain ineliminable moral factors and social ideals. Added to these features are (9) a causal-evolutionary account of scientific insight, and (10) a fundamentally economic characterization of theory-acceptance.

In my judgment, the point most worth reflecting on is that for Peirce all ten factors are "intrinsic" to science and all are involved in an "internal" account of scientific development. The last five do not compromise or even qualify the first. In fact, far from compromising any features of the classical picture, the social and historical factors are seen to be partially constitutive of "scientific rationality," "scientific progress," and "the realistic reach of science."

One's stance on the issue of the rationality of scientific explanation and scientific change is as much a function of the scope of one's conception of rationality as it is of any particular historical contention; and, similarly, one's stance on the issue of the realistic reach of science is as much a function of one's conception of reality as of any historical story of what scientists do. It is my contention that there is a symbiotic relationship between the articulation of defensible abstract notions of "rationality" and "reality" and familiarity with the concrete development of human cognitive accomplishments.

Hence, part of the explanation of Peirce's ability to satisfy himself that all of the aforementioned factors can be woven together into an internally coherent account of science would be in terms of his richer (or at least broader) conceptions of "rationality" and "reasoning," conceptions which he gets in turn from reflecting on the history of thought. Speaking approvingly of Lavoisier, he identifies as one of the latter's major accomplishments the articulation of "a new conception of reasoning as something which is to be done with one's eyes open, in manipulating real things instead of words and fancies" (CP 5.363). Peirce himself was to continue this line of development and expand the concepts of rationality and reasoning in the direction of further concreteness by including historical, social, institutional, and valuational factors as well. As the concept of rationality expands, the number and kind of factors it is rational to take

into account in accepting or deciding among scientific theories correspondingly expands. Conversely, the number and kinds of extra-rational
factors contract.

And this is not ad hoc or conventional. Illuminating concepts do not
descend from a Platonic heaven but are fashioned through their own historical dialectic. This is particularly true for fundamental normative notions such as *rational* and *real,* and Peirce would defend *his* formulation
of such notions in terms of their ability to shed light on the history of
and practices embedded in our cognitive enterprises. They emerge from
the process they are endeavoring to illuminate. This does not mean that
there is no room at all for the internal-external distinction with regard to
the history of science, and no place at all for an articulation of nonrational
factors influencing the development of science. But it does mean that we
should not be too quick to assume that historical, social, and even moral
factors are automatically to be thought of as nonrational external factors
vis à vis the structure and development of science.

NOTES

1. The numbers in the text refer to the standard Peirce editions in the conventional way. CP for *Collected Papers of Charles S. Peirce,* ed. Hartshorne, Weiss,
and Burks; W for *Writings of Charles S. Peirce,* ed. Fisch, Moore, and Kloesel
et al.; MS for Peirce manuscripts as catalogued in *Annotated Catalogue of the Papers
of Charles S. Peirce,* ed. Robin.

2. For an excellent discussion of this dimension of abduction, see Timothy
Shanahan, "The First Moment of Scientific Inquiry: C. S. Peirce on the Logic of
Abduction," in *Transactions of the Charles S. Peirce Society* 22 (1986):449–466.

3. For a discussion of this point, see C. F. Delaney, "Peirce's Critique of Foundationalism," in *Monist* 57 (1973):240–251.

4. This section draws on my "Peirce on the Conditions of Possibility of Science" in *Charles S. Peirce and the Philosophy of Science,* ed. E. Moore (Tuscaloosa,
Ala.: University of Alabama Press, forthcoming.)

THE ORIGINS OF MANNHEIM'S
SOCIOLOGY OF KNOWLEDGE

Fritz Ringer

The remarks that follow are based largely upon my *Decline of the German Mandarins*, which was written, partly under the influence of Karl Mannheim, as an experiment in the historical sociology of knowledge.[1] The book deals with what I would now call German academic culture. By an "academic culture" I mean, on the one hand, the *institutions, practices,* and *social relations* that obtain in an academic community and, on the other hand, the *beliefs,* including incompletely conscious beliefs, held within that community about its practices of research and teaching. I consider that the beliefs involved may be treated as *ideologies* in the broader sense of that term; that is, they may be partly explained in terms of the relevant institutions, practices, and social relations. Sometimes, they are also ideologies in the narrower sense of that term, in that they tend to legitimate and to preserve the existing social system.

1. German Academic Culture and the Mandarin Thesis

In the case of the "German mandarins," I focused upon the beliefs current among German academic humanists and social scientists between about 1890 and 1933, a period which many of them explicitly characterized as one of cultural and intellectual crisis. My argument was—and still is—that their responses to this intellectual crisis were partly shaped by their sense of a decline in their own social position and cultural leadership. If I am right about this, then Mannheim's sociology of knowledge itself can be at least partly understood as a product of intellectual *and social* crisis. That is what I will try to show, and I will begin with a brief sketch of the social background.

Not only did industrialization come relatively late in Germany, educational modernization came relatively early. As a result, an educated upper middle class of civil servants, Protestant pastors, lawyers, doctors, secondary teachers and university professors achieved a particularly prominent position in nineteenth-century German society. The "mandarins," members of the university-educated or "academic" professions, made up an educated stratum (*Bildungsschicht, Bildungsbürgertum*) that was more a *status* elite than an economic *class* in Max Weber's terms. The social prestige of the highly educated, their style of life and their self-image were based more on their learning than on aristocratic birth on the one hand, or on wealth and economic power, on the other. Their close ties to the monarchical civil service gave them a degree of political influence, at least during a transitional period in German history, and they claimed a broader cultural leadership as intellectual notables as well. Institutionally, it was the revitalization of the German universities during the late eighteenth and early nineteenth centuries that secured their position, together with the early emergence of a certified corps of university-educated secondary teachers, and of a highly developed scale of educational qualifications and entitlements (*Berechtigungen*), which was tied to merit principles of recruitment in the civil service. The preeminent place of the German university professors and the outstanding achievements of German university scholarship during the nineteenth century were built on these social foundations. The German academics were "mandarin intellectuals," partly because they were the most prominent representatives of the "mandarin" elite as a whole. But they also controlled the standards of access to that elite, and they were its natural spokesmen. They formulated and expressed its political and cultural aspirations, its "ideology."

From the late nineteenth century on, however, the social position and cultural leadership of the German mandarin intellectuals came under increasing pressure from changes within the educational system as well as in the larger environment. Industrialization, when it came, proceeded swiftly. It was accompanied by an unusually high degree of corporate concentration on the one hand, and by the rapid advance of working-class organization, on the other. The growing power of money and of "the masses" confronted each other in an undisguised conflict of material interests. The high capitalist class society made traditional status conventions appear increasingly irrelevant, even as technical "civilization" threatened to overwhelm the inherited norms of humanist culture. In secondary and in higher education, substantial enrollment increases and the rise of "realistic" or technical studies raised the spectres of "massification" and of "utilitarianism," while the advances of disciplinary specialization threatened the moral and personal significance assigned to learning in the neohumanist and idealist philosophies.

In response to these converging pressures, a creative and progressive minority of academic "modernists" (as I call them) attempted to "translate" vital elements of the mandarin heritage in ways that might ensure their continued relevance. An even smaller group, which included Mannheim, advanced toward radical criticisms of their tradition. But the large majority of "orthodox" mandarin intellectuals persisted in an exclusively defensive position that ultimately took on escapist and purely irrational dimensions, under the impact of defeat, revolution, and inflation, during the Weimar period.

2. Mandarin Ideology of Bildung

Social and intellectual historians have given too little attention to middle-class ideals of education. Apparently obsessed with entrepreneurial individualism as the root of "bourgeois ideology," they have largely ignored advanced education and intellectual "merit" as sources of middle-class self-definitions and middle-class self-esteem. The fundament of German "mandarin" individualism, in any case, was the concept of *Bildung*, meaning education in the large sense of self-development or "cultivation." One can find it in a standard encyclopedia of the interwar period; or one can follow the subtle analysis of a Georg Simmel some decades earlier; its salient implications remain the same.[2] To begin with, *Bildung* as a process entails an interpretive or "hermeneutic" relationship between a learner and a set of texts. The texts are objectively given; in neo-idealist terminology, they make up a suprapersonal realm of "objective cultural values."

The learner's "understanding" of these texts is more than analytical or intellectual, for he is said to "absorb" the "values" transmitted by the texts. In one version of the tradition, he is pictured as empathetically identifying with the author and in effect "reliving" (*nacherleben*) or *reproducing* the experiences that gave rise to the text. This identificationist or subjectivist model of textual interpretation was not only a constant methodological temptation in German humanistic scholarship; it was also particularly rich in its ideological yield, for the reader could be imagined transformed by the value-laden contents of his texts. As Max Weber observed in a similar context, the canonical sources of the tradition were thought to have charismatic qualities that enriched and "elevated" those who "made them their own."[3]

In a more complex version of the hermeneutic relationship, it was conceived as a dialectic *interaction* between the reader and the text. Here the reader actively posited *possible* interpretations, which the text then "showed" to be more or less effective in clarifying and integrating what at first appeared obscure or incoherent. The reader's active contribution to this process made sense of another claim that typically figured in definitions of *Bildung*. In Simmel's version, this was the thesis that "cultivation comes about only if the contents absorbed out of the suprapersonal realm seem, as through a secret harmony, to unfold only that in the soul [of the reader] which exists within it as its own instinctual tendency, and as the inner prefiguration of its subjective perfection."[4] The reader, in other words, is utterly unique; his self-development is the fulfillment of a unique potential; there is a "secret harmony" between what the texts "unfold" within his soul and what already "existed" there to begin with.

If most German academic humanists were more or less consciously committed to the concept of *Bildung* from the late eighteenth century on, then much is explained that would otherwise remain merely given. Thus the modern German research university drew some of its vitality from the neo-humanist enthusiasm that also inspired a new vision of education. The birth of the research seminar and the subsequent expansion of the "philosophical" faculties were linked to the emergence of the philological and interpretive disciplines, which initially shaped the dominant paradigms of exact scholarship or *Wissenschaft*. In nineteenth-century German historiography, what may be called the *principle of empathy* demanded that historical epochs be understood "in their own terms," or that the past-minded historian "put himself in the place of" the historical agents he seeks to comprehend. In philosophy, the post-Kantian Idealists were dedicated to the image of mind unfolding and comprehending itself in its creations. The word *Geisteswissenschaft* did not come into common use until the later nineteenth century; but the interpretive tradition that really defined it was, of course, much older.[5]

The neo-idealist revival of the *Geisteswissenschaften* that began with the work of Wilhelm Dilthey in the 1880s was not so much a new departure as an effort to clarify a well-established pattern of interpretive practice. One of the difficulties it faced was precisely the one just raised. Is interpretation based upon the "reliving" of the experiences "behind" the text and thus upon the reproduction of inner states, or is it a less subjective but more complicated procedure? Support for the latter view can be found in Martin Heidegger, in the late works of Dilthey, and of course in the more recent elucidations of Hans-Georg Gadamer.[6] Yet the tendency to construe the hermeneutic relationship as an empathetic *Erleben* was particularly prevalent among German humanists during the intellectual crisis of the Weimar period.

The notion of *Bildung* as the unfolding of a unique potentiality too was rich in implications. It differed radically, not only from any view of education as the "socialization" of the learner by an external agent, but also from any mere superaddition of information or of analytical skills. The cultivated individual, moreover, is literally incomparable; he resists any "abstract" or "reductive" characterization that might make him a predictable agent in the manner of the utilitarian rationalist or of "economic man." To be committed to this *principle of individuality*, whether in full consciousness or not, is to be guided toward certain analogous schemes of thought about change, about the relationships of the particular to the general, and of the individual to the group. Thus change is likely to appear as the development of a unique whole "from within," or as the actualization of a preexistent essence, not as a "mechanical" rearrangement of identical constituent units. A grouping is likely to be conceived as a configuration of unique elements in particular relationships to each other, rather than as a mere aggregate of similar parts. In the human studies, the principle of individuality favored an emphasis upon the interpretable individual and upon networks of interpersonal relationships. In the German historical tradition, nation-states and epochs as well as persons could be conceived as unique individualities, rather than as products of timeless laws. This view was codified in Wilhelm Windelband's 1894 distinction between "nomothetic" and "idiographic" disciplines, in which idiographic description in the cultural sciences was held to focus upon the unique and the particular.[7]

Thus the idea of self-cultivation shaped methodological preferences in the human studies. It also profoundly affected the concept of *Wissenschaft*, which encompassed all systematic disciplines, including the interpretive ones, of course. There was a common belief that productive involvement in research should have the effect of *Bildung*. The original scholar was meant to emerge from his activity enriched in mind *and person*. In the late nineteenth and early twentieth centuries, this expectation was also expressed in the recurring proposition that *Wissenschaft* should engender *Weltanschauung*, a comprehensive and partly evaluative orientation toward the world.[8] The pursuit of truth was to lead to something like integral insight and moral certainty, or personal knowledge, or wisdom.

To the extent that *Wissenschaft* was linked to the objective of *Bildung*, moreover, the hermeneutic disciplines were assigned a primary role.

Although the classical secondary schools taught mathematics in Germany as elsewhere, practical and experimental knowledge was at least theoretically undervalued and rather difficult to conceptualize. Laboratory science depends upon controlled intervention in an environment. Yet German treatises on *Bildung* and *Wissenschaft* rarely included positive references to practical activity. On the contrary, they usually inveighed against instrumental or "utilitarian" conceptions of knowledge, and they tended almost automatically to identify "pure" *Wissenschaft* as impractical.[9] It was as if a symbolic hierarchy extended downward from abstract theory to experimental or causal analysis, and finally to merely "technical" or applied studies.

It should be added that there was a change in the meaning of *Bildung* sometime between 1800 and 1900, a change that can be described in Mannheim's terms as a shift from a forward-looking or "utopian" emphasis to a defensive or "ideological" one. Around 1800, the idea of self-enhancement through *Bildung* was a socially progressive and universalist challenge to permanent social distinctions based on birth. Advanced education was not in fact available to everyone, but it seemed universally accessible to talent *in principle*. The emerging educated middle class could in good conscience regard itself as an "open" or "merit" elite, a new aristocracy of intelligence and personal worth. By around 1900 or 1920, in sharp contrast, advanced education itself had taken on the character of a distinguishing social privilege. With the full institutionalization of the credentials system, educational qualifications had become routine sources of social status. An established educated upper middle class now sought to check the influx of new social groups into the universities, and thus to reduce the competition for places in the "academic" professions.

As the concept of *Bildung* took on a socially confirmative significance, some of its other implications changed as well. Thus there was an unmistakable shift in the relationship of the mandarin intellectuals to the state. In Wilhelm von Humboldt's early writings, he had insisted that human improvement can come only from the development of free individualities in interaction with each other. This was the *cultural* individualism that so impressed John Stuart Mill. Even in Humboldt's projects for the reorganization of Prussian higher education in 1809–1810, he saw the state as providing no more than a material environment for the autonomous life of *Wissenschaft*. Nevertheless, the institutional arrangements he actually made or conceded gave considerable scope to state intervention in university affairs. Indeed, to several of his contemporaries and to many German academics of later eras, this did not seem troublesome; or it seemed less and less troublesome. For they tended to regard the existing state as an adequate embodiment of the "cultural state" (*Kulturstaat*), the disinterested supporter and earthly representative of their national culture. Especially as they began to see themselves as a threatened minority, the mandarin intellectuals moved toward an ever firmer commitment to the bureaucratic monarchy, which sustained their institutions, protected their social position, and accepted their claim to speak for the nation as a whole.

3. The Crisis of Wissenschaft

From around 1890 on, German university professors in the humanities and social sciences expressed a sense of crisis that reached its greatest intensity during the interwar period. They wrote of a "crisis of culture" and, by the 1920s, of a "crisis of *Wissenschaft*" as well. They were concerned partly with structural transformations in the educational system that were commonly perceived as forms of modernization and democratization. Most of them opposed these changes or sought to reverse them. They accordingly used the ideology of *Bildung* in a conservative form to resist cultural "levelling" and the supposed advances of "utilitarianism" in science. At a deeper level, they were oppressed by a sense that they were losing their former authority, not only in cultural questions, but in social and political life as well. "Mind" appeared to have forfeited its influence in public life; for ideas and principles played a shrinking role in the organized confrontations among economic organizations and political machines. Before 1918, the most orthodox among German university professors liked to think, against strong evidence to the contrary, that the bureaucratic monarchy could "rise above" class conflict and reverse the disaffection of "the masses" by pursuing a paternalist program of "social policy." Economic individualism and unrestrained capitalism found few supporters in the German academic community; the mandarin intellectuals were not "bourgeois thinkers" in that sense of the term. Yet many of them identified with the conservative and "national" forces in Wilhelmian politics, distrusted potentially democratic alternatives, and directed their deepest hostility against Social Democracy and the supposed "materialism" of "the masses".

During the Weimar period, the orthodox majority of German university professors supported the "national" opposition to the new regime. Unable to perceive democratic liberalism as a genuine political principle, and unwilling seriously to address the distributive questions that strained the Republic's parliamentary system, they became addicted to moralistic

attacks upon modern "interest politics." Since they had no part in the conflict of immediately *economic* interests between capitalists and workers,
they saw themselves as *absolutely* disinterested, able to stand "above" the
"materialistic" politics of the contending parties. Striking a characteristi-
cally "apolitical" pose, they preached the primacy of the "national community" over its parts, or the need for an "idealistic" alternative to economic
class conflict. Some dreamed of an "intellectual" or "spiritual revolution"
that would restore the empire of "mind" in public affairs, and such "idealistic" prophecies of course had very material political consequences.

The minority I have called "modernists," to be sure, took less one-
sided positions. Having been relatively critical of the Wilhelmian social
and political system, they supported the genuinely republican parties after
1918. Most of them were guided less by genuine enthusiasm for democracy, not to mention socialism, than by a sense of realism, and by the hope
that the Republic might be encouraged to pursue moderate policies. Some
of them were determined cultural individualists or "liberals" in some sense
of that term; others more closely resembled the type of the reformist conservative. All believed that the most vital elements in their tradition could
be preserved and transmitted to a wider audience in an inescapably more
democratic age. This was an intellectually fruitful position; for it caused
them to reexamine their intellectual heritage in an effort to "translate" its
soundest conceptions and thus to perpetuate them in a new environment.
In almost every discipline and especially in the social sciences, some of the
most prominent innovators were modernists, who critically reexamined
and reformulated vital aspects of the German scholarly tradition.

A very few of the modernists, in fact, may be identified as "radical
modernists" or simply as radical critics, in that they were driven into more
thoroughly heterodox paths. Degrees of radicalism were not only individual responses to unusual and distancing experiences, from contacts outside
the academic world to encounters with anti-Semitism or a close reading of
Hobbes; they were also immediate consequences of intellectual crisis and
incongruity. Once dislodged from the position of naive adherence, the
critics of orthodoxy could be precipitated into a characteristic chain of re-
versals that nevertheless reflected the tradition they challenged. Thus
German idealism provoked self-conscious anti-idealisms that are hard to
imagine in other intellectual fields. The philosopher Ernst von Aster, for
example, complained of the "merciless moralizing" that often took the
place of political analysis in the German academic debates of the 1920s.
The rhetoric of "apolitical idealism" virtually forced dissenters into a debunking stance. They had the choice of unmasking the nonspiritual in-

terests actually served by such rhetoric, of crudely reducing the much-cited good of the whole to the interests of its members, or of countering elevated laments about lower-class "materialism" in Bertold Brecht's language: *"Erst kommt das Fressen, dann die Moral!"* (First eats, then morals!).[10] Some of Mannheim's work, it seems to me, must be understood in this context, which is not to exclude the possibility that he imitated certain orthodox patterns of thought, even while sharply attacking others. But I will come back to that issue.

While most German academics of our period were troubled by structural changes in education and in politics, they also expressed much anxiety over the advance of disciplinary specialization. Most of them were deeply involved in specialized research themselves. Yet they could not shake the sense that something vital to them was being undermined, and that their practice was becoming incongruent with their ideals. They not only feared a kind of cognitive atomization and incoherence; they also felt that specialization threatened the old relationship between empirical *Wissenschaft* and idealist philosophy.

This helps to account for the almost automatic association of specialization with "positivism." The latter in turn was hardly ever described approvingly or in detail; for *self-confessed* positivists were rare to nonexistent at German universities between the 1890s and the 1930s. Thus the label "positivism" was almost invariably used in a derogatory sense, and the "positivists" were typically thought guilty of *unacknowledged* fallacies, chief among them the belief that the search for law-like regularities is the main task of the interpretive and historical disciplines as well. Indeed, even unreflected research *practices* could be viewed as positivist, if they envisaged a theory-free adding up of facts, or if they were guided by a strong causalist program. Obviously, all forms of determinism, "materialism," or doctrinaire Marxism were considered positivist in tendency, as were "atomistic" or otherwise reductive analyses of complex mental states or social groupings. Indeed, positivism was seen as a kind of intellectual acid, a potentially disastrous dissolvent of wholistic concepts, traditional beliefs, and socially integrative certainties. To "overcome" the problems raised by specialization and positivism alike, it was widely held, there was an urgent need for a revitalization of philosophical idealism that would also reinstate *Wissenschaft* as a ground for an integral and partly normative *Weltanschauung*.

During the Weimar period, the revulsion against specialization gave rise to repeated calls for intellectual "synthesis." Initially, 'synthesis' meant no more than a drawing together of discrete research results, and it was recommended more often by modernists than by orthodox academics. But it gradually became a predominantly orthodox slogan, and it took on an ever broader meaning. Thus the neo-idealist revival of the *Geisteswissenschaften* since the 1880s was reinterpreted to signify a spiritually profitable engagement with the values embedded in great texts. The rhetoric of *Erleben* was used to suggest an identificationist account of interpretation, just as "phenomenological" methods were taken to authorize a direct apprehension of "essential" meanings. A few scholars, including Max Weber, warned against an obsession with intuitive insight and vital experience. But the stance Weber took in his famous lecture on "Learning as a Vocation" remained a minority position, and almost a foil for repeated expressions of dissent from it. [11]

The identificationist construal of historical interpretation probably aggravated a further dilemma that was intensively discussed during the 1920s, though it originated a good deal earlier than that. This was the "problem of historicism" (*Historismus*), which was carefully analysed by Ernst Troeltsch between 1918 and 1922. In Troeltsch's account of it, the problem arose because the historical method revealed all values and convictions to be expressions of particular historical contexts, so that no unconditional certainties could be rescued from the limitations of historicity. [12] This is not the issue mainly referred to in Anglo-American discussions of "historical relativism," which has more to do with the difficulty of obtaining objective *knowledge* of the past than with the precariousness of present-day *value judgments*. It is the idiographic doctrine which suggests that epochs are unique totalities that can be understood only in their own terms. But if that methodological commitment is taken quite seriously, then the historian's own standpoint is inseparable from his particular historical situation. His norms and judgments too are fatally entangled in the flux of history. That is the "problem of *Historismus*" as it confronted Karl Mannheim, among others, during the "crisis of *Wissenschaft*" of the 1920s.

4. Mannheim's Sociology of Knowledge in Relation to the Crisis

Against this sketch of the social and intellectual background, I want now to indicate some of the ways in which Mannheim's sociology of knowledge reflected its origins in the Weimar crisis of *Wissenschaft*. Thus an assumption that has probably been made in other intellectual environments as well was particularly prevalent in the German academic culture of the 1920s. This is the conviction that certain methodological or even

epistemological positions are linked to particular socio-political preferences. As an example, consider the debate over the young discipline of
sociology in 1919 and 1920. Carl H. Becker, the reformist Secretary for
university affairs in the Prussian Ministry of Culture, which was headed at
that time by a Social Democrat, suggested that sociology was particularly
suited for the urgent task of "synthesis." It could help to compensate for
the excesses of specialization, while also fruitfully involving German
scholarship in the pressing social and economic problems of the day. Becker's suggestion provoked a sharp response from two orthodox academics,
who promptly identified sociology with socialism. One of them, the arch-
conservative historian Georg von Below, claimed that German university
professors were already very much engaged in political life; Becker was
presumably unhappy only because they generally repudiated the Socialist
Republic. As for the insights of sociology, they were merely weaker versions of what the German Romantics had taught about the rootedness of
the individual in his national culture (*Volksgeist*). To substitute the new
sociology for these Romantic doctrines was to open the way for the ma-
terialist positivism developed in France and England. Becker's wrong-
headed recommendation of sociological "synthesis" was presumably due to
his Marxist sympathies.[13]

Or consider a manifesto issued by members of the Vienna Circle in
1929. Writing as exasperated outsiders, they attacked the "growth of
metaphysical and theologizing tendencies" in German academic philosophy. They announced that most so-called philosophical problems were
products of semantic confusion that could be analyzed out of existence. A
new kind of philosophy would henceforth work directly with the specialized disciplines, helping them with the clarification of their methods. The
authors of the manifesto also expressed their sympathy for the progressive
social and political movements of the day, noting a "curious unanimity"
among themselves on issues separate from their main philosophical concerns. Why was agreement on scientific issues in fact accompanied by political consensus?—Rudolf Carnap speculated that "those who hold on to
the past in the social field also cultivate . . . (outdated) positions in metaphysics and theology."[14] It is interesting that Carnap thus essentially rat-
ified von Below's association of positivism with socio-political radicalism,
which would certainly have surprised American radicals of the 1960s.

In a somewhat different vein, finally, consider some definitions proposed by Max Scheler, who practiced what he considered the "sociology of
knowledge" during the mid-1920s. Scheler distinguished three "forms of
knowledge": the "knowledge of achievement" (*Leistungswissen*), the

"knowledge of cultivation" (*Bildungswissen*), and the "knowledge of salvation" (*Erlösungswissen*). By the knowledge of achievement he meant knowledge, presumably of regularities and causal relationships, that permits those who possess it to intervene successfully in the natural or social world. For this form of knowledge, Scheler was prepared to accept Max Weber's self-denying exclusion of *Wissenschaft* from the realm of ultimate value judgments. Not so for the knowledge of *Bildung,* in which man transcends practical needs to 'deify' himself, making his understanding a microcosm of the universe. The "knowledge of cultivation" could also be translated as "personal knowledge" or simply "wisdom"; Scheler thought that it had to encompass a *Weltanschauung.* In the "knowledge of salvation," of course, man approaches the great questions of metaphysics and of religion. [15]

I am saying that the "crisis of *Wissenschaft*" brought into open debate a set of questions about the practical implications and the moral uses of knowledge that are normally answered in a more tacit way, if at all. The widespread anxiety over the declining influence of "mind" caused various styles of thought to be examined with a view to their spiritual or ideological efficacy. The attacks on "positivism," the calls for "synthesis" and for a revival of "idealism" reflected a programmatic or even tactical approach to intellectual issues that probably aggravated the general sense of crisis. Moreover, the German university professors were introduced in a particularly abrupt fashion to the language of modern politics. In that language, as Mannheim pointed out, the views of opponents can be debunked by an "unmasking" (*Enthüllung*) that shows them to be mere rationalizations of concrete interests. Thus the orthodox mandarins themselves routinely accused the working class of "materialism," while the radical modernists saw the "merciless moralizing" of anti-Republican academics as a front for less elevated objections to democracy. It is certainly not surprising that in Mannheim's *Ideology and Utopia,* the phenomenon of "unmasking" provided the starting point for a sociological approach to knowledge, and especially to knowledge that is engaged or "active," constituted with a view to social *practice.*

Yet, while Mannheim's accounts of "unmasking" and of ideology generally reflected the influence of Marxism, and especially of Georg Lukacs, his sociology of knowledge also owed much to certain aspects of the German hermeneutic tradition. This is especially clear in his early essays, "On the Interpretation of *Weltanschauung*" (1921) and on "Historicism" (*Historismus,* 1924). [16] Here Mannheim argued that the unity we detect in the various manifestations of a past culture, from art and religion to philosophy, must be traced to an underlying *Weltanschauung* that is not itself a set of theoretical propositions, but an implicit, *"atheoretical"* orientation that then expresses itself in explicit philosophies, formal works of art, and so on. In a way, a *Weltanschauung* may be considered a synthesis of its various articulations; indeed, Mannheim explicitly linked the interest in *Weltanschauung* to the new striving for intellectual "synthesis." Older studies of such specific cultural expressions as art styles, religious beliefs or philosophical doctrines were being drawn together in the broader focus upon the underlying *Weltanschauungen*.

These *Weltanschauungen*, according to Mannheim, are not "given" us in the same way as the facts of the natural universe. Rather, we seem to have a "pretheoretical" knowledge of them. We may try to state this knowledge in a systematic way; but this is clearly an ex post facto clarification. Mannheim apparently believed in something like an intuitive or empathetic understanding, and he occasionally came close to an identificationist account of interpretation. He suggested that we are most likely to understand cultures similar to our own, just as we will best comprehend our fifty-year-old parents when we ourselves reach that age. At the same time, he insisted that all interpretation is "active" in the sense that it involves our own standpoint, that it draws upon our own purposes and values. He was not completely clear about just how this happens, or about how we distinguish between more or less adequate interpretations, though he did say that they must be consistent with the cultural expressions that confront us. He explicitly held that several equally coherent readings of a historical culture are possible, and that each age must reinterpret the past afresh.[17]

Mannheim's obligations to his intellectual environment are even clearer in his comments upon the issue of historicism, which largely follow the work of Ernst Troeltsch. Like Troeltsch, he stressed the strictly time-bound character of all cultural orientations and beliefs. We have utterly abandoned the Enlightenment faith in timeless norms and truths, he wrote in effect, for historicism has become central to our world view. We define our situation and our aspirations in historical terms. The Truth that interests us is the truth about the historical process. Following Alfred Weber, Mannheim argued that some aspects of historical change may be understood as cumulative progress, chiefly in science and technology (the realm of "civilization"). Certain other portions may be grasped in a Hegelian "rational-dialectic" manner; for the later stages in the development of philosophy, for example, may be seen to supersede and yet preserve (*aufheben*) the anterior ones. Yet in the evolution of the more atheoretical dimensions of culture, of religion, of the arts and of *Weltanschauung* itself, there are no such rational continuities. Here each historical culture can only be understood directly and in its own terms. To lament the danger of "relativism" in all this, according to Mannheim, is to obtrude the contrast with an absolute standard that is simply no longer warranted. Though it is not easy to follow his arguments here, he believed that we must and can make our own cultural choices in a historical or "dynamic" framework, achieving some sort of "synthesis" between our historical understandings and our projects for the future.

5. Ideology and Utopia

Mannheim's 1927 essay on "Conservative Thought," while a brilliant piece of intellectual and social history, did not address the methodological problems of the "sociology of knowledge." I will therefore now focus upon his 1929 *Ideology and Utopia,* his major work before 1933, or perhaps ever. His overall thesis in this work, of course, was that all theories and other cultural phenomena must be understood in their social and historical contexts. He described ideas as being "bound to a situation," and he emphasized the relationship between knowledge and "existence." He tried to show that we cannot account for the genesis of an idea, or even fully describe it, without some reference to its "situation," meaning its relationship to its intellectual environment as well as its roots in some "real" conditions of life.

Turning to the modern problem of ideology, he began with the characteristic phenomenon of mutual "unmasking," which has already been discussed. People often see the arguments of their opponents as conscious or unconscious lies, as specific distortions of reality occasioned by their interests. To move from this "particular" to the "total conception of ideology," one has to recognize that ideological distortion is not typically as superficial or as individual a matter as a lie. Given his social situation, one comes to understand, the opponent is incapable of unbiased perception. His total outlook, his unconscious assumptions, and the whole structure of his thought is affected; in Marxist terms, he is suspected of "false consciousness." The sociology of knowledge is born when, in a further step, one moves from the "special" to the "general form of the total conception of ideology." This happens, Mannheim wrote, when "the analyst has the courage to subject not just the adversary's point of view but all points of view, including his own, to ideological analysis."[18]

An ideology, in these terms, is a situationally conditioned or situationally distorted view of reality, and any viewpoint may be more or less successfully subjected to ideological analysis. Mannheim sometimes treated a utopia as a special type of ideology, while also suggesting the possibility of a reactionary utopia. At other times he equated a utopia with a progressive or revolutionary outlook, an ideology with a backward-looking mentality. Much of the analytical framework of *Ideology and Utopia*, as we noted, was Marxist. Economic class interests played a major role in the "existential determination" of thought. Yet in writing about social groups as carriers of ideologies, Mannheim specified that he meant "not merely classes, as a dogmatic type of Marxism would have it, but also generations, status groups, sects, occupational groups, schools, etc."[19] His prior treatments of *Weltanschauung* and of *Historismus*, moreover, continued to guide him in important respects. They had set the stage for the claim that men's "socio-historical situations" affected their perceptions of the world at a "pretheoretical" level, prior to all analysis. This might make ideological divides as difficult to bridge as the differences between autonomous cultural worlds. Was not relativism therefore a serious problem for the sociology of knowledge?

While conceding a nonideological realm of factuality, but only for essentially trivial propositions, Mannheim anticipated the charge of relativism with a preemptive attack upon his potential critics. They had their eyes on mathematics and were mostly neo-Kantians, he claimed. Behind their "idealistic" conception of knowledge as purely theoretical, there lay the vision of the contemplative life, which in turn stemmed from a specific (pretheoretical) philosophy of life. After all, the "type of knowledge represented by pure theory" was only a "small segment of human knowledge." In addition to it, there was also knowledge linked directly to action, in which "the concepts and the total apparatus of thought are dominated by, and reflect, this activist orientation."[20] Here Mannheim wrote as a self-consciously radical critic of the mandarin tradition of "pure" and "impractical" *Wissenschaft*. He saw this tradition as an ideology in what he called the "evaluative" sense of that term, as a disguised defense of the status quo.

In a somewhat more conventional defense of the sociology of knowledge, Mannheim proposed to use the techniques of the new subdiscipline to *cleanse* social theory of ideological elements. Here he addressed men of Max Weber's convictions, who meant to separate scholarship from value judgment and thus to approach objectivity. If that is your aim, he argued in effect, you must be interested in what I can tell you about the influence of context on thought. For it is only an awareness of such possible sources of distortion that can help you to eliminate them.

Even while offering such therapeutic services to his natural critics, however, Mannheim persistently urged upon them a more "dynamic" view of knowledge in his theory of "perspectivism" or "relationism." Comparing "truth in itself" to the Kantian "thing in itself," he suggested that it could be empirically replaced by the sum of possible experiences of it. In the same way, every system of active knowledge, every ideology, is really a perspective upon the truth. Thus we need not despair of knowledge simply because we are forced to recognize its relational character. To comprehend all relevant perspectives upon a social situation really would be fully to know it. Perspectival propositions are not without truth value; for once we have understood the standpoint of another social group, we can usually translate its reports upon a social situation into our own perspective. Much of our social knowledge is probably based upon triangulations of this sort.

Above all, as Mannheim insisted, a more complete perspectival understanding, in a relational system of social knowledge, must subsume more partial viewpoints, and thus approach an ever more comprehensive insight into social reality, which itself is partly conceptual in character. Adequate relationist knowledge is thus neither as unstable nor as one-sided as its "absolutist" critics would have us believe. Moving through a series of actively oriented "syntheses," as Mannheim explicitly named them, perspectivism may achieve a dynamic universality more fruitful than the purely contemplative knowledge of the objectivist. In any case, an activist synthesis of possible perspectives, for Mannheim, was the ideal outcome of relational social analysis.

The difficulty was that Mannheim had to identify a real social group that could achieve such an outcome. His axiom that all active knowledge of society is "existentially determined" absolutely required that the capacity for synthesis be as thoroughly rooted in the situation of the synthesizers as any other, more partial perspective was in that of ordinary classes, status groups, generations, and so on. No form of knowledge could be posited that did not reflect an actually experienced social position. A correlate in social reality therefore had to be found for the synthetic function, and for the ability to rise above the limitations of partial perspectives. In part, Mannheim found this correlate in the phenomenon of social mobility. When individuals migrate from one socio-economic context to another, or when whole social groups move to new positions, he argued, novel viewpoints are necessarily superimposed upon older ideologies, and people become accustomed to relational thinking. This strikes me as a reasonable claim; it resembles my earlier suggestion that rapid social change may help to create a sense of intellectual incongruity and crisis.

6. The "Free-Floating Intelligentsia"

Mannheim moved into a much more problematic position, however, when (again following Alfred Weber) he identified the "free-floating intelligentsia" as the privileged agent of relationist synthesis. Even on the individual level, he argued, the intellectual often experiences several social situations. Typically, he leaves the social context in which he grew up in order to enter his profession. As a group, the intelligentsia thus comes to include members from a variety of social backgrounds. All these members then commit themselves to a new social role *as intellectuals.* They have no immediate stake in the struggles among the main contenders in the capitalist class system. It is their duty to understand and to communicate with each other and with the other groups in their society. In the ensuing debates among them, the influences of their situations are at once revealed and put in perspective. Unless they succumb to the temptations of cognitive "absolutism," they emerge from these experiences with a well-developed capacity for interpretation and for relational synthesis.

It is worth emphasizing that some of Mannheim's assumptions about the intellectuals were simply false in regard to his own environment. Thus German university professors of his time were not recruited in anything approaching representative proportions from all sectors of society.[21] The huge majority of them came from upper middle-class backgrounds, especially from the educated upper middle class. In fact, they were no more democratic in their social origins than the entrepreneurial elite, and certainly less diverse, socially, than the parliamentary politicians of that period. Mannheim must have known that his radically modernist outlook was shared by *very* few of his colleagues. But this did not prevent him from imagining the intellectuals as a progressive force in society. Though he clearly did not expect them to champion a revolutionary transformation of society, he did assign them the task of preserving a dynamic and partly utopian perspective upon the present. It is unclear how he reconciled these expectations with his own experience.

It is quite clear, however, that in one important respect, Mannheim fell prey to an ideological misperception that was quite characteristic of his immediate environment. Like many of his colleagues, he apparently thought the intellectuals capable of rising above all limitations of perspective and ideology, simply because they were not directly involved in the conflict between capitalists and proletarians. Since they had no *economic class* interests of the usual sort, he credited them with a purely disinterested perspective. He thus came very close to the apolitical posture of orthodox German academics who saw themselves as "idealistic" opponents of parliamentary interest politics. Though in many respects a self-consciously radical critic of the German mandarin tradition, Mannheim here revealed his own obligations to its habitual perspectives. He was determined to find a relationist equivalent for the absolutist notion of objective truth. Driven by this need, he succumbed to a clearly tendentious elevation of the intellectuals above the class conflicts of modern times.

To me, Mannheim's example suggests that the historical sociology of knowledge must hold fast to the regulative ideal of objectivity. We may suspect ourselves of failing to reach it, but we cannot abandon it as an implied maxim of scientific discourse. To be shown the ideological limitations of a perspective is to be obligated to change or to enlarge it. In any case, the logical or methodological problem of objectivity cannot be resolved by inventing such sociological surrogates for it as Mannheim's free-floating intelligentsia. No absolutism could be as damaging to thought as the assumption of an intellectual community that is factually, not just ideally, free of ideological entanglements.

7. The Divide between the Natural and the Human Sciences

In conclusion, let me comment briefly upon Mannheim's suggestion that his sociology of knowledge was in some way less applicable to the natural than to the human and social sciences. He repeatedly referred to "special fields of knowledge, such as mathematics or physics," to the "so-called exact modes of knowing," to the world of the measurable, or to "strata of reality which (are) accessible to a formal quantitative approach, or at least to subsumption under generalizations." This rather thinly charted realm of what he also liked to call "positivist science" he contrasted with the world of ordinary, qualitative experience, with practically oriented knowledge, or with the "so-called pre-scientific inexact mode of thought" which "cannot be readily detached from the . . . vital impulses which underlie it or from the situation in which it arises." "The peculiar nature of political knowledge, as contrasted with the exact sciences," he stipulated, "arises out of the inseparability, in this realm, of knowledge from interest and motivation."[22]

In further characterizing this realm of inexact but vital thought, he occasionally evoked neo-Romantic themes, along with certain positions in the post-Diltheyan debate over the Geisteswissenschaften, the role of "idiographic" knowledge, and the problem of historicism. He wrote of "the immediate and direct perception of totalities," of seeking "a science of that which is in process of becoming, of practice and for practice," of a "middle road between abstract schematization and historical immediacy," and of "the type of knowledge which seeks qualitative understanding and which tends. . . . to affect the whole subject" (like Scheler's *Bildungswissen*). But I need scarcely emphasize the breadth of Mannheim's formulations and the extent of his obligations to the rhetoric of the cultural crisis. I do not see how anything more rigorous than an *ad hoc* distinction between Mannheim's two realms could be built upon these foundations.

Indeed, Mannheim himself undercut his distinction in several ways. He insisted that the type of thinking characteristic of mathematics and physics was "applicable only under quite special circumstances," circumstances he never fully specified. He repeated the characteristic claim that positive science could not "exhaust the fullness of reality," since it neglected the "wealth of the unique, concrete phenomena." He pointed out again and again that "the intellectualistic conception of science underlying positivism" was "rooted in a definite *Weltanschauung*," a presumably outdated form of bourgeois rationalism. At the same time, he argued for an *enlargement* of the traditional territory of science:

> The fact that political science in its spontaneous form does not fit into the existing framework of science . . . should be a stimulus to the revision of our conception of science as a whole. Only after the juxtaposition of the different modes of knowledge and their respective epistemologies can a more fundamental and inclusive epistemology be constructed.[23]

The more inclusive epistemology he had in mind presumably encompassed sociological "relationism" and perspectival synthesis not only in the human and social sciences, but in all modes of knowledge.

The full scope of the synthesis Mannheim intended may be inferred from some remarkable passages on the situation of the natural sciences in his day.

> In the quantum theory . . . it is impossible to speak of a result of measurement which can be formulated independently of the measuring instrument. . . . Thus the thesis arose that position and velocity measurements (for electrons) are expressible only in "indeterminate relations" . . . which specify the degree of indeterminacy. . . . According to Einstein's relativity, (the absolute velocity of bodies in motion) is, in principle, not determinable.
>
> If we followed this trend of thought, which in its unformulated relationism is surprisingly similar to our own, then the setting-up of the logical postulate that a sphere of "truth in itself" exists and has

validity seems as difficult to justify as all the other existential du-
alisms. . . . Because, as long as we see only relational determinabil-
ities in the whole realm of empirical knowledge, the formulation of
an "as such" sphere has no consequences whatsoever for the problem
of knowing.[24]

As I have tried to explain elsewhere, I believe that the sociology of knowledge is no less applicable *in principle* to the natural than to the human and
social sciences.[25] But my subject here is Mannheim, and all I want to say
about him is that he offers no secure support for any absolute divide between the social study of science and the analysis of belief in general.

NOTES

1. Fritz K. Ringer, *The Decline of the German Mandarins: The German Academic Community, 1890–1933* (Dartmouth: University Press of New England, 1990).

2. Ibid., 86, 107.

3. Ibid., 179.

4. Georg Simmel, "Der Begriff und die Tragödie der Kultur," *Philosophische Kultur: Gesammelte Essais* (Leipzig: Klinkhardt, 1911).

5. Ringer, *Decline of the German Mandarins*, 90–99, 102–103.

6. Ibid., 315–334; Hans Georg Gadamer, *Wahrheit und Methode* (Tubingen: Mohr, 1975).

7. Ringer, *Decline of the German Mandarins*, 324–325.

8. Ibid., 103–107.

9. Ibid., 109–113.

10. Ibid., 236–241 for the situation of the radical modernists; the Brecht is from the *Dreigroschenoper* (*Threepenny Opera*), near the end of Act III.

11. Ibid., 384–403 on 'synthesis', and 352–366 on the Weber debate.

12. Ibid., 340–345.

13. Ibid., 228–230.

14. Ibid., 308–310.

15. Max Scheler, *Die Formen des Wissens und die Bildung* (Bonn: F. Cohen, 1925); Scheler, *Die Wissensformen und die Gesellschaft* (Leipzig: Der NeueGeist Verlag, 1926).

16. Karl Mannheim, "Beiträge zur Theorie der Weltanschauungs-Interpretation" and "Historismus," in Karl Mannhiem, *Wissenssoziologie: Auswahl aus dem Werk,* ed. Kurt H. Wolff (Neuwied: Luchterhand, 1970), 91–154, 246–307. An English translation of "On the Interpretation of Weltanschauung" is available in a reader edited by Wolff, as well as in Karl Mannheim, *Essays on the Sociology of Knowledge,* ed. P. Kecskemeti (London: Routledge & Paul, 1952). The "Historismus" essay originally appeared in *Archiv fur Sozialwissenschaft und Sozialpolitik* 52 (1924): 1–60.

17. I am neglecting Mannheim's distinction between 'objective meaning' (i.e., harmonic relationships in music, socially constituted acts like 'alms-giving'), 'intended expressive meanings' (showing pity or benevolence, conveying melancholy), and 'documentary meaning' (unintended reflection of a *Weltanschauung*). Only the last of the three is clearly at issue in the essay.

18. Karl Mannheim, *Ideologie und Utopie* (Frankfurt, 1978); trans. by Louis Wirth and Edward Shils, as *Ideology and Utopia: An Introduction to the Sociology of Knowledge* (New York: Harcourt, Brace, 1936), esp. p. 77 for passage cited.

19. Ibid., 276.

20. Ibid., 295.

21. My doctoral student David Vampola is currently reanalyzing the biographical data on German university faculty from 1864 on that was originally collected during the 1950s by a group of Göttingen sociologists led by Helmuth Plessner.

22. Mannheim, *Ideology and Utopia,* 1–2, 165–166, 171, 175, 190, 291, including for what follows.

23. Ibid., 1, 164–167, and esp. 164, 292 for inset quotation.

24. Ibid., 305–306.

25. Fritz Ringer, "The Intellectual Field, Intellectual History and the Sociology of Knowledge," *Theory and Society* 19 (1990): 261–294.

SOCIAL THOUGHT AND SOCIAL ACTION

Martin Hollis

Guinea pigs do not read books. Biologists do. They read books by biologists and sometimes by philosophers or sociologists of science. They have ideas about how science is and ought to be conducted, not only as a search after truth but also as an institutional activity in need of funding. They have ideas about science in society and society in science. Also they are citizens of a world wider than the laboratory and, when they don their white coats, they do not hang up their other selves along with their hats. The social scientist, peering thoughtfully into the biology departments, finds its inhabitants peering thoughtfully back. This social dimension of science is a special case of the universal social fact that human beings have ideas in their heads. It therefore saddles philosophers and sociologists of natural science with the double hermeneutic involved in thinking about people who think. But at least reflexivity stops there. Biologists think about guinea pigs. Guinea pigs do not read books.

1. International Relations: A Triple Hermeneutic

When the topic is social scientists, the hermeneutic is triple. For instance, American foreign policy-makers certainly read books. Their fancy has been caught in recent years by game theory, as purveyed by the approach to the science of international relations currently known as neo-realism.[1] One sees the attraction, especially for anyone disposed to think of the international world as a formally anarchic state of nature where nation-states pursue their individual national interests. For example, the arms race has many game-theoretic features and it is worth trying to identify the precise game involved. Are the U.S.A. and U.S.S.R. like Texas teenagers of the 1950s, each armed with the family car and hurtling towards one another down a blacktop road to settle which, if either, will swerve? If so, the game is Chicken. Or is each side locked into a dominant logic, which bids each side to defect from any agreement to disarm, whatever the other does? In that case the game is the Prisoner's Dilemma. Neither reading is very cheering for the rest of us but at least the implications may differ. Rational "chickens" do well to invest in a reputation for ferocity, but will swerve if their bluff is called. Rational "prisoners" are willing to contribute to a Leviathan whose sword is too sharp for defection to be prudent, but will ride free if they can. Or so says one version of the theory of games and it, as least, whets a lively interest in identifying the games which nations play.

But that sets a peculiar question. It takes two to play Chicken. Before the State Department plays as it thinks best for a "chicken" to play, it needs to be clear that the Kremlin also takes the game to be Chicken. To play Chicken against a "prisoner," whose reading of a finite Prisoner's Dilemma is that one should always defect, can be fatal. So what is the Kremlin thinking? This general Other-Minds problem has two instant complications. One is that "the Kremlin" thinks only what persons with roles in the Russian decision-making process somehow combine to think. The other is that game theory is more American than Soviet, and it is not plain that Russian policy-makers are thinking in precise game-theoretic terms at all. Neither complication can be dealt with easily in a theory of games which standardly works with an ideal-type case, where all agents are fully rational and know that all other agents are similarly rational.

Although this is not the occasion to explore the point, it serves to make us ask how the theory of games relates to the world which it analyzes. A plausible suggestion is that nations play whatever games they believe themselves to be playing. If the U.S.A. and U.S.S.R. mutually take the game to be Chicken, then a game of Chicken is thereby in progress; and otherwise not. Unlike biological guinea pigs, which have no opinions about evolutionary strategy to worry evolutionary game theory, human decision-makers inhabit a world which is as they collectively define it. In the words of Thomas's useful epigram, "things defined as real are real in their consequences." The suggestion then yields the further twist that game theorists, by putting game theory into the heads of policy-makers, create the world which they analyze.

If so, social science here reveals a social dimension radically unlike any in natural science. But the suggestion cannot be altogether right as it stands. Game theory was formulated by Neumann and Morgenstern in the 1940s as a descriptive analysis of typically "economic" interaction in markets where individuals choose rationally in the light of their preferences and information. It did not create the markets which it described. Still less did it create the international world to which theorists of international relations were quick to apply it. Only later still did foreign policy-makers get to hear of it. States have played games, one might say, for as long as princes have had preferences and a shrewd idea of what other princes were up to. Viewed from this angle theories of "economic" inter-action idealize and formalize no differently from theories in physics and, like physics, have an antecedent world to describe and analyze.

Enter Mr. Gorbachev. He reads books, or at least has plenty of advisers who do. Yet he seems not to have the hang of game theory at all. For instance, he lately sent a Soviet admiral to the Foreign Affairs Committee of the U.S. Senate to announce, among other things, that the Russian sur-face fleet had not put to sea for eighteen months and could well be scrapped. At about the same time, an American public opinion poll asked respondents which nation presented the greatest threat to the U.S.A., and found that, whereas 22 percent named Russia, 75 percent named Japan. This sounds like an empirical test of relevance for neo-realism, and one which the theory fails. Yet that would, of course, be naive. Perhaps Mr. Gorbachev understands the game very well and has donned sheep's cloth-ing so as to lull American sheep into dispensing with their sheep dogs. In that case, as the Pentagon has been quick to point out, the rational re-sponse is for America to up its defenses in the face of so devious a threat.

The example shows nothing simple but it does indicate a looseness of fit between theory and facts. The hypothesis that the U.S.S.R. is a self-interested, rational agent is confirmed both by aggressive and by eirenic behavior, at least in the eyes of the Pentagon. This need not discredit its claim to scientific status, since deep scientific assumptions are never as falsifiable as a schoolroom version of Popper might seem to demand. But it does invite recognition of a further social dimension of science. Defense costs money. It is not only the *raison d'être* of the armed forces, the Defense Department and all who serve in them, but also the bread and butter of large industries with powerful lobbies. Could it be that vested interests have a hand in what neo-realists present as a disinterested search after the truth?

The question prompts us to reflect that the science of international re-lations has a history. It dates, roughly, from the end of the 1914–1918 war and a determination by persons of good will to entrench peace in the world. Out of a previous motley of diplomatic history, comparative law, and political philosophy there emerged an intellectually organized con-viction that war resulted from misunderstanding and could be prevented by enlightened institutional arrangements. The League of Nations was the symbol of this idealism and was intended to be its reality too. But the 1939–1945 war soon scotched such hopes and, in its aftermath, a tough-minded realism came to dominate the academic discipline of international relations in Britain and America. This was a self-conscious attempt to apply scientific method, conceived in positivist terms, to international relations, conceived as the objectively identifiable behavior of nation-states. Realism in various forms has remained dominant and has outlasted the positivism once so widely professed in social theory and philosophy.

The 'neo' in 'neo-realism' marks a refurbishing of a realism which took the state as the principal unit of the international system.[2] Its retort to those who point to the growing influence of economic agencies, like transnational corporations and banks reaching across state boundaries, has been to emphasize the growth of state intervention in economic matters. Its retort to those who emphasize individual decision making by personalized elites in specific historical contexts has been to import the neoclassical microeconomic theory of the firm, with its account of how rational units accommodate to market forces. Game theory, with nation-states as the players, comes in very handy. At the same time these are the tunes which the American government likes to hear. Realism sets objective parameters to the scope of foreign policy and licenses the accumulation of power, partly by viewing power as the motive force of international politics and partly by endorsing a fact/value distinction which sets aside questions of ethics. The science of international relations has been heavily funded by government agencies, which, in paying the piper, can be claimed to have called the tune.

Symbiosis between paymaster and piper is always a feature of expensive science, and should not be described too crudely. Paymasters know only roughly what tunes they want to hear. Pipers live by finding new ones and, even if the former held the purse, the latter are the authorities on good music. Each educates the other in the realities; and symbiosis deepens as the pipers' tunes come to animate the actions of the dancers who pay for them. Less allegorically, the relationship illustrates the two chief aspects of Kuhnian paradigms. On the one hand, a paradigm is marked by a set of intellectual presuppositions too broad, entrenched, and regulative to be falsifiable, at least until so many anomalies have built up that the barriers to a fresh paradigm crack. Mr. Gorbachev is no more a clear counterexample to realism than were Galileo's first observations the obvious defeat of Ptolemy. Anyone seeking to account for a general scientific view needs to look to more than the deliverances of reason and experience, even supposing that these are neutral and objective sources. On the other hand, a paradigm is marked by institutional practices, which regulate a scientific community and its research procedures. These practices are not

finally distinct from the other institutions of the wider society and are up-
held by an authority wider than scientific truth. On both counts, an open
society whose institutional beliefs are wholly guided by reason and wholly
subject to criticism is a myth. Science is bound to have a social dimension
and the science of international relations is no exception.

In pointing out that intellectual presuppositions and institutional practices both stand outside the schoolroom canon of rational science, Kuhn
issued an exciting invitation to a sociology of knowledge. But it was not
a one-sided invitation to trace intellectual outcrops to their roots in social
systems and power structures. Witness the case of international relations.
Institutions of all kinds embody ways of thinking about the world, and
governmental agencies are no exception. Hence the invitation is also to
understand the symbiosis of science and society from the inside. The Pentagon no doubt has much else on its mind but the search after truth is
certainly part of its concern. Symbiosis is a matter of sense as well as
of dollars.

A theme is now ready to emerge. Every science has a social dimension,
as may be noted from two points of view. Even cognitively, since there is
more to the search after truth than the acquisition of beliefs warranted
by reason and experience, a study of scientific beliefs needs to include
their cultural context. Secondly, even if the search after truth were cognitively self-contained, science is an organized and expensive collective
action. Since there are many truths which could be the subject of the
search, one can usefully ask social questions about why paymasters pay
more willingly for some tunes than others. All this is the standard business of a sociology of knowledge. The social sciences, however, have a further social dimension, because they are, so to speak, tied to their own tail.
They study human guinea pigs, who, unlike the four-legged kind, have
ideas in their heads. Neo-realism may be an unusually pure case of the
ideas which inform action being taken from the science which studies the
action; but I regard it as typical of what is true in a more diffused way
whenever the social sciences study a society which takes notice of them.
Again the matter can be noted from two points of view. Cognitively, the
search after truth has a moving target which shifts in response to the
search itself. Institutionally, the paymasters are not inert objects or blind
forces but thinking agents whose ideas come from somewhere. Connecting
the two dimensions is the thought that, when the sociology of knowledge
studies the natural sciences, it takes biologists as its guinea pigs. Separating the two dimensions, however, is the fact that real guinea pigs do
not read books.

To pursue the theme, I must sharpen an implicit distinction between external and internal analysis. That is best done, I think, by starting from Max Weber's demand that any account of the social world be adequate both at the level of meaning and at the causal level:

> Without adequacy on the level of meaning, our generalisations remain mere statements of *statistical* probability, either not intelligible at all or only imperfectly intelligible . . . On the other hand, from the point of view of sociological knowledge, even the most certain adequacy on the level of meaning signifies an acceptable *causal* proposition, only to the extent that evidence can be produced that there is a probability . . . that the action in question *really* takes the course held to be meaningfully adequate.[3]

This is a thoroughly teasing demand, partly because the causal level is glossed in Humean terms, which one might widen to challenge, and partly because, to my mind, Weber never comes clean about the relation of the two levels. Does action *"really"* take its course at the level of meaning, with the causal level merely a reassuring check that the proposed understanding is accurate, or at the causal level, with meaning merely an initial pointer, or at some unified level achieved when both heuristics are satisfied?

The ambivalence is not resolved by Weber's firm statement at the start of *Economy and Society* that "the science of society attempts the interpretative understanding of social action." Having said that action includes "all human action in so far as the acting individual attaches subjective meaning to it," he then offers a marvelously neat definition of social action as action "which takes account of the behaviour of others and is thereby oriented in its course." In that case, one sees why game theory is so promising for a Weberian social science. But this leaves it unclear whether its final claims rest at the level of meaning, the causal level, or both. Meanwhile Weber's insistence on individual action as the starting point threatens to beg a large question about social structure. Individualist accounts of social structures can certainly be offered but, conversely, so can structural accounts of individual action. For the moment, let me remark only that structural accounts need not be causal. In the dispute between causal explanation and interpretive understanding, *both* parties can go either way on whether institutions are prior to actions.

As to construing the "causal" character of "causal explanation," there is no short way to sum up current disputes in the philosophy of science. But it may still be instructive to revert to a remark by Condorcet in his *Sketch for an Historical Picture of the Human Mind* (1794, 'Xth Stage'). Writing on a crest of Enlightenment optimism and looking ahead to future scientific conquests, he declared:

> The sole foundation for the belief in the natural sciences is this idea, that the general laws dictating the phenomena of the universe are necessary and constant. Why should this principle be any less true for the development of the intellectual and moral faculties of man than for the other operations of nature?

It remains broadly true, I think, that the key to the natural sciences is still held to lie in "general laws dictating the phenomena of the universe," to the exclusion of older ideas about meaning or moral function. But the idea that they are "necessary and constant" marries what would now be thought unequal partners. If *constant* is uppermost, then laws are at heart statistical and any necessities are at most psychological, as in Hume (and Weber). If *necessary* is uppermost, then constancy is reliable only when it is underwritten by natural necessities, which call for a realist theory of explanation. This dispute remains central to the nuanced arguments between realism and anti-realism, and I shall not try to settle it here.

The claims of "understanding" to primacy depend on taking "the intellectual and moral faculties of man" to be peculiar in the order of nature. Action occurs in particular historical contexts, which are ideal in the sense of being distinguished by shared intersubjective meanings. Meaning is, as Dilthey put it, "the category which is peculiar to life and to the historical world," adding for the benefit of those tempted by a Hegelian World Spirit: "Life does not mean anything other than itself. There is nothing in it which points to a meaning beyond it."[4] Understanding proceeds by reconstruction of the meaning of actions in their historical context. How, precisely? Weber's individualist answer is to work initially within an assumption that action is rational and interaction the sum of individually rational actions. This is to be done with the aid of "ideal types," the clearest of which is the "economic," or, in its liveliest current version, game theory. But Weber also recognized "sociological" ideal-types, like bureaucracy, and it is far from plain that they can be given an individualist construal. The mark of social action from this more holistic standpoint is that the actors follow rules which they did not invent, at any rate individually, and that the meaning of action is to be found by reconstructing these rules. Current hermeneutics is as divided about the social and individual components of action as are theories of causal explanation about "necessary and constant."

Return to Mr. Gorbachev and the problem which he sets for theories of international relations by seeming not to play the game and, equally, not to follow the habitual rules of the Soviet political system. It involves, of course, a fascinating first-order problem about what will happen next. But I shall focus on the second-order problem of how we should think about institutions, if we are to make sense of attempts to make sense of Mr. Gorbachev. Institutions occur twice in this second-order question, once in the context of Mr. Gorbachev's actions and once in the context of scientific theories to account for them. The second-order problem is fascinating too.

I have, in effect, been sketching a conceptual space with two axes, one marked "Explaining/Understanding" and the other "Individualism/ Holism." All four quadrants are habitable, including their borderlands. Very briefly, causal explanations range from systemic theories at the holist end to psychological ones at the individualist end. As a robust example of the former, there is Kenneth Waltz's account of international relations as the behavior of nation-states in response to the demands of "the international system," which has its own dynamic. The system is at present "bipolar," a notion so defined as to yield strong functional properties which explain national adaptations, almost as if we were dealing with a planetary system. Such pure systemic functionalism is rare these days and even Waltz has modified his position so that structures only "shape and shove," thus giving the units of the system some scope for contributing to its overall development. Meanwhile, at the other extreme, the units can be analyzed into human individuals and then synthesized through a theory of individual interaction. This is one attraction of microeconomic decision theory and game theory as a strategy for explaining how markets and, by analogy, international exchanges work. Although a rampant individualism is nowadays more common than a pure holism, there is an evident temptation to compromise when thinking about organizations. For instance, one might want to look outside an organization for the sources of its goals, power, and prospects of survival but inside it for its processes of individual decision-making. Indeed compromise is inevitable, as soon as microexplanations are cast in terms of individuals whose preferences are determined exogenously.

Equally briefly, keys to "understanding" can be ranged according to the view taken of the relation of social rules to individual reasons. Here one might reflect that there are two ways to construe Wittgenstein on following a rule. In the holistic direction, there is his famous utterance that "What has to be accepted, the given, is, so to speak, *forms of life*."[5] It

seems to suggest that actions are to be not only identified but also found
their whole significance by reference to meaning-rules, which, ultimately,
are the ramifications of what defines some particular form of life. In that
case actors' reasons are finally the appropriate expression of what the rules
require, and reconstruction goes by enhancing the context accordingly.
Conversely, however, "knowing how to go on" is never a mechanical process and there is a thoroughly constructivist reading of Wittgenstein on
offer. Here rules are not, so to speak, scripted in advance of how individuals interpret them, and even a form of life is ultimately no more than an
agreement in judgments which is widespread and durable. Since both
readings have virtues, a compromise is again tempting, with the idea that
action is rule-governed so construed that rule-followers have latitude in
negotiating their own interpretations of the rules which constitute and
regulate their practices.

I do not mean to imply that there is safety in compromise, as if holism and individualism could live together in comfort by taking in each
other's washing. Thus the first-order question about Mr. Gorbachev's future leads swiftly to a question about the nature of power, where compromise sums the problems rather than factoring them out. The same goes for
compromises between explaining and understanding, when one asks how
the world as seen from within relates to the world analyzed according to
what is deemed necessary and constant about its workings. Thus, one
might declare piously, where science succeeds, the world goes as it is expected to go. But when this platitude is addressed to the social world, it
becomes radically ambiguous. Does it mean that, since human intellectual and moral faculties are as predictable as the other operations of nature, social science is a search for the antecedent causes of social behavior?
Or does it mean that, since people act in the light of what they expect of
others, the social world is created by expectations which are partly shaped
by the social sciences themselves? No doubt, one may reply "a bit of
both." But that involves dealing with the puzzles of both, as well as making sense of their relationship.

2. The "Strong" Program

To focus these very general remarks, I revert explicitly to the two social
dimensions of science identified earlier. One was the scope for social elements in the business of science, created by the limitations of reason. The
other was the special feature of social science that it lives in symbiosis not
only with its paymasters, as does natural science, but also with its subjects

(including the paymasters). The second dimension, I shall contend, upsets a familiar compromise between explaining and understanding, which might seem right for the first.

Consider a "Strong Program" in the sociology of knowledge, which distinguishes sharply between intellectual systems and social systems, and tries to explain the former as an effect of the latter.[6] An intellectual system is an interconnected set of beliefs, a web one might say, expressing the order which the holders find in their experience. Each strand in the web has some internal support, as judged by criteria of rationality which are internal to that intellectual system. Witness the belief systems of, for instance, the Nuer, the preformists, or the Catholic church; the web need not be exhaustively or exclusively rational, even by its own standards, and hence not static. As that group of examples shows, religious, scientific, or any other belief-systems are all grist to the mill in the same terms, which do not involve an outside assessment of their truth. A social system, on the other hand, is a network of roles, grouped into institutions and constituting a society, together with the distribution of power which regulates it. Although there is often feedback from intellectual to social, basically the former evolves in response to pressures from the latter and a Strong Program's research brief is to illustrate the process, especially in the history of science.

The compromise here is to give the task of delineating systems of belief to understanding and then to account for them by causal explanation. Beliefs are to be identified from within and explained from without, with emphasis on what is intersubjective in both cases. The Program is thus profoundly anti-Cartesian and embodies a relativism congenial to postmoderns. The relativism has a strong and a weak version. In the strong one, the truth or falsity of the beliefs is irrelevant to their true explanation, and the task of understanding involves no external judgments of truth. "Knowledge for the sociologist is whatever men take to be knowledge. It consists of the beliefs which men confidently hold to and live by."[7] In the weak version, there may be separate questions of truth but the external explanation bypasses them and explores the social dimension of science independently. Either way, the intellectual is relative to the social, and the Program does not distinguish science from religion, ideology, or metaphysics in this regard.

I do not in fact agree that knowledge for the sociologist is whatever men take to be knowledge, since I do not accept that an independent natural world enters the story only because men hold beliefs about it, which make the same sense whatever the truth about the external world, if indeed there is any such thing. But, setting this aside for the moment, I want to raise questions about the "social system" which is invoked as an explanatory variable, and so about the root distinction between intellectual and social. Institutions sound pretty solid entities, wielding a power which is entirely real, until one stops to think about them. It then becomes plain, I submit, that a division between ideas and social things makes no sense at all.

The dispute between individualists and holists over the key to understanding can be thought of as a tug-o'-war centered on the character of roles. On the one hand, a role is a set of normative expectations, whose source is a prior set of social positions or institutional arrangements. From this point of view, Mr. Gorbachev is interchangeable with whoever occupies those positions and, were he run down by the proverbial bus, Soviet foreign policy would continue as before. On the other hand, normative expectations sit pretty loosely on role-players. Roles cannot be fully scripted in advance of situations, and conflict is endemic both within and between the several roles which most of us play. Interpretation is part and parcel of the demands of office and it extends to negotiating amendments to the roles and rules with the aid of others. From this point of view, Mr. Gorbechev has his own power, even if it depends on recognized authority, and he is by no means interchangeable.

The common ground in this dispute is that, to put it elliptically, institutions think. Constitutive and regulative rules are not just devices for bringing social order out of individual anarchy. They also order and legitimate beliefs about human nature, human intercourse, and even, some thinkers maintain, the natural world. Individualists then try to cash out this metaphor by insisting that only individuals think and hence that institutional thinking is a sum or deposit of individual contributions. Holists counter by insisting that thought, like language, is irreducibly social. Both parties are committed, however, to a constructed element in social facts. Keynes once compared the economy to a beauty contest so conducted that the winner does not win because she is prettiest but is prettiest because the judges severally have judged that other judges, similarly guided, expect her to win. That captures the constructed element nicely.

Take this view seriously and one sees how the social sciences are tied to their own tail. They are like the competitors' agents in a Keynesian beauty contest, each lobbying the judges to believe that other judges will vote for their competitor. Whether the lobbying is done in a language of positive science or romantic poetry is a matter of fashion. If it succeeds, then verily it has guided its victims to the truth. This is a limiting case of a confidence trick which goes all the way down. In everyday life, the mug who is led to believe that the Statue of Liberty is for sale as scrap is sadly mistaken. But, if *everyone* comes to believe that the Statue of Liberty is for sale, then indeed it is.

Neo-realist game theory is peculiar in that its tail makes a short loop through small decision-making elites. It thus illustrates the presence of a scientific component in institutional thinking unusually well. But it does not illustrate a pure Keynesian beauty contest because its guinea pigs are role-players with more in their heads than foreign policy. They are networked into wider and different social systems, which constrain as much as enable their international activities. These constraints are not unlike those placed on the institutional activities of biologists by their need to be accurate about real, four-legged guinea pigs, which, as remarked, do not read books. But that holds only for the initial round of questions. The constraining American or Soviet role-players outside the foreign policy arena do have ideas in their heads. They include, ultimately, those distant but nonetheless constraining and enabling elements, the ordinary citizens of the U.S.A. and U.S.S.R. The final constructivist question can be posed only at this degree of distance and diffusion. How deep lies the truth in the apothegm that "fifty million Frenchmen can't be wrong"?

More soberly put, the question is whether, socially speaking, what is external to each is also external to all. For the world of nature and the natural sciences, I strenuously maintain that it is. Guinea pigs are not to be internalized to biology for purposes of analyzing the social dimensions of that science. But this does not settle matters for the social sciences. In the Christian story, God created the natural world but left the social world to Adam and Eve and their descendants. Each generation of descendants inherits a past which constrains as well as enables. But, even if it is false for a single generation that the social world is however it is understood to be, it may still be true for the sum of generations.

Whatever the final truth about social facts, there is no denying some self-fulfilling element in shared expectations. That is implicit in the definition of social action as action which takes account of the behavior of others and is thereby oriented in its course, as is seen when one looks at the actions of several agents together. Where each is guided by expectations about others also so guided, the outcome is a function of what it was expected to be.

This is explicit in game theory, especially for games with multiple equilibria. It is also crucial for many economists, especially those of the Austrian school. But it is often then muted by glossing "expectations" as "rational expectations," which are regarded as predictions of the sort which any rational scientific observer makes. To bring out the creative or generative character of expectations, we should notice the presence of normative expectations too, in the sense involved in the concept of a role and applying to social actors, rather than to scientific observers. Expectations which guide the choice of how to go on in an underscripted role differ from scientific predictions. They depend, furthermore, on what theories or models of the social world social actors have in their heads, and there remains the twist that a social theory or model, if accepted by all involved, tends thereby to prove itself the winner. Biologists' rational expectations about guinea pigs are simply predictive. Their social expectations have a normative dimension.

3. Objectivity and Expectations

These last few pages have been written from the side of understanding and will be resisted by advocates of a Strong Program and the universal scope of causal explanation. The crux is how best to conceive of institutions. It seems to me a mistake to rely on a sharp distinction in kind between intellectual systems and social systems, by analogy with a distinction between mental and physical systems. Just as one may refuse to separate persons into mind and body, one may certainly refuse to separate social thought from social action. Institutions are real, even physical, in their consequences, because they think and, in thinking, translate social thought into social action. Since they do not all think alike, the outcome of social action also shapes social thought. This goes for all manner of institutions, for the science and theology departments of the University of Notre Dame, the Catholic Church, the CERN laboratory in Geneva, the Pentagon, and the Politburo alike. These are all animated intellectual systems made flesh in the players of the games which constitute and regulate the social world.

In harping on the illiteracy of guinea pigs, I have been taking a stand against the species of relativism which internalizes fact to theory or, more grandly, nature to culture and disclaims the relevance of truth to the explanation of belief. A stand is not, of course, an argument, and the matter is too intricate to pursue here. But I register it because, in anchoring biology to guinea pigs and then distinguishing Mr. Gorbachev from a guinea pig, I may seem to have internalized social facts to social thought. So here is a brisk defense of objectivity across the board.

International relations are a game, if not in the formal sense defined by game theory, then at least in the broader, more Wittgensteinian sense that those involved are maneuvering in an arena governed by man-made rules. Since some power grows out of the barrel of a gun and the rules are, to say the least, fragile, the game differs from, for instance, chess or even domestic politics. But much of the action is communicative and thus relies on rules of interpretation, normative expectations, and, in short, constraints and enablements typical of games. The international game is unusually vulnerable to invasions which change its rules. But, since the invaders are usually pursuing aims due to other games and since they are influenced by theories about the situation, we are dealing with matters of degree. In a game with a rigid constitution, like chess, the aim is fully specified independently of theories about how best to achieve it. Even so, a theory of good tournament play needs to allow something for whether it is in circulation among the players. The more fluid the constitution of a game and the more complex its intersection with other games, the larger this recursive element becomes. Is this a threat to objectivity and an invitation to relativism?

I think not. Consider a symptomatic difference between weather forecasting and traffic forecasting. If all sailors hear a gale warning and change course, the gale still occurs but no one is caught in it. If all motorists avoid an impending traffic jam, there is no jam. This typifies the suggested divide between natural and social sciences. But it does not cost the social sciences their objectivity, as if they could study traffic flows only in a world without car radios. Questions of what people are likely to do when fed forecasts of what they are likely to do certainly have quirks. For instance, a book revealing how to make a million dollars on the stock exchange cannot possibly have a million satisfied readers. But the reasons for disappointment are wholly objective. If it is true that expectations make the social world go round, then it is as solid a fact as any known to physics.

Social facts may, in that case, involve relations in basic and often peculiar ways, demanding an epistemology with concepts like *perspective* and *feedback*. But that gives no hostages to the kind of relativism inherent in a Strong Program. It does not undercut epistemic distinctions between true and false, rational and irrational beliefs. Here lies a minefield, I admit, and, to keep out of it, I pick my words with care. A recursive element in the relations among social thought, social action, and social facts is of interest to relativists and anti-relativists alike. But both parties can analyze it consistently with their own view. Nothing said so far is meant to strengthen either hand.

4. Conclusion

I have been working within a conceptual space organized around the two axes, Explaining/Understanding and Individualism/Holism, in the spirit of my earlier remark that all four quadrants are habitable. I shall stay neutral between individualists and holists, but shall finally sum up in favor of understanding as the more revealing angle on the social dimensions of science.

It is uncontentious that every sociology of science needs to be adequate at the level of meaning and hence must *identify* beliefs by construction from within. Since even a Strong Program agrees, I shall take this much as read. More contentious, perhaps, is the case offered for saying the same of institutions, since there are accounts of institutions so systemic and functional that it can seem not to matter how institutions think. But, since so many chief advocates of a Strong Program are philosophers, I shall risk taking this as read too. So far understanding is uppermost. But that does not touch the crucial issue of how organized beliefs, once identified from within, are to be accounted for.

Consider first the double hermeneutic involved in interpreting the behavior of biologists who interpret nature. The initial round tells us that biology is a game whose overt imperative is the search after truth but whose moves are underdetermined by an appeal solely to what reason and experience warrant. That creates an opening for the suggestion that the biological game has social determinants. Notice, however, the apparent concession that where a scientific belief is warranted by reason and experience, there is no opening for social determinants. It may still be interesting to ask why governments fund research on nerve gas but the answer will not explain why biologists believe that nerve gases are lethal. Meanwhile, let us agree that there is an opening for social explanation of any research program whose scientific prospects are speculative. This is a matter of relating scientific games to social games. But the relation need not be construed along lines set by theories of causal explanation as found in the game of science. Whether it should depends on the final truth about naturalism or the thesis that, since nature includes human beings and institutions, there is finally only one method of analysis, causal explanation. If naturalism is false, then the method called for is again one of understanding.

Now consider the triple hermeneutic involved in interpreting the actions of social scientists who interpret the actions of institutional role-players. Social science, too, is a game whose overt imperative is truth but whose moves are underdetermined by the warrants of reason and experience. But if the truth about social actors is some function of what they expect of others, who include, directly or diffusedly, the social scientists who put ideas about others into their heads, then the relation of social science to society is not that of natural science to nature. Here the final question is whether there are social facts not only external to each but external to all. The triple hermeneutic suggests that social life is what it means and that there is nothing in it which points to a meaning beyond it.

This suggestion has come through just strongly enough, I hope, to worry naturalists without encouraging relativists. On the other hand, the data of social science are games and actions which are as discerned from within, and the social dimension of social science is an irreducible feature of its subject matter. On the other hand, some games point beyond themselves and these pointers are not all to be internalized. Two groups obtrude. One comprises the games of religion, ethics, and political aspiration, whose variety is endless but whose core is an attempt to fuse fact and value through understanding how to live better. Here I shall stay silent about whether the meaning involved succeeds in pointing beyond the human condition. The other comprises the games of natural science, where the pointers are to an external world but not one with the sort of meaning peculiar to life and the historical world. That commits me both against the moral naturalism which tempts the green movement and, epistemologically, against a hermeneutic takeover bid for the natural sciences. My case rests with the one undoubted fact in this paper. Guinea pigs do not read books.

NOTES

1. I shall be drawing on M. Hollis and S. Smith, *Explaining and Understanding International Relations* (Oxford: Oxford University Press, 1990) and acknowledge with thanks that I owe my acquaintance with that science to Steve Smith. I thank him also for comments on a draft of the present paper.

2. The classic source for realism is Hans Morgenthau, *Politics Among Nations* (New York: Knopf, 1973), originally published in 1948. The leading neo-realist text is probably Kenneth Waltz, *Theory of International Politics* (Reading, Mass.): Addison-Wesley, 1979), although, as noted later, it emphasizes the properties of the system as determinants of national behavior. Game theory is of service insofar

as states act rationally within systemic parameters and of still greater service to neo-realists with a more anarchic view of the international system; witness for instance the essays in Kenneth Oye, ed., *Co-operation Under Anarchy* (Princeton: Princeton University Press, 1986).

3. This and other quotations are from *Economy and Society* (1922), as translated by E. Matthews for *Weber: Selections in Translation*, edited by G. Runciman (Cambridge: Cambridge University Press, 1978). See p. 15 (his italics).

4. *Gesammelte Werke*, edited by B. Groethuysen (Stuttgart: Teubner Verlag, 1926), vol. 7, 24.

5. *Philosophical Investigations* (Oxford: Basil Blackwell, 1953), vol. 2, 226.

6. See, for instance, David Bloor, *Knowledge and Social Imagery* (London: Routledge & Kegan Paul, 1976), esp. 4–5, and, for further discussion, my essay, "The Social Destruction of Reality," in M. Hollis and S. Lukes, eds., *Rationality and Relativism* (Oxford: Basil Blackwell, 1982), 67–83.

7. David Bloor, *Knowledge and Social Imagery*, 2.

GOOD SCIENCE AS BAD HISTORY:
FROM ORDER OF KNOWING
TO ORDER OF BEING

Thomas Nickles

[T]he past must be forgotten if it is not to become the gravedigger of the present. . . . [T]he unhistorical and the historical are equally necessary for the health of an individual, a people and a culture.
—Friedrich Nietzsche

His writing is not about something; it is that something itself.
—Samuel Beckett on James Joyce[1]

1. Introduction

While a college undergraduate, I arrived at my calculus class early one day to hear another student rehearsing Zeno's paradoxes, which he had encountered for the first time. He then remarked forcefully that Zeno must have been a simpleton, since all he had to do to solve these puzzles was to apply a little calculus. As if the calculus were available to Zeno (and as if elementary calculus suffices to handle all of the paradoxes)! My fellow student surely realized that the calculus was not invented by the ancient Greeks, for our textbook contained little snippets about Newton, Leibniz, Cauchy, and other great mathematicians. His idea seems to have been that the calculus is so obvious that all the Greeks had to do was open their minds to grasp it. Since they failed to do this, they must have been fools.

Some years later, I read Herbert Butterfield's delightful little book, *The Whig Interpretation of History* (1931), and learned that the student's diatribe against Zeno has a name. It was a particularly glaring instance of the "Whig fallacy." Actually, 'whiggism' or 'presentism' (as it is also called) does not label a single, well-defined mistake but rather a family of related historical fallacies. The underlying sin is that of reading history backward, of interpreting and evaluating the past in terms of the present, or in terms of what came later. One form of the whig mistake is that it makes

85

history self-explanatory and therefore viciously circular—rather like a silly time-travel series recently shown on American television. We all tend to project current knowledge of outcomes backward upon our decisions (Fischhoff, 1975), a tendency that becomes an occupational hazard for historians. Historians are, of course, wise after the event, and it is more difficult than might be imagined for them to avoid projecting some of this hindsight back into the historical actors, who thereby gain a measure of foresight or prescience. "The United States is what it is today because Mr. Jefferson and the other Founders could see into the future, and they acted and wrote so as to bring about the particular future they wanted." "Newton possessed a special ability, unavailable to others, to see into the structure of the universe." These two examples illustrate what we may call the "prescient genius" variety of whiggism. Another form is that of my fellow calculus student: what we take to be obvious (but what we only learned in class a month ago) ought to have been equally obvious to the Greeks— unless they were dolts. Our problems must have been their problems, our options their options.

Reading Butterfield's and Thomas Kuhn's historiographic essays (1977) converted me into an historicist, someone who believes in "the historicity of all things"—a conveniently ambiguous phrase.[2] All the things that we take as obvious had historical origins. They had to be made or learned by a long, historical process of trial and error.[3] Marx (1844) noted that even "the cultivation of the five senses is the work of all of previous history." Kuhn and other science studies experts have shown how this thesis is recapitulated in the ontogeny of the individual scientist being trained into a specialty discipline. She must learn how to see the objects of her study and not to see other things. The desired knowledge is not simply "given" by nature. Marx's Hegelian observation indicates that history is *creative*. This is a key tenet of most versions of historicism and one of many ways in which history and historiography (history as written) take over functions traditionally ascribed to God. The circularity version of the whig error then amounts to reducing historical creation to immediate self-creation.[4]

"Avoid whiggism!" has been the rallying cry of the movement to professionalize history of science over the past four or five decades, a movement that more recently has spilled over into other science studies disciplines, and even into philosophy. Since it has become a defining characteristic of some of these specialty disciplines, this anti-whiggism has naturally produced an "I am more anti-whig than thou" syndrome, frequently visible in book reviews and the like. To get some feeling for this competition, the reader might challenge a friend to see who can find more and deeper whig errors in the statement:

On January 15, 1784, physicist Henry Cavendish entered his laboratory, exploded some hydrogen in oxygen and showed that water was a product of the two gases, thereby giving a deathblow to the Greek theory of the elements.[5]

The new generation of sociologists and anthropologists of science (whom I shall call the "new wave" experts, for lack of a better term[6]) claim to find more whig mistakes in naive historical accounts than have the professional historians themselves. The new wavers can "out-anti-whig" the original anti-whigs, and in several ways. First, they reject so-called internalist histories that describe and explain scientific work as the application of logical and methodological rules. Indeed, they reject the older internalist-externalist distinction itself. They tend to dismiss any appeal to rationality as a kind of theological move.[7] Second, in their studies of training, expertise, and judgment, they spell out in greater detail the epistemological consequences of the "learning to observe" point made by historians.

Third (and of primary interest here) is their charge that much historical work contains a residual whiggism, because historians stick too closely to what Andy Pickering (1984a and 1984b) has termed "the scientist's account" of research. Historians allegedly retain the scientists' practice of "putting the phenomena first." By explaining discoveries in terms of the causal influence of the entities reportedly discovered, by explaining the process of research in terms of the products, historians continue to invert history. This practice is unhistorical in smuggling in precognition, in taking as given and unproblematic what had to be historically constructed by human activity, that which now needs historical explanation. At its worst, the critics complain, such work becomes self-explanatory, viciously circular. History may be creative, as historicists claim, but it is not self-creative in this direct and immediate way. The sociological critics therefore aspire to a higher standard. A thoroughly anti-whig account must take every piece of information, even the data of empirical science, as *factum*, not *datum*. Accounts of the givens, the unhistorical atoms or "black-boxes" of the science textbook, must be expanded until each of those taken-for-granted items can be displayed as a product of a complex, constructive, sociohistorical process.

Fourth is a great irony in a subject full of ironies. Some science studies experts hint that the discipline of history itself, the discoverer of whig bias and the champion of its eradication, history-writing *as such,* turns out to be a whiggish enterprise, because it is unavoidably retrospective. Historians cannot help looking at things in reverse, from present to past; for they already know how things turned out. Retrospective biases are impossible to eliminate completely, even by studying historical controversies from a nonmember's point of view (as do Shapin and Schaffer, 1985). The only "pure" way to study science is therefore to look at the ongoing work of contemporary science, especially controversies that have not yet been closed, or perhaps to do "discourse analysis." Hence some new-wave social anthropologists of science claim to occupy a privileged position in the science-studies professions. Their work alone can be unbiased.[8]

We may look upon the epistemological developments of new-wave science studies as an attempt to "de-transcendentalize" the subject by denying all forms of precognition or foresight. Such a strategy amounts to methodological solipsism of a social variety. Admittedly, 'social solipsism' sounds like a contradiction in terms, but it signifies that, for all we know, human beings face the epistemic project of developing a coherent world picture *alone,* with only the "naturalistic" resources[9] left to us by natural selection. All we have is each other, so to speak. To be sure, a community of supportive but critical colleagues is more than the Cartesian solipsist had; but also much less, since our community cannot underwrite its methodology by appeal to the existence of a nondeceiving God. As far as we know, human beings have had to build up the entire fabric of knowledge by trial and error, with no illuminationist help along the way; that is, with no help from the gods or from any godlike intellectual powers of our own. Even if there is a God who speaks to us, we must determine "from the inside" whether it is indeed God speaking and what He is saying. And scientific methodologists today would deny that appeal to God carries any epistemic weight.[10]

I think that methodological solipsism of this social variety is correct, and I endorse it. However, anti-whiggism in its latest forms goes beyond this, in my judgment. Insofar as it does, I am forced to reject it, historicist though I am, as an untenably strong form of historicism. To combat these excesses is the central purpose of my paper. In my view we must temper our historicism with pragmatism. If you like, we must add to the strong historicists a dose of Nietzsche, Peirce, James, or Dewey. I agree with the pragmatists that a pure, disinterested, "spectator" account of knowledge, characteristic of most epistemology from Descartes forward, neglects the life of action. This insight I extend to historical knowledge, which has become spectator knowledge *par excellence.* In our case, the active agents include not only scientists but also the contributors to science studies, insofar as they attempt to theorize and explain and not merely to describe passively, and insofar as they make normative, methodological claims, critical judgments, and policy recommendations. In short, I believe that excessive anti-whiggism in science studies results in an oversimplified, passive, spectator historiography of science.

Andy Pickering is the contemporary science studies expert who best exemplifies both of these tendencies of thought—strong historicism *and* pragmatism. I shall play the latter off against the former. Insofar as he takes his pragmatism seriously, as he ought, the excesses of his anti-whiggism should vanish, yielding a more Deweyan sort of balance. Or so I shall argue. But before taking a closer look at Pickering's anti-whiggism, let me introduce another bit of background.

2. The Discovery-Justification Distinction

Attacks on "the" discovery-justification distinction have also been characteristic of the newer branches of science studies, since a main use of that distinction had been to mark off the process of scientific investigation from its logical products and to minimize the interest of the former. As with anti-whiggism, the new-wave science studies practitioners claim greater purity than others who have criticized the distinction and its uses. By the latter I mean the philosophical "friends of discovery" and their effort to soften up the old distinction sufficiently to permit epistemological investigation of the process, the practice, of scientific research.

As before, the new wavers insist that an inversion of the older analysis is necessary. Where philosophers have traditionally devoted nearly all of their efforts to the context of justification, sociologists have, in effect, devoted nearly all of theirs to the context of discovery or rather "construction." Bruno Latour (1987), for example, carefully distinguishes *science in action* from finished science, but he attends to the former. This way of stating the inversion may be misleading, however, for some science studies experts would do away with the discovery-justification distinction altogether. As with their rejection of whiggism and the internal-external distinction, they feel that the stronger the denial the better.

The attacks on whiggism and on the discovery-justification distinction do not merely run in parallel; they intersect. Once one finishes studying science in action, including the closure of controversy, what else is left? The so-called logical product is just that, it might be said, nothing more than a (temporarily?) stable product of that investigative process. As a knowledge product, it must be approached "from the inside," from the activity side, in the forward direction, and not transcendentally and retrospectively. The new wavers claim that in studying science as a logically analyzable product, either alone or as a subject that merely complements process studies, as some friends of discovery do, one necessarily looks at science backwards, from the wrong end. In fact, they say, the discovery-justification distinction positively conceals, even from friendly philosophers, what the actual practices of knowledge production are like. For philosophers allegedly cannot avoid seeing the final logical outcome as foreordained in the "discovery" process leading thereto (Latour and Woolgar, 1979), a malady that is the logicians' counterpart to the *precursoritis* of whig historians[11] and that underestimates the contingency of historical developments. Philosophers assume that the substantive and methodological black-boxes present at the end (e.g., the accepted reality of a new micro-particle and knowledge of good ways of detecting it) were there operating all along, guaranteeing victory for the winning side, even while they were the center of controversy. This is Pickering's (1984b, pp. 406ff) complaint about philosophers' and historians' use of "the scientists' account."

Although I am a philosopher, I must agree with the critics that philosophers over the last century have shirked, even obstructed, the task of studying some of the most interesting problems of scientific cognition and learning. There is no denying that misuse of the discovery-justification distinction has helped to seal off the research process from philosophical investigation.[12] However, at the risk of sounding stodgy, I do not believe that dismissing all discovery-justification distinctions is a promising strategy. Although I am a friend of discovery, it has never been my plan of attack to obliterate all forms of the distinction. As with the internal-external and theoretical-observational distinctions, the problem is surely that we have lumped too many, context-sensitive differences into one large, "absolute" distinction. Indeed, rejecting all forms of the discovery-justification distinction invites the opposite mistake of thinking that there is no useful distinction to be made between process and product or between earlier and later phases of research, in which the later phases are based on the products of the earlier.

On the latter view, the research process becomes a seamless fabric, not something repeatedly redesigned in the light of its own products. The status of claims and techniques remains essentially the same throughout, and epistemologically profound changes do not occur—at least none that science studies analysts themselves can embrace and use. On this view of professional propriety, the analysts must remain completely impartial to the debates and completely noncommittal as to the reality of the discoveries claimed by historical agents. This means that any significant changes that occur in the activities of scientific research communities cannot be explained by appeal to newly gained knowledge of the natural world but can only be explained in terms of social attributions of success, the formation of social power structures, and the like. A difficulty with this view is that, once science studies experts begin to question, reflexively, the privileged status of appeal to social forces and structures, as in fact they are now doing, the whole explanatory exercise is placed in jeopardy. This is a claim that I shall defend.

Much of the confusion about what is and what is not permitted in studies of science stems from the ambiguous status of philosophy, history, and the other science studies disciplines. Some practitioners see themselves as engaged in the larger scientific enterprise of understanding and changing the world, while others restrict the role of science studies analyst to that of a distanced, nonmember of the communities studied—yet still, somehow, a *scientific* observer making use of scientific methods. It is not yet clear how it is possible to study science scientifically without begging crucial questions one way or the other.

I shall defend a broadly "bootstrap" account of the growth of knowledge in which (1) research transforms itself by putting to work as taken-for-granted tools what were once contentious conjectures or techniques, (2) scientists' appeal to the new discovery claims to help explain the successes and failures of the previous course of research is part of what licenses those claims as genuine discoveries ("they work!"), and (3) historians, methodologists, and policymakers may legitimately give these discoveries a similar explanatory role.

The discovery-justification distinction I defend is a process-product distinction that recognizes the "phase changes" that occur in research when once-contentious claims or procedures become tools that successfully transform subsequent research. As such, the distinction marks the modest, fallible, modern-day counterpart to the Aristotelian transition from mere order of knowing to the intelligible order or order of being. As a pragmatist, however, I should prefer to speak of order of doing and making rather than merely of an order of being.

My position rejects *both* of the following, polar-opposite readings of the process of investigation leading to a discovery or invention. Each reading blurs the process-product distinction, but from opposite sides, as it were. The first characterizes the product in terms of the early stages of the process that eventually produces it, while the second characterizes the process in terms of the logical form of the final product. The "forward" reading commits a genetic fallacy by supposing that the nature of the product is determined by its conditions of origin in the early stages of the research process that produces it, and, accordingly, that the process never appreciably changes in character over time. Meanwhile, the "backward" reading whiggishly reads the logical character of the "final," textbook product back into the nature of the research process, even in its early phases, a sin that typifies logical empiricist accounts of scientific research as well as the rhetoric of scientific publications (see section 3 below). If philosophers and working scientists are attracted by the logical positivist pole, new-wave sociologists are tempted by the opposite pole.

Neither extreme allows for significant conceptual and methodological change. To that extent, *both* are unhistorical. That logical positivists and other philosophers have a tendency to commit whig fallacies, to read the past in terms of the present, has long been recognized. But it is equally a mistake to press anti-whiggism so strongly as to fall into a genetic fallacy. In the sciences no more than in other developments do its conditions of origin fix for all time the character of an institution, movement, or other cultural product. The early phases of research do not fix the character of the later phases or products, however much the rhetoric of publications may mask this dialectical or "bootstrap" process.

Apart from its negative role of screening off most of scientific activity from philosophical investigation, the discovery-justification distinction *has* played another, more positive role: it suggests that research falls into stages or phases. For me the above-mentioned idea of phase transitions—from order of knowing to order of being, or rather, to order of *doing* and making—is one key to an adequate account of research. Accepting this idea, however, implies no commitment to any of the "stage theories" by which philosophers have divided research into a rigid succession of two or more stages. First there was the two-stage model. This converted the discovery-justification distinction from a logical distinction between process and product into a temporal distinction between two kinds of *processes*: discovery-cum-construction on the one hand and testing and other justificatory activities on the other. Then, ten or fifteen years ago, several philosophers proposed a three-stage model, in which a stage called "pursuit," "heuristic assessment," or "preliminary evaluation" was interposed between the "initial" discovery and "final" justification. [13]

While the stage models did call philosophical attention to the research process, a topic that logical empiricists had neglected, they displayed research in a form that was both truncated and too linear or sequential. For example, they tended to confine innovation to the initial, discovery and pursuit stages of research, whereas the sort of logically and temporally articulated account of research that I defend allows for much of the innovation to enter the story during and *after* the justification or reception stage.

3. Single-Pass Versus Multi-Pass Conceptions of Science

In this section, I further articulate and illustrate my conception of scientific development by contrasting it with both standard philosophical and new-wave sociological accounts. I employ a vehicle that I have used before (Nickles 1987, 1988), a mini-critique of Sir Peter Medawar's celebrated attack on the scientific paper as a fraud.

> The scientific paper is a fraud in the sense that it does give a totally misleading narrative of the processes of thought that go into the making of scientific discoveries. (1964, p. 43)
>
> It is no use looking to scientific 'papers', for they not merely conceal but actively misrepresent the reasoning that goes into the work they describe. Only unstudied evidence will do—and that means listening at the keyhole. (1969, p. 7)

Medawar makes an important point, of course, one that anticipates much valuable work in science studies. The course of the preceding research cannot be accurately determined by reading the published papers. As everyone realizes, scientific papers are full of objectifying rhetoric suggesting, for example, that the experiments performed simply "opened a window on the world."[14] Further, the logical form of the final arguments might not be apparent in any of the preceding work. According to Medawar, this is most unfortunate, for a paper should merely report on the *previous* investigation and not become part of the ongoing process of investigation itself.

While I am fully sympathetic with Medawar's call for the study of scientists in action, his way of putting the point misleads. He does retain a sort of discovery-justification distinction but in the traditional form that has a consequence—of separating off the writing of papers from the "real" activity of doing science—exactly opposite of the one I want. For Medawar, the creative work (including the testing and justification process) ends before the paper is written, and any departure the paper makes from a simple historical report on the research is therefore a distortion, a fraud. But it is a mistake to think that published papers should serve as accurate *narrative reports,* as trustworthy historical accounts of the work previously undertaken. The chief purpose of scientific papers is surely to make claims and to argue for them, to contribute to scientific debates. First papers concerning experimental results are usually composed during the final stages of the work or immediately thereafter and obviously must interpret any novel results. Later papers typically engage in some reinterpretation and placement of the work within a larger theoretical framework or research tradition.

The new-wave analysts recognize these things, of course, yet I still detect a genetic bias—a "Medawar bias," as we might call it—in their tendency to treat scientific papers as little more than deliberate misrepresentations of the "real" scientific work.[15] The upshot has been a curious agreement of some "rationalist" philosophers and "ethnographic" sociologists that scientific papers are only tenuously related to research activity. But while these philosophers have taken the finished papers as the real science and ignored the vagaries and vicissitudes of the research process as logically uninteresting or confused (insofar as the final logical results cannot be read back into it), the sociologists have done roughly the opposite and have considered the papers illegitimate insofar as they do not accurately reflect the earlier stages of research. I reject both positions.

To be sure, many papers contain historical sections that masquerade as descriptive reports of previous activity. Nigel Gilbert and Michael Mulkay (1984) dismissively label these "folk history." But even these sections[16] are often more revealingly construed as a continuation of the scientific work than as an attempt to write professional history. The main purpose of these "historical" sections is surely not to report the history as it actually happened but to describe those developments that are now, as *presently* interpreted, deemed significant in heuristically and epistemically locating and justifying the *present* position. This is more than rhetorical overlay, and I see nothing wrong with it.[17] And *of course* this and other devices omit much of what happened in the "original" context of discovery, for that is precisely their purpose—to *wean* the claimed results from the earlier phases of discovery and the contingencies of their contexts. To change the metaphor, this process corresponds to Brunelleschi's removing the scaffolding from his dome. A certain amount of "deconstruction" did not destroy everything but, on the contrary, left the magnificent result to stand on its own.

The view that scientific papers should only describe previous research activity manifests what I call the linear, *one-pass* or *single-pass* conception of science. This style of paper writing reminds us of the "inductivist" papers submitted to the Royal Society three hundred years ago.[18] However, for

Medawar and his followers, reportage is also the desirable style for the modern, hypotheticalist research format: a well-written scientific paper should describe in turn the research problem, the hypotheses proposed, the manner in which the latter were tested by deriving predictions and performing experiments, and the conclusions that were drawn from those results.

The alternative view is that scientific work is *multi-pass* and that the overall research process is dialectical or self-transforming, often in unintended ways. There are various kinds of feedback loop in which the preliminary results of one bit of work are reprocessed and refined, often modified substantially. The process is both irreducibly logical and irreducibly social, in ways at which I can only hint here. We might term it "social construction by reconstruction." Once a rough and ready problem solution is published, it can in turn become an object of study by others, search spaces of possible solutions can be constructed around it, and so on. As a result of successful tinkering and rethinking, mistakes and blind alleys are eliminated, procedures are streamlined, noise is reduced, new procedures and standards emerge, and the very conception of the problem may be fundamentally altered so that what was formerly an ill-structured problem becomes well-structured. [19] Once the search space is neatly characterized, more powerful solution techniques can be applied or developed. What was once a mere conjecture, a stab in the dark, may eventually become an established *fact,* which might in turn be generalized into a well-founded *law*-claim or, still better, made into a routinized technique or *method,* a powerful *epistemic amplifier* for efficiently producing large quantities of new knowledge. Such procedures can sometimes be automated in laboratory equipment or commercialized outside the laboratory, a point to which I shall return.

Notice that the reconstructions I am talking about are not the rational reconstructions of professional philosophers or the narrative reconstructions of professional historians. Rather, they are internal to the work of scientists and essential to that work. These reconstructions do not fall outside of the historical process of scientific development; they are part of that process. Fabricating them is part of the work of the research scientist, the critical reviewer, and to some extent even the textbook writer.

I am not criticizing the new wavers alone. [20] In fact, they more than anyone have documented this process of internal transformation or redigestion. They have been more careful observers and readers of scientific work than philosophers. And yet they retain the Medawar bias in tending to treat such reconstructions as mere rhetorical overlay. [21]

My main point so far is nicely captured by my second motto: Samuel Beckett remarking of James Joyce that "His writing is not about something; *it is that something itself.*" Even in the quasi-historical remarks of their papers, scientists are not writing *about* science; they are *doing* it. Frederic L. Holmes writes,

> Far from being a distorted version of something the scientist has already done, the scientific paper is an essential phase of the investigation itself. Writing the paper is a central act within the creative process. (1986, p. 229)

Employing examples ranging from Lavoisier to Krebs, Holmes indicates several ways in which the writing constitutes part of the research. Some of Lavoisier's most important ideas emerged over successive drafts of his papers. That should not surprise us, for it is obviously the case in our own writing in the science studies disciplines. Why should scientists be totally different?

The reconstruction and weaning processes occur on many levels, at many scales, from the single investigator, a Darwin or a Faraday looking over his notebooks and jotting down new thoughts and new wrinkles on old ones, all the way up to a community's revolutionary recharacterization of a whole period of previous work, not to mention technological applications to the "real world." A good deal of reprocessing is already done in the writing of the original scientific papers as they are outlined and subsequently move through successive drafts. But reprocessing can occur again and again at later stages. The contents of one or more papers may be redigested later, both by their original authors and by other investigators. What philosophers of science used to worry about as the theory-ladenness of observation reports is actually a more general, historical-interpretive phenomenon that applies to the reinterpretation of scientific papers as well.[22] After several cycles or "passes," the original work (which usually still receives the lion's share of the credit) may be transformed beyond recognition.

Thus if Kuhn (1978) is right (as I think he is), much of the innovation described as "Max Planck's discovery of the energy quantum" was actually accomplished by Einstein and Ehrenfest in 1905–1909, not to mention several other writers over the next quarter century. In their work, Einstein and the other physicists attributed to Planck a solution that Planck never offered and later explicitly repudiated (the early quantum theory, with free energy quanta) to a problem that Planck never entertained (the problem-complex that Ehrenfest later dubbed "the ultraviolet catastrophe," and to which Rayleigh had called attention already in 1900 and Lorentz soon after). This was largely because Einstein and Ehrenfest whiggishly projected *their* problems back into Planck and misread him as addressing those problems. However, it is also true that there was something there in Planck's writing to misread, that is, more than Planck himself consciously intended to put there.

Several historians and sociologists have made a similar claim about Mendel's biological "quantum theory," his alleged discovery of the gene and its later rediscovery by De Vries, Correns, and Tschermak. As Brannigan (1981) sums up the affair, Mendel, like Planck, was actually a classical thinker. The status of Mendel's work has curiously changed with each context from within which it has been viewed—whether that of his contemporaries, that of De Vries, Correns, Tschermak, or that of still later investigators. [23]

At less dramatic levels, examples can be multiplied. [24] Still pretty dramatic is Cannizzaro on Avogadro. On standard accounts, Avogadro, in an almost universally ignored paper of 1811, advanced the thesis that, at standard temperature and pressure, equal volumes of any gases contain equal numbers of particles (see note 5). Cannizzaro allegedly rescued "Avogadro's law" from oblivion at the Karlsruhe conference of 1860. According to Brooke (1981), however, in 1858 and succeeding years, Cannizzaro successfully advanced his own project of finding a unified system of atomic weights for chemistry by creatively adapting the much earlier work of Avogadro to his purpose.

While I do not want to say that all science is like this, either in misreading previous work or in transforming it so completely, it is surely true that frontier research rarely survives in its original form. The textbook and *Handbuch* versions rarely resemble the original papers. Nor do I say that it is necessary to positively misread people in this way in order to model one's own work on theirs . . . but it helps. Being a sensitive historian conflicts with the economy of scientific research, as Kuhn (1977) noted long ago. Anything helps that deforms X's problem situation or techniques into your own. Such transformations may be an aid to modeling your efforts on work on a different problem or, more intimately, to your seeing them as a literal continuation of the old line of investigation.

I conjecture that all of the whig shortcuts and simplifications noted by Butterfield and others can be helpful in guiding current research, in bootstrapping the past into a future. At the very least, it would be an interesting topic for science studies to investigate misreading and other whiggish moves as ways of finding and applying scientific precedents to current scientific research programs.[25] In *The Englishman and His History* (1944), a book published more than a decade after *The Whig Interpretation of History* (1931), Butterfield himself emphasized that whig moves are ideal for repairing ruptures, for sewing up gashes in society that threaten to separate our causes from the main concerns of our fellows and from the past. To be sure, telescoped, whig history can also be used to create the appearance of revolutionary break, in retrospect. In fact, I think most of Kuhn's revolutions are like this. But in the service of future action, this is just the other half of the same story—for scientists it is a powerful heuristic both to align their work with certain research traditions and concrete precedents and to sharply distinguish it from others.

Polanyi (1958), Kuhn (1962), Toulmin (1972), and, more recently, Pickering (1987a and forthcoming) have all emphasized the importance of direct, concrete modeling of scientific work on particular antecedents or exemplars, usually in contrast to rule-guided accounts of research. I am sympathetic with such accounts, but I believe that the manner in which the antecedent models are found and employed needs much study. My suggestion here is that whig moves provide part of the answer.

Now whig fallacies are, by definition, fallacies of historiographic interpretation; whereas scientists, as such, are not historians. Nonetheless, as they pick and choose among possible antecedents as models for their own work, scientists engage in quasi-historical interpretation. Thus we may extend talk of whig moves and whig fallacies to working scientists, just as Butterfield himself extended it to politicians and judges, who, after all, are not historians either. Moreover, notoriously, the whiggish reinterpretations that motivate successful scientific work tend to stick, to become part of the scientists' informal history of their subject and, unless explicitly corrected, to be taken over, *faute de mieux*, by historians. As citation analysts have noted, the very fact that creative scientists standardly cite an older work as a precedent confers a new, contemporary interpretation upon that work.

In helping one to relate the work of others to one's own problems, as a guide to future action, whig reinterpretations of previous work in the light of one's own aims can be invaluable. It is hard to see how scientists could do good research without being whiggish in these ways. In fact, my working title for this paper was "Whiggism as good science and bad history." It parallels the topic: "Whiggism as good common law and bad history," for in legal practice (by contrast with legal historiography), one also looks to the past for antecedents of present cases. In common law the appeal to precedents may be stronger than in science, for legal judgments in present cases are largely justified by citing the rulings of relevant precedents.

(However, it would be rash to say that appeal to scientific precedents has a merely heuristic function.) A compensating difference between science and law is that modern science transforms itself (making previous work obsolete) more rapidly than the law. Scientific precedents more obviously become tools for change. My topic also parallels (or partially coincides with) the topic: "Whiggism as good teaching and bad history" or "as good applied history of science and bad history" (Heilbron 1987, pp. 557–558, Klein 1972).

The young author of *The Whig Interpretation of History* was himself still puritanically one-pass in his own anti-whiggism, in his view that genuine historical research ends with the prying of historical facts from primary sources and that any form of inference, interpretation, later reinterpretation beyond this, or any *use* of historical research as a practical tool in politics, is whiggish overlay (Butterfield 1931, p. 7). Later, as we have seen, he mellowed.[26]

4. Pickering (and Others) against Circularity

Against this background, let us consider Pickering's well-known brief against putting the phenomena first.

> The distinguishing feature of the scientist's account is that the primary explanatory load is put upon natural phenomena: these *come first* and are used to explain scientists' experimental and theoretical practice. . . . [H]istorians have had some difficulty in seeing their way past the key element of the scientist's account: few of them have been able fully to escape from the scientist's habit of *putting the phenomena first,* of using natural phenomena to explain scientific practice. . . . Typically, historians ask why one scientist *succeeded* in observing some historically-accepted phenomenon while others *failed.* (1984a, p. 86)

If Pickering's charge against historians is correct, it removes from them the main advantage of hindsight, the capability of exploring (naturalistically, in terms of our own, "correct" knowledge) and of *explaining why* distant controversies turned out as they did. What we should put first is scientific practice, not the weak-neutral currents or the quarks allegedly discovered:

> I argue that the reality of the weak neutral current was the *upshot* of particle physicists' practices, and not the reverse. (1984a, p. 87)

In his book, *Constructing Quarks,* Pickering rejects the

> circular idiom . . . whereby the product of a historical process, in this case the perceived reality of quarks, is held to determine the process itself. (1984b, p. x)

Now if these and similar passages by Harry Collins and other writers were intended only to deny precognition to the historical actors, they would surely be correct: people cannot know and use at one time what they only acquire later.[27] However, Pickering et al. clearly want to make a stronger claim, that denying precognition entails rejecting as viciously circular anything like the scientist's account, whether offered by scientists themselves or by historians.

In *Constructing Quarks*, Pickering traces the alleged explanatory circularity not only to the epistemological circularity of prescience (knowing in advance what only came to be known later) but also to a corresponding causal circularity in nature that the explanation apparently presupposes, the absurd assumption that something can be self-creating, can pull itself into existence by its own bootstraps, like the picture of the hand drawing itself. Pickering's point is that the discovered micro-particles (for example) are created by the very (high energy) experiments that investigators use to "detect" them. The scientist's account goes wrong by appealing to these created entities to explain the activities that produced them.

This does not mean that we are left with a "social" account of science, pure and simple, for Pickering joins those sociologists who reflect the above line of criticism back upon strong social constructivism itself. We cannot take society or social forces as "given" or as simply discovered there in the social world any more than we can take natural or psychological categories as given.[28]

Although it is hard for most philosophers to understand these constructivists as anything other than idealists of some kind, that is a misleading characterization; for the new wavers are trying to "get off" the Kantian pendulum that swings between metaphysical realism and idealism, between *noumena* and *phenomena,* object and subject. They are certainly not idealists of a traditional variety. Idealists say that the world is our *intellectual* creation, whereas the social constructivists say that scientific phenomena cannot even exist, let alone be known, until the right set of material and interpretive *practices* is in place (or rather, the phenomena and the social practices come into existence together). It is *no entity without activity*! It is practical knowledge and know-how that largely dictate (or construct) reality. This view apparently contains a dose of the old pragmatic "maker's knowledge"; it hints at the *verum/factum* theme found in "modern" writers from Bacon to Vico and beyond, only it is closer to Bacon than to Vico in holding for the natural sciences as well as the social.[29]

If this is idealism, it is a pragmatic idealism. Better not to call it "idealism" at all, given the importance of *material* practice. In more recent writings, Pickering (forthcoming) emphasizes the irreducible role of the material world in experimental work. He explicitly regards his current project as a pragmatic account of research. It is one that I find promising.

On a sympathetic reading of Pickering and precursors such as Latour and Woolgar (1979), they are neither idealists nor instrumentalists, for they do not deny that there is a real, material world or even that the socially created world has a material dimension. Rather, for them high-tech science is highly *artificial*. We do not simply go out and look at unadulterated nature. The events we detect are so highly contrived and constrained as to be "man-made." Esoteric particles almost come stamped "Made in Fermilab" or "CERN Made," and by the year 2025 the more reliable phenomena will no doubt be "Made in Japan." According to the constructivists, these experiments carry a Baconian forcing of nature to an extreme degree, so far that, ironically, the scientific laboratory comes to screen us off from the natural world. The medium of inquiry creates its own message, nay its own world.[30] In denying that the world of high-tech science discloses to us the real world—nature—the sociologists are, in effect, vindicating Aristotle's claim that constraining nature only produces monsters, artificial rather than natural phenomena. Or are they? For 'artificial' does not mean 'artifactual' in the pejorative sense.[31] Pickering, for example, does not suggest that particle physics is plagued by shoddy research. One way of looking at the issue is to say that technoscience is transforming the world, but that the new world is important to make and study for all that and not to be dismissed as a monster.

Latour and Woolgar made a similar point in *Laboratory Life* (1979), and Latour (1987) has further developed the idea in what I call his *termite model* of research and applied science. Before they can extend their science and technology out into the world with any assurance, Latour says, technoscientists must first reconstruct the world as a kind of extension of the artificial conditions of the laboratory, just as termites can increase their range of operation only by extending their little tunnels. The main difference, as I understand Latour, is that our scientific tunnels are made of paper; the world is reduced to paper or to what Latour calls "immutable mobiles," a more technoscientifically advanced form of wood pulp than that of the termites. I allude to his account, in the latter chapters of *Science in Action*, of how scientific and technical information is brought back to, measured, documented, and conveniently packaged, in "centers of calculation." Latour stresses paper and inscriptions where Pickering would not, but for the moment I am not concerned with *their* differences.

Now I myself find such analyses attractive up to a point, but I should prefer to say that our research results are accounts of a world that can be described in more than one way, instead of saying that all our expertise is confined to the laboratory and cut off from the real world. In order that scientific and technological work will hold up in alien environments, it must be weaned from its idealized conditions of origin in the laboratory. It is a matter of decontextualizing it so that it can exist outside the context of discovery. In any number of cases, as I shall illustrate below, we have been able to do that successfully. Items that we could hardly get to work in the laboratory, during early phases of discovery and development, are now taken for granted in the darkest jungles. Moreover, we can deny that high-tech laboratories screen us off from the world without being forced to say that "all the world's a lab."

Of course, weaning is a matter of degree. Where philosophers have too quickly shifted focus from historical context to universal truth, socio-historians have been impressed by how much our sciences—even the more abstract ones—bear the mark of human cognitive capacities and interests, both in general and in historical particulars. My response to the latter is that such an historical perspective leaves ample room for decontextualization and for the emergence of results that are cross-culturally and trans-historically robust.

To be sure, using statistical methods to study what happens when penicillin or cataract surgery is applied in the outback does extend methods of laboratory control to the world at large. Moreover, the (humanly constructed) statistical categories may in some sense create the phenomena being studied. But it is also beyond question that these research applications can make a difference (in health, say) that the local residents easily recognize in their own terms. Increased life expectancy, a primary goal of Bacon and Descartes, has been achieved. This is a hard fact, not a mere social attribution. Furthermore, now that the testing phases are over, all sorts of vaccines and other remedies are automatically mass-produced and administered just about everywhere, under nearly any conditions. Similarly, gasoline engines and TV sets were once confined to laboratories for research and development, and were extremely difficult to operate and to reproduce. Now, alas, they are almost everywhere. Thus technoscience is not *so* laboratory-dependent.

This is the obvious reply to overdone, artificial world accounts and to the circularity objection. A pragmatist will want to avoid blanket statements here. Some areas (e.g., high energy physics, cosmology) seem more highly artificial than others (e.g., solid state physics, molecular biology).

Yet even here we are able to extrapolate beyond the laboratory to some practical applications and to conclusions about the interior of stars millions of light-years away, and even about the beginning of the universe. Recall Comte's positivistic pessimism about such matters and how quickly he was shown wrong. Thus are the bonds of the laboratory broken!

An equally obvious constructivist response is a more moderate version of the laboratory-constructivist position, one that derives from Marx on the construction of the natural world. The fact that something works in the outback demonstrates the success of our efforts to "civilize" the outback, to introduce artificial structures not otherwise found there—aqueducts, terraced fields, clinics. Like the birds and the earthworms, we construct our life-world, our environment, our niche in the material environment. Moreover, beyond the reach of our space missions, we cannot alter the larger universe; and insofar as something is beyond our direct experimental manipulation and control, our understanding is suspect (Hacking, 1988).

Who wins the debate? Surely there is truth in both positions. The question largely rests on a false dilemma. Insofar as discovered phenomena are made, they are not, of course, purely discovered, not waiting there to be uncovered in just that form. Yet, taking a cue from Aristotle, we can say that the material aspects of the phenomena are still there *potentially* in those cases in which doing X to nature (by means of a specified human practice) will regularly produce phenomenon Y. And that is just the sort of reliability that technoscience strives to achieve and often enough does achieve. In other words, we can still make sense of the idea of a phenomenon or technique waiting to be discovered. Of course, our theoretical representation of the phenomenon may not be unique and the aspects of nature to which we attend will be culture-relative. But so what?

I do not want to diminish the importance of the socio-cultural contribution to our scientific knowledge: it needs the emphasis that Pickering and others are now giving it. Different interests and categories of description might yield quite different (though complementary) accounts of nature. Even if our theory happens to be correct, that does not make it the One True Theory. Nonetheless, it is surely also true that, *relative* to a given system of theory and practice, we can regularly produce Y by doing X; and that the success of producing Y cannot always be explained in purely social terms.

The upshot is that we must sometimes put the natural phenomena first in order to avoid a circularity in *social* accounts. Or rather, neither sort of account can stand on its own without collapsing into vicious circularity.

They are mutually entangled and potentially mutually supporting in an explanatory context. By pressing their admittedly interesting point about artificiality too far, some new wavers mistakenly impute circularity to *any* explanatory appeal to nature.[32] Does anyone seriously want to reject the strong conviction of scientists and the rest of us that the phenomena can be first in the *causal* order, the order of nature, the order of being, even though they are not first in the order of evidence, the order of knowing?

No precognition is required in order to understand how the causal traces of something can aid in its own discovery, given the availability of suitable practices. But here we do have something of a bootstrap mechanism or at least a knowledge amplification mechanism. The underlying cause is not simply given; we have to puzzle it out. But it is partially self-revealing. We can piece together knowledge of causal traces and eventually produce a higher-grade outcome, perhaps even knowledge of an ahistorical reality. This puzzling ability may be what Aristotle had in mind in his problematic, inductive ascent to apodictic causal knowledge.[33]

Admittedly, the old Aristotelian (medieval) distinction between order of being and order of knowing, *ordo essendi* and *ordo cognoscendi,* is subject to criticism on both epistemological and metaphysical grounds. However, the distinction I am invoking is only an ordinary, everyday one that anyone might be brought to admit. For sometimes things *are* self-revealing. That is how we find mice in the cupboard, ore deposits in Colorado, helium on the sun, electrons, and even neutrinos.

My point is not diminished by the existence of error and controversy in science. Scientific controversies are wonderful loci of science-studies research, but their invocation does not magically demonstrate the truth of social solipsism in the extreme form that denies human beings any meaningful interaction with the natural world. The social solipsist argument concerning the word of God and other nonnatural forms of illumination (sketched in section 1) cannot be *simply and directly* extended to the natural world. For one thing, we have gained considerably better evidence for (and control over) one than the other. This whole matter calls for considerably more attention than it can receive here. I shall only observe that "there was a controversy about the existence and nature of Xs" does not entail that "Xs themselves could have played no role in resolving the controversy." We might dub this fallacy *appeal to controversy.*

Finally, once scientists think they know how nature works, why cannot they review the course of the investigation with new understanding of what was going on? This is how scientific research *does* proceed on a multi-pass account. Moreover, scientists do not wait until controversies are settled before doing this. On the contrary, doing this is *how* controversies are settled, in part. It is hardly news to be told that scientists are constantly proposing explanations or models to account for everything from how the samples got contaminated to why the data curves have an unexpected bump, to why the previous model worked here but not there, why this experiment or theory or person or laboratory or technique succeeded and that failed. How else does one learn from trial and error? There is nothing causally circular here, for scientists actually do this.

And if scientists do this, why are not historians and methodologists of science free to do it, too, with their materials?[34] There is nothing prescient or otherwise circular in an historian's careful reference to mechanical reality, as *we* now understand it, to explain Galileo's or Newton's or Lagrange's successes and failures, or to the structure and function of the pancreas, as *we* now understand it, to help explain Claude Bernard's work in Paris, that of Frederick Banting and his colleagues at Toronto, or the recent failure of a biotech company in California working on pancreatic tissue cultures.

5. Symbiosis and Consilience: Nonlinear and Social Support

I now discuss aspects of Pickering's position in more detail. I hope the discussion will indicate the relevance of recent work in science studies to some neglected problems concerning the growth of human knowledge.

First, Pickering rejects Harry Collins's *experimenters' regress* as based on a false dilemma. Collins's idea is that experimental evidence (including replication) in science has roughly the same status as the *given* in traditional empiricist epistemology: it is essentially circular or regressive. Collins writes:

> This is a paradox which arises for those who want to use replication as a test of the truth of scientific knowledge claims. The problem is that, since experimentation is a matter of skilful practice, it can never be clear whether a second experiment has been done sufficiently well to count as a check on the results of a first. Some further test is needed to test the quality of the experiment—and so forth. (1985, p. 2)

In effect, Pickering (1987b) rejects Collins's position as too positivistic, too verificationist, too linear-foundational. Something can count as evidence without there being any conclusive evidence. At best, Collins's predicament applies to the earliest stages of novel research. In later, more mature, research, there exist judgmental constraints sufficient to avoid this circularity.

(Pickering dislikes the term 'constraint' but I use it in the flexible sense of Nickles, 1980. See also Baigrie, forthcoming).

Where circularity *does* arise, Pickering says, is in the combination of experiment *plus* theory. Each depends on the other for its perceived validity. Here he employs his much-quoted term 'symbiosis', meaning the mutual dependence of experimental and theoretical practice. More recently, he speaks of "mutual (or interactive) stabilization." But cannot he avoid vicious circularity again at this level by recognizing the existence of less-than-conclusive constraints? As many commentators have pointed out, the constraints imposed by experimental and theoretical practice, equipment, and achieved results are more confining than Pickering allows.[35]

On the other hand, these factors are *mutually* supporting, so do we not have circularity still? No, as shown by the fact that success is not guaranteed. Like most business ventures, most scientific ventures fail. "Nothing succeeds like success"—a bootstrap slogan if there ever was one.[36] And nothing fails like failure. As a pragmatist himself, Pickering is prepared to appreciate the importance of something's working or failing to work, in the absence of some final determination of truth or reality.

Second, an objection of vicious circularity implies that the support relation among the items is linear-foundational. Yet Pickering's idea of symbiosis or mutual support suggests a nonlinear conception of justification, according to which A and B can be mutually supportive without circularity. After all, mutual support does exist in nature, in the way the members of a building or an arch support one another, for example. Brunelleschi's dome again comes to mind. This model contrasts with the "brick wall" model of the classical, linear, foundational tradition in epistemology, in which each brick represents a cumulative increment of knowledge supported only by the bricks below it. The emphasis on symbiosis is further evidence of a revival of interest in the Whewellian topics of consilience and robustness. Consilience is achieved when distinct research pathways lead to the same result. Similarly, a result is robust when it is invariant over changing circumstances, including changes of technique.[37]

All this has an evidential ring. Although symbiosis may look viciously circular, it is noteworthy that researchers often have failed to achieve it. In at least some cases, the symbiosis represents an epistemic achievement. Accordingly, I think we need not accept Pickering's own suggestion that the circularity is evaded only by a social power-play, that the phenomena achieve reality only because there is an informal, mutual arrangement of the "I'll scratch your back if you scratch mine" variety. Early in the process of discovery, the connections are fragile, even circular. But with some cooperation from both nature and society, robust, multiply-connected results may emerge, permitting the field to mature.

Third and more controversially, Pickering's symbiotic alliances of interests need not be irrational but may actually have a logical dimension. By that I mean that the social relations may instantiate "logical" relations of an epistemically interesting variety. Conversely, the interests of these subcommunities provide a kind of "social" or "causal" backing for those logical or methodological principles that its members have found to work on epistemological grounds. Logical and social support, reasons and causes, can be less at odds than one might imagine. I do not want to claim anything so simple as a one-to-one relationship here, but for every variety of consilience or robustness that one can think of, there seems to be a social counterpart. This suggests a broadened conception of methodology, wherein it is not confined to logical relations among propositions but extends also to economy of research, including the economical organization of the research communities (Nickles 1989a and 1989b).

Fourth, Pickering (1987a and elsewhere) neatly welds past to future by seeing scientific decisions as optimizing interests, as applying expertise already acquired to the new problem. In fact, he aims to spell out Kuhn's tantalizing old suggestion that all scientific research consists of analogically modeling new work on old, in concrete ways. Here is where the whig moves that I mentioned before come in handy. The future is constructed from the past—not just from any element of the past but from those that appear to work for the kinds of problems at hand. While nothing like the cumulative, foundational view of knowledge is operative here, the selection process is epistemically relevant.

Fifth, Pickering is well aware of the multi-pass, transformative nature of scientific work. This provides him with the resources for seeing research as a noncircular way of bootstrapping stabilized past results and practices into a future. It will require much effort to spell this out, of course, but until we try, the circularity objection (as I understand it here) seems premature. Naturally, such a bootstrap procedure will, in an innocuous way, put the established phenomena first. At an elementary level, scientists put the phenomena first when constructing scientific explanations. Once a scientific claim is reasonably settled, they do not hesitate to use the newly accepted entities and processes in new research or, if necessary, to appeal to them in order to explain away some once worrisome results that complicated the research leading to their own discovery. This is obviously possible because it is done all the time.

Sixth, as the classical pragmatists attempted to reduce past and present to future in their pragmatic theory of meaning, by reducing meaning to future consequences, so Pickering in effect tries to reduce epistemic justification or acceptance to heuristic appraisal, that is, to the estimate of the promise or the future fertility of a problem, research proposal, program, hypothesis or technique:

> Quite simply, particle physicists accepted the existence of the neutral current because they could see how to ply their trade more profitably in a world in which the neutral current was real. (1984a, p. 87)

This is an extremely important idea, but it ultimately fails as the *sole* component of justification. It is insufficiently multi-pass and cannot handle the difference between accepted work that opens up a field, such as that of Watson and Crick, and accepted work that effectively closes down a field, such as the Hilbert proof that solved the last main problem of invariant theory.[38] Pickering (and everyone else) needs to be able to distinguish this sort of "final closure" from other forms of acceptance and rejection.

Seventh, Pickering is right, however, in holding that heuristic appraisal is a topic more central, even to epistemic justification, than most people think. In effect, he calls attention to the importance of heuristic judgments in relation to the, not one but *two* kinds of underdetermination on which sociologists have focused much of their efforts. The first, Duhemian, underdetermination has to do with the context of justification.

Philosophers have discussed epistemic justification endlessly and have remarkably neglected heuristic justification by comparison. But the latter pervades scientific practice and is surely as important as the former. Research decisions rest, one way or another, on an appraisal of what is worth pursuing and what is not. In fact, it is immediately apparent that epistemic justification depends on heuristic appraisal in a very practical way. Here is where the first, Duhemian, sort of underdetermination enters, the type most often discussed. Researchers attempting to justify a claim or technique face potential difficulties at every point. There is an entire spectrum of possibilities here, ranging from the "all possible objections" of the philosophical skeptic to the small subset of possible objections that will actually be raised by real opponents. Many of the first sort will never be considered (e.g., the possibility that the entire universe came into existence five minutes ago, complete with historical traces). Other possible criticisms may be considered briefly and rejected on the ground that they cut equally against all scientific work (e.g., various fallibilities of human cognition, also logical problems of induction) and still others because they equally challenge the researchers' primary competitors in that specific field and thus get no purchase in this local context of justification. Lying between the two extremes are the possible difficulties raised by the original researchers themselves, either in informal discussion or in technical reports and published papers, for the express purpose of forestalling critical responses from real opponents. Every researcher wants to avoid looking foolish to the next generation of graduate students, but in discussion the researchers will consider most seriously those objections likely to be raised by opponents who have the resources to carry out their critical threats in practice. It is one thing to criticize someone's work *in abstracto;* it is another to be able to furnish contrary results.[39] Accepted results are those that are constructively cited by others and for which the potential difficulties do not become live difficulties, or else die away in the wake of responses because no one who really counts sees any point in further challenging the position. Meanwhile, opponents do their own heuristic assessment of the likelihood of their being able to do enough to make an objection stick with the time and resources they are willing to commit to such an effort.

The kinds of logic-based confirmation and disconfirmation moves that philosophers study almost exclusively are in scientific practice underlain by clusters of heuristic appraisals, including heuristic appraisals of others' heuristic appraisals. The vast majority of these fertility assessments remain unnoted in published accounts of the work. I claim that it is largely the practical judgments of heuristic appraisal (judgments that the approximations are good enough, the experiments sufficiently well designed, the evidence strong enough that no one can get far by challenging them), themselves informed by the results of previous epistemic appraisals, that close up the gap between Duhemian logical underdetermination and practical decision-making and that stop the regress of justification in practice. Informed judgment is a necessary supplement to logical argument. Beyond a certain point, leading researchers find it unfruitful to demand more evidence or more convincing responses to objections. These will be "negative" heuristic appraisals (that such-and-such is not a promising line of criticism, for example), and they are appraisals of possible objections rather than of the central scientific theses themselves; but they remain heuristic appraisals for all that. In this sense, epistemic justification is what the community lets the claimant get away with.[40]

But it is that other sort of underdetermination—the openness of the future stressed by the classical pragmatists, Peirce, James, and Dewey—

that makes heuristic assessment a most exciting topic. No matter how they are construed, established methodological rules do not suffice to determine future research in detail. As I see it, heuristic appraisal is the locus at which the past is tentatively mapped onto conjectured futures, where available resources are selected and reconfigured as instruments for making a future.

Pickering is the science studies practitioner who best exhibits the pragmatic orientation that I find attractive; hence I have focused on him. It may be that I have over-interpreted his anti-whiggism, so that the tension between it and his Kuhnian emphasis on modeling the future on the past is largely my own creation. Perhaps he is now concerned only to avoid precognition and to gain an adequate recognition of the socio-cultural determinants of research. Perhaps he would not extend his warnings against putting the phenomena first to those areas of science in which the posited entities are less problematic than quarks or less obviously the product of human technological culture. Even so, his spirited remarks do provide an occasion for engaging once again the momentous debate between naturalists and historicists. And if Pickering might now moderate his own circularity charge, it is being urged as strongly as ever in other quarters.

I am puzzled by the sociologists' continued enthusiasm for the circularity objection, once precognition has been eliminated, and by their overzealous pursuit of anti-whig ideals. I am puzzled not only because these excesses are untenable but because, in pressing their objections, the new wavers are unduly limiting their own explanatory ambitions. For it appears to me that the sociologists themselves are contributing to the development of the very resources necessary to advance a plausible, explanatory account of the development of human knowledge, an account which is no longer a one-track, "social" account. They officially reject one-pass conceptions of science. They reject linear, foundational conceptions of scientific justification. In recent years, most of them have set aside their earlier, doctrinaire anti-realism. As I read them, several leading constructivists now admit a weak sort of internal realism or a pragmatic realism. This implies that some questions are empirical at least in the sense that whether or not something works is not entirely up to us, no matter how much our community may desire it. In *Science in Action,* Latour says that the social student of science should not, on his own, reopen black-boxes any more than he should close them. Whether they are to be opened or not depends on whether the scientists themselves find occasion to open them through actual controversy. We might say that science studies experts increasingly adhere to a constraint of *historical nominalism,* which asserts that possible difficulties are not to be given the same weight as actual difficulties. This change represents a shift from earlier days, when new-wave sociologists acted very much like philosophers, indeed more so. For these sociologists, everything that was not dictated by logic was a point of openness and thus of possible controversy, and therefore should be treated as if it were a locus of *actual* controversy with some possible skeptics in some possible culture. Philosophers have always felt it necessary to explore the entire space of possibilities rather than just the local region around the "world historical point" of historical actuality. The early new wavers found many more potential sources of difficulty than philosophers had recognized, and they exulted in outdoing the philosophers at their own game. But lately, the sociologists have shown more restraint in such matters than philosophers have. The openness question has now been turned around, as we have seen in the example of Pickering, so that it is no longer a question of justifying claims so much as seeing how forward-looking scientific practice is able to "cut down" this openness in formulating definite research projects that produce specific results. Roughly speaking, openness has become a problem of understanding context of discovery, not (only) context of justification.

6. *Bootstrapping the Past into a Future*

One way of putting my main point is that extreme historicism is self-defeating. It is too strong even as a constraint on historiography if it confines historical writing to descriptive, specialist monographs that risk no theoretical interpretations or explanatory inferences beyond the primary source material. And it is certainly too strong if it is made a condition of adequacy on other science studies disciplines engaged in methodological debate, policymaking, and culture critique.

To say that all our competences and all our concrete human developments are products of history means that historically produced resources are the only ones available to each generation, including our own. We have no alternative but to construct the future out of the past. However, this does not mean that the construction process itself must be historicist. It must be historical, of course, i.e., part of an historical process; but it will rarely be historicist. "The historicity of all things" never meant that all things are *produced* by anything like historical research, a view that confuses history as the unfolding of events with history as a scholarly discipline.[41] To do science or politics is not to do history. In his essay,

"The Advantages and Disadvantages of History for Life" (1874), Nietzsche went so far as to claim that all great historical developments came into existence in an unhistorical atmosphere. That is a bit strong, but we should take note of his point.

Clearly, the most urgent problems of life, including the scientific life, are not problems of understanding historical developments. They are, roughly, problems of how to build the future, both in one's own career and in the larger community. Yet the only resources given to a generation to make something of are those bequeathed to it by its previous history. Whether or not those resources are employed by historically sensitive individuals, they must be used whiggishly, at least in the sense that the problems of these individuals will rarely be identical with the older problems from which the resources derive. Even the application of traditional ways to current situations is whiggish in this respect: the new cases to which they are applied are not identical with the old; and insofar as the new applications become exemplary of the tradition, they alter that tradition. Traditional practice evolves.

Perhaps whiggism is not the only way to effect conceptual and practical change (whether witting or unwitting) but, again, being a whig surely helps. For example, sticking precisely to the original, historical signification of terms would obstruct historical development rather than stimulate it. Such a policy would be as inimical to conceptual change as operationism and earlier movements that aimed to make scientific language pure and constant.[42]

Given my central thesis that we should be (moderately) anti-whiggish when studying history for its own sake but we may be appropriately whiggish when undertaking other projects, where does that leave philosophy and the science studies disciplines? Are they essentially historical disciplines or are they, on the contrary, continuous with natural science? This, of course, is a false dilemma; they are something of both. Hence they need not be slavishly anti-whig. Whether and when depends upon the context. If one cites historical actions and their upshot as evidence for or against a methodological thesis, one should get the history right as far as that is relevant to the problem at hand, but some abstraction from historical details will be required. It is certainly permissible to use historical evidence for nonhistorical purposes, to support a normative, methodological thesis or policy decision, for example.[43]

Attend to the following words of wisdom:

> We are all of us exultant and unrepentant whigs. Those who, perhaps in the misguided austerity of youth, wish to drive out that whig

interpretation . . . are sweeping a room which humanly speaking-cannot long remain empty. They are opening the door for seven devils which, precisely because they are newcomers, are bound to be worse than the first. (Butterfield 1944, pp. 3f)

These are the words of none other than Herbert Butterfield in a book written some dozen years after *The Whig Interpretation of History* and referring back to it. His main point in the later book was that whiggism has been politically and culturally valuable as the chief mechanism for wedding past to future, for legitimating future change by reference to past policies, traditions, and cultural forms that are whiggishly adapted to the program of the reformists. Thus whiggism helps to solve the major problem we face as we *make* history, as we alter our former ways of life, as "we live forward" (in the words of Dewey, 1917). I have tried to extend the point to science.

7. *Concluding Remarks*

In this paper I have assumed or defended the following theses. (1) Scientific theory and practice are entirely products of human historical development (though that practice may discover entities that are not themselves the products of human historical development). (2) In particular, there is no human precognition that could have guided this development. (3) Rather, human knowledge has grown by means of a self-transforming, dialectical or "bootstrap" process, rooted in variation, selective retention, and triangulation of historically available resources. We want to avoid a direct, creationist epistemology just as we do a creationist biology and economics, in favor of an account of the emergence of self-regulating, self-developing systems. The selection of results and methods has been based mainly on success or failure (sometimes as perceived by us, sometimes not). (4) Epistemic amplification has occurred in several ways: through factual discoveries, by generalizing factual knowledge into law claims, and by converting substantive knowledge into knowledge amplifiers in the form of new methods and techniques ("each chief step in science has been a lesson in logic," as Peirce (1877) put it) or entire *Denkstile* (Hacking, in this volume). (5) Often the most successful steps have become "black-boxed" and taken for granted by later generations, who employ these capacities and their products as "givens" rather than items that were once constructed. In these cases the apparatus of construction and maintenance has become invisible and remains so as long as things work well enough. Examples of such steps are the development of human perceptual capacities and (at another level) the modern notions of experiment, evidence, laboratory, predictive test, and mechanical explanation. More local examples are afforded by almost any body of truly innovative work.

(6) Historians and other science studies experts should be historicist (anti-whig) in disclosing the historical process by which these black-boxes were constructed. An historical account that assumes them to be available from the beginning of the work that produced them either takes them as self-evident and needing no explanation at all or renders them self-explanatory products of prescient agents. (7) However, historical explanations are not restricted to actors' accounts. Historians are free to employ later (current) knowledge in order to help us understand an historical episode (e.g., why no one succeeded in producing effect E by means M), as long as the later knowledge is not attributed to those agents. In other words, historians are permitted to "detach" the best-established contemporary claims from the story of history and to use those claims to explain the very history that produced those claims. They can use our knowledge of electrons to help explain the discovery/construction of electrons, why some constructions worked and others did not. Future changes in our own knowledge may require changes in our historical accounts, but so what? It is futile to require that historians seek a standpoint outside all history in order to achieve infallibility. If that is what strong historicism requires, then it is clearly self-defeating.

(8) We must be still more tolerant of whiggism on the part of "working scientists." The greater the depth of the layers of thought and practice that historians disclose retrospectively, the greater the magnitude of the creative changes that the historical agents had to make in the "forward" direction to arrive at our present viewpoint (though not, of course, as a goal they were capable of entertaining at the time). (9) Yet few of the agents who effected these changes did so with an historians' sensitivity to the sources. That is fortunate, since strongly historicist attitudes would surely have hampered much of the work. (10) An unfortunate and unintended byproduct of historically insensitive work is that the present conception of the past work on which it was based becomes the "default" historical interpretation. This is true even if the scientists in question did not consciously reinterpret previous work as a guide to their own but merely cited it as a precedent.

(11) To sum up, then, within the limits on anti-whiggism already indicated: we should tolerate a whiff of whiggism in the "backward" direction, but only enough to allow historical accounts to be appropriately explanatory (without attributing prescience to the agents); but we should

be tolerant of whiggism in the "forward" direction, on the part of the practitioners attempting to progress beyond our current understanding of the world. An anti-whig account of working forward is nearly as problematic as whig history itself. (12) This means that our anti-whiggish historical accounts usually must treat scientists (as such) as whigs. (13) While self-explanation of the precognitive sort is to be rejected, the epistemic enterprise as a whole—the self-transformative process from cave dwellers to the present—must for that very reason be self-explanatory at a different level; for there is nothing else in terms of which to explain it. In this (limited) sense, the human epistemic enterprise *is* self-creation!

(14) Some leading sociologists of science are too historicist insofar as they do more than is necessary to avoid precognitive accounts, accounts that attribute to historical agents knowledge they could not have possessed. They make whiggish behavior on the part of the scientists either impossible or undesirable. Despite their emphasis on contingency and openness, their accounts unduly limit the options of scientists and restrict the resources of science studies into the bargain. (15) As a result, they shun the epistemological task of giving an account of the growth of human knowledge just when they have provided some promising means toward a solution. These science studies experts are able to locate black-boxes and hidden knowledge amplifiers, and to disclose something of their structure, but they think it illegitimate to use this knowledge to explain human epistemic progress. Why? Because they believe either (a) that their social analyses always "deconstruct" the black-boxes or (b) that their strong historicism implies relativism. Either way, we dare not judge one social product as superior to another but must limit our accounts to noting the social attributions of the historical agents. That is, we cannot say that move X was found to work better than move Y in situation Z but only that more, and more powerful, historical agents *attributed* success to X than to Y.

(16) Such a strong historicism engenders passivity. It induces a passive, "spectator" theory of knowledge of the past and neglects the fact that the various members of contemporary communities are not (merely) students of the past but builders of the future. It is no accident that pragmatic writers who promote the active life of future-making, of constructing a particular future from a previously "open" future, were not strong historicists of the anti-whig variety. The leading examples are Nietzsche and the American pragmatists. They were historicists in a moderate sense, but they all recognized that the life of action is a life relatively insensitive to history (at least in the way that professional historians should be

sensitive). They used their historicism, with its emphasis on contingency, to support their belief in an open (undetermined) future and to empower their readers to assume a more active role in making their own futures. It is probably because philosophers of science tend to be more interested in the future than the past that they conflict with their science studies colleagues at this point.

(17) Furthermore, an historicism that limits us to talk of social attributions of success and failure, and excludes judgments of "objective" success and failure on our part, is ultimately self-defeating. It paralyzes social studies of science by refusing to allow us to detach previous results as genuine results to be used as opposed to mere social attributions of results. But if social studies experts are never in a position to use the fruits of previous learning, how can they hope to explain anything at all, including how black-boxes were successfully produced and made invisible, by people employing previously black-boxed procedures? Science studies analysts apparently face the following dilemma. Objective success and failure are either determinable on some occasions or not. That is, claims of success and failure are (sometimes) detachable from claims about the social attribution of success and failure, or they are not. If they are, then we can appeal to pragmatic successes and failures to help explain the growth of knowledge. If not, then science studies accounts of scientific and technological activity have no explanatory force either. I seize the first horn of the dilemma, the "active" horn. I agree that social attribution is important in accounts of scientific development but deny that it screens us off from the world.[44] If it did, it would equally screen us off from social attributions of historical agents as well as any other "facts," and we should have a regress of social attributions of attributions. At some point we must go beyond "they say it works" to "it works." We must temper our historicism with a dose of (pragmatic) naturalism.

(18) The grand irony is that a defensible historicism does not rule out a bootstrap account of the development of knowledge; on the contrary, it requires it! Once we take the rejection of precognition completely seriously, this argues *for* the existence of nonlinear, bootstrap—and in that sense self-explanatory—processes of knowledge amplification rather than against it. For, assuming that skepticism is false and that we do have knowledge, how else could we have gone from essentially zero knowledge to the knowledge we have today? In this large sense, which nowhere implies a vicious circularity, our world of knowledge *is* self-created and so, in some sense, *is* self-explanatory, in principle. At the risk of sounding too much like Kant, I ask: How is our knowledge possible? My insistence on

a thoroughgoing, self-transforming, multi-pass account of scientific inquiry is my own, weakly Hegelian, "dialectical" step toward an answer.
It is only *weakly* Hegelian because, for one thing, it presupposes no transcendent Reason that shapes the overall developmental process.

In Aristotle's account of knowledge, last in order of knowing is first in
order of being. It remains rather mysterious to us how Aristotle makes the
transition from his inductive order of knowing to his necessary order of
being. And if we abandon his theory of the intellect and his equation
of the intellectual order with order of being, this becomes even more
problematic.

If their work is to advance, scientists must, somehow, make the transition from the order of knowing to the order of being in order to use and
reflect on their previous work in what turns out to be a self-transforming
manner. Roughly, last in context of discovery is first in order of *explanation*. At some point, they must make the judgment "enough support" and
detach claims or techniques from a context of discovery and social attributions of success, taking them as reliable enough to use as resources in
further work. The same holds for science studies practitioners insofar as
they wish to explain anything.

Aristotle's project was "foundational" insofar as we can apply that modern, epistemological label to him. By now, we have shown all foundational
accounts of knowledge to rest upon one or another mysterious, question-
begging, self-certifying claim or capacity. Yet a moderate historicism itself implies that any adequate account of the growth of knowledge will be
broadly circular. The growth of knowledge will have the character of a
self-transforming, ultimately self-supporting or "bootstrap" process in the
sense that no Archimedean point has ever been available to provide leverage for the epistemic enterprise.

Now the "givens" of traditional philosophies are nonexistent, as such,
but some talk of givens surely signals (to us) the existence of concealed
social mechanisms, black-boxes of the kind that social studies experts are
beginning to open. I would only insist that one may open such a box in
order to find out how it works and whether it works well enough to keep;
and not only to "deconstruct" it as a mere social device. Although all such
devices are fallible, some of them are surely reliable and useful, else it is
difficult to explain their persistence across different historico-social formations. Indeed, without them it is difficult to explain our survival.

For an epistemologist wanting to locate as many of these black-boxes
as possible and to find out their internal structure, how they work,
sociological work looks helpful, initially. Yet sociologists tend to leave

epistemologists with a contemporary version of the puzzle about Aristotle. For these very accounts seem to make the transition from one order of thinking to another (or to the order of doing) somehow impossible or illegitimate or unintelligible, both to working scientists and to science studies explanations and evaluations of their work. This seems to me a failure in reflexivity[45] and a great opportunity missed. How *do* we know what we know? Shouldn't it be one goal of science studies to explain this? I had thought the aim of the original, Strong Program was to employ scientific methods in order to understand science itself.

NOTES

This paper makes use of work on social epistemology originally supported by the John Dewey Foundation and work on heuristic appraisal and scientific problem-solving supported by the U.S. National Science Foundation. I am grateful to both organizations. Ernan Mc Mullin's abundant comments improved the clarity of both the language and the thoughts expressed. Criticism of excessive anti-whiggism was a feature of a surprising number of papers (in addition to my own) at the 1991 History of Science Society and Society for the History of Technology joint meeting in Madison, Wisconsin. I mention especially Stephen Brush, "Should Scientists Write History of Science?" The "critical problems" papers from this conference are to be published.

1. The first motto is from Nietzsche (1874, 12). The second is quoted by Shapin (1984), who uses it for a different purpose. It fits mine so well!

2. In order not to beg questions, I do not simply assume that historicism, as I use the term, implies relativism, the view that all forms of life are equally good, epistemically and morally, and hence that there is no progress. Historicism in my sense holds that everything human (including our knowledge of the natural world and, indeed, everything else) has a history and is subject to future change but entails nothing about the progress of any particular enterprise relative to a particular standard. Whether an enterprise has progressed over time is an open question. I do assume that progress is possible, by accumulation and transformation of useful results and by improving the known reliability of a particular item that "survives the test of time." While the vagaries of history may seem to favor relativism, history can also provide a laboratory for establishing consilience and robustness, a point to which I return later.

3. Campbell (1988, 1990) convincingly rejects epistemologies employing any sort of prescience or illumination (that is, any sort of self-certifying intuition rather than normal, "naturalistic" ways of coming-to-know), and he sketches an evolutionary account of the growth of our capacities for knowing. Sellars (1963, ch. 5) mounts an effective attack on philosophical theories of the given.

4. Before whig historians embraced the idea of progress, early seventeenth-century whigs were insensitive to the creative force of history, to essential change

over time (Butterfield, 1944). For them there was no real history in the historicist sense. Much later, Hegel and Marx did consider history (both as acted and as written) to be the history of the self-creation of human beings, but this process is not circular in the way that whiggish, "immediate self-creation" is.

5. Adapted from Asimov (1982, p. 201). Compare the following (self-contradictory) statement:

> In 1811 the difficulties attending the application of the law of volumes had been cleared up by an Italian physicist, Amedeo Avogadro . . . . Avogadro was little known in Italy and still less abroad. His important memoir appeared in French in 1811, and another in 1814. His work passed unnoticed and a similar theory was advanced in 1814 by Ampère. (Partington 1957, p. 208).

See the discussion in section 3 below.

6. 'New-wave' is intended to contrast the sociological work of the Edinburgh Strong Program, the Bath relativist program, the York discourse-analysis school, and related, more recent developments in sociology and anthropology of science (especially in France, Holland, and America) with the older sociology of science exemplified by the work of Robert Merton and his associates. As I use the term, it is neither laudatory nor pejorative.

7. More than a century ago, Marx (1844) lauded Feuerbach for showing that "philosophy is nothing more than religion brought into thought and developed by thought."

8. It would seem, however, that such work cannot capture that bit of historicist wisdom contained in Hegel's famous remark that the owl of Minerva flies out only at dusk. Unfortunately, Hegel's invocation of reason at this point has helped to give historicist, "bootstrap" accounts of the growth of knowledge a bad name.

9. My naturalism is weaker than the old empiricist and positivistic naturalisms, modeled on physical science; weaker than the new naturalisms, based on biological or psychological reductionism; and weaker even than the socio-naturalism of Bloor's (1976) version of social interest theory. Naturalism, as I am using the term, implies that neither the natural nor the social world is simply given to human knowledge.

10. On the other hand, whether or not they were justified in doing so by our lights, many investigators were motivated by religious convictions that underwrote their beliefs that the world is intelligible to human reason and that natural knowledge is worth having. This was especially true during the heyday of natural theology, from Newton to Darwin.

11. By 'whig precursoritis', I mean the strategy of forcing as many precursors as possible into the role of anticipators of later work and reading the latter back into the former in order to "explain" the later work as an outgrowth of the earlier, whether or not there was any historico-causal connection. See the reference to Hull in note 23. I do not, of course, deny that later work does build on previous work.

12. Curiously, the discovery-construction process is sealed off in standard positivist and Popperian treatments of science not for the usual reason that discovery has been reduced to routine but, on the contrary, because it is like Wittgenstein's "beetle in the box" in that it can be anything at all and hence is of no epistemic significance. Therefore, only confirmation or justification is epistemologically relevant.

13. See, e.g., Laudan (1977), Schaffner (1980), Curd (1980).

14. Still, as Holmes (1981) points out, even published papers provide an expert historian with more material for historical reconstruction than sociologists appreciate. (Look, for example, what Heilbron and Kuhn (1969) found in Niels Bohr's famous 1913 papers.) Moreover, Holmes adds, competition for priority and the need for professional advancement imply that scientists normally publish many of their significant ideas as soon as they can. It was Planck's series of articles over several years that enabled Kuhn (1978) to reconstruct his research program in such detail. Finally, Holmes notes how combining laboratory notebooks or diaries, when available, with published papers can yield a fairly reliable account of discovery paths. Apart from Latour, "ethno" sociologists tend to undervalue public texts (it is in their professional interest to do so), which partly explains the vehemence of their attack on the construction of texts and their lack of patience in interpreting them.

15. For example, see Bloor (1976), Knorr-Cetina (1981, pp. 127ff), Woolgar (1988). Collins (1984, p. 170) writes:

> [A]s long ago as 1963 Medawar wrote an article called 'Is the Scientific Paper a Fraud?' Understanding has advanced considerably since then and in particular we now know the research paper presents an unrealistically ordered, logical and consensual account of scientific practice.

But why consider a research paper an account of scientific practice? Bloor (1976) argues that logic and forms of reasoning are only *post hoc* rationalizations of scientific work rather than explanatory determinants of it. While there is some truth in Bloor's point (see my treatment of logics of discovery, 1990), it overlooks not only the positive research contribution of paper-writing but also the Hegelian point that the logic may articulate something implicit in the scientific practice.

16. I mean the historical paragraphs in research papers, not the retrospective reflections of explicitly historical intent by Great Men—though, to the extent that the latter authors are attempting to reinterpret their own work in the most favorable light, the point might be extended even to them.

17. See MacIntyre (1977) on the role of history in scientific justification. Analysts as sophisticated as Gilbert and Mulkay (1984) retain something of a one-pass conception of science (see below), as if what scientists identify as a "key experiment" can only be key if it was crucial at the time it was reported, and any later change of status is on a par with the Russians denying that there was a battle of Stalingrad. Many things that Gilbert and Mulkay find odd about scientists'

reporting can be explained by taking into account retrospective reconstruction of a perfectly legitimate sort.

18. Dear (1985) and Shapin (1985) explain, somewhat differently, why the early papers were presented as personal reports. See also Holmes (1986) and Bazerman (1988, Part II).

19. See Simon (1973). It is perhaps harder to relate well-structured problems to messy nature, but that is another issue. Without doubt, it has been accomplished on numerous occasions. Not infrequently, the upshot of research is a solution to a problem that could not even be formulated at the outset.

20. Nor am I the only one to notice the disparity between theory and practice in the new-wave work. Lenoir (1988, p. 8) observes that:

> In contrast to the relatively straightforward production line reification of theoretical statements into facts described by Woolgar and Latour, Holmes [1985] emphasizes a more complex interactionist perspective with numerous feedback loops linking theory and practice . . . .

21. See the references in Note 15.

22. For example, what Shapere (1982) and Pinch (1984) have said about observational data being theoretically reinterpretable at successively higher levels of description can be adapted to the interpretation of what is really going on in a scientific publication.

23. I am interested here in whiggish moves that help advance one's actual research at the time. In this respect the Mendel case is marginal, according to Brannigan (1981). Insofar as the "rediscovery" of Mendel did not appreciably alter the course of later work but only helped to resolve a priority dispute about new work already accomplished, then Mendel had no significant impact on the development of genetics and was not even part of the so-called "Mendelian" community; and his work is of largely antiquarian interest. For Hull (1989), such labels as 'Mendelian' and 'Darwinian' identify populations of historically (causally) related individuals rather than collections of similar ideas. By contrast, Kalmus (1983, p. 76), evaluates all aspects of Mendel's work *except* its causal, historical impact. I am inclined to agree with Hull, whose approach was applied to the label 'Aristotelian' by Grant (1987).

Giambattista Vico seems to play a Mendel-like role in some branches of social science. The first step in the "reification" of Vico is to characterize him as a genius whose reception was delayed until long beyond his own time. ('Reification' is a term used by Brannigan in this context.) The explanation for this delay—that he was too far ahead of his time to be understood by his contemporaries—also seemingly justifies neglecting his own historical context. Step one opens the way for step two. Contemporary structuralists, historicists, etc., can now read their own (conflicting) views back into Vico in order to tell us what he really meant, how he addressed *our* questions.

24. This phenomenon is common in scientists' retrospective accounts of their own work, e.g., Max von Laue's report on X-ray diffraction in Munich. See Forman (1969). "Defining the problem situation by projecting the solution backward" (Forman 1968, p. 158) is a favorite bootstrap device. It has been said of many, including Descartes and Freud, that their work invented the problem for which it provided the solution.

25. Hints toward such a study may be found in Latour (1987) and Hull (1979, 1989), for example, not to mention Kuhn (1978) and Pickering (1984a and 1984b). See also Fuller (1988, p. 144) and the Oldroyd-Lynch (1989) exchange.

26. Butterfield (1944) was less linear and more inclined to a whiggish, "bootstrap" view of historical development.

27. This may have been what Collins meant when he wrote:

> [S]ince the consensus is not known while it is being formed, nothing related to knowledge of the ultimate consensus can have played a part in scientists' decisions about how to act in order to form the consensus (barring precognition). Thus, data based on that consensus must be irrelevant to rational-actor explanations of its formation . . . . If what one is seeking to investigate is scientist-actors' parts in the construction of scientific knowledge it is no use using the outcome of the process as part of the explanation of the outcome. On the one hand, this is circular, on the other hand, if such a method could be used then it would be possible to short-circuit the whole process of the development of knowledge; those who had access to the relevant data could reveal it—reveal what is true, rational etc.—and there would be no need to do much scientific work other than a few detailed measurements. (1981, p. 222)

28. For reflexive attacks on sociologists' own manner of putting the phenomena first, see Woolgar (1981), Yearley (1982), and Latour (1987 and this volume). While I agree, of course, that social categories cannot be taken as given, any more than natural ones, I would insist that one can put the phenomena first in careful explanatory accounts, in sociology as well as in natural science. Something already black-boxed can later be *used*. Incidentally, a partial explanation why scientists put the phenomena first is that the implicit rules of attribution of "discoveries" demands it (which "rules" help to stabilize the community). Latour observes that a scientist wants to enroll others as allies but also to control them so that his work is not transformed out of recognition, with corresponding loss of credit. I suggest that the rules of discovery-attribution assign credit to the original work even when the extent of later transformation is recognized. This practice by itself makes scientists' accounts look more whiggish than they really are. And hence the reification of Mendel, Banting, et al.

29. On maker's knowledge, see Pérez-Ramos (1989) and Funkenstein (1986).

30. Some philosophers also have dropped broad hints in this direction. Compare Cartwright's Aristotelian world picture (1983). She holds that phenomeno-

logical laws tend to be closer to the truth than the basic theoretical principles from which they are allegedly derived. The most general laws of physics "lie"; approximations and idealizations are needed to make them fit the real world. Advocates of the semantic view of theories (e.g., Giere, 1988), stress that theories describe only ideal models that must be fitted to local bits of the real world by means of approximations and idealizations. See also Levins and Lewontin (1985), Hacking (1983, ch. 13, and 1988), Ackermann (1985), and Feyerabend (1989). Hacking's contribution to the present volume and his forthcoming book, cited therein, further develop his ideas. Meanwhile, Kuhn is completing a new book that will restate and defend in linguistic terms his notion that scientists under different paradigms live in different "data" worlds while residing in the same "stimulus" world. See Kuhn (1991).

31. Hacking (1988) notes that 'artificial' is a highly ambiguous term and that the sociologists' talk of reality differs from that of philosophers.

32. Note the curious parallel to operationist accounts of theoretical entities. Since 'electron' is defined in terms of certain experimental operations and particular phenomena that they produce (namely, what theoretical realists would call the *evidence* for electrons), we are not allowed to appeal to electrons as the underlying causes that explain this evidence. That would be to confuse causal explanation with definition. Strong social-constructivist views appear to waver between saying that social practices define the "discovered" entities and saying that they fully create or cause those entities (rather than vice versa). See also note 43.

33. See Feyerabend (1989) on the general problem of reasoning from idiosyncratic historical changes to history-independent facts and laws.

34. There are many ways in which careful historians may legitimately use current scientific knowledge to illuminate the past. For some references, see Kragh (1987, ch. 14), Hull (1979, 1989), and Gorman and Carlson (1989). Margolis (unpublished) maintains that current knowledge of the basic correctness of the Copernican hypothesis permits us to ask and answer questions (such as why it took so long to arrive at Copernican conclusions) that we should not otherwise have hit upon. I think questions of this kind can be legitimate, but there are whig dangers, as pointed out by James (1985).

35. E.g., Gingras and Schweber (1986). But see Pickering (1990) on conservative appeals to constraints.

36. I recognize that this slogan and others, e.g., the pragmatist's "it works" and the evolutionary epistemologist's "blind variation plus selective retention," are question-begging if amplified into universal, context-free claims. For it is precisely the point of the "phenomena first" sort of sociological critique that success is not its own explanation, that success and failure are culturally defined. I would only insist that they are not always *totally* culturally determined. Again, increased life expectancy is a hard fact, not a mere social attribution.

37. See Wimsatt (1981) on robustness and also Latour (1988) on "Einsteinian" relativity.

38. Fisher's (1966) account is now being challenged by Karen Parshall in lectures. If this example should fail, there are many others. Nickles (1989c) is a general discussion of heuristic appraisal.

39. For example, Garvin's critique of Weber's claim to have detected gravity waves had more impact on the community than similar attacks because Garvin had set up his own apparatus and produced empirical results. This case is discussed by Collins (1985).

40. I don't mean to suggest that every claim not explicitly rejected by the community is accepted. Many are just ignored. In other cases, the community fails to apply its own critical standards. Heuristic appraisal of a more positive variety will figure in the explanation of why some claims are accepted for use in further work.

41. Students of history sometimes forget that only very rarely were the history-makers they study historians themselves. Most scientists are unaware of some of the people we label their antecedents, let alone careful students of the previous work.

42. A priggish historicism would reduce ideas to one-criterion concepts as rapidly as do verificationist theories of meaning of the positivist-operationist variety. On such a principled view, as Putnam (1975) noted, we could not say that Einstein greatly advanced the study of gravitation but must instead say that he changed the subject, since he was not talking about gravitation in the strict, Newtonian sense at all. Compare note 32.

43. It may seem that my forward whiggism contradicts MacIntyre's (1977) Vichian thesis that "Scientific reason turns out to be subordinate to, and intelligible only in terms of, historical reason" (66); but I think not. In my view, specific techniques as well as larger methodological strategies can only be epistemically evaluated against their historical record of success and failure, in comparison with their predecessors and competitors. (Even here, one should not forget the importance of future-oriented, heuristic appraisal.) I agree with MacIntyre: "It is because only from the standpoint of the new science can the inadequacy of the old science be characterized that the new science is taken to be more adequate than the old" (69), a statement that fits well with Butterfield's mature position. The position is whiggish, since it implies that we assess our own efforts in relation to the past—but in terms of our *present* conceptual framework, interests, and standards.

44. I am not invoking either nature or society as some sort of theological given. There is a middle position between eschewing the use of previously developed tools and results, and taking them as theological givens. Again, as Latour says, we may use what has previously been black-boxed and is working well enough that the box has not been opened.

45. Of course, there are several dimensions of reflexivity and symmetry. I have not attempted here to justify taking historically robust "scientific" results more seriously than, say, the practices of a so-called "primitive" tribe. Obviously, I would try to do this in terms of scientific results "working" more reliably.

REFERENCES

Ackermann, Robert. 1985. *Data, Instruments, and Theory.* Princeton: Princeton University Press.

Asimov, Isaac. 1982. *Asimov's Biographical Encyclopedia of Science & Technology,* 2nd ed. New York: Doubleday.

Baigrie, Brian. "Scientific Practice: The View from the Tabletop," in *Tabletop Experiments,* ed. Zed Buchwald, in press.

Bazerman, Charles. 1988. *Shaping Written Knowledge: The Genre and Activity of the Experimental Article in Science.* Madison: University of Wisconsin Press.

Bloor, David. 1976. *Knowledge and Social Imagery.* London: Routledge.

Brannigan, Augustine. 1981. *The Social Basis of Scientific Discoveries.* Cambridge: Cambridge University Press.

Brooke, John. 1981. "Avogadro's hypothesis and its fate: A case-study in the failure of case studies," *History of Science* 19:235–273.

Butterfield, Herbert. 1931. *The Whig Interpretation of History.* London: Bell.

———. 1944. *The Englishman and His History.* Cambridge: Cambridge University Press.

Campbell, Donald. 1988. *Methodology and Epistemology for Social Science.* Chicago: University of Chicago Press.

———. 1990. "Epistemological Roles for Selection Theory," in *Evolution, Cognition, and Realism,* ed. Nicholas Rescher. Lanham, Md.: University Press of America.

Cartwright, Nancy. 1983. *How the Laws of Physics Lie.* Oxford: Clarendon Press.

Collins, Harry. 1981. "What is TRASP?: The radical programme as a methodological imperative," *Philosophy of the Social Sciences* 11:215–224.

———. 1984. "When do scientists prefer to vary their experiments?" *Studies in History and Philosophy of Science* 15:169–174.

———. 1985. *Natural Order.* London: Sage Publications.

Curd, Martin. 1980. "Scientific discovery: An analysis of three approaches," in Nickles (1980a), 201–219.

Dear, Peter. 1985. *"Totius in verba:* Rhetoric and authority in the early royal society," *Isis* 76:145–161.

Dewey, John. 1917. "The need for a recovery of philosophy," in *Works,* vol. 10, 3–48. Carbondale: Southern Illinois University Press.

Feyerabend, Paul. 1989. "Realism and the historicity of knowledge," *Journal of Philosophy* 86:393–406.

Fischhoff, Baruch. 1975. "Hindsight ≠ foresight: The effect of outcome knowledge on judgment under uncertainty," *Journal of Experimental Psychology: Human Perception and Performance* 1:288–99.

Fisher, Charles. 1966. "The death of a mathematical theory: A study in the sociology of knowledge," *Archive for History of Exact Sciences,* 3:137–159.

Forman, Paul. 1968. "The doublet riddle and atomic physics *circa* 1924," *Isis* 59:156–174.

———. 1969. "The discovery of the diffraction of X-rays by crystals; A critique of the myths" (plus Ewald's reply), *Archive for History of Exact Sciences* 6:38–81.

Fuller, Steve. 1988. *Social Epistemology.* Bloomington: Indiana University Press.

Funkenstein, Amos. 1986. *Theology and the Scientific Imagination.* Princeton: Princeton University Press.

Giere, Ronald. 1988. *Explaining Science.* Chicago: University of Chicago Press.

Gilbert, Nigel, and Michael Mulkay. 1984. "Experiments are the key: Participants' histories and historians' histories of science," *Isis* 75:105–25.

Gingras, Yves and Silvan Schweber. 1986. "Constraints on construction," *Social Studies of Science* 16:372–383.

Gooding, David, Trevor Pinch, and Simon Schaffer, eds. *The Uses of Experiment: Studies of Experiment in the Natural Sciences.* Cambridge: Cambridge University Press.

Gorman, Michael, and Bernard Carlson. 1989. "Can experiments be used to study science?" *Social Epistemology* 3:89–106.

Grant, Edward. 1987. "Ways to interpret the terms 'Aristotelian' and 'Aristotelianism' in Medieval and Renaissance natural philosophy," *History of Science* 25:335–358.

Hacking, Ian. 1983. *Representing and Intervening.* Cambridge: Cambridge University Press.

———. 1988. "The participant irrealist at large in the laboratory," *British Journal for the Philosophy of Science* 39:277–294.

Heilbron, John. 1987. "Applied History of Science," *Isis* 78:552–563.

Heilbron, John, and Thomas Kuhn. 1969. "The genesis of the Bohr atom," *Historical Studies in the Physical Sciences* 1:211–290.

Holmes, Frederic L. 1981. "The fine structure of scientific creativity," *History of Science* 19:60–71.

———. 1985. *Lavoisier and the Chemistry of Life.* Madison: University of Wisconsin Press.

———. 1986. "Scientific writing and scientific discovery," *Isis* 77:220–235.

Hull, David. 1979. "In defense of presentism." *History and Theory* 18:1–15.

———. 1989. *The Metaphysics of Evolution.* Albany: State University of New York Press.

James, Frank. 1985. "The creation of a Victorian myth: The historiography of spectroscopy," *History of Science* 23:1–24.

Kalmus, H. 1983. "The scholastic origins of Mendel's concepts," *History of Science* 21:61–83.

Klein, Martin. 1972. "The Use and Abuse of Historical Teaching in Physics," in *History in the Teaching of Physics,* ed. Stephen Brush and Allen King. Hanover, N. H.: University Press of New England.

Knorr-Cetina, Karin. 1981. *The Manufacture of Knowledge.* Oxford: Pergamon Press.

Kragh, Helge. 1987. *An Introduction to the Historiography of Science*. Cambridge: Cambridge University Press.

Kuhn, Thomas. 1962. *The Structure of Scientific Revolutions*. Chicago: University of Chicago Press.

———. 1977. *The Essential Tension*. Chicago: University of Chicago Press.

———. 1978. *Black-Body Theory and the Quantum Discontinuity, 1894–1912*. Oxford: Oxford University Press.

———. 1991. Presidential lecture, Philosophy of Science Association. *PSA 1990*, Vol. II, 3–13.

Latour, Bruno. 1987. *Science in Action*. Cambridge: Harvard University Press.

———. 1988. "A relativistic account of Einstein's relativity," *Social Studies of Science* 18:3–44.

Latour, Bruno, and Steve Woolgar. 1979. *Laboratory Life*. London: Sage.

Laudan, Larry. 1977. *Progress and Its Problems*. Berkeley: University of California Press.

Lenoir, Timothy. 1988. "Practice, reason, context: The dialogue between theory and experiment," *Science in Context* 2:3–22.

Levins, Richard, and Richard Lewontin. 1985. *The Dialectical Biologist*. Cambridge: MIT Press.

MacIntyre, Alasdair. 1977. "Epistemological crises, dramatic narrative and the philosophy of science," *Monist* 60:453–472. As reprinted in *Paradigms and Revolutions*, ed. Gary Gutting. University of Notre Dame Press, 1980, 54–74.

Margolis, Howard. Unpublished. "Copernican reality and Ptolemaic belief."

Marx, Karl. 1844. *The Economic and Philosophical Manuscripts*.

Medawar, Peter. 1964. "Is the scientific paper fraudulent?" *Saturday Review* (1 August): 43–44.

———. 1969. *The Art of the Soluble*. New York: Barnes & Noble.

Nickles, Thomas. 1980a. *Scientific Discovery, Logic, and Rationality*. Dordrecht: Reidel.

———. 1980b. *Scientific Discovery: Case Studies*. Dordrecht: Reidel.

———. 1987. "The reconstruction of scientific knowledge," *Philosophy and Social Action* 13 (1987): 91–104.

———. 1988. "Reconstructing science: Discovery and experiment," in *Theory and Experiment*, ed. D. Batens and J. P. Van Bendegem. Dordrecht: Reidel, 33–53.

———. 1989a. "Justification and experiment," in Gooding et al. (1989): 299–333.

———. 1989b. "Integrating the science studies disciplines," in *The Cognitive Turn: Sociological and Psychological Perspectives on Science* (Sociology of the Sciences Yearbook, 1989), ed. Steve Fuller, Marc de Mey, Terry Shinn, and Steve Woolgar. Dordrecht: Kluwer, 225–256.

———. 1989c. "Heuristic appraisal: A proposal," *Social Epistemology* 3:175–188.

————. 1990. "Discovery logics," *Philosophica* 45:7–32.

Nietzsche, Friedrich. 1874. *On the Advantage and Disadvantage of History for Life,* trans. Peter Preuss. Indianapolis: Hackett, 1980. Part 2 of *Unzeitgemässe Betrachtungen.*

Oldroyd, David. 1989. "Why not a Whiggish social studies of science?" (with reply by William Lynch and rejoinder by Oldroyd). *Social Epistemology* 3:355–72.

Partington, J. R. 1957. *A Short History of Chemistry,* 3rd ed. New York: Harper.

Peirce, Charles. 1877. "The fixation of belief," in *Collected Papers,* vol. 5, 358–387. Cambridge: Harvard University Press, 1931–1935.

Pérez-Ramos, Antonio. 1989. *Francis Bacon's Idea of Science and the Maker's Knowledge Tradition.* Oxford: Oxford University Press.

Pickering, Andrew. 1984a. "Against putting the phenomena first: The discovery of the weak neutral current," *Studies in History and Philosophy of Science* 15:85–117.

————. 1984b. *Constructing Quarks: A Sociological History of Particle Physics.* Chicago: University of Chicago Press.

————. 1987a. "Models in/of scientific practice," *Philosophy and Social Action* 13:69–77.

————. 1987b. "Forms of life: Science, contingency and Harry Collins," *British Journal for the History of Science* 20:213–221.

————. 1989. "Living in the material world: On realism and experimental practice," in Gooding et al. (1989), 275–297.

————. 1990. "Beyond constraint: The temporality of practice and the historicity of knowledge," Conference on "Philosophical and Historiographical Problems about Small-Scale Experiments," University of Toronto, March 1990. Forthcoming in *Tabletop Experiments,* ed. Zed Buchwald.

————. Forthcoming. "Openness and closure: On the goals of scientific practice," in *Experimental Enquiries,* ed. Homer Le Grand. Dordrecht: Kluwer.

Pinch, Trevor. 1984. "Towards an analysis of scientific observation," *Social Studies of Science* 15:3–35.

Polanyi, Michael. 1958. *Personal Knowledge.* Chicago: University of Chicago Press.

Putnam, Hilary. 1975. *Philosophical Papers.* Cambridge: Cambridge University Press.

Schaffner, Kenneth. 1980. "Discovery in the biomedical sciences: Logic or Irrational Intuition?", in Nickles (1980b), 171–205.

Sellars, Wilfrid. 1963. *Science, Perception, and Reality.* London: Routledge.

Shapere, Dudley. 1982. "The concept of observation in science and philosophy." *Philosophy of Science* 49:485–525.

Shapin, Steven. 1984. "Talking history: Reflections on discourse analysis," (comment on Gilbert and Mulkay). *Isis* 75:125–128.

————. 1985. "Pump and circumstance: Robert Boyle's literary technology," *Social Studies of Science* 14:481–520.

Shapin, Steven, and Simon Schaffer. 1985. *Leviathan and the Air-Pump*. Princeton: Princeton University Press.

Simon, Herbert. 1973. "The structure of ill-structured problems." *Artificial Intelligence* 4:181–201. Reprinted in *Models of Discovery*. Dordrecht: Reidel: 1977, 304–325.

Toulmin, Stephen. 1972. *Human Understanding*. Princeton: Princeton University Press.

Wimsatt, William. 1981. "Robustness, reliability and multiple-determination in science," in *Scientific Inquiry and the Social Sciences: A Tribute to Donald T. Campbell*, ed. Marilynn Brewer and Barry Collins. San Francisco: Jossey-Bass, 124–163.

Woolgar, Steve. 1981. "Interests and explanations in the social study of science," *Social Studies of Science* 11:365–397.

———. 1988. *Science: The Very Idea*. London: Tavistock.

Yearley, Steven. 1982. "The relationship between epistemological and sociological cognitive interests: Some ambiguities underlying the use of interest theory in the study of scientific knowledge," *Studies in History and Philosophy of Science* 13:353–388.

STATISTICAL LANGUAGE, STATISTICAL TRUTH AND STATISTICAL REASON: THE SELF-AUTHENTIFICATION OF A STYLE OF SCIENTIFIC REASONING

Ian Hacking

It is a philosophical task in our times to connect:

(1) Social studies of knowledge, of the sort pioneered by David Bloor and Barry Barnes in Edinburgh, but now quite common in Europe, especially in the United Kingdom.

(2) Metaphysics, particularly the debates that resulted from Hilary Putnam's series of revised positions, beginning with the scientific realism founded on his theory of reference, but proceeding to his rejection of such metaphysical realism, and his advocacy of internal realism, recently the focus of attention in the United States.

(3) The Braudelian aspects of science, that is, the long-term slow-moving, persistent, and accumulating aspects of the growth of knowledge. Braudel, in caricature, wrote of the Mediterranean as a Sea around which nothing much happens besides shifts in climate and topography; the chief effect of civilization in Greece was to turn a forested peninsula into a rockheap. [1]

The task of connecting (1)–(3) was trivial when the whole of science was thought of as gradual Braudelian accumulation. We had (2) a metaphysics of a real world to which true propositions correspond, (3) a permanent, if sometimes subdued, will to find out the truth, and (1) types of civilization or social order—ours—that fostered ingenuity, honesty, innovation, and the growth of knowledge. That vision has fallen from favor. It may seem odd that I do not even mention a fourth item that needs reconciliation with the three that I do list—the structure of scientific revolutions. I omit it because (1)–(3) are contraries precisely because of Kuhn's work. My paper discusses a problem that takes Kuhn for granted in the background. Since he published in 1962, three types of inquiry have almost ceased to speak to each other, namely:

A. Newly gained analyses of, and case-studies of, the fleeting "microsocial" interactions of knowers and discoverers, their "macrosocial" relationship to larger communities, and the material conditions and objects in which the discoveries are made and which they are about. At this level, the relevant events last a week or at most a few decades.

B. Current philosophical conceptions of truth, being, logic, meaning, and knowledge.

C. Models of relatively permanent, growing, self-modulating, revisable features of science. Such features might begin in a lot of delicate interplays of needs, interest, and power struggles that cry out for detailed examination of a microsocial sort. Their persistence demands another analysis. The result of their persistence is a body of what is counted as objective ways of determining the truth, of settling belief, of understanding meanings, a body of nothing less than logic itself.

Philosophers, historians, and sociologists have brilliantly energized studies of (1) and (2). Putnam's metaphysics has redrawn the contours of discussion, while the plethora of perhaps misleadingly titled "social" studies of science has opened new vistas. The social construction of scientific facts school does not mention Putnam nor does Putnam mention it. Neither has much use for big units of philosophico-historical reflections. The mighty have fallen. Paradigms are distinctly out. Putnam, following Peirce, speaks grandly of what would ideally be known late in the day as a result of unceasing honorable inquiry. But this is not a vision of any actual science in the long term, for unlike Peirce, Putnam says little enough about how the inquiry is conducted. Putnam is concerned not with reasoning but with pure reason. The increasingly common references to Kant in his work are no accident. They reveal the extent to which he has lost interest in how we find out, in the details of how scientists actually carry on. Instead his papers are full of fables, science fictions used to make philosophical points, delightful to read, but the very opposite of factual microsociology.

The constructionalists form a different contrast. They study the first shift at the factory of facts. Quitting work early in the day, they leave us in the lurch with a feeling of absolute contingency. They give little sense of what holds the constructions together beyond the networks of the moment, abetted by human complacency. We now need to examine something in between timeless metaphysics and the momentary social conjunctures. What will serve?

I want something both social and metaphysical and propose my concept of a "style of reasoning."[2] It is an irrevocably metaphysical idea, yet styles, like all else human, come into being through little local interactions. So styles help fulfill the task of bridging (1) and (2). And what are "styles"? I took the name "style of reasoning" from A. C. Crombie, who, in a paper of 1978, listed six very familiar items. The only thing unusual was that he took them to be the core list of "styles of scientific thinking in the European tradition."

(a) The simple postulation established in the mathematical sciences.
(b) Experimental exploration and measurement of more complex observable relations.
(c) Hypothetical construction of analogical models.
(d) Ordering of variety by comparison and taxonomy.
(e) Statistical analysis of regularities of populations and the calculus of probabilities.
(f) Historical derivation of genetic development.[3]

These "styles" did not stay in one community or wither away. They run the world. A style of scientific reasoning is put in place in a network of people, answering to the needs, interests, ideology, or curiosity of some of its members, defended by bluster or insidious patience. But when it becomes fixed as a new way to truth, it needs no support or rhetoric, for as it assumes self-confidence it generates its own standard of objectivity and its own ideology. It starts by being pushed and shaped by social vectors of every sort; we end with a self-sustaining mode of knowledge. It becomes less something molded by interests, and more an unquestioned resource upon which any interest must draw, if it ever hopes for the accolade of objectivity. And it further determines how people conceive of themselves and their world, opening new horizons, but also constraining the possible forms of knowledge.

The relatively slow-moving, curiously permanent evolution of ways in which we know, find out, and evolve skills of thinking, asking, and investigating is eminently Braudelian. For example, once people began to reason like Euclid, they continued to do so, off and on, and always can do so, once they see how it goes. When (to use Althusser's catchy phrase) a legendary Thales "discovered the continent of mathematics" we began postulational reasoning, the deduction of or speculation about the consequences of precise assumptions. That way of thinking has grown, reconceived itself, abandoned old aspirations and achieved new heights. It is the accumulation not so much of knowledge (which even in mathematics is commonly superseded) as of ways of finding out. I am inclined to say much the same of laboratory science, which, whatever its antecedents, began to assume its present power in the world only in the "scientific revolution." But here my example is Crombie's (e), especially the fixation of the statistical style of reasoning during the nineteenth and early twentieth centuries. It has the great merit of being relatively recent so that we can almost see new kinds of objectivity emerging before our very eyes. It has also, over the past decade, benefitted from a great deal of new scholarship.

The following essay is in two parts. In Part I ("The Metaphysics of Styles") I sketch out the general idea of a style of reasoning, and its connection with truth, meaning, and verification. Then in Part II ("The Styles of Statistics") I show how the brazen metaphysical claims that I make are exemplified in a surprisingly unadventuresome way by statistical reasoning. In passing, I shall observe that as this style of thought evolved, every social dimension is on show. If you want interests, we have interests. If you want rhetorical devices, we have those. And institutions, modes of legitimation, takeover battles, constructions, uses of power, networks, intimations of control, and much, much more. Yet as the style becomes increasingly secure, these are decreasingly relevant to its status. The style ends as an autonomous way of being objective about a wide class of facts, armed with its own authority, and available as a neutral tool for any project or ideology that seeks to deploy it. It provides new criteria of truth, new grounds for belief, new objects about which there can be knowledge. It generates the very stuff about which we do metaphysics. Thus do I address the ask of connecting (1) social dimensions, (2) metaphysics and (3) a long-term, "Braudelian" aspect of science, namely styles of reasoning.

1: The Metaphysics of Styles

We can tell a good deal without much speculation, reasoning, or active reordering of and intervention in the world. That means: we do not need *any* style of reasoning to find out lots of things, because we do not need, literally, to reason. We can just go and look, and find out whether some sentences do in fact correspond to the way the world is. The banal fact that there are such "observation statements" does not imply that our remarks about what we notice or check out by looking and listening are in some way privileged, basic, or foundational. Of course what we see is affected by what we expect, by our neighbors, by our education, and by our past experience. But I say this not to defend the idea of observation, whose real-life complexities I have amply examined elsewhere, but instead to address correspondence theories of truth. And I do *that* not because I have any investment in them, but because *I do not think styles of reasoning come into play for sentences to which a correspondence theory applies.*

It is now rather fashionable to decry correspondence theories, often using that wonderful canard of William James: "copy theory of truth." Philosophers neatly divide into two camps: those who say correspondence is worthless, and those who say that a correspondence theory, accompanied by a sound theory of reference, is the only one that makes sense. I may for the moment be unique in holding the only commonsense view, that correspondence theories are on the right track for some but by no means all declarative sentences. I stated this obliquely some time ago, but the point may need recapitulation.[4]

The core objection to a correspondence theory is that there is no way in which to identify the facts to which a statement corresponds, independently of the statement itself. That is true in general, but not of a lot of the run-of-the-mill sentences of the sort beloved by logicians—subject-predicate, and subject-relation-object—the kind codified in first-order logic, and using commonplace "observational" common nouns and verbs. In a debate with P. F. Strawson, J. L. Austin had a tidy way of overcoming the standard objection, insisting that we do often have independent ways of telling what a subject term refers to and what a predicate term denotes. We can then identify the fact to which "my shoes are black" refers by independently identifying the shoes and the blackness. That is Austin's doctrine of cap-fitting.[5]

That idea depends upon a supposedly outmoded classification of "observational" terms. It is outmoded in philosophy of science, maybe, but not among progressive psycho-anthropologists, who contend that there are "basic-level" concepts that are relatively stable among languages. They are expressed by short words. They have fairly standard prototypical examples that are elicited in standard testing of virtually all speakers of a language. George Lakoff has provided an excellent resumé of these ideas.[6] I have no trouble with a correspondence theory for sentences whose terms designate basic-level concepts. Those are the sentences that, even though we sometimes deduce them from evidence, we also can tell to be true or false, on occasion, just by looking. That is the humdrum fact that provides the sound core to the idea of observation sentences.

In contrast, there are many typically complex questions that can be answered only by a process of reasoning. Indeed, it makes sense to ask them only against a background of ways of acceptably reasoning towards their answer. The answers make sense only in the context of a style of reasoning. Many ways of reasoning have been developed, "discovered." A style of reasoning grows, together with questions that it can help answer, and with the truth-conditions of the sentences on which it bears. In these cases, Moritz Schlick's motto, that "the meaning of a sentence is its method of verification," points in the right direction. This implies a radically non-correspondence theory of truth. I have no wish to discuss theories of truth here, but these excellent if hackneyed models, correspondence and verificationism, serve my purpose of establishing that I do not think there is one theory of truth, or one semantics, that applies to all contingent empirical sentences investigated in the sciences.

Schlick did not think of "methods of verification" as having histories, and he seems to have had little sense of the motley of methods that we use. Our methods of verification have different historical trajectories, each within its own timeframe. My own study of the statistical style illustrates this. Putting such considerations aside for a moment, let us suppose that the truth conditions of some sentences are determined by the ways in which we reason to them. And suppose that a style becomes a standard of objectivity because, to use Peirce's phrase, it has the "truth-producing virtue." There then arises a suspicion of circularity. I embrace it, I welcome it. For there *is* an odd way in which a style of reasoning and truth-conditions of some sentences are mutually self-authenticating. The truth is what we find out in such and such a way. We recognize it as truth because of how we find it out. And how do we know that the method is good? Because it gets at the truth.

The style of reasoning dictates constraints on the truth and establishment of the sentences that it defines. The actual truth value of those sentences is external to the style: what is true in no way depends upon the style of reasoning. The truth does not depend on how we think. But that a certain complex sentence is a candidate for the truth may depend upon there being a style of reasoning, because there is no truth-or-falsehood in the matter, independent of the style of reasoning. There is not a prior truth, deeper, original, independent of reason, dwelling in the very interstices of the world, and which is discovered by reasoning ("correctly") according to some style. Nor do we discover the styles that then enable us to unearth and finally state the hitherto unstatable but pre-existing truth. The truth-or-falsehood and the style grow together. And as I shall show in Part II, this abstract metaphysics becomes rather modest common sense when we begin to look at a historical example.

This body of doctrine is not as relativist as it may sound. A style of reasoning, once in place, is not relative to anything. It does not determine the standard of objective truth. It is the standard.

1.1. META-CONCEPTS

I should begin by comparing and contrasting my idea of a style of reasoning with more familiar notions. We have just passed through a quarter century in which philosophical discussions about science were couched in terms of governing meta-concepts that are now disdained by the microsociologists. Kuhn's paradigms, Lakatos's programs, Holton's themata: extending our net beyond mere science, there are Foucault's discursive formations and Wittgenstein's language games. Do they have a common trait, aside from their flamboyant generality and abstractness? I shall discuss this under four heads, *possibility, exclusivity, historicity,* and *exemplification.*

Possibility. All the meta-concepts have to do with possibilities and constraints. All are Kantian. My "style of reasoning" is from the same bag. We should not give all the credit for this family of ideas to a faceless Kant. The more immediate filiation of Kuhn, Holton, and Foucault is with Alexandre Koyré. Koyré's conception of a dominating Platonic idea constraining the possibilities of thought and structuring experience had an extraordinary power on his audience and readers. Herbert Butterfield's bluff English metaphors, "picking up the other end of the stick" and "putting on a new thinking cap," capture some of Koyré's immediate attraction.[7] I know from discussions with him that Crombie's styles have the same filiation as do some of the ideas of Holton and Foucault.

Another meta-concept might seem in the offing here: "conceptual scheme." And so it is, in the sense in which one immediately takes the phrase. What is a conceptual scheme but an end of the stick, a thinking cap? But Quine preempted the phrase and took it to mean a set of sentences held for true. That is not in the realm of possibility but of actuality. If I were to try to reclaim the phrase for common usage, I would say that a conceptual scheme is a set of sentences that is up for grabs as true or false, a set of sentences that might be true. I think of a style as determining just such a set.

Exclusivity. Kuhn presented competing paradigms and Lakatos described rival programs as mutually exclusive, not as a matter of logic (as would be the case for incompatible Quinean schemes) but as a matter of thought and action. A generation after those authors, we are not in need of their hyperbole, and admit that a person can in a single mind entertain two "incommensurable" paradigms, and that a laboratory director may support two conflicting research programs within the same building. Nevertheless, competing paradigms or research programs do tend to drive each other out. They constrain possibilities: not only do they open doors, but they also close them. That is less true of Holton's themata. One can contemplate the possibility that the world is atomistic, and also that it is continuous, and apply one type of analysis to one problem, applying the other to a closely related difficulty. But in the grandest sense that Holton has in mind, themata do tend to be hegemonous, so that one cannot wholly subscribe to contrary themata: when Boyle believed that the world is made up of atoms and the void, a world of continuous variation and plenitude did not make sense to him.

Here is one respect in which my "styles" are quite different from more famous meta-concepts. Styles may have to fight to become established, but once they are mature and confident they do not even tend to exclude each other. The six that I have listed above are interwoven. They are not contraries but simply different, and can all be called upon in a single research project.

When it comes to possibility and constraint, the meta-concept of a language game is trickier than the others. Readers of Wittgenstein will quarrel little with the following unambitious remark: for speakers who participate in a language game, some speech acts are possible and some not; a language game has to do with what makes sense. Language games are the unstatable boundaries of the possible. Perhaps somebody has already called them the post-modern version of the scaffolding of which we read in the *Tractatus*. But I do not believe that from within the text of Wittgenstein himself we will find much support for the idea of competing language games.

Michel Foucault's sketched archaeology of knowledge is concerned with the way in which within a "discursive formation" certain sentences attain positivity, i.e., can be determined as true or false within the procedures authorized by the formation. My discussion of styles appropriates much Foucault, as I understand him. There is a big difference, too. His archaeology is self-consciously non-Braudelian.[8] His *epistemes* come into being and later perish at two moments of transformation. My styles are evolutionary, and might be with us evermore. Thus exclusivity is one dimension on which to range the meta-concepts under discussion, and my styles are the least exclusive of all.

Historicity. Aside from language games, all these meta-concepts historicize Kant. Georges Canguilhem was precise when he spoke of Foucault's "historical a priori." Paradigms and research programs are historical objects. To test the assertions of Kuhn or Lakatos, you must dig out some historical detail. Paradigms flourish for brief and glorious moments. By comparison Holton's themata seem timeless. Has not atomism been with us always? Yet Holton's interest is above all historical, to see how an ongoing theme is deployed in successive problem situations, in successive eras of science. Styles of scientific reasoning are equally historical entities, with a past, present, and future. They can also just die.

Wittgenstein alone had no lust for historicity. His language games are not in time. In this as in many other domains that vex contemporary philosophers, he is the odd man out, the restless Cartesian of the twentieth century. As part of the normal rewriting of our day, he must of course be historicized; people attempt this by appropriating his phrase "form of life" and regarding forms of life as historical entities. That is not Wittgenstein, but it does suggest another item to add to my roster of historiographic meta-concepts. Just as we have historicized Kant, so people are beginning to historicize Wittgenstein. Tim Lenoir does this in his discussion of German physiology in this volume, and David Bloor does so under the title "Left and Right Wittgensteinians."[9]

Exemplification, not definition. Paradigms, research programs, themata, discursive formations, language games, forms of life—these have been powerful words. They are used for vigorous metaphysical, epistemological, and methodological theses. But the concepts are never exactly defined. Instead their authors present plentiful examples together with some characteristics and differentia. I must now do the same for styles, begging for the same indulgence as my predecessors. I provide paradigmatic examples, illustrations, commentary, and application, but no precise definition.

1.2. STYLES

Crombie spoke of "styles of scientific thinking in the European tradition." I choose "reasoning" over "thinking" because I am more concerned with what is said than with what is thought. More importantly, reasoning is not, as I understand it, a purely sedentary art. It includes a lot of doing, not just arguing or thinking.

The pedigree of the phrase "style of thinking" is by no means immaculate. Precedents are found in the writings of memorable German thinkers, including Oswald Spengler, Edmund Husserl, and Ludwig Fleck. The English "style of thinking" is a term for intellectuals to toy with, whereas Fleck's term *Denkstil* was part of more common speech, loosely employed, and in little need of definition. *Jüdisch Denkstil* was a handy epithet of the Nazis. At the time that I encountered Crombie's use of "style of thinking" I also found the phrase in essays by the high energy physicist and cosmologist Steven Weinberg, the linguist Noam Chomsky, and the historian Winifred Wisan.[10] During 1980, I read the draft of an enormous book by Crombie, *Styles of Scientific Thinking in the European Tradition*. It had six parts, corresponding to the six styles already mentioned, the fifth of which was statistical and probabilistic. The trajectory of each style was laboriously traced, with myriad citations, as far back as there are any records of "the European tradition."[11] Crombie's list of styles is, *ex cathedra*, the set of standard examples for the use of the word 'style', just as Holton's examples form the paradigms for 'themata'. We may want to divide, combine, recluster, or supplement his examples, but we know where to start.

I am not happy with the word 'style'. I would not want to hang anything on the distinctions about style made by critics of art or literature, or by practitioners of aesthetics. Nor should we be tempted to, for there is at least this great difference: the *style empire* or *Jugendstil* flourish for short periods of time after which they cease and can at most be imitated ("nurtured in tragedy and perished amid disaster" says my faithful *Encyclopedia* of the "empire style" of furniture, meaning that it began in the years of terror and ended with the defeat of Napoleon I). Crombie's styles are long-lived and cumulative. We live in a world where his six are inextricable from scientific enterprises. We could say that fads and fashions in apparel take the word 'style' in the direction of ultimate transience, while Crombie is chasing it in the opposite direction in the hope (which I do not share) of finding an irrevocable teleology.

There is a further disadvantage to the word, that we have the idea of personal style. We have management style, style when doing the Australian crawl. That leads at once to seedy jokes or tawdry irony. And what style of reasoning did Ronald Reagan use? What style are you using yourself? "O my! In this very paper you have given us a new style of reasoning!" Crombie's styles are completely impersonal, anonymous, just like Foucault's discursive formations. They became, like a language, there to be used, canons of objectivity. They were indeed formed and fixed in social traffic. We can find spokesmen for a style, a Hobbes or a Boyle, say, but we shall not find an author. We shall find authorities, but oddly enough, once the style is fixed, the experts get their authority from the style.

2: The Styles of Statistics

2.1. USES OF PROBABILITY

"Statistics" has three importantly different roles: descriptive, inferential, and modeling. We can simply enumerate and report how many of this, that, and the other fall under various classifications. That is description. Then there is statistical inference in which we reduce data, infer generalizations, or decide what is to be done in the light of data and goals. Thirdly, we build mathematical models, using the concept of probability, to represent some structure we dimly perceive in reality. The probabilities of modeling are often called objective probabilities; those of inference, inductive or subjective. They are inextricably related. Many types of statistical inference rely on probability models. In the old days, statistical descriptions were digests of enumerations and had little enough to do with modeling. In this century, they are derived from initial data by means of a host of inferential technologies.

If we include statistical descriptions, it is obvious that "the statistical style" is ancient. Since I shall be talking almost entirely about the nineteenth century, it is well to make this point clear. The fourth book of the Pentateuch is called Numbers because it is about a census of Israel. Numbering is about as deep in the Jewish and the Christian tradition as could be. King David commenced the Temple to atone for his census of Israel and Judah. [12] And Jesus was born in a manger because his parents were en route to be counted and taxed in their home town. [13] Statistical description is so common among civilizations that it can be called a universal of human governance, a product of those two other universals of orderly society, recruitment and taxation.

But does statistical description, the result of mere enumeration, deserve to be called "reasoning"? Yes. As I understand reasoning, it is not just sentential, not just thinking and mulling. The doing in the case of a census description is also extraordinarily complex. When General Joab numbered Israel and Judah he did not "observe" in the way we observe that there are three people in the corner, nor count as when we count the people in the room. He had to organize, choose marshalls, devise a coding method, make tests to find out which marshalls were faking numbers; every one of these activities was integral to the reasoning. The data were not passive, awaiting collection; they were moved, ordered, coerced. The operation took nine months and twenty days and, like many a modern census, gave incompatible answers. [14]

2.2. THE TRAJECTORY OF THE STATISTICAL STYLE

I am able to use the statistical style as an example because there have been so many recent and excellent publications on the topic. My own version of events, on which of course I draw in what follows, is to be found in *The Taming of Chance*.[15] In order to follow subsequent sections we nevertheless require here the briefest outline of the development of the statistical style. The story of Joab makes plain that it did not begin in 1820 or whatever. But it was of little importance—certainly unworthy of Crombie's canonization among the top six styles—until a sequence of events during the nineteenth and early twentieth century. My own periodization goes as follows. I hope that the dates are so exact that no one will take them seriously. They are markers. I shall very briefly explain my names.

1640–1693 the emergence of probability
1693–1756 the doctrine of chances
1756–1821 the theory of error, and moral sciences I.
1821–1844 the avalanche of printed numbers, and moral sciences II.
1844–1875 the creation of statistical objects
1875–1897 the autonomy of statistical law
1897–1933 the era of modeling and fitting.

My names are idiosyncratic but my periods are not. The avalanche of printed numbers coincides with Harald Westergaard's "Era of Enthusiasm" for statistics, 1820–1848. He emphasized that the events of 1848 drew to a close a period of fetishistic counting prompted by belief in utilitarian reform. Lorraine Daston rightly groups the period covered by my first four units as "Classical Probability" terminating about 1840. Stephen Stigler with equal good reason divides his "History of Statistics" in two at 1827, the death of Laplace. That conveniently separates what Stigler calls the "Gauss-Laplace synthesis," providing an essentially complete theory of errors, from the new era in which the problem was the assessment of information about mass phenomena, primarily social phenomena.[16]

Those authors have well explained the phenomenon they wish to highlight with their dates. I use signal events to indicate my interests. I have described the events around 1660 in *The Emergence of Probability*. In 1693 or thereabouts Bernoulli began the work that culminated in his celebrated theorem, the first central limit theorem—the next being due to De Moivre. In 1756 came the last edition of De Moivre's *Doctrine of Chances*, and the beginning of Lambert's studies of error. That is at the same time as the start of the rationalist conception of what were called moral sciences and whose noblest advocate was Condorcet. From the point of view of mathematics, this was the time of the theory of errors; but it was also the period of Enlightenment moral science. The year 1821 marks the first of the statistical publications about Paris and the Seine department. From then, or a little before, the printing of *public* statistics (as opposed to those privy to the government) ran rampant. Moral science and moral analysis became the names not of what we now call "rational choice theory" in the style of Condorcet, but of the statistics of moral deviancy, also called moral science, but in a completely new sense of the words, which is why I speak of moral sciences II, 1821–1844.

In 1844 Quetelet objectified the mean of a population. I shall describe this in a little detail below in the section titled "New Objects." In 1875 statistical laws were used not only to describe but also to explain phenomena, as I discuss under "New Explanations." By 1897 chance (as Peirce had written in 1892) was pouring in at every avenue of sense, Durkheim's *Suicide* to right and Mallarmé's most celebrated poem ("A throw of the die will never annul chance"), to left. Those great works were two culminations of 1897, which also marked the beginnings of Karl Pearson's chi-squared, published in full detail in 1900.

These periods single out a series of distinct stages in the fixation of the statistical style of reasoning. It is there that we find the material mesh with my metaphysics. This is because we can exhibit, without any exaggeration, the classes of sentences that became possible, sentences that had no clear sense, certainly no defined truth value, until the time span indicated. Very commonly, the sentences quite literally did not exist; neither they nor their translations are to be found among the entities uttered, inscribed, or even thought. When they had existed earlier, the conditions of their truth changed. I shall speak not in metaphors but with citations. Indeed, were I not propounding metaphysics, no one would think twice before assenting to my claim, "these are new sentences with new meanings, new truth-conditions, new objects, new classifications, and new criteria for verification."

2.3. NEW SENTENCES

It is a trifling matter to check that most statistical sentences on view in textbooks, laboratory handbooks and notebooks, internal company audits, research papers, gallup poll results, TV commercials, sports broadcasts, expert testimony on risk, fault trees, stockbroker's reports, sex manuals, parapsychology, agricultural gazettes, catalogues of quasar and other astrophysical objects, dispositions made by the World Health Organization, and the official statistics of every nation just did not exist at the beginning of the period under scrutiny, 1821. Not only were the sentences not uttered, but also they could not have been understood. We take for granted that most of the sentences are either true or false. No one will dispute the fact that sentences such as these were not inscribed in 1821. I urge that they did not have truth values. I do not mean that a sentence uttered now, say "the gross national product of Württemberg in 1817 was 76.3 million adjusted 1820 crowns" has no truth value. I mean that such a sentence uttered then would have had no truth value, not only because "gross national product" was not defined, but because there was no procedure of reasoning about the relevant ideas.

But surely some such sentences had truth values! For example, "the population of New York City in 1820 was 123,706" (as determined by the census). Of course, but I hope I have laid grounds for doubt above, in mentioning the biblical censuses. In America there was indeed a rather ramshackle procedure that led to that very sentence about New York in 1820, a procedure constituted in a rush with funds voted by Congress in the nick of time, and census takers hired entirely on grounds of political patronage. Forms were completed, knockers knocked, answers given, sums tallied, and the end product was this number, 123,706. We are inclined to say, that was the procedure, in which we have no exact trust. We conclude that the population was only somewhere in the neighborhood of 124,000. We do not and never will know the exact figure. But at least there was a fact of the matter, was there not?

There were some facts of the matter. For example, having recalculated many a sum I am completely confident that some errors of addition were made in the course of enumerating New York City. People "always" made mistakes; moreover, these mistakes in arithmetic would have been acknowledged then, had they been brought to anyone's attention (well, I ignore graft). The truth conditions for the arithmetical sentences had long been in place. That is less clear about the sentences stating the number of people. The population is not the number of living human bodies inside a certain perimeter at a certain moment, but rather the number of people who inhabit New York on a certain day. Transients are to be excluded— yet it will not even have been a fact, of many a person, that they were or were not "transient" until much later.

I do not believe that there is a sequence of sentences, "the population of New York on 1st January, 1820, was 100,000" [100,001, . . . , 159,999], exactly one of which was true. But surely I know the population was between 100,000 and 160,000! Of course. But that is not like saying that the number of people in this room is between 44 and 59. With those small numbers I believe that one sentence in the sequence "44 people in the room" [45 . . . 59] is true. The truth-conditions of "between 44 and 59" is a disjunction of the truth-conditions of "44 in the room" . . . "59 in the room," and each of those typically has definite truth-conditions defined by counting and the like. But none of the sentences "There were exactly n people in New York City, on 1st Jan., 1820" has such a truth condition.

It was for just such a reason that the economist J. B. Say urged, around 1820, that there is no such thing as the population of France. Of course, he had a political agenda as well. His position is no longer viable. But this is not because there is a number, the population of France on a certain day, that we have circumscribed with greater care than in 1820, and have better means of determining. We have, as it happens, almost entirely lost interest in total population. We direct attention to subgroups by age, origin, occupation, interest, income, and inclination. The standard view at present is that populations and subpopulations are not most accurately determined by exhaustive enumeration every decade, but by quite small stratified samples. The very idea of representative sampling was a novelty a century ago. But do we not at least know now that stratified sampling yields the most accurate estimates of subpopulations? The technique was introduced in the late 1930s, in the United States, when Jerzy Neyman was brought over from London in order to help work out a technique for cheaply avoiding errors in the census and the like.[17] And we now believe these techniques work well, i.e., are on the whole accurate. But what is the measure of accuracy? Correspondence with a true number known independently of any statistical method? No. Reliability itself determined statistically. We have probabilities of probabilities, or more sophisticated tools such as variance and confidence intervals.

I do not claim that this procedure is circular. There is no logical error that impugns its validity. On the contrary, it is precisely what is objective. It is what the statistical style teaches as valid assessment. This is bootstrapping. The statistical style of reasoning improves upon itself, where improvement is judged by its own standards. I believe that something like this happens with every style of reasoning. The self-authentification of the statistical style differs only in its unusual transparency.

2.4. NEW CLASSES

I have said that even the census sentences of the form "The number in class C is n" acquire truth value within a system of reasoning. That supposes that the class C exists and is waiting to be counted. We must add to the doing in statistical reasoning the creation of new classes. In almost every decade, every country with an active statistical bureau produces a new set of classifications. These are, of course, partly a response to internal changes in the population or in the interests of authorities. New trades develop, new kinds of objects are owned, and new groups become "social problems" whose extent must be determined. Functionaries decide what classes shall be counted and how they shall be defined. Commonly they are well in advance of popular distinctions, rather literally bringing the distinctions into being. In an earlier era, Karl Marx read the statistical reports of the factory inspectorate and the like. It is a small joke that they, rather than he, contributed the most to class consciousness. For they devised the classes and obtained data from the mill-owners, who had not thought of their workers falling into those classes. Thereafter they and their workers conceived themselves as within that frame of work within the factory, and factories were redesigned and trade unions organized to accommodate these differences in the classes of employees.[18] If we see a style of reasoning as inseparable from the institutions that deploy it, we find new and complex relations between the style and the sentences that it brings into being.

2.5. NEW LAW-LIKE SENTENCES

Throughout the nineteenth century, German statisticians resisted the very existence of statistical laws of social groups, but these were readily embraced in the more atomistic and individualistic west. In France, it was laws of misbehavior that seemed to leap from the pages of official statistics. A whole range of phenomena now seemed subject to inexorable law, which had hitherto seemed the province of free choice: crime, suicide, and the like. That created a famous problem of statistical determinism.[19] Let us consider, however, not the mawkish question of freedom but continue with the arid matter of new laws of nature and society. Two new kinds of fact emerged: first, the number of suicides, sorted by region, age, sex, cause, health, marital state, social class, time of day, time of year, existence of suicide notes. Secondly, dispositions and regular tendencies to suicide according to the preceding classifications, expressed as probability distributions. Sentences able to state this second tier of "facts" came into being, in a new modality. They were the expression of social laws, laws hitherto unimagined.

The most fascinating laws (especially in France) were moral, but laws of other kinds of deviation, such as physical infirmity, may have had more consequence. We know exactly when and how and why some of these "came into being." Two sets of biological regularities had been well known from 1660, namely birth and death. These were spoken of in terms of law, the law of mortality, or the law that slightly more boys were born than girls. They were couched in terms of probability. Biostatistics stopped exactly there until 1825. In that year, a Select Committee of the House of Commons addressed the problem of sickness premiums for Friendly Societies, small mutual-benefit clubs of working men. As always at the start of a new class of sentences, there was immediate political motivation. The societies were suspect as covers for illegal Combinations (trade unions) but the primary interest was more philanthropic (viz. concerned with the worker's good but acting so as to maintain moral fiber and the social structure). What were actuarially sound sickness premiums? The national actuary John Finlaison asserted in testimony that "life and death are subject to a known law, but . . . sickness is not, so that the occurrence of the one may be ascertained, but not so the other."[20] He made clear that not only did he know no such laws, but that they do not exist. The Select Committee searched Europe for contrary belief but found none—except in one document compiled by the Highland Society of agricultural reformers in Scotland, completed in 1824. Suddenly it seemed that there could be laws of sickness, and the worlds of medicine and sickness insurance never looked back. Finlaison protested the Scottish figures had to be wrong, because the sickness rate was so much less than shown at musters of the British Army stationed at home—the beginning of a lesson not really enforced before that great statistical reformer Florence Nightingale. But probabilistic laws of disease did come into being almost literally at once; in the 1830s, medical studies were full of them. I do not here imply that disease had not secretly been following its allotted rates of spread, decline, and fall. I mean that law-like sentences about disease rates did not exist, and had even, by some of the most scrupulous observers, been excluded as stemming from a false analogy between disease and death.

I need hardly emphasize that the sequence of events is susceptible of almost every type of microsociological analysis ever proposed. At the banal level of interests of an overt material or political sort, we find the entrenched concerns of employers fearing strikes, the military fearing exposure for incompetence, the utilitarians seeking stability in the laboring force, the resistance of the insurance companies to reduced premiums, and so on and on. In Latour's account of actants, networks, and alliances, we are particularly struck by the alliance between specifically Scottish working men, with their concerns for good health, and the London administrators. The story can be elaborated for chapters. Here we find the proximate causes of the emergence of a new type of medical law. Nevertheless, once this kind of law is in place, it is largely independent of the proximate causes, and becomes a new standard of objective fact of which we can have objective knowledge. The same remark may be made at the end of each of the following sections; I shall not repeat it.

2.6. NEW OBJECTS

The coordinates of an archipelago, the position of a planet at a moment, the velocity of light in a vacuum, the atomic weight of an isotope of chlorine, the gravitational constant: given a scale for measurement, these are all definite numbers given (or so we say when not in a skeptical mood) by nature. The theory of errors was devised for such quantities. Its immediate application is a theory about the best estimate, based on a number of slightly discrepant measurements, and a measure of the dispersion of the readings. In the standard theory, for which Gauss and others provided elegant motivations, the best estimate is usually the mean and a measure of dispersion (the probable error, or, later, the standard deviation) is used as an indicator of accuracy. All this was in place by the early 1800s, and all subsequent theory of error is only a set of more or less ingenious footnotes to the work of Gauss and Laplace.

Tables of deviancy seemed to show that averages—of conviction rates for crimes against the person, of suicides classified according to region, season, sex, and method—were pretty constant. The average was the arithmetic mean, but it was not "natural" to transfer the theory of error to social statistics. Scholars have asked why it took so long, but they have done so only because it later *seemed* "natural."[21] The former manifest difference between geodesy or astronomy, on the one hand, and social or biometric statistics, on the other, was simply erased. That was in 1844.

In a few brief pages published that year, Adolphe Quetelet gave three examples. First he tabulated readings at Greenwich, followed by computations illustrating the mean and the probable error. Secondly, he suggested that if one could on plausible nonstatistical grounds divide a set of readings into two groups, with different means and smaller probable errors, one could conjecture that there were two distinct quantities under measurement.[22] Thus one would find that the readings were not homogeneous. Third, he directed us to measurements made on a large number of different individuals, to wit, the chest diameters of 5,738 Scottish soldiers. These are so distributed about their average, he said, that it is just as if one typical Highlander had been measured by an incompetent tailor with a definite probable error. The distribution is that of the law of error, or, as we say now, the normal distribution or bell-shaped curve. At that time he had so few data upon which to draw for purposes of illustration that he used a digest, prepared perhaps by a student, of a summary of information collected by a contractor and published in Edinburgh over a quarter century before.[23] Before Quetelet's kind of inquiry, such data were of scant anecdotal interest.

Quetelet brought into being a new kind of object: not the average of the diameters of these 5,738 chests, for that type of number had been around for quite some time. His new object was the population characterized by a mean and a standardized dispersion. The mean and dispersion are now thought of as objective properties of some part of the world, as "out there" as the location of a planet. Conversely, the old-fashioned kind of population—Scotsmen, or Highland crofters, or whatever—was replaced or at any rate paralleled by a more abstract concept of a group of individuals whose attributes are represented by the law of error. Populations can be split into two more homogeneous lots by the formal technique of distinguishing two means and smaller dispersions around each mean. Quetelet was not a eugenicist, but one of his immediate aims was the characterizing of the subpopulations of Europe, groups that would not necessarily be separated by any traditional boundary.

Philosophical talk of creating new objects, populations and phenomena is tricky. There is a spectrum of philosophical opinion. To start at one end, consider the population of "homeless" camped on the streets of major American cities. Whatever its causes, this population is a distinct one that did not exist a decade ago, even if its members were mostly members of other populations that shifted to this one. There is no hint of nominalism in saying that this is newly created. Moving along the spectrum, I myself am happy to say that people created lasers and also the phenomenon of lasing—nothing lased until people made it do so. Many more conservative philosophers of science resist what I say, but such statements do not reveal me as a closet constructionalist. Going further along the spectrum, some have said that a new object, the solar system, and its center, the sun, came into being after Copernicus. That is clearly a more radical use of "new object" than my commonplace and commonsense remark about lasers. And there are more radical versions of "new object" than the remark about the sun, versions that tend toward what I once called linguistic idealism.[24]

Where, on this spectrum of philosophical radicalism, should we place remarks about the mean of an attribute of a social or biological population? To say that it is a new kind of object, presented to the world in 1844, is to be more radical than to say that lasers are a new kind of object, and lasing a new kind of phenomenon. It is less radical than saying that the solar system and the sun were new kinds of objects. They were, to a conservative mind, old objects reclassified. That is not true of the new kind of population and its statistical parameters. There were no such objects under *any* description.

Quetelet's move in 1844 was a decisive advance for the statistical style of reasoning, because it created discourse about a new class of entities and their measurements. This discourse could not exist without the importation of probabilities and the Gaussian law of error. Had it not been for this move, there might have been no such thing as Crombie's "the statistical analysis of populations and the calculus of probabilities." There might have been two distinct things, statistics and probability.

2.7. NEW EXPLANATIONS

In daily life, we commonly try to explain unexpected events or puzzling occurrences. The target is the particular. In the sciences we explain phenomena, what happens or can be made to happen as a rule. There are overlaps, as when a particular surprise is shown to be an instance of an explicable phenomenon, and also when the phenomenon is singular, as the extinction of the dinosaurs. Philosophers of science have recently been sidetracked into analyses of explanation of the particular. They ponder puzzles that arise when an individual event falls under a merely statistical law. Here I attend instead only to "scientific" explanation of a phenomenon by showing how it arises from known laws or facts of a general kind.

The statistical style furnished no such statistical explanations until 1875. There were descriptions and predictions. There was the trap of statistical determinism and the associated devolution of morality. If Tom Gradgrind is one of a class of whom a fixed law-like proportion steal, was not there bound to be theft by many of these miscreants? Is not Tom's crime explained and thereby excused? Such were the preoccupations of the 1850s, made memorable in Dickens's parodying, in *Hard Times,* of the statistical style or "S-s-stutterers" as Cissy called it.

Galton furnished the first statistical explanation of a phenomenon (as opposed to a singular fact). Donald MacKenzie wrote one of the first, and best, "social construction of scientific knowledge" books around the

Galtonian tradition of biometrics.[25] That reminds us once again how the proximate causes of an event in the trajectory of a style of reasoning are subject to social analysis. Here I attend to a feature slightly different from that studied by MacKenzie. Galton knew that gifted and retarded families produce unusual offspring, but also that children of the outstanding parents tend to be less exceptional than their parents. This "regression towards mediocrity," as he called it (both from above and from below) was a phenomenon that he established by descriptive statistics. It baffled him—until he showed that it was a mathematical consequence of the fact that the relevant attributes in the population were distributed according to the law of error. As we now say, regression toward the mean is deducible from the supposition that the population has a normal distribution. Many more explanations followed. The statistical style had created a matrix from which a whole generation of new, complex, sentences would be born. The sentences that expressed the explanations simply did not exist until the person whom we call Quetelet had brought into being discourse about these new objects, populations with means, dispersions. The use of these sentences in the sentence or sentence sequence of the form "explanandum explains explanans" required further developments which we call the invention of regression analysis. A few years later correlations were added to the body of technique that could, among other things, furnish a new kind of explanatory paragraph.

2.8. NEW CRITERIA

Few of the populations studied by Quetelet "really" had a normal distribution. Like all other styles the statistical one leap-frogged along on the backs of propaganda-exemplars based on optimism, error, exaggeration, or sometimes deceit. Why do I speak of error? Because we now have criteria for goodness of fit that became settled at a later state in the trajectory of the statistical style. Quetelet's table of Scottish girths only very roughly fit the normal distribution, and his other examples tend to be worse. Quetelet did have a technique for comparing an empirical distribution (say of heights of Union soldiers in the American war) with a mathematical curve. But it was a matter of comparison, not of testing. Good tests (by modern criteria) did develop in Germany around 1875 at the hand of the economist Lexis and others. These were long ignored by the Anglo-Americans, who thought that statistical laws had the form of equations containing a number of constants, called parameters, that were fixed by nature. For example, the mean of a normal distribution, and a measure of dispersion, determine precisely the normal law attributed to a phenomenon. The German measures in contrast were typically nonparametric (in today's terminology) because the Germans did not believe in the new objective laws of what they called *Queteletismus*. One of their aims, in line with their total skepticism about statistical law, was to show how much irregularity is to be found in empirical statistics. The ecological niche for nonparametric theory was located in Eastern Europe, in Berlin, and St. Petersburg. London was the locale for parametric approaches.

Parametric theory—that is, much standard "Anglo-American statistics" until recently—can be regarded in two ways, realistic and positivist. The realist says that in describing a population as normally distributed, with mean mu and variance sigma, one is making exactly the same sort of statement as in saying that the latitude of the tip of the archipelago is 57° 37′ 26″ S, or that the atomic weight of chlorine is 34.651. The positivist view is that one is only representing the population *as if* its attributes were the product of a stochastic device whose results are normally distributed. The difference was not felt keenly. Those who were inclined to the positivist understanding were positivist about all quantities—Karl Pearson, for example. In either interpretation, statistical hypotheses—an increasingly well-defined class of sentences—stated that certain quantities associated with a population were distributed according to a mathematical law in which there were free parameters such as the standard deviation or the correlation coefficient. The statisticians saw themselves as estimating these unknown parameters, assessing the fit of an empirical distribution to a family of curves, of testing the significance of a treatment upon a population whose distribution and range of parameters was specified in a model, and, in the late stages, as assessing the "operating characteristics" of a decision procedure for accepting or rejecting statistical hypotheses. All of these procedures were themselves couched in terms of probabilities. In broad outline, the ideas can be perceived in earlier writings—the theory of confidence-intervals in Laplace or A. A. Cournot (1843) for example. But the self-conscious general application of the ideas came later: the conditions of assertibility of statistical hypotheses are themselves to be determined by using the statistical style of reasoning, and in terms of yet a new layer of sentences that themselves are statistical.

Thus theories of statistical testing and estimation conform all too readily to my thesis about statistical language, statistical truth, and statistical reason. I claim that testing procedures, which provide criteria for the acceptance and rejection of statistical hypotheses and statistical models, determine the meaning of the sentences expressing the hypotheses and the models. This is an overt verification theory of the meaning of statistical sentences. I did not inaugurate it: it is full-fledged in R. B. Braithwaite's *Scientific Explanation*. I did follow that approach in *Logic of Statistical Inference* a quarter century ago.[26] There is, then, the danger that my example of a style of reasoning will be defeated by its own success. "Yes, of course we see the introduction of new criteria for the assertibility of statistical statements, and that assertions about probability are themselves assessed using probabilities. The statistical style has indeed evolved by bootstrapping, but the example is unique!" Such are the risks of proving a point. I do not claim that the argument will go in the same way for Crombie's other styles of reasoning. I claim that it will go in different ways, which require as much detailed elaboration for those cases as the ones that I draw upon for the present essay.

2.9. NEW INTERSUBJECTIVITY

Within an objective theory of probability such as that favored by Jerzy Neyman, there is only one type of meaning for statements of probability, whether they occur in assessments of a method of testing ("the probability of wrongly accepting an hypothesis is only 0.05") or in statements about a part of the world under investigation ("the probability of infection after three weeks decreases to 0.05"). The meaning may be the same (for example, on a verification theory, always given in terms of meta-statements of acceptance and rejection) but the use and role is very different. The infection statement tells us something about transmission of disease; the statement about the test seems to tell us something about the test. But its role is primarily not to say something about this test but to provide a protocol for the intersubjective comparison of tests. Reflect on the litany of statistical chants, "5 percent significance level," "95 percent confidence," "P value in a chi-squared test of 3," and what the newspapers now give us in reporting opinion polls, "These results are considered to be accurate to within 3 percentage points 19 times out of 20." The last is closest to plain English, but people are too scared to ask what it means. It is not literally true that if this poll were taken many times, 19 out of 20 of the results would be within 3 percent of the true value (whatever "true value" is supposed to mean). Instead, these numbers indicate that a general protocol has been used, and provide a method for qualitative interpoll comparisons.

A technology of intersubjectivity has come into play. I suspect that this is a uniform feature of all styles of reasoning, although the protocols of intersubjectivity will differ at different epochs within one style, and will be different for different styles. The difference for different styles is perhaps a tautology: we could use the mode of intersubjectivity to characterize the style. We have proof procedures in mathematics, experimental controls in the laboratory sciences. In statistics we have these measures that are essential to legitimation, to publication, to authority: the confidence level, for example.

The technology of statistical intersubjectivity is now, if not hard-wired, thoroughly softwared. You buy a program such that if you use it, and do not cheat elsewhere, you are assessing data in an objective way. That is now what it means to be objective about statistical data. I am not denying that this is objective. To do so (as some, alas, do) is to suggest that there is some other standard of objectivity for statistical sentences. On the contrary, these sentences get their meaning precisely within this technology of objectivity.

I shall not pause to consider conceptual disagreements about the foundations of statistics, fierce battles between "Bayesians" and "orthodox statisticians." This is often presented as a difference between subjective and objective ideas about probability. Do they matter? It is true that different schools will give you different advice about how to design experiments, but for any given body of data they agree almost everywhere. The disputes are of measure zero in the space of intersubjective analysis of actual data. There is an important story to be told here about the ways in which foundational issues have been used to mask the regimentation of reason that is so characteristic of that great epistemological and metaphysical success story of our century, the calculus and language of probabilities. But that philosophical exercise demands both mathematical and historical exposition beyond the scope of this discussion. I shall only warn against words. The existence of a subjective school may seem to count against my claim that statistics has provided criteria of objectivity. In fact, the most dogmatic statisticians have been Bayesian. After the Second World War some writers, such as the French mathematician Allais, saw adolescent Bayesianism as the march of American stormtroopers across the European mind.[27] Where "objective" statisticians, such as that authoritarian giant R. A. Fisher, said that statistics could only present objective comparisons of data, leaving free-thinkers to judge as they wanted, the subjective theory was explicitly intended by that mild and generous soul, L. J. Savage, as a mode for disciplining your own mind.

2.10. THE TASK RECALLED

We should try to connect, I said at the beginning, social studies of knowledge, metaphysics, and the Braudelian aspects of science. Styles are Braudelian. The seeds of statistical analyses of population are as ancient as counting; I took biblical examples only for reasons of familiarity. Since 1821, there has been a lot of activity on the probability-and-statistics front, yet in earlier writings I found it entirely natural to describe even that in geological terms ("the avalanche of numbers," yes, but also "the erosion of determinism"). When we look at any individual incident we shall see a mass of social detail to which I have merely alluded (e.g., the worry about weekly premiums for Friendly Societies of working men). We also see certain global characteristics (e.g, the fascination with deviancy and the drive towards not just normalization but the very concept of normalcy). There is also a phenomenon of different statistical ideas developing in different "ecological niches"—compare Paul Forman's famous thesis that Weimar Germany was peculiarly suited to the advent of the new quantum mechanics. I have illustrated at length in *The Taming of Chance* how French culture was curiously receptive to the idea of statistical law, while this was thoroughly resisted in Prussia—a fact of great importance, once, to the sociology of statistical knowledge, but now irrelevant to modern statistical practice.

A style of reasoning becomes largely independent of all these early proximate causes of different sorts, ranging from ecological niches spanning more than half a century of development to meetings of a Parliamentary committee lasting a couple of weeks. The extent to which a style retains the more global characteristics associated with its maturation is a matter for open and ongoing inquiry. Is statistical thought intrinsically dedicated to normalization and control of people? Must it be so, as part of a historical a priori resulting from its initial conditions of possibility? Those are questions for future reflection.

The intersection of the proximate social causes and the Braudelian thrust of a style of reasoning should not, I think, create any philosophical perplexity. How could things be otherwise, if there is any stability at all in our patterns of reasoning? Little incidents and global needs bring ideas into being. Certain of them become part of the fabric of our thought, our very canons of objectivity. That is not surprising.

I have been driven to provocative statements only at the level of metaphysics. There the interplay between the proximate social causes and the long-range organization of reasoning becomes vital. This is because I claim that sentences get truth-conditions at definite moments of time, and those moments are the product of the social. At the same time, those sentences and their modes of verification become taken for granted within the grand march of the style of reasoning. As soon as one starts talking in this way, or in my annoying section titled "Metaphysics" early in the essay, one seems on the edge of speculative gobbledygook. On the contrary, I have illustrated how all the talk about styles and sentences and truth-conditions and verification-theory-of-meaning is to be taken in a literal and unadventuresome way. The assertion that the statistical style of reasoning is self-authenticating turns out to be correct, a rather old-fashioned conclusion given heightened significance.

Is the result some kind of "relativisim" about truth and styles of reasoning, some kind of "anti-realism"? No. That by which we investigate reality is not relative to anything, and the aspects that we call the real determine what is true or false according to our criteria. Yet our styles and our truths do not exist until we bring them into being. Objectivity is not the less massive, impenetrable, resistant, because it is the product of our history. But when we get close enough to run our hands across this rock—or rather, conglomerate—we shall feel its fissures and notice how different is its texture from that smooth surface that we seem to observe from afar, before we attend to the innumerable details that are its only origin and which constitute its substance.

NOTES

1. I owe the Braudel metaphor to Peter Galison, *How Experiments End* (Chicago: Chicago University Press, 1987), 246.

2. The title of the present paper alludes to Ian Hacking, "Language, Truth and Reason," in M. Hollis and S. Lukes, *Rationality and Relativism* (Oxford: Blackwell, 1982), 48–66. See "The Accumulation of Styles of Scientific Reasoning" in Dieter Henrich (ed.), *Kant Oder Hegel* (Stuttgart: Klett-Cotta, 1983), 453–462. These two papers are combined and condensed in "Styles of scientific reasoning," in John Rajchman and Cornell West (eds.), *Postanalytic Philosophy* (New York: Columbia University Press, 1985), 145–163.

3. A. C. Crombie, "Philosophical presuppositions and shifting interpretations of Galileo," in J. Hintikka, D. Gruender, and E. Agazzi (eds.), *Theory Change, Ancient Axiomatics and Galileo's Methodology, Proceedings of the 1978 Pisa Conference on the History and Philosophy of Science* (Dordrecht: Reidel, 1981), vol. I, p. 284. He has more recently published an account of the concept of style in general and of these six styles in particular in "Designed in the mind," *History of Science* 26 (1988): 1–12.

4. I. Hacking, *Representing and Intervening* Cambridge: Cambridge University Press, 1983), 145. My discussion of observation, alluded to in the preceding paragraph above, is found in chs. 10 and 11.

5. J. L. Austin, "Truth" and "Unfair to Facts," in his *Philosophical Papers* (Oxford: Clarendon Press, 1961), 85–122.

6. George Lakoff, *Women, Fire and Dangerous Things: What Categories Teach About the Human Mind* (Chicago: Chicago University Press, 1986).

7. Herbert Butterfield, *The Origins of Modern Science* (London: Bell, 2nd ed., 1957), 1–4. The book is based on lectures at Cambridge commenced in 1948, and is written under the spell of Koyré.

8. *The Archaeology of Knowledge* (London: Tavistock, 1972) begins by saying just that, on pp. 3–21 of the English edition.

9. Michael Lynch, "Extending Wittgenstein: The Pivotal Move from Epistemology to the Sociology of Science" and David Bloor, "Left- and Right-Wittgensteinians," in Andrew Pickering, *Science as Practice and Culture* (Chicago: Chicago University Press, 1991).

10. For references to these authors, see my first paper cited in note 2 above.

11. The book took longer to complete than expected, but from July 1990 has been with the publishers (Duckworth, London), in three volumes. I am very glad of this, for Crombie has fleshed out the idea of a style with a rich plenitude of historical example.

12. He had been "moved" or "provoked" to take the census by either God or Satan (depending on whether you read 2 Sam. 24:1 or 1 Chron. 21:1). On either story, God was furious with David, and offered him a choice of (a) 3 months famine, (b) 3 months of constant defeat by enemies or (c) 3 days of pestilence. David chose the third as the least evil, but after the plague had killed 70,000 men, God repented and made David build the Temple. The "Satan" of the King James Bible is for the difficult Hebrew word also rendered "adversary."

13. The "taxed" of the Authorized Version is better rendered "enrolled," which means counted and taxed; Augustus wanted not only revenue, but also a head count for military purposes.

14. How many men able to bear arms? 800,000 in Israel and 500,000 in Judah? (2 Sam. 24:9). Or 1,100,000 in Israel and 470,000 in Judah (1 Chron. 21:5). It does not help that in Chronicles we are told that Joab refused to count two tribes, Levi and Benjamin. The Chronicles numbers obviously cannot be the Samuel numbers, less Levi (in Israel) and Benjamin (in Judah). The same census was referred to. The disagreement does not show that the Bible is inconsistent but that the reasoning around a census is tricky.

15. Ian Hacking, *The Taming of Chance* (Cambridge: Cambridge University Press, 1990). For a collective study, containing work by authors of individual books cited below, see Lorenz Krüger et al. (eds.), *The Probabilistic Revolution*, 2 vols., (Cambridge, Mass.: MIT Press, 1987).

16. Harald Westergaard, *Contributions to the History of Statistics* (London: P. S. King, 1932). Stephen Stigler, *The History of Statistics: The Measurement of Uncertainty before 1900* (Cambridge, Mass: Belknap Press, 1986). Lorraine Daston, *Classical Probability in the Enlightenment* (Princeton: Princeton University Press, 1988).

17. See Margo Conk (Anderson), "The 1980 Census in Historical Perspective," in William Alonso and Paul Starr (eds.), *The Politics of Numbers* (New York: Russell Sage Foundation, 1987), 155–186.

18. I began to argue this in "Biopower and the Avalanche of Printed Numbers," *Humanities in Society* 5 (1982): 272–295. A much more detailed examination of the effects is given by Alain Desrosières and Laurent Thevenot, *Les Catégories socioprofessionelles*, (Paris, 1988), and other work by these two authors.

19. See Theodore M. Porter, *The Rise of Statistical Thinking, 1820–1900* (Princeton: Princeton University Press, 1986), ch. 6, and Ian Hacking, *The Taming of Chance* (Cambridge: Cambridge University Press, 1990), chs. 14, 15.

20. Full information is found in my *Taming*, ch. 5.

21. Hilary Seal, authority on the mathematics of error, is an example of someone who presents the slow transfer as a mystery. See his essay, "The Historical Development of the Gauss Linear Model," reprinted in E. S. Pearson and M. J. Kendall (eds.), *Studies in the History of Statistics and Probability* (London: Charles Griffin, 1970), vol. 1, 207–230.

22. Quetelet actually is closer to the case of social statistics than my statement here suggests.

23. The digest is reproduced and recalculated by Stigler, pp. 207–8. The original summary was intended to show that different regions of Scotland have different biometric characteristics, that is, that the population was inhomogeneous—that is why I charitably suppose that Quetelet never saw the data, *Taming*, ch. 13.

24. In *Why Does Language Matter to Philosophy?* (Cambridge: Cambridge University Press, 1975), 182. The phrase has since been used by both G. E. M. Anscombe and Hilary Putnam with slightly different meanings.

25. Donald MacKenzie, *Statistics in Britain, 1865–1930: The Social Construction of Scientific Knowledge* (Edinburgh: Edinburgh University Press, 1981).

26. R. B. Braithwaite, *Scientific Explanation* (Cambridge: Cambridge University Press, 1953). I. Hacking, *Logic of Statistical Inference* (Cambridge: Cambridge University Press, 1965). Isaac Levi was the first to show me, many years ago, how incredibly "verificationist" these books are.

27. I shall not cite other twentieth-century statistical works referred to, such as those by Savage or Fisher, on the grounds that they are well-known to philosophers, but it is worth giving the title of one of the most vigorous critical papers here: Maurice Allais, "Le comportement de l'homme rationnel devant le risque: Critique des postulats et axiomes de l'école americaine," *Econometrica* 21 (1953) 503–546.

PRACTICAL REASON
AND THE CONSTRUCTION OF KNOWLEDGE
The Lifeworld of Haber-Bosch

Timothy Lenoir

My aim in this paper is to argue for the central role of practical reason in contextualist accounts of science. Contextualist accounts are frequently criticized for being anti-rationalist and anti-realist. I disagree. Knowledge is socially constructed, but on that account it is not fictional, subjective, arbitrary, or arational. Theoretical reason, however, does not capture the processes that produce knowledge. Foresaking retrospective, spectator accounts of knowledge, we must give up foundationalist epistemology and think instead about the production of knowledge. Validating or justifying scientific theories through the logic of scientific explanation is only one (small) part of the production of knowledge, and for my present purposes not its most interesting part. Explanation belongs to the process of reflection upon an already made object: it relies on the process of arriving at community consensus through argument, construction and adjustment of criteria of evaluation, and formation of belief. In contrast, the production of knowledge must be seen as socially embedded action aimed at sustaining and extending a lifeworld. When we view knowledge production as purposeful activity within a form of life, we focus not on the logic of validation but rather on the rhetorics of persuasive argumentation, the processes through which we make choices within contingent situations, and the decisions we take in realizing and practicing our form of life. We find ourselves, in short, in the domain of practical reason, where the most appropriate model for rationality is intentional action rather than abstract mathematical demonstration. Objective (scientific) knowledge is something we make drawing upon our social, cultural, and material resources. Instruments, experiments, and practices—habits or ways of doing things—are the means through which we construct and stabilize nature.

The relationship between "nature" and the things we make was much discussed at the turn of the twentieth century in philosophical disputes between self-styled realists and rationalists on the one side, and persons who identified themselves as pragmatists and phenomenalists on the other. Anglo-American pragmatists inspired by Charles Sanders Peirce, most notably William James, John Dewey, and Ferdinand Schiller, and German phenomenalists, Ernst Mach and Wilhelm Ostwald, were all concerned about the relationship of practice and practical reasoning to theory. Waging a stout-hearted campaign against a theory-dominated approach to science, they emphasized the role of the interested subject in the production of knowledge; at the same time they worked to account for the power of theories and the relation of mathematics and logic to the external world. The pragmatists' concern with the relation among practice, intentional action, and mathematics was shared by the pragmatically oriented mathematician, Felix Klein, who sought the foundations of mathematics in a constructivist "*Anschauung.*" Like the pragmatists, Klein wanted to ground abstract mathematical thought and scientific theory in the more immediate, everyday world of unarticulated practices and familiarity with the machines used to control, define, and "carve out" an environment. Coming from the quite different perspective of phenomenology, Edmund Husserl also emphasized the centrality of the interested subject in knowledge production, and the works of James and Klein were crucial to Husserl in elaborating his own practical orientation to the foundations of mathematics. Husserl did not reflect in a deep or critical way on industrial science, however, and his general philosophical orientation was motivated by concerns different from those of Klein. Nevertheless, through his formulation of the notion of the "*Lebenswelt,*" Husserl extended the pragmatic approach beyond the domain of scientific practice to culture more broadly conceived. Certain features of Husserl's discussion of knowledge as a culturally situated enterprise are crucial to our own current debates on the social construction of knowledge, particularly our recent concern with practice, instrumentation and skill.

My aim in this paper is, first, to elaborate the pragmatist conception of knowledge production as cultural production in the service of a form of life. I will then illustrate this view by pursuing a concrete passage of knowledge production contemporary with the work of the pragmatists in a domain which they regarded as emblematic of their program: namely, thermodynamics and the energeticist program of Wilhelm Ostwald.[1] Within work on energetics I will treat matters relating to the theory of gas reactions, the third law of thermodynamics, and especially the Haber-Bosch process for synthesizing ammonia from the elements, seen by contemporaries as one of the primary achievements of the new discipline of physical chemistry.

1. Nature Humanized

It is in every way appropriate to focus on industrial science in discussing pragmatist and constructivist views of natural science and objective truth. Peirce, James, Dewey, Husserl, Klein, the creators of the Kaiser-Wilhelm-Institutes, and the major industrialists shared a view of the relationship between practice and objective knowledge. While certainly not the first to have made the distinction, they all insisted on discriminating between "nature" and "nature humanized." Nature taken in and of itself abstractly, fixed and isolated from man, James asserted, is nothing but sensible flux. In James's view, talk about reality 'independent' of human thinking is a hard thing to find.[2] Nature, the nature that is the object of knowledge, is *nature humanized:* the world of objects produced through human intervention:

> In our cognitive as well as in our active life we are creative. We *add,* both to the subject and to the predicate part of reality. The world stands really malleable, waiting to receive its final touches at our hands. . . . Man *engenders* truths upon it.[3]

James insisted that the position here advocated not be confused with a sort of Kantian idealism. Nature humanized was not the product of categories of reason produced independently of and *before* the beginning of an external world. Rather along with Peirce and Dewey, James endorsed a dialectical, historical engagement with the world out of which rational categories gradually emerge through interested human action.[4] This brand of radical historicism, then, was committed both to a genetic theory of truth and to a pragmatic form of realism with broad-ranging consequences:

> *The alternative between pragmatism and rationalism, in the shape in which we now have it before us, is no longer a question in the theory of knowledge, it concerns the structure of the universe itself.* On the pragmatist side we have only one edition of the universe, unfinished, growing in all sorts of places, especially in the places where thinking beings are at work.[5]

Implicit in the pragmatist notion of the universe as a project finished only by human labor is the view that the production of nature and the generation of society are codependent processes. Peirce insisted on this in his discussion of "the real," which involved the "notion of a community, without definite limits, and capable of a definite increase in knowledge."[6] Peirce defended the radical position that "reality depends on the ultimate decision of the community."[7] The production of nature, the real, is at the same time the generation of consensus within a community. From the related notions of objective nature as nature humanized and the pragmatist conception of truth, which emphasized the role of convention and practical intervention, it followed that the order of nature is bound up with the right ordering of social production. Truth, James tells us, is not agreement with some preexistent, independent reality: "Truth for us is simply a collective name for verification-processes, just as health, wealth, strength, etc., are names for other processes connected with life, and also pursued because it pays to pursue them. Truth is *made,* just as health, wealth and strength are made, in the course of experience."[8] The direct analogy to social processes of production was intended to draw attention to the interested, purposeful character of knowledge production. At the same time the pragmatic conception of truth leads to a parallel notion of the social construction of nature, for truth, in James's view, is constructed in accordance with human purposes:

> Human motives sharpen all our questions, human satisfactions lurk in all our answers, all our formulas have a human twist. This element is so inextricable in the products that Mr. [Ferdinand Canning Scott] Schiller sometimes seems almost to leave it an open question whether there be anything else. "The world," he says, "is essentially ὕλη, it is what we make of it. It is fruitless to define it by what it originally was or by what it is apart from us . . . ; it *is* what is made of it. Hence the world is *plastic.*"[9]

James was careful, however, to distance the pragmatist position from a naive relativism which treats nature as a simple reification of social convention. Crucial to the pragmatist project is the notion that nature is not a simple projection of ideas; nor is nature determined by society. Nature is plastic but not infinitely malleable. It resists, and in doing so actively participates in forming our purposes. Speaking of Schiller, James says:

> Mr. Schiller admits as emphatically as anyone else the presence of resisting factors in every actual experience of truth-making. . . . All our truths are beliefs about 'Reality'; and in any particular belief the reality acts as something independent, as a thing *found* not manufactured.[10]

James, speaking on behalf of his Anglo-American pragmatist colleagues, argues the crucial point that the socially constructed character of nature is erased, leaving nature standing in our beliefs as something found, as a world of objective entities determining our knowledge of them. But neither James nor his pragmatist colleagues investigated the processes directly involved in that construction, and the manner in which those active processes are silenced. To have done so consistently with their historicized conception of truth and pragmatic realism would have entailed a culturally embedded historical account of controversy. Such an account should aim at revealing how the closure of controversy brings with it the stabilization of facts, values, and standards and their silent but actively present insertion in machines and social practice. That, of course, was not their project. That this project should be undertaken, however, was the view of Edmund Husserl.

Husserl argued that ever since Galileo and Descartes, modern natural philosophy sought to deny the role of interested subjectivity in the constitution of truth. Galileo, Husserl wrote, had abstracted from subjects as persons and removed all reference to the cultural properties which are attached to things in human praxis. Descartes's "dualism" of mind and matter completed Galileo's efforts at "idealization," resulting in the idea of nature as an independent world of bodies operating in terms of a self-enclosed natural causality in which every occurrence is determined unequivocally and in advance.[11] Husserl saw that to reinsert the interested subject into accounts of knowledge production was to engage in a return to origins:

> It did not enter the mind of a Galileo that it would ever become relevant, indeed of fundamental importance, to geometry, as a branch of a universal knowledge of what is (philosophy), to make geometrical self-evidence—the "how" of its origin—into a problem. For us, proceeding beyond Galileo in our historical reflections, it will be of considerable interest to see how a shift of focus became urgent and how the "origin" of knowledge had to become a major problem.[12]

Husserl pursued epistemology without foundations, a radically historical enterprise of unpacking the sociological, psychological and cultural historical networks through which humanized nature is produced. This historical enterprise could not be a mere history of ideas, however. The objective of this historical program was to reveal the labor—in the form of technologies and practices as well as practical reasoning—involved in the coproduction of nature and society. In order to carry out the program, Husserl added the idea of the *Lebenswelt* to the pragmatist notions of humanized nature and truth as something we make. The notion of the *Lebenswelt* is fundamental to exploring the amazing fit between mind and nature so admired by rationalists, for it empowers an investigation of how practices and concepts are intertwined.

2. *Lebenswelt, Logic, and the Laws of Nature*

Klein adopted the pragmatist view that our concepts and theories about nature are tied deeply to the instruments and practices through which phenomena are produced and stabilized. Viewed in this light, it makes little sense to draw a distinction between pure and applied science, between science and technology. This interdependence of technology and science in the production of knowledge is at the same time the coproduction of a lifeworld.

The futility of distinguishing pure and applied science was a theme familiar to the natural scientists, state administrators, and industrialists who founded the Kaiser-Wilhelm-Institutes early in this century. Felix Klein, no stranger to the empyrean realms of pure mathematics, urged the Prussian minister of education and culture, Friedrich Althoff, to disrupt the pattern of institutional segregation of the disciplines then prevalent, the tendency of mathematicians and physicists to pursue their work independently of engineers. The Berlin mathematical establishment labeled Klein a "compiler," "blender," and "faiseur," because of his tendency not to pursue mathematics *"um der Sache willen."*[13] In a memorandum urging the creation of an interdisciplinary institute bringing mathematicians, physicists, and engineers together in a cooperative arrangement with industry, Klein argued that one should return to the conception of mathematics predominant during the eighteenth and early nineteenth centuries in the writings, for example, of Gaspard Monge and Poncelet, before idealists had begun to spin their webs of pure reason.[14] "Pure" mathematics in their sense had never existed. The abstract mathematics of the great mathematicians such as Gauss had always been fueled by constant contact with consideration of concrete, material problems. Klein compared mathematics to a tree that drives its roots ever deeper into the earth at the same time that its branches develop.[15] The roots of the tree, its real foundations, are in the earth. Klein objected to the notion harbored by pure mathematicians and physicists, such as Kronecker, that the object of science is explanation. Science, according to Klein, cannot be separated from human purpose, and the object of science is to assist in achieving human purposes. "The object of science is not to explain nature—which in the final analysis it is incapable of doing—but rather to command nature. . . . It should never be forgotten that there is a creative technology which transforms [*umsetzt*] the statements of theoretical science in actuality."[16] In his attacks on the notion of pure mathematics, Klein spoke of the need to pursue a program unifying what he called "non-empirical" mathematics concerned with its own constructions and "empirical" mathematics whose fields were geometry and mechanics. The sources of both forms of mathematical thought were phenomenal experience. Mathematics, for Klein, is an idealization of the phenomena. Crucial to this program was a proper conception of *"Anschauung"*—intuition. Klein defined it as a reflective form of memory, an inborn talent which develops unconsciously and which includes the "motor senses" of the engineer as well as the "undefined sensibility" possessed by a person experienced in arithmetical calculations. Klein's notion of *Anschauung* was not passive. In physics, he claimed, it works as "a kind of interpolation" which lays weight on certain kinds of general conditions. This active *Anschauung*, informed by human intentions, provided the material for logical constructions: "I claim that mathematical intuition understood in this sense always precedes logical thought and therefore in every moment always possesses a wider domain than logical thought. . . . Logical consideration acquires its authority only after the *Anschauung* has done its work of idealization."[17] For idealist mathematicians, such as Hilbert and Kronecker, mathematics comes first and then the world. In Klein's program the world comes first. The connection between the world and mathematics is provided by *Anschauung*, an acquired competence which physicists and engineers share with mathematicians.

Though differently motivated, Husserl's views on the relationship among mathematics and the world were much of a piece with Klein's. But Husserl went further than Klein in considering the culturally embedded character of the relationship among theory and practice, and between logic, mathematics, and the world. Like Klein, Husserl stressed the role of subjective intentionality in the constitution of objects. Constitution does not come about for Husserl simply as a result of acts of consciousness. Not invented by consciousness, the world enters in the form of a certain givenness, an ego-foreign element, a constraint. From his earliest investigations on the foundations of geometry, Husserl emphasized the association of conscious acts with acts of bodily movement and routine practice. The body for Husserl is the center of all orientation in the world. Subjectively initiated bodily movements are essential to the perception of concrete objects, and kinesthesis is crucial to the constitution of visual space and the objects within it. Intentional acts are embodied in what Husserl calls *Aktgebilde*, action-structures similar to Klein's "motor senses"; they become the basis of empirical *Anschauung* or intuition. In this move, however, Husserl does not reduce all conscious acts to a foundation of bodily movement or perception; similarly, he does not reduce theoretical practice to the domain of know-how or practical action. Each has its own set of objectives. While operating in parallel, they interact with one another in dialogic fashion.

This discussion of mathematical expressions follows Husserl's treatment of the relation of language, speech acts, and the world. Both mathematical and verbal statements are embedded in what he calls the lifeworld. The meaning of the statement, "The blackbird is flying off," does not derive from a direct perception; for it can have meaning even in the absence of an objective occurrence of the sort referred to by the statement. Husserl accounts for this possibility:

> This expression of a perception is not the object of the utterance [*Wortlautes*], but rather the concern of certain *expressive acts*. In this context "express" means the expression animated by its total sense, which is posited here in a certain relation to the perception, which for its part is called "expressed" on account of this relationship. Included in this is that between perception and statement another action is inserted (or an *Aktgebilde*). I say an action because the expressive experience has an intentional relationship to something objective whether or not a perception accompanies it. This mediating act must function as that which actually gives meaning. The mediating act belongs to the meaningfully functional expression as its essential content and is the condition that the meaning is the same whether a perception covered by it is associated to it or not.[18]

The action-structures are not in themselves the structures of language, as Husserl's contemporaries Ferdinand de Saussure and Roman Jakobson might argue; rather they mediate between these and the external world. As the source of explicit experience, the action-structures are, in a sense, the evidentiary basis of the world as it is given to us and at the same time the conditions for its linguistic expression. In other places Husserl describes them as the structures through which things are simply given to us in intuition as being "itself-there." In other words, they are dispositions and intuitive acceptances. The totality of these dispositions makes up the lifeworld.

Both Klein and Husserl emphasized practical reason and the role of technical and social practice in the construction of knowledge. Rationalists treated concepts as independent from material practice. Husserl and Klein, like James, believed that concepts and practices come packaged together.[19] Mathematical constructs and the laws of nature "work" not because of some miraculous fit between idea and independent object, but because conceptual structures emerge out of a dialogic engagement with the world of material practice. In the pragmatist conception, humanized nature is achieved by human purpose materialized through human agency or intervention—in short, through labor. New truths, according to James, are added to old truths, adapting to and at the same time altering old truth. In this process the practices embodied in the performative actions of our everyday lifeworld are crucial. In Husserl's account, performative actions, concepts, and language are fused by practical reason in the course of constructing facts. The structures of these performative actions are embedded in what he refers to in the previous quotation as *Aktgebilde*, or in Klein's terminology, the "motor senses" of the scientist or engineer. But while enabling abstract thought, the practices organizing performative action remain implicit by being embedded in habit, and hence they remain silent. Late in his career Husserl wrote:

> Like all cultural acquisitions which arise out of human accomplishment, they [the practices underlying pure mathematical thought] remain objectively knowable and available without requiring that the formulation of their meaning be repeatedly and explicitly renewed. On the basis of sensible embodiment, e.g., in speech and writing, they are simply apperceptively grasped and dealt with in our operations. Sensible "models" function in a similar way, including especially the drawings on paper which are constantly used during work, printed drawings in textbooks for those who learn by reading, and the like. It is similar to the way in which certain cultural objects (tones, drills, etc.) are understood, simply "seen," without any renewed process of making intuitive what gave such properties their true meaning. Serving the methodical praxis of mathematicians, in this form of long-understood acquisitions, are significations which are, so to speak, sedimented in their embodiments. And thus they make mental manipulation possible in the geometrical world of ideal objects.[20]

Husserl regarded the lifeworld as the precondition for science. He argued that science presupposes the lifeworld as the unquestioned ground of its investigations. Even if the idealizing Galilean scientist focuses his or her interests on objective nature, the subjective-relative is still functioning, not as something irrelevant that has to be passed through but as that which ultimately grounds theoretical and logical validity. According to Husserl, the lifeworld constantly functions as *subsoil*, "its manifold prelogical validities act as grounds for the logical ones, for theoretical truths."[21] The realm of original self-evidences and goals constituting the lifeworld is the mediator among logic, mathematics, and nature:

> Objective theory in its logical sense (taken universally: sciences as the totality of predicative theory, of the system of statements meant "logically" as "propositions in themselves," and in this sense logically joined) is rooted, grounded in the life-world, in the original self-evidences belonging to it. Thanks to this rootedness objective science has a constant reference of meaning to the world in which we always live, even as scientists and also in the total community of scientists—a reference that is to the general life-world.[22]

For purposes of the themes I will be treating later in this paper, it is important to stress the broadly cultural character of Husserl's lifeworld. Husserl's notion contrasts sharply with some other formulations, such as Wittgenstein's notion of forms of life, in its inclusion of the *total* set of intuitive assumptions, habits, cultural practices broadly construed, and especially larger social and cultural interests—what might best be termed positive ideologies in the Gramscian sense or legitimating narratives in the sense of Lyotard. Wittgenstein's notion of form of life, which he analogized to language games, is much more localized and subject to change, as evidenced by the frequent explication of it in terms of gestalt-switch analogies, and more recently as laboratory or disciplinary cultures. In this sense, Wittgensteinian forms of life are very close to Thomas Kuhn's notion of paradigm or disciplinary communities.[23] The difference between the broader Husserlian-Jamesian cultural concept of the lifeworld and the Wittgensteinian form of life is the implication of its being more firmly rooted in the practices of everyday life—hence the greater difficulty in displacing or radically changing it. It is this relatively conservative, long-term stability of the lifeworld that is essential to the pragmatic realism of the position I have been sketching.

In its broadest sense, then, a lifeworld is the system of dispositions generating the cultural—including the technical—practices of a particular society. However, even though lifeworlds encompass the codes for practical activity, they cannot be described by a set of rules either explicit or implicit. They are not algorithms for action.[24] In discussing lifeworlds we must adopt a localized historical stance and follow the actors themselves as they engage in purposeful activity; for in this way we are faced with the "transposable dispositions"[25] orchestrating their strategic moves as they deliberate about concrete alternatives. Always confined to such localized passages as controversies, we cannot completely describe a lifeworld;

rather we must narrate how people within a lifeworld react to events in their history or act to achieve particular purposes.

Recent treatments of forms of life and lifeworlds by Steven Shapin and Simon Schaffer and by Michael Baxandall exemplify this historically localized approach to the study of interested subjectivity and knowledge production. *Leviathan and the Air Pump,* Shapin and Schaffer's study of the "form of life of experimental philosophy," reveals the way in which the social and linguistic practices—the conventions, practical agreements, and labor—embodied in the construction of facts and the doing of science were integrated into patterns of activity supporting the larger polity in Restoration England. Central to their study is the notion that the generating and protecting of knowledge is a political problem; for particularly in times of political crisis and social turmoil solutions to the problem of knowledge are also solutions to the problem of social order. Boyle's program for experimental philosophy could assist in guaranteeing political order and restoring right religion to society because the community of experimental philosophers served as the model of an ideal, stable society. Crucial to its ability to play this role was the manner in which the practices of experimental philosophy were integrated into the body of practices essential to the polity. Boyle's life form of experimental philosophy made use of three technologies: the material technology of the air-pump; a literary technology suitable for multiplying the witnesses to an experience; and a social technology involving open dispute and toleration within the space of the laboratory. These same practices were either identical or closely analogous to religious and legal models of authority through witnessing. Shapin and Schaffer, then, use the term "form of life" to denote a consciously deployed set of strategies to promote a constellation of interests.

The concept is used more broadly by Michael Baxandall to include not only conscious strategies (discursive and otherwise) but also unarticulated dispositions, feelings, and practices. Baxandall's *Painting and Experience in Fifteenth Century Italy* provides an excellent illustration of the way in which an integrated system of habits and dispositions—what Baxandall calls "the period eye"—grounds a particular lifeworld. The Bellini we see now was not the painting a fifteenth-century viewer experienced. Baxandall argues that a fifteenth-century painting's ability to represent something meaningful to a contemporary viewer depended upon that viewer's possession of a complex web of interdependent skills, many of which are no longer part of our cultural formation. An example of the interdependence of social practices and the representations they enabled was the mathematical technique, widespread among Italian merchants, of gauging, a method using π to estimate the volumes of barrels, cylinders, and cones. Painters commanded this skill as well, and they could activate it in their viewers by depicting objects used in typical gauging exercises—columns, barrels, cisterns, towers—in the construction of perspectival spaces and figures. This skill supported the painters' explorations of perspective as well as their viewers' abilities to interpret these explorations. The lifeworld was a resource of dispositions supporting both visual experience and painting practice.[26] In short, just as in Husserl, the theory of perspective works *because* of the practices it draws upon. No less important is the point that the body of skills and the configuration of practices constituting the lifeworld *precede* and enable the representation. The practices of representation link up with our world because they are formed in cooperative, symbiotic fashion as an extension and part of the fabric of everyday practices—including the organization of the discourses and institutions of power—coordinated in the service of a lifeworld.

This conception of the relationship among practice, mathematics, and the world was understood by Felix Klein, and it provided the basis of his proposal for an interdisciplinary institute. Klein believed that mathematicians would profit from an abstract consideration of machine design, and that physicists and engineers as well as industrialists would similarly profit from the abstractions of the mathematicians. Klein was not arguing here for an institute that would survey the different disciplines with an eye to their potential for solving problems posed by industry and the development of new products. Rather he saw the very purity of those disciplines to consist in a deep immersion in the machines and practices in which nature is given.

Klein's point was made perhaps better by the creators of industrial research. The physical chemists educated in the laboratories of Wilhelm Ostwald in Leipzig and in the new research labs in firms such as Rudolf Knietsch's lab at BASF in Ludwigshafen understood that many major advances did not result from simply applying scientific theory ready-made for the task. A point argued recently by Thomas Hughes with respect to inventors like Thomas Edison and Elmer Sperry is equally applicable here.[27] This first generation of industrial scientists scoured the scientific literature, used scientific theory, even employed scientists when necessary. Scientific theory assisted them in their attempts to solve problems. It helped in constructing and refining models, but it did not create the new technology. For the most part these new industrial scientists believed that invention followed from experiment, from reasoning with physical metaphors, from constructing and refining models, not from the manipulation of mathematical formulae. Science quite frequently failed the technology.

Emil Fischer also emphasized the deep interactions between scientific theory and scientific practice. In his view, the great recent developments, particularly stereochemistry and the physical chemistry of gas reactions, had all been connected with refinements of experimental method,[28] especially increased importance of determining molecular weights, control of gas reactions at extremely high temperatures, and fractionation at low temperatures.[29] Like Klein he recognized the codependence of his science and his lifeworld. Fischer believed that his generation was living in a new scientific-technological age with completely new knowledge requirements. It was an age of technological enthusiasm and of system builders. Crucial were the period's concern with dynamical processes, integration and control of resources, more efficient conversion of present energy resources, and the development of new energy sources. But all of this was to be placed in the service of Fischer's primary goal, the synthesis of materials crucial to a mass industrial economy. In fact, like a true system builder, Fischer argued that the object of scientific research should be to learn to imitate nature as perfectly as possible in order to improve upon it, to go further in the construction of an environment completely subservient to human purposes. It was difficult to imagine, he often said, that human artifice could produce basic foodstuffs more efficiently and more cheaply than plants do,[30] but it just might be possible.[31] In various contexts where he set forth the problems facing science, Fischer emphasized three main points: (1) the need to isolate the principle compounds that served as the building blocks of organic nature—carbohydrates, proteins, sugars, purines, nucleic acids, and polypeptides—and to synthesize these materials "in purer form than nature herself";[32] (2) the need to investigate key physical-chemical reactions at extreme conditions such as high and low temperatures; (3) the construction of a network of basic research institutes in the physical, chemical, and biological sciences focused on understanding the substances, processes, and technologies at the heart of the new industrial economy.

When Fischer spoke of the Kaiser-Wilhelm-Institutes as basic research institutes, he meant that they should be concerned with generalized problems of importance to the scientific disciplines, technologies, and industrial processes at the core of the political economy. Highly specific, specialized research could be carried on in university laboratories or even industrial laboratories. The institutes he envisioned were all to be guided by a strategic postulate: "Think separately but experiment in common."[33]

The two pillars of the network of institutions he envisioned were a Kaiser-Wilhelm-Institut for coal research and a Kaiser-Wilhelm-Institut for physical chemistry. The rationale for the institute for coal research was most revealing of his expansive viewpoint on basic science. It was not just because the coal industry was powerful and would hence serve as a useful patron for scientific research; rather it was because carbon and carbon compounds were fundamental to so many domains of current science, technology, and medicine. Fischer envisioned a network of investigative enterprises centered on coal which would branch out in one direction into institutes concerned with determining fundamental constants and processes in physical chemistry and thermochemistry and in another direction into institutes concerned with synthesis and assimilation of organic materials. Better understanding of physical chemistry and thermochemistry would enable the investigation of more efficient uses of fossil fuels. Given the roughly 85 percent energy loss in the conversion to mechanical work, Fischer argued that coal hydrogenation should become a national high-technology research priority, for it would produce a more efficient fuel and reduce dependency on foreign supplies of petroleum. Investigation of fossil fuels was at the same time a bridge to the investigation of metabolism, and through it to the investigation of growth, nutrition, and reproduction. Understanding carbon compounds was the key to organic synthesis. By commanding the processes of organic synthesis, one could turn to the real land of opportunity, the synthesis of proteins, and ultimately to the control of cellular processes:

> Perhaps we can sustain even greater expectations. Chemical synthesis is in many respects superior to nature herself, because it commands other resources. . . . With the entry of synthesis not only has artificial fabrication begun but variation of the products. Something similar has happened with the synthesis of sugar and the purines. If the same success could be achieved for the elements of life, should it not be possible to acquire a radical chemical influence on the development of life? Experimental biology has achieved noteworthy results through selection, crossing, and inheritance. . . . But how much more impressive might the phenomena be if we succeed in changing the chemical building materials of the cell and at the same time tricking them? Certainly that will require much cunning on the part of the experimenter. But if chemists and biologists join forces and undertake this task of exploring the appropriate subjects with the proper tools, success is not so improbable. Thus I see, half in a dream, the emergence of a synthetic chemical biology, which

invades the domain of life just as thoroughly as chemistry and physics have long since done for inorganic nature.[34]

3. The Lebenswelt of Ludwigshafen: Haber, Bosch, and Ammonia Synthesis

When Fischer spoke of the fruitful interactions occurring between advances in technological practice and theoretical science in his discussions, the paradigm he invoked was the synthesis of ammonia and the development of the Haber-Bosch process. The 1890s had been a period of enormous technological change in the chemical industry. The demise of the Leblanc soda process and the growth of several industries, particularly in dyestuffs, textiles, glass, soap, paper, metals, pharamaceuticals, and fertilizers, all stimulated an unprecedented demand for soda and alkalies of all sorts, as well as nitrates and various acids. Sulfuric acid production, the recovery of sulphur and ammonia, the preparation of chlorine for bleaching and numerous chlorinated compounds were all central to these expanding industries. Stimulated by the introduction of the Solvay process, German chemists and chemical engineers expanded around it by developing electrolysis and the contact method—the use of catalysts—in sulfuric acid production. Understanding, controlling, improving, and expanding these chemical processes became the goal of intense scientific inquiry. Crucial to these purposes was a deeper understanding of chemical equilibria. The problem of predicting the conditions for chemical reactions had troubled chemists throughout the nineteenth century. Catalogues of affinity relationships had proven unable to answer the mysteries of why some chemical reactions go and others do not. More importantly, the new contact methods and the pressing concerns of industry for efficient methods capable of massive yields forced attention on the question of determining just how far and how fast a chemical reaction would go before it reached equilibrium. Chemists needed to understand the dynamical process of chemical reaction, and a new breed of researchers turned to physics, especially to thermodynamics, for their models. Around the year 1900 several chemists started to investigate chemical equilibria in terms of thermodynamics; among them were Wilhelm Ostwald, his student Walther Nernst, and Fritz Haber.

Fritz Haber's interest in ammonia synthesis was prompted by a request made in 1903 from two industrial chemists, the Margulies brothers, who owned the Österreichische Chemische Werke in Vienna. The Margulies had obtained minute quantities of ammonia from reactions of hydrogen with nitrates of calcium, lithium, and magnesium. Haber decided to enter into a consulting agreement to assist them in determining whether their technical process could be improved and made practicable by investigating the equilibrium conditions of ammonia. Gas reactions do not generally go through to completion but halt at equilibrium points. At low temperatures gases react sluggishly with respect to one another, whereas at high temperatures the reaction velocities are less of a problem, so that equilibrium phenomena come to the fore. Hence Haber investigated the dissociation of ammonia and its reformation in an equilibrium condition at high temperature. After a number of experiments Haber found equilibrium established by passing nitrogen and hydrogen over a catalyst of finely granulated iron on a bed of asbestos at around $1000°C$ and at atmospheric pressure. In these experiments Haber found that the speed of reaction was too slow at temperatures less than $1000°C$. Even at higher pressures, he noted, the condition of equilibrium was still unfavorable at lower temperatures. He did not try working with extremely high pressures, however, for "practical reasons, which require no explanation." Autoclaves, small ovens and circulation equipment then available in the chemical industry could not withstand pressures above 25 atmospheres. Gas canisters of hydrogen and oxygen achieved pressures of 200 atmospheres when filled according to the Linde liquefaction method, but these pressures were reached either at normal or very low temperatures. Operating with high pressures in large scale high temperature apparatus was simply unthinkable.

After completing this study in 1904, Haber turned to investigating the equilibrium conditions for all the principal gas reactions of interest to the industrial processes of his day. These were primarily the permanent gases. His object in this work was to adapt the principles of thermodynamics to the determination of general laws of equilibrium for chemical reactions. In constructing theory, Haber adopted the phenomenalist point of view. Leaving the atomic hypothesis aside, he declared his purpose to be the application of the mechanical theory of heat to chemistry by restricting himself "to the heat and work effects of masses directly perceptible to our senses."[35] Accordingly, in adapting the mechanical theory of heat to his purposes, Haber replaced the notions of free and bound energy in Helmholtz's classic treatment of the subject with reaction energy and latent heat, arguing that latent heat is something concrete, measurable, and appealing directly to the senses, whereas bound energy is an abstraction. Determination of a sensible measure for the reaction energy, or the force driving a chemical reaction, was a tricky matter, however. The application of the mechanical theory of heat to chemistry differs from other types of consideration of work, energy, and heat, where the determination of the force to be measured proceeds by setting up some opposing or compensating force, such as a balance and weights in the case of mechanical forces, or opposing electrical forces in the case of electrical measurements. Haber noted that it was impossible to set up an opposing chemical force to measure the driving force of a chemical reaction. On the other hand, he argued, every isothermal chemical reaction which proceeds with the production of the maximum amount of mechanical or electrical work, such as in a galvanic cell, is connected with the appearance and disappearance of definite quantities of sensible heat. Therefore, the heat that appears or disappears (i.e., becomes latent) when the maximum electrical or mechanical work is generated by a chemical reaction progressing at constant temperature and constant composition can serve as the measure of the reaction energy or work obtainable from the reaction. Writing the energy obtainable in the form of mechanical work as A, the accompanying decrease of the total energy as U, and the heat used up in the process as $-q$, Haber wrote as his fundamental equation

$$A - U = -q \tag{1}$$

Given this general equation Haber set out to find the relationship between the latent heat and temperature of a chemical reaction. Consideration of work, energy, and temperature for an ideal gas under isothermal expansion produced the relationship

$$-q = T \frac{\delta A}{\delta T} \tag{2}$$

In chemical reactions involving gases, the reaction heat, Q, can be substituted for the decrease of total energy, U, so that upon substitution, Haber was able to rewrite the fundamental equation as

$$A = Q + T \frac{\delta A}{\delta T} \tag{3}$$

Haber gave separate demonstrations of this relationship for the assumption of constant volume and constant pressure. In what follows, I will be primarily interested in the case assuming constant pressure.

Haber focused his attention particularly on the temperature coefficient $\delta A/\delta T$ in the equation (3), showing its equivalence to ΔS, or change of "entropy," introduced by Clausius into the theory of heat. In terms of an infinitely small isothermal change, where an infinitely small amount of maximum work, dA, is done, the reaction heat, $-dq$, and entropy are related by the equation

$$-S = -\int \frac{dq}{T} \tag{4}$$

Haber's main contribution was to make entropy considerations primary in the study of gas reactions. Previous investigators had sought to bypass the role of entropy in chemical reactions by invoking the principle of Berthelot, which equated A and U, provided that changes of state were excluded. Berthelot had excluded changes of state in order to eliminate latent heats, realizing that they would disturb the relation. Haber observed, however, that according to the fundamental equation, latent heats could only really be excluded when a reaction takes place at absolute zero. In every other case concentration relations and temperature would produce a difference between A and U:

> At ordinary temperatures of about 20°C, which does not lie very high on the absolute scale ($+293°$), and in the really important regions of greater concentrations, the differences between A and U is not as a rule very great, and Berthelot's rule affords a useful approximation. This rule, however, cannot be applied to gas reactions, for these often take place at temperatures which are higher by many thousands of degrees.[36]

Haber concluded this discussion by noting: "The significance of entropy in the simplest changes of substances is therefore patent."[37] Equating reaction heat and reaction energy was thus permissible most of the time, particularly in the range of low temperatures where, for most reactions, changes in entropy are inconsiderable. But in order to achieve exacting control over chemical reactions where large temperature changes played a role—and for a form of life centered on synthetic chemical technologies this was the desideratum of the day—*it was crucial to take changes in entropy into account*. This, in my view, was the crucial difference, the watershed that transformed the laws of thermodynamics from abstract mathematical concerns to the pulsating heartbeats of a lifeworld.

Haber's concern with latent heat and entropy led him to devote more exacting attention to determining all the elements affecting the fundamental equation over a large range of temperatures, and especially at high temperatures. Thus, where previous investigations of chemical equilibria had concentrated on the effects of mass action alone, Haber argued that changes in specific heats and reaction heats had to be considered as well. Reaction heat changes with temperature and the change generally depends on the specific heats of the substances formed in the course of the reaction. The consequences of this problem were great when it came to evaluating the fundamental equation (1). The difficulty was that the effect of temperature on specific heats could only be expressed by means of an empirical approximation formula.[38] Furthermore, in order to introduce the dependence of reaction heat on temperature, it had to be assumed that gaseous reactions can be carried out at absolute zero without the gases losing their ideal properties. These two assumptions required the use of Kirchhoff's law in order to evaluate the fundamental equation. Kirchhoff's law permitted the empirical determination of reaction heat in terms of temperature according to the relation

$$Q_T = Q_0 + \sigma_p'T + \sigma''T^2 + \ldots \tag{5}$$

Where Q_T is the reaction heat at temperature T, Q_0 is the reaction heat at absolute zero, σ'_p is the difference of mean specific heats of factors and products entering into the reaction at constant pressure, and σ'' is the specific heat at constant pressure (the latter term has no subscript, because it is the same whether at constant volume or at constant pressure).

Haber used these theoretical considerations to derive a general equation representing the free energy to do work at some temperature T. He proceeded by substituting term-by-term in equation (3). Thus for Q_T he substituted the approximation formula given by Kirchhoff's law in equation (5). He next derived a substitution for the entropy term by integration of equation (4), which involved consideration of the change in entropies of the separate components entering a gas reaction and the entropy of the resulting gas mixture. Where Q_T is the heat of reaction at absolute zero, ln is the natural logarithm, v' is the number of molecules taking part in the reaction, p and p' are the partial pressures of the reactants, σ' and σ'' are constants dependent upon the specific heats at constant pressure, and k is the integration constant, equation (3) could be rewritten as

$$A = Q_0 - \sigma_p T\ln T - \sigma''T^2 - RT \sum v'\ln p' + \ldots + kT \tag{6}$$

Haber's interest in constructing a generalized theory of gas reactions expressible in a set of fundamental equations was frustrated by the persistent need to resort to empirical generalizations, rules valid only within specific domains, and "reasonable" extrapolations between the ideal and actual conditions. Among these were the assumptions that reaction heat does not change with increasing temperature,[39] the assumption that the specific heats of gaseous compounds are made up additively of the specific heats of the gaseous components, and the assumption that the specific heats of factors and products are the same for all temperatures,[40] all assumptions he adapted to his purposes by introducing approximation formulae. Within limits these difficulties confronting theory could be made acceptable. The main problem in evaluating the equation, however, was the recalcitrant constant, k. Haber discussed at length the difficulties connected with determining the constant, concluding that the equation could only be used if k and the specific heats of the reacting gases could be empirically determined for some temperature.[41]

Haber also went on to consider conditions under which the constant could be eliminated altogether. In a discussion of the significance of the constant, k, he showed that in a reaction proceeding reversibly at concentrations which are equal to 1 and at temperatures of 1° absolute, the constant k is equal to the change in entropy. Assuming that Berthelot's principle, the notion that reaction energy and reaction heats are equal—$A=Q$—holds at absolute zero, and that it is most likely true at 1° absolute as well, Haber was able to conclude that at 1°, and hence at 0°, $k = 0$. In effect, then, Haber was arguing that Berthelot's principle would hold at absolute zero, if the change of entropy ΔS is also zero at absolute zero. The solution to all the problems in evaluating the fundamental equation would, therefore, disappear if $k \rightarrow 0$ in the neighborhood of absolute zero. Haber was sorely tempted by this beautiful assumption, but he resisted making it on the grounds that too little was known about specific heats at extremely high and low temperatures:

> We cannot decide in this way whether a perceptible difference between A and Q does not exist, though small in comparison with Q_0. But, unfortunately, this is a crucial point. For although we can certainly neglect k at a temperature of 1° absolute, this does not help us at all, for we never observe gas reactions at such low temperatures. But if the observations are carried out at 2000° absolute, kT is two thousand times greater than k at 1°, and we do not know whether we can neglect kT or not.[42]

The prescience of these reflections did not escape Walther Nernst. In 1906, Nernst took up the problem of determining chemical equilibria.[43] In his work, he traced much of the same ground as Haber, and indeed, Haber's *Thermodynamik technischer Gasreaktionen* was fundamental to his work. I am not concerned with Nernst here or with his formulation of the third law of thermodynamics first broached in the 1906 paper but rather with the consequences his work had for the problem of ammonia synthesis. As the basis of his *Wärmetheorem* Nernst postulated the conditions concerning heats of reaction, reaction energies, and entropy changes discussed by Haber at absolute zero. Nernst was arguing that an additional law of thermodynamics, one which postulated the conditions described by Haber at absolute zero, was required in order to complete the job of understanding changes of state and chemical reactions in terms of the first and second laws. In order to determine the correct relationship between the reaction energy and reaction heat, it was necessary to determine the integration constant in the integrated form of Haber's fundamental equation (the second law formulation of chemical reactions) linking the two, and this could not be done without a further postulate concerning the mode of behavior in the vicinity of absolute zero. In his efforts to confirm the Third Law, Nernst devoted the main part of his experimental work to examining specific heats at low temperatures. But before departing the domain of high temperatures, he made a crucial observation which redirected Haber's efforts.

As noted above, Haber and van Oordt had proceeded experimentally in finding the equilibrium condition for ammonia, which they set at about 1000°C at one atmosphere. Assuming his *Wärmetheorem*, Nernst could make an absolute calculation based on known thermal constants. His calculations from theory led to a temperature of 620°C for the equilibrium condition at atmospheric pressure, rather than the value some 400° higher determined experimentally by Haber. Nernst suspected that Haber and van Oordt's experimental procedure was insufficiently precise, and he decided to undertake experiments of his own.[44] In his investigation of ammonia synthesis Nernst focused on determining the relevant constants only by means of a method which produced a high yield of ammonia. For this purpose he chose to examine the equilibrium point under *high pressure* so that more easily measurable quantities of ammonia could be detected. He used an electric oven which could withstand pressures of between 30– 75 atmospheres and temperatures between 700–1000°C. This method indeed produced results which fit well with the theoretically expected values. At the meeting of the Bunsen Society in Hamburg in May 1907, Nernst revealed the line of reasoning from the heat theorem and his own experimental results, and in the discussion of his paper with Haber, Nernst suggested that a process more suitable for industry would be a catalytic method of synthesis operating at a lower temperature but at very high pressure.

Haber took up this challenge and began exploring a variety of catalysts, eventually hitting upon osmium as the most favorable. About this
same time, in the beginning of 1908, he broke off his relation with the
Margulies brothers and entered into a contract with Badische Analin und
Soda Fabrik (BASF). Haber was able to construct a laboratory model of
the process for synthesizing ammonia. In his benchtop model (Figure 1)
nitrogen and hydrogen were mixed in a compressor, K, at about 150–200
atmospheres and passed through a reaction chamber, R, heated to 500–
600° and containing pulverized osmium as catalyst. The ammonia was
then separated out and cooled, A, while the remaining gases were recir-
culated back through the system by another pump, U. This method produced approximately 8 percent volume concentration of ammonia per hour.

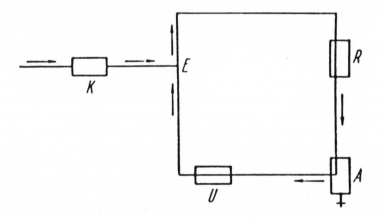

Lest we suppose that the theoretical difficulties in understanding and
controlling the gas reaction were over after Nernst had developed his
Wärmetheorem, it is worth noting the further development of concepts
needed to turn the demonstrated existence of ammonia synthesis from the
elements in a toy-sized, laboratory model into a practicable industrial process. In this passage of knowledge construction, actors are weaving a fabric in many directions simultaneously, linking some strands to established
models and practices as they simultaneously transform them in the process. As we have seen, this fits the view of knowledge production advocated by James, Klein, and Husserl, who emphasized that the concepts at
the core of a program of investigative research are not invented in a vacuum and then attached to empirical practices; rather they come packaged
with the practices themselves.[45] The very construction of the concepts is
intertwined with the practices which put them into operation, give them

empirical reference, and make them function as tools for the production of knowledge. For the brief examples we have considered, it is clear that in order to develop new conceptual structures, it is necessary to expand, alter, and reshape the body of empirical practices.

It is important to emphasize the manner in which the evolving conceptual structures are embedded in the network of investigations and the practices they depend upon. The developments we are tracing did not emerge from the elaboration of a single discovery or the elaboration of a single concept—such as change in entropy. The conceptual structure emerged as cloth from a loom, gradually but whole. The concepts of entropy change, reaction velocity, catalysts, and even the atom all evolved together and depended upon one another for mutual support. In the midst of contingency and circumstance, practical reason solidifies its object through bootstrapping, relating independent streams of investigation through fruitful metaphors and analogy.

This dialectic between the web of practice and concept is evident in Haber's discussion of suitable "reaction velocities" in *Gasreaktionen* and in his 1908 synthetic ammonia patent. In his historical reflections on ammonia synthesis, Bosch's assistant, Alwin Mittasch, identified the consideration of the velocity of a reaction as the watershed between the "old" and the "new era" in understanding chemical reactions. Whereas previous investigations had treated the formation of a gas compound as an instantaneous reaction dependent on a condition of *"status nascendi,"* in which nitrogen and hydrogen, for example, were brought together in the right concentrations under the right conditions, the thermodynamic approach emphasized the time involved in a reaction, and the fact that it might go through several stages with the formation and dissolution of intermediate compounds on the way before reaching an equilibrium in which a reversible reaction of reactants and products occurred. Mittasch argued that the new generation's experience with physical chemistry, particularly the law of mass action and the determination of equilibrium constants it enabled, formed the practical foundation for this new way of treating chemical reactions.[46] As a result, focus shifted to experimental work on establishing reversible reactions, preparing much of the ground for Haber's treatment of the problems of ammonia synthesis. Experimental work by William Ramsay in 1884 had established that dissolution of ammonia into its elements occurs at temperatures between 500–830° over a bed of asbestos wool as catalyst. Ramsay's experiments showed, furthermore, that the dissolution of ammonia is never complete, indicating that an equilibrium is established somewhere within this temperature range and that a reversible reaction occurs leading to the production of a small amount of ammonia. Haber set out to measure precisely the factors entering the equilibrium condition and to capture this small amount of ammonia. Haber's process for ammonia synthesis comes to equilibrium with a generation of heat: $N_2 + 3H_2 \leftrightarrows 2NH_3 + 22$ kcal. Given the small amounts of ammonia generated (approximately one percent), Haber was keen to speed up the reaction rate in order to make the process commercially viable. One way to increase the reaction rate was to increase the temperature. But increasing temperature favors an endothermic reaction and hence drives the reaction to the left in favor of generating reactants, reducing the already small yield of ammonia. At lower temperatures, around 300°, the percent of volume NH_3 could be increased to 2.2 percent (still miniscule compared to the near 100 percent volume production for sulfuric acid), but at these lower temperatures the reaction proceeds very slowly, and in addition, catalysts failed at these lower temperatures to speed up the reaction. A compromise solution used catalysts to increase the reaction rate, operating at a temperature sufficiently high to speed the rate of reaching equilibrium yet not so high as to drive the reaction too far backward: all in all, a very tricky business.

Haber's work embodied exactly the fruitful sort of interactive engagement with technical practice that Felix Klein maintained would invigorate theory. Haber's efforts to construct a theory of gas equilibria was deeply embedded in current experience and practices with gas reactions. His was not a "purist" consideration abstracted from the industrial production of ammonia.[47] In Haber's treatment of reaction velocity, scientific-technical objectives were indistinguishable from industrial concerns. In his theoretical inquiries, he sought a measure for the total quantity of ammonia that could be generated per day by a high-pressure, high-temperature apparatus operating catalytically in an economically efficient manner. Haber called this measure the *"Zeitraumausbeute,"* or space-time utilization. Thus, explicit formulation of the concept of reaction velocity required the simultaneous formulation of suitable catalysts. Crucial from the point of view of potential industrial development was the amount of ammonia produced per cubic centimeter of the contact space per hour. Obviously these two concepts together indicated the efficiency of the process. In order to interest a large chemical firm like BASF in the process, Haber had to provide the intellectual tools enabling the design of a large production facility aimed at constant throughput and maximum yield. As one scaled up from laboratory model to pilot plant and then to production facility, it was essential not to be vague about the size and the temperature of the contact oven, the sorts of catalysts that should be employed, the length of time the gases needed to contact the catalyst in order to produce a cost effective yield, the velocities at which the gases had to circulate in the reaction chamber, and so forth. Independently of the technical difficulties of building such a facility—to which we will turn momentarily—the costs involved were enormous. The outcome had to appear more than just feasible. Even though, as I have argued, the laws of thermodynamics and the principle of mass action were developed out of a direct consideration of machines and technical processes, they only provided the broadest framework for understanding what was going on.[48] Making ammonia, and lots of it, required an entire fabric of interdependent concepts and practices.

Haber's presentation of his theoretical work on the thermodynamics of technical gas reactions was indebted to this interlocking of theory development and practice, and he was extremely cautious about forming generalizations that were inaccessible to exacting experimental verification. His development of theory retraced the ground which had already been technically mastered.[49] He began with the analysis of processes well understood in terms of thermodynamics, such as the action of galvanic cells. He then extended this theory through suitable analogies and plausibility arguments to the field of gas dynamics, selecting as his working examples the "Hargreaves process" for the sulphate formation and the "Deacon process" for chlorine production. There were sound pragmatic reasons for proceeding in this fashion. Groping in new, uncharted territory, Haber found that empirical data on specific heats, heats of reaction, and temperatures of dissociation derived from the best understood technical processes offered a guide to generalization. In each of these areas various phenomenological rules had been worked out, such as the Kopp-Naumann rule, which states that the specific heat of a solid molecule is equal to the sum of the specific heats of the component atoms, or the Desperez-Pictet-Trouton rule, according to which the quotient of the heat of vaporization of homogeneous liquids divided by their absolute boiling-point under atmospheric pressure is a constant. Phenomenological rules of this sort provided Haber with a bridge to move from the solid to gaseous states, increasing the generality of his model. Consistency of theoretical foundation was not an issue at this point. It was rather the endpoint he hoped to attain. Thus, at certain stages in his discussion, Haber uses work dependent on atomism as a postulate, while in the later stages of his theoretical construction he abandons it:

Many important discoveries have undoubtedly been made by the help of atomistic considerations. . . . On the other hand, Gibbs, Helmholtz, Planck, and Mach have shown that the theory of heat becomes simpler and more convincing when stripped of its atomistic clothing. This especially applies to the work of Mach. If we abandon the atomistic basis and no longer consider the peculiarities and movements of molecules imperceptible to all our senses, and consider instead those qualities of heat and work—things directly accessible to our senses corresponding to molar quantities—the view of Clausius and Buff [the assumption that specific heats of gaseous compounds are made up additively of the specific heats of the gaseous components (TL)] loses the nature of a postulate, which it possessed with Clausius, and becomes simply a statement of experimental fact. It is in this sense that Planck introduces it into his thermodynamic treatment, while we, because of the poor confirmation which experiment affords it, do not use it in our general considerations.[50]

As we have seen, William James, Felix Klein, and Edmund Husserl attacked a theory-dominated historiography depicting the fit between equations and the real world as a miraculous occurrence possible only in a world in which an underlying truth is captured by the equation. In considering how the equations of Haber and Nernst came to fit the phenomena, we should examine the ways in which experience with the concrete practices and objects within a lifeworld preconditions theory. We ought, therefore, to bear in mind that the principal figures involved—Haber, Nernst, Robert Bosch, Robert Le Rossignol, Alwin Mittasch, and scores of technicians—learned their chemistry, physics, and engineering mechanics in theory and in practice in the same environments using the same problems, machines, and models as objects of study. The apparently miraculous convergence of theoretical and technical practice was facilitated by the passage of persons through both the sites of theoretical knowledge production in Berlin (Charlottenburg) and Leipzig, and the industrial sites of technoscience, particularly the research labs at BASF. During exactly the same period (late 1890s through 1907) that Ostwald (Leipzig), Knorre (T-H Berlin)—who taught both Haber and Bosch—Haber, and Nernst were trying to extend thermodynamics to dynamical equilibria for the permanent gases central to industrial production, Knietsch, Knorre, and Bosch were trying to engineer plants for production of sulfuric acid, liquefaction of chlorine, and production of nitrous acid, the latter crucial to nitrate production. High theory and material practice could be fitted to one another smoothly because the sites in which those practices evolved were linked through many levels of personnel, problems, and machines. This point is illustrated most dramatically in the case of Robert Bosch.

Bosch came to the work on ammonia synthesis fully equipped with a repertoire of the most advanced practical skills in the chemical industry. The son of a gas and water plumbing manufacturer and installer, Bosch had studied metallurgy and mechanical engineering at the Technische Hochschule in Berlin before going on to the University of Leipzig to study physical chemistry with Wilhelm Ostwald from 1896 to 1899.[51] During these years Ostwald was particularly concerned with electrochemical processes and catalysis. In his last year of study, Bosch immersed himself in the new research in spectral analysis at Leipzig. It is important to emphasize that Bosch received a practical as well as a technical education. During the summers he served an apprenticeship in metallurgy at the Krupp high-temperature oven works in Neuweid. He learned several trades, including that of machinist. After completing his studies Bosch started work at BASF. He first entered the "Hauptlaboratorium" where the individual talents of the new apprentices were surveyed before assigning them to specific research lab or production-line divisions. Bosch was quickly sent off to work in the lab of Rudolf Knietsch. This was the glamour lab of BASF, where the synthetic production of indigo had been worked out just two years prior to Bosch's arrival. Bosch was put to work on the development of a process for producing phthalic acid anhydride, an intermediate used in the synthesis of indigo, by oxidation of naphthalene with sulfuric acid. In connection with the indigo blue project at BASF, Knietsch had also been the man who had worked out both the catalytic contact process for sulfuric acid production and the process for liquefying chlorine, which depended on the development of compressors for bringing chlorine gas into contact with a coating of sulfuric acid on the parts of the pump. The phthalic acid lab worked in close connection with the sulfuric acid plant. Thus, Bosch spent his apprenticeship acquiring hands-on experience with the new techniques of catalytic contact as well as with the new high-pressure technology used in liquid chlorine and sulfuric acid production. He contributed to the phthalic acid process by developing a more efficient gas oven, which enabled a major expansion of the plant.

Bosch's first encounter with the problem of ammonia synthesis took place well before his meeting with Haber in July 1909. Indeed, Bosch had been assigned the task of confirming Ostwald's synthesis method in 1900. After careful attempts at duplicating the procedures outlined by Ostwald, Bosch submitted a report indicating that the method would not work, and that impurities in the iron catalyst had enabled Ostwald's model to generate ammonia during laboratory trials. The directorship of BASF did not abandon the project at this time, however, and Bosch was assigned the task of exploring other paths to nitrogen fixation. From 1904 to 1907 he worked on methods involving the action of nitrogen on a glowing mixture of barium carbonate and coal barium cyanide. In the course of this work he was given his own laboratory.

Bosch's training and experience gave him a certain sensibility for technical solutions in the field of gas dynamics, the sort of sensibility that would enable him to glance at a model or drawing of a theory and make the snap judgment that it would or would not work. By this I do not mean that he was without theoretical knowledge. Indeed, as mentioned above, he had studied experimental physics, what was then known of thermodynamics, and physical chemistry. But his theory was embedded in his practices and in the devices he worked with daily. The description of his first encounter with Haber's ammonia device illustrates this point. On the day that Haber demonstrated his ammonia synthesis model, Haber and his technical assistant, an Englishman named Robert Le Rossignol, set up the device in Ludwigshafen but could not get it to work properly. The gaskets on some of the high pressure fittings blew out before the desired equilibrium point was reached. Bosch suggested repairs and minor reconstruction which got the device running once again, but he had to leave before the demonstration was complete. He told Haber and Le Rossignol that he did not need to see the conclusion of the demonstration: he knew it would work.[52]

I have argued that theoretical practices need to be assembled, that they are jerry-built from results in other domains. But the same is true of technical practices. I am not attempting to argue that Bosch had some privileged practical insight which enabled him to see immediately that Haber's process would work and then proceeded straightaway to translate it into pieces of hardware. Indeed, when Bosch got to work on Haber's device back in his lab in Ludwigshafen he saw that a large scale version of that machine was unworkable. The principle would work, however. Theory had done this much: it had demonstrated that under high temperatures and pressures of about 200 atmospheres, ammonia synthesis in suitable yield was possible. What was now required was a large scale plant which embodied that principle. To bring this about Bosch had two challenges: first, to develop apparatus capable of operating with corrosive gases at high temperatures and high pressures well in excess of operating conditions known at the time; secondly, to construct a durable and relatively inexpensive catalyst for the ammonia reaction. Haber had used osmium in his device, and it worked beautifully. But osmium was a rare metal and an extremely expensive element. In fact, it was only because BASF owned the world's supply of osmium at the time that they entertained the notion of developing Haber's patent.

Bosch had to construct an entire new generation of apparatus from the ground up. He did this by assembling persons from diverse parts of the chemical industry under the single roof of his own lab. Here he broke with company policy at BASF and was frequently reprimanded for raiding other divisions which were supposedly off-limits to him.[53] At BASF the various departments and labs were not supposed to exchange information. If a machine was to be built a design had to be sent to the machine shop. Different chemical labs did not exchange personnel. The reason for this was concern about control over the knowledge base at the heart of the enterprise. With all the processes, both patented and unpatented, in the different departments of a concern like BASF, it was deemed crucial not to allow workers access to every part of the plant. Bosch simply ignored these strictures. He roamed through the different labs and divisions of BASF inquiring into whatever interested him. Much to the chagrin of foremen and other lab directors, he recruited persons with expertise he thought might be useful to his project. He brought these persons together in his own lab, encouraging them to exchange their viewpoints and experience with one another. Of this period he later noted: "In our projects, I have frequently learned that in order to strike out in new directions, experience can be drawn from any corner. One must not only know chemistry and physics but must also learn what is going on in marginal fields. Precisely in the marginal fields is where the future lies."[54] In this environment of close interaction under Bosch's careful and demanding scrutiny the first high pressure apparatus was machined, fitted, remachined and refitted until levels of precision were reached far exceeding anything done elsewhere in the industry. The group designed entirely new types of compressors and pumps, the most innovative of which was the so-called "mole pump" which was sealed into the gas flow pipes so that it was inaccessible. The pump had to operate for months at a time in an extremely corrosive gas mixture. The process of gas synthesis had to be monitored step-by-step throughout the system, a task which involved installing 1,630 measuring gauges for quantity, pressure, and temperature, 80 analytical registration instruments, and 2,170 temperature gauges. Many of these measuring apparatuses were of completely new design.[55] The entire ammonia synthesis plant required forty people monitoring 2,100 measurement stations.[56] These massive demands of innovation and expertise were met because Bosch created an environment where a repertoire of diverse practical experience honed through work on the most advanced technologies of the chemical industry was linked in an interactive network with laboratory skill and theoretical practice.

Between 1909 and 1912 Bosch assembled a group of chemists, engineers, machinists and highly skilled workers in his lab, 180 persons in all. They worked closely with one another in developing new apparatus requiring completely new levels of high-precision work. Bosch proceeded by dividing up into teams and assigning different research problems to each team. The team working on catalysts was headed by Alwin Mittasch, a gymnasium teacher who had studied physical chemistry and catalytic contact methods with Ostwald in Leipzig. The Mittasch group conducted over 20,000 experiments in determining the composition of the appropriate catalyst.[57] In the course of this work, they revolutionized understanding of the processes of catalytic action in gas reactions and the phenomena connected with reaction velocities. Almost every assumption guiding previous work on catalysis was revised in the course of this work. They discovered, for example, that Haber's assumption that one had to have an extremely pure metal to serve as a catalyst was incorrect. The most successful catalysts were amalgams of two, three, or more different metals. Surprisingly, optimal results depended upon each component having an affinity for either hydrogen or nitrogen, but not both. This work broke new ground for the development of the entire theoretical understanding of catalysis. The stabilization and control of the synthetic ammonia process led to an expanding web of related concepts and practices outside the immediate domain of Bosch's lab.

Similar path-breaking work resulted from the development of the high-pressure/high-temperature contact oven. The achievement of this technical feat reveals further the extent to which Bosch relied on the network of technical skill and practical experience as a resource for extrapolation. The early ovens Bosch constructed all burst after a few working hours. In order to make progress in this area, Bosch decided to draw directly upon Haber's experience in building his own model oven. He sent a machinist from the BASF workshops to learn directly from Haber's own technician, Le Rossignol, and from their machinist, Kirchenbauer, the workings of their oven. Le Rossignol had improved upon and patented valves for operating at high temperatures and pressures in the ovens, and Kirchenbauer had patented conical shaped gaskets for operating in these conditions.[58] Constructing larger ovens operating at full capacity for lengthy periods of time, however, required heroic measures. Investigation revealed that the hydrogen at high temperature was attacking the steel and weakening it by removing carbon in the form of methane. Bosch's solution to this problem was to run the process through two tubes, one serving as an inner sleeve for the other. The inner sleeve was made of perforated soft iron, while the outer tube was of hardened steel. Bosch's device, which earned him a Nobel Prize, was indebted to the practical experience of Knietsch, who had confronted similar problems in developing the catalytic contact method for sulfuric acid production. In that case, the highest yields of sulfuric acid were achieved by keeping contact pipes relatively cool and at the same time bringing the gases into intimate contact with the platinum catalyst. Knietsch's solution, like Bosch's after him, was to perforate the plate upon which the catalyst rested.[59] To be sure, the problems were not identical. But working in Knietsch's sulfuric acid lab at BASF familiarized Bosch with a repertoire of technical "tactics" which served him well when he attacked problems he could construe as analogs to problems he had seen previously. The methods Bosch used in arriving at this invention were no less important than the invention itself. As in the case of catalysis, the solution and stabilization of one technical problem was achieved through the expansion of the web of concepts and practices to other domains. New research instruments and materials issued from this process, strengthening and anchoring the original set of concepts and practices. Thus, Bosch employed high-powered microscopes in studying the structure of the metals and even experimented with the development of x-ray crystallography in this context as a research tool useful for understanding material structures of relevance to the chemical industry. He investigated numerous new alloys of steel for high pressure work, including alloys of tungsten, chrome, and vanadium.

In the years that followed, once the basic techniques and methods had been developed around a working plant, separate workshops were established for ovens, for compressors and pumps, and for other parts of the entire system.[60] Where initially the different components of a system had been fabricated and assembled in one lab, eventually this work was divided between independent research and production units; in the case of catalysts, alloys, and instruments entire scientific disciplines split off from their original site of technoscientific production. Skilled workers as well as sites multiplied. The initial group of technicians under Bosch's supervision trained others in the precision and rigor of the new high-pressure, high-temperature technology. In this fashion, through the assembly of a wide variety of skills and practices, their operational packaging with theoretical concepts, and their repetition in the day-to-day work of the laboratory, the pilot plant, and eventually the full-scale ammonia factory, the habits, dispositions, and "motor skills" or *Aktgebilde* (action-structures) Klein and Husserl referred to were woven into a strong fabric. Through reproduction at other sites, these skills and habits, together with high-pressure/high-temperature apparatus and theoretical understanding of its workings passed into the domain of everyday practice of industrial engineers, chemists, and physicists. This multiplication of technical culture constituted a lifeworld.

4. Values and the Practice of a Lifeworld

Earlier I drew a parallel between the lifeworld described by Husserl and the cultural practices implicit in Baxandall's period eye. In the technical culture I have been describing, the analogs to the mathematical practices of gauging and calculation with π shared by Baxandall's Quattrocento artists and viewers were the principle of mass action, determination of equilibrium constants, Nernst's *Wärmetheorem*, methods for determining reaction velocities, activation curves for catalysts, Kirchenbauer gaskets, steel alloys, Le Rossignol valves, spectrographs, magnetometers, and ultraspectrometers. All of these became a commonly assumed base of theoretical practices, techniques, and artifacts essential to the chemical work of theoreticians like Nernst, experimentalists like Haber, Mittasch, and Paul Gmelin, and industrial engineers like Bosch. This repertoire of habits and dispositions was an enabling resource; the orchestrated practices and technologies physically embodied in Ludwigshafen could serve as a powerful source of technical intellectual tools, as well as of images and metaphors for thinking constructively in other domains.

I want to conclude by emphasizing the further ideological, value-constitutive component of the lifeworld. Again Baxandall's description of Quattrocento merchant-oligarchic culture is a direct parallel to the modern, technocratic, industrial-scientific lifeworld I have been describing. The physical layout of the ammonia factory, depicted in Figure 2, embodies the modernist concern with large, self-contained and self-regulating systems expressed by Fischer, Haber, and entrepreneurs such as Emil and Walther Rathenau. Efficiency, flow, system, precision control—mastering the processes of nature in order to synthesize materials more completely under our control—all of those values, purposes, and

Die Ammoniak-Hochdruck-Synthese der
Badischen Anilin- & Soda-Fabrik, Ludwigshafen a. Rhein

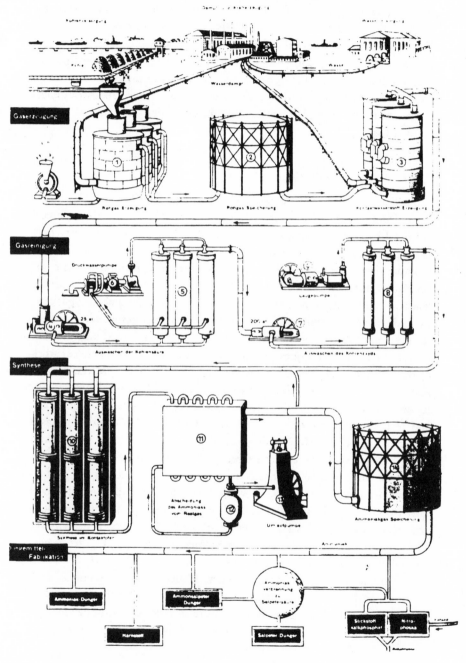

the dispositions to pursue them constituted a lifeworld. We see it materially embodied in the pilot ammonia factory in Ludwigshafen and even more completely realized in the full-scale factory constructed in nearby Oppau in 1913. In Oppau the land was specially filled and hardened in order to bear up the weight of the huge high-pressure/high-temperature apparatus operating at peak efficiency and precision. More than the massive buildings and equipment depicted in Figure 2, the plant was its own model city, built literally from the ground up, symbolizing through the synthesis of a man-made environment the mastery over nature that went on inside the contact ovens—streets laid out in a perfect grid, rail connection, central electric power plant, and telephone system with several hundred units connected by an automated switching center, the first of its kind in Germany, constructed a decade before such telephone systems were in widespread public use.[61] This lifeworld also undergirded the organization of the Kaiser-Wilhelm-Institutes and Emil Rathenau's creation of the Allgemeine Elektrizitäts Gesellschaft (AEG). Each of these concerns expressed Emil Fischer's enthusiasm for fashioning forms of organization appropriate to the production of knowledge for the new age.

In the shaping of this new age, aesthetic values were to play a crucial role. Artists, architects, and designers joined forces with industrialists to transform society through the creation of a new aesthetic culture. Through organizations such as the Deutsche Werkbund, which linked a group of twelve architects and designers, including Hermann Muthesius and Peter Behrens, with twelve commercial firms, a cooperative endeavour of technology, industry, the natural sciences, and art aimed at renewing German nationalism. This lofty goal was to be attained through applying modern industrial processes to the objects of everyday life, such as chairs, eating utensils, tea kettles, and lamps. In the process, industrial designers would become artists, the traditional division between art and technology would be overcome, and aesthetic practice would be invigorated by its active integration with industrial means of production. All these benefits depended on new forms of collective organization and cooperation between the arts and industry.[62]

A case in point: Peter Behrens, who as chief architect and designer for AEG was closely associated with Emil Rathenau. Behrens was one of the new breed of avant-garde artists who believed that engineers expressed in their industrial designs the principles of modern technology, such as efficiency, flow, and system. Behrens wanted to provide the machines and buildings of the new industrial revolution with the aesthetic forms that expressed these principles. As he put it, his goal was to "achieve those forms that derive directly from and which correspond to the machine and machine construction."[63] He designed factories, electrical appliances, exhibitions, and graphics that celebrated the spirit of large-scale production and business organization. His famous design of the AEG turbine factory, with its monumental scale and regular design elements, manifested the concentrated power, order, precision, and regularity of the production methods inside the plant, as well as of the machines produced there. Contemporaries saw this logical and unified building as a symbol of what it enclosed.

Technical and economic efficiency became part of the design itself. Walther Gropius, a colleague of Behrens in the Deutsche Werkbund, shared the commitment to constructing revolutionary new architecture based on specialization, organization, and centralization. Factories and other industrial buildings would embody the spirit of this new age just as cathedrals had expressed the culture of the middle ages. Gropius personified the mastery of the new forces of production at the heart of the second industrial revolution.[64] Like Walther Rathenau, he was also an entrepreneur. Not satisfied with only designing buildings, he presided over the technical, economic, and organizational aspects of construction as well. With Martin Wagner and Ernst May he pursued his interest in large housing projects, designing model houses suited for large-scale, systematized, and rationalized manufacture. He made efficient organization and vertical integration of production his explicit goals. Builders of modern dwellings should, he argued, employ mass production methods, factory assembly-line processes, flow charts, and other control techniques in executing architectural projects.[65]

Among the concepts central to this lifeworld were the laws of thermodynamics, and particularly the third law. It, too, expressed this drive for efficiency, flow, control, system, and above all synthesis. Through the work of Haber, Bosch, and his team of laboratory workers this law and the fabric of concepts that gave it meaning and shape became integrated into concrete engineering practice, just as it was embodied in the high-pressure/high-temperature technology of the new chemical processing plants. Like Baxandall's Renaissance community of merchants and viewers of paintings who were all familiar with the practices of gauging, scientists and engineers—and others such as Rathenau, Behrens, and Gropius, who attended to the forces of production—in the early decades of this century actively constructed laws of nature and the materials essential to the co-production of their lifeworld.

NOTES

I am grateful to Nancy Cartwright, Lorraine Daston, Peter Galison, Klaus Hentschel, Fritz Ringer, Cheri Ross, Simon Schaffer, and Norton Wise for their careful reading and comments on early drafts of this paper. Cheri Ross has also provided invaluable editorial assistance.

1. For William James's enthusiastic endorsement of the work of Mach and Ostwald, see William James, "What Pragmatism Means," pp. 29–30, and "Pragmatism and Common Sense," p. 93 in *Pragmatism: A New Name for Some Old Ways of Thinking*, and "Humanism and Truth," p. 206–207, in *The Meaning of Truth*, in A. J. Ayer, ed., *William James: Pragmatism and the Meaning of Truth* (Cambridge, Mass.: Harvard University Press, 1975).

2. James, "Pragmatism and Humanism," 119. Peirce defended the same position, and he, too, was careful to disclaim that external objects are reifications of the mind: "there is no thing which is 'in-itself' in the sense of not being relative to the mind, though things which are relative to the mind doubtless are, apart from that relation." See "Some Consequences of Four Incapacities," in Philip P. Wiener, ed., *Charles S. Peirce: Selected Writings (Values in a Universe of Chance)* (New York: Dover, 1966), 68–69.

3. James, "Pragmatism and Humanism," 123.

4. Ibid., 120: "We 'encounter' it [sensible reality] (in Mr. Bradley's Words) but don't possess it. Superficially this sounds like Kant's view; but between categories fulminated before nature began, and categories gradually forming themselves in nature's presence, the whole chasm between rationalism and empiricism yawns."

5. Ibid., 124. Elsewhere, speaking to the same issue, James writes that the previous fifty years had brought about fundamental changes in the notion of scientific truth: "So also the 'laws of nature,' physical and chemical, so of natural history classifications—all were supposed to be exact and exclusive duplicates of pre-human archetypes buried in the structure of things, to which the spark of divinity hidden in our intellect enables us to penetrate. The anatomy of the world is logical, and its logic is that of a university professor, it was thought. Up to about 1850 almost everyone believed that sciences expressed truths that were exact copies of a definite code of non-human realities. But the enormously rapid multiplication of theories in these latter days has well-nigh upset the notion of any one of them being more literally objective kind of thing than another. There are so many geometries, so many logics, so many physical and chemical hypotheses, so many classifications, each one of them good for so much and yet not good for everything, that the notion that even the truest formula may be a human device and not a literal transcript has dawned upon us. We hear scientific laws now treated as so much 'conceptual shorthand,' true so far as they are useful but no farther. Our mind has become tolerant of symbol instead of reproduction, of approximation instead of exactness, of plasticity instead of rigor. 'Energetics,'

measuring the bare face of sensible phenomena so as to describe in a single formula all their changes of 'level,' is the last word of this scientific humanism, which indeed leaves queries enough outstanding as to the reason for so curious a congruence between the world and the mind, but which at any rate makes our whole notion of scientific truth more flexible and genial than it used to be. . . . Truth we conceive to mean everywhere, not duplication, but addition; not the constructing of inner copies of already complete realities, but rather the collaborating with realities so as to bring about a clearer result." Quoted from "Humanism and Truth," (1904), 206–207.

6. Peirce, "Some Consequences of Four Incapacities," 69.

7. Ibid., 72.

8. James, *Pragmatism*, 104.

9. Ibid., 117.

10. Ibid., 117.

11. Edmund Husserl, *Die Krisis der europäischen Wissenschaften und die transzendentale Phänomenologie: Eine Einleitung in die phänomenologische Philosophie, Husserliana*, vol. 6, translated by David Carr (Evanston, Ill.: Northwestern University Press, 1970), 60.

12. Ibid., 29.

13. Herbert Mehrtens, *Moderne—Sprache—Mathematik: Die mathematische Moderne um die Jahrhundertwende und ihre Gegner* (Berlin: Unpublished Habilitationsschrift, 1989), 166.

14. Discussed in Karl Heinz Manegold, "Felix Klein als Wissenschaftsorganizator: Ein Beitrag zum Verhältnis von Naturwissenschaft und Technik im 19. Jahrhundert," *Technikgeschichte* 35 (1968): 177–204.

15. Felix Klein, "Über Arithmetisierung der Mathematik (1985)", in *Felix Klein: Gesammelte mathematische Abhandlungen* (Berlin: Springer, 1921–1923), vol. 2, 240.

16. Felix Klein, "Autobiographische Skizze," *Mitteilungen des Universitätsbundes Göttingen*, 1923, Part I, 199.

17. Klein, "Arithmetisierung der Mathematik," 237. Quoted by Mehrtens, *Moderne—Sprache—Mathematik*, 169.

18. Husserl, *Logische Untersuchungen*, vol. 2, 551–552.

19. Dagfinn Föllesdal argues that James played a crucial role in the development of Husserl's views on the foundations of logic, mathematics, and their relation to empirical practice. Husserl owned both volumes of James's *Principles of Psychology* (London: 1890), and studied them carefully in the mid-1890s. The role of pragmatist thought and empirical psychology is evident throughout the papers written in the period between 1886–1901. See Edmund Husserl, *Studien zur Arithmetik und Geometrie. Texte aus dem Nachlaβ. 1896–1901*, in *Husserliana. Edmund Husserl Gesammelte Werke*, volume 21, Ingeborg Strohmeyer, ed. (The Hague: Martin Nijhoff Press, 1983). Also see Dagfinn Föllesdal, "Husserl on evidence and justification," in Robert Sokolowski, ed., *Edmund Husserl and the*

Phenomenological Tradition: Essays in Phenomenology, (Washington, D.C.: Catholic University Press, 1988), 107–129, especially p. 118.

20. Edmund Husserl, *Die Krisis der europäischen Wissenschaften und die transzendentale Phänomenologie: Eine Einleitung in die phänomenologische Philosophie, Husserliana*, vol. 6, translated by David Carr (Evanston, Ill.: Northwestern University Press, 1970), 26–27.

21. Husserl, *Krisis der europäischen Wissenschaften*, 124.

22. Ibid., 130.

23. I am grateful to Peter Galison for calling my attention to this feature of Wittgensteinian forms of life. At issue in the Wittgensteinian "form of life" is the commitment to framework relativism. See Peter Galison, "Aufbau/Bauhaus: Logical Postivism and Architectural Modernism," *Critical Inquiry* 16 (1990): 709–752. Galison develops this point more explicitly in "Context and Constraints," paper delivered to the British Society for the Philosophy of Science, September 1990.

24. Pierre Bourdieu has discussed the difficulties in treating a form of life as a system of rules that might be articulated like a generative grammar. See Pierre Bourdieu, *Outline of a Theory of Practice* (Cambridge: Cambridge University Press, 1977), see especially 1–30; 72–93; 96–97; 109–110; 123–124. In an important discussion of the relation of theory to practice and of unarticulated versus articulated knowledge, Michel de Certeau makes the distinction between "tactics" and "strategies." Certeau's discussion of Foucault and Bourdieu is brilliant. See Michel de Certeau, *The Practice of Everyday Life* (Berkeley: University of California Press, 1984), 49–90.

25. See Bourdieu, *Outline of a Theory*, 72.

26. See especially Michael Baxandall, *Painting and Experience in Fifteenth Century Italy* (Oxford: Oxford University Press, 1972), second edition, 1988, 45–56, 81–108.

27. See Thomas P. Hughes, *American Genesis: A Century of Invention and Technological Enthusiasm, 1870–1970* (New York: Viking, 1989).

28. Emil Fischer, "Antrittsrede als Mitglied der Akademie der Wissenschaften zu Berlin (1893)," in *Emil Fischer: Untersuchungen aus verschiedenen Gebieten*, M. Bergmann, ed. (Berlin: Springer, 1924), 702.

29. Fischer, "Neuere Erfolge und Probleme der Chemie (1911)," *Untersuchungen*, 757, 760.

30. Fischer, "Proteine und Polypeptide (1907)," *Untersuchungen*, 756.

31. Fischer, "Die Kaiser-Wilhelm-Institute (1915)," *Untersuchungen*, 805–806.

32. Fischer, "Proteine und Polypeptide," *Untersuchungen*, 755–756; and "Neuere Erfolge und Probleme der Chemie," *passim*.

33. Fischer, "Bergrüβungsansprache bei der Eröffnungsfeier des I. Chemischen Instituts der Universität Berlin am 14. Juli 1900," *Untersuchungen*, 728.

34. Fischer, "Die Kaiser-Wilhelm-Institute," *Untersuchungen*, 808.

35. Haber, *Thermodynamik technischer Gasreaktionen* (1905), translated by Arthur Lamb (London: Longmans, Green and Co., 1908), ix.

36. Ibid., 26.

37. Ibid., 83.

38. $c = a + bT + cT^2 + \ldots$, where c is the specific heat at constant volume and a and b are constants. Haber noted that "our observations are hardly accurate enough to allow us to determine more than the first two constants . . ." ibid., 48.

39. Ibid., 65–66.

40. Ibid., 47.

41. Ibid., 47.

42. Ibid., 42.

43. Walther Nernst, "Über die Berechnung chemischer Gleichgewichte aus thermischen Messungen," *Nachrichten von Gesellschaft der Wissenschaften zu Göttingen* (1906), 1–40. The best discussion of Nernst's work in thermodynamics is Erwin Hiebert, "Nernst, Hermann Walther," in Charles C. Gillispie, general editor, *Dictionary of Scientific Biography* (New York: Charles Scribner's Sons, 1970), vol. 10, 432–453.

44. This is recounted by Nernst in his book, *Die theoretischen und experimentellen Grundlagen des neuen Wärmesatzes*, (Halle: W. Knapp, 1918).

45. The symbiotic relationship among practice, experiment, and concepts is also emphasized by Andrew Pickering in his essay review of Harry Collins' book, *Changing Order*. See Andrew Pickering, "Forms of life: Science, contingency and Harry Collins," *British Journal for the History of Science 20* (1987): 213–221, especially p. 216. The most detailed study of this "packaging process" is Frederic Lawrence Holmes's examination of Lavoisier's "investigative enterprise." See Frederic L. Holmes, *Lavoisier and the Chemistry of Life: An Exploration of Scientific Creativity*, (Madison, Wis.: University of Wisconsin Press, 1985), especially xv–xxii, 46–62, 63–128 *passim*.

46. Alwin Mittasch, *Geschichte der Ammoniaksynthese* (Weinheim: Verlag Chemie, 1951), 48.

47. This point is emphasized throughout Mittasch's memoire. See Mittasch, *Geschichte der Ammoniaksynthese*, 73.

48. Nancy Cartwright discusses the relationship between phenomenological laws and theory in *How the Laws of Physics Lie* (Oxford: Oxford University Press, 1983).

49. See especially the seventh lecture, "The Determination of Gaseous Equilibria. Theoretical and Technical Observations Regarding Related Subjects," in Haber, *Thermodynamik*, 245–314.

50. Haber, *Thermodynamik*, 67–68.

51. Biographical details on Bosch are from Karl Holdermann, *Im Banne der Chemie. Carl Bosch Leben und Werk*, (Düsseldorf: Econ-Verlag, 1952), 23–65.

52. Ibid., 69–70.

53. Ibid., 70–74.

54. Quoted from Holdermann, *Im Banne der Chemie*, 76.

55. Paul Gmelin, who worked in Bosch's lab and developed many of the new measuring instruments, discussed the new requirements of technical measurement in the chemical industry introduced by the Haber-Bosch Process and the resulting increased research demands these placed on the physical foundations of technical measurement. See Paul Gmelin, "Physikalische Technik in der anorganischen chemischen Technik," *Die Chemische Fabrik 3* (1930), numbers 44, 45, 46, and 47.

56. See Holdermann, *Im Banne der Chemie*, 115–117.

57. Discussed at length in Alwin Mittasch, *Geschichte der Ammoniaksynthese*, 87–134.

58. The importance of the practical knowledge exchanged in such site-visits was emphasized by Mittasch in his account of ammonia synthesis. See Mittasch, *Geschicte der Ammoniaksynthese*, especially p. 93.

59. See Rudolf Knietsch, "Über die Schwefelsäure und ihre Fabrication nach dem Contactver-fahren," *Berichte der deutschen chemischen Gesellschaft 44* (1901); 4069–4115, especially 4086–4087.

60. Holdermann, *Im Banne der Chemie*, 79.

61. See Holdermann, *Im Banne der Chemie*, 119.

62. I am particularly indebted to two essays by Frank Trommler for this interpretation. See Frank Trommler, "Vom Bauhaussstuhl zur Kulturpolitik: Die Auseinandersetzung um die moderne Produktkultur," in Helmut Brackert and Fritz Wefelmeyer, eds., *Kultur: Bestimmungen im 20. Jahrhundert* (Frankfurt: Suhrkamp, 1990), 86–110; and Frank Trommler, "Technik, Avantgarde, Sachlichkeit: Versuch einer historischen Zuordnung," Götz Großklaus and Eberhard Lämmert, eds., *Literatur in einer industriellen Kultur* (Stuttgart: J. G. Cotta'sche Buchhandlung Nachfolger, 1989), 46–71.

63. Quoted by Tilmann Buddenseig, *Industriekultur. Peter Behrens und die AEG 1907–1914* (Berlin: Mann, 1979), 15.

64. See Winfried Nerdinger, "Vom Amerikanismus zur Neuen Welt," in Winfried Nerdinger, *Walter Gropius. Der Architekt Walter Gropius. Zeichnungen, Pläne und Fotos aus dem Busch-Reisinger Museum der Harvard University Art Museums, Cambridge/Mass. und dem Bauhaus-Archiv Berlin*, (Berlin: Mann, 1985), 8–32.

65. This point is emphasized by Thomas P. Hughes in *American Genesis: A Century of Invention and Technological Enthusiasm*, especially 314–319.

ESSENTIAL TENSIONS—PHASE TWO: FEMINIST, PHILOSOPHICAL, AND SOCIAL STUDIES of SCIENCE

Helen E. Longino

In the last ten to fifteen years, feminists from various disciplines have articulated a number of challenges to conventional wisdom about the sciences. In this endeavor they have been joined by other critics both within the sciences and working in the social studies of science, although often to different ends and with different analytical tools. It is such differences in ends and in analytical tools that provide a starting point for these reflections on the relations between feminist approaches to science, philosophy of science, and social studies of science.

Feminist analysts' proposals about the role of gender and of gender ideology in the sciences implicitly challenge at least two intradisciplinary points of consensus. Interestingly these points of consensus are themselves issues of *inter*disciplinary dissensus. The normative aspirations of much philosophy of science stand in troubled tension with the descriptive results of much work in sociology, anthropology, and, to a lesser extent, history of science. Feminist science studies themselves are in disagreement over basic methodology. This disagreement has at least two sources: one, which I have discussed elsewhere,[1] is a question about the most effective strategy for undermining the hegemony of scientism; another is the inability of either strictly normative or strictly descriptive analyses of the construction of scientific knowledge to fully meet the demands of the feminist agenda.

This essay will begin with an exploration of the multiple tensions among the three bodies of inquiry mentioned in its title. I propose that the position some feminist thinkers about the sciences have called feminist empiricism offers, if not a resolution of these tensions, at least a ground upon which to negotiate them. In my book, *Science as Social Knowledge*,[2] I develop a position I call contextual empiricism which I wish to recommend as a form of feminist empiricism. This form of empiricism differs in certain crucial respects from the neoclassical empiricism of Hume and the modern empiricism of the logical positivists. Feminist, or contextual, em-

198

piricism offers an account of knowledge as partial, fragmentary, and ultimately constituted from the interaction of opposed styles and/or points of view. Rather than a foil for postmodernism, it is more appropriately understood as itself postmodernist in spirit.

Let me begin by outlining what I take the feminist agenda to be, and the tensions in which it finds itself vis-à-vis the dominant traditions in philosophy and social studies of science. I will then summarize the relevent elements of the contextual empiricist account of inquiry with a view to indicating how it is possible within this account to reconcile the claim that scientific inquiry is value- or ideology-laden *and* that it is productive of knowledge. I will conclude by proposing that such an account goes further towards meeting the methodological needs of feminist science studies than present alternatives.

1. The Challenge to Philosophy and Social Studies of Science

Feminist scholars have developed a multifaceted critique of the sciences, addressing issues of professional structure and the experiences of women within that structure, issues of content, and issues of methodology. As regards professional structure, historians of science have documented the exclusionary practices adopted both in Europe[3] and in the United States,[4] which involve the exercise and legitimation of discriminatory policies, the channeling of women into fields that become *ipso facto* less prestigious, and the metaphoric appropriation of scientific inquiry as a domain of male activity.[5] Other historians have studied the experiences of individual women in the sciences, examining how gender affected their work, both its content and its career structure.[6] As regards content, historians of science have documented the role of (male supremacist or misogynist) gender ideology in the scientific study of females and of reproduction in biology from Aristotle to Darwin.[7] Contemporary scientists and analysts of science are continually uncovering such ideology in specific current research programs in sociobiology, developmental biology, behavioral biology, and the biology of cognition; and in some cases offering alternative approaches to that so criticized.[8] In addition researchers have begun to identify the use of gendered metaphors in the description of (non-gendered and non-sexed) natural processes, for example in the analysis of intracellular processes involving the nucleus and cytoplasm.[9] Finally, a number of feminists both in and out of the sciences have argued that establishment science is characterized by explanatory models and frameworks that privilege relationships of control in the analysis of natural processes.[10] They both argue that this represents another level of expression of gender ideology in the sciences and urge the development of other models emphasizing not control by a relatively autonomous "master" entity, but complex interaction and mutual influence among the various factors involved in natural processes, including, for some, the researcher.

This summary survey of the multiplicity of projects carried out under its aegis suggests that the feminist study of science has (at least) a double agenda, critical and constructive:

1. identification of masculinist ideologies in the content and methodologies of scientific inquiry;
2. identification of liberatory or emancipatory potential in the sciences, or at least a transformation of the sciences for feminist ends.

The first of these tasks is often presented as the task of purging the sciences of illegitimate elements introduced by the bias of practitioners; the second as the task of envisioning a new science. The first presupposes some common criteria of evaluation according to which the influence of social values is inappropriate in the sciences. The second requires criteria of acceptability other than those that validate theories feminists find objectionable.

Is there an account of inquiry which makes it possible to satisfy all aspects of this agenda? Feminist scientists have looked to philosophical accounts of scientific inquiry to ground their critiques. The philosophical traditions most often invoked either explicitly or implicitly in the gender and science literature are positivist empiricism or Kuhnian wholism. These are deployed respectively in defense of internalist or externalist accounts of knowledge or belief formation. Philosophers have typically been concerned with the normative question of good reasons, or of what counts as a genuinely justificatory argument in the sciences. The version of Kuhn that is invoked is the version that has found its way into the social studies of science, that is, a Kuhn that licenses, or even mandates, accounts of knowledge construction that appeal to causes other than what the philosopher would recognize as good reasons.[11] Each of these approaches can ground different aspects of the feminist enterprise. And indeed, reading feminist texts we find positivist forms of empiricism invoked to support the condemnation of masculine bias in the sciences as bad science, while Kuhnian wholism, or its descendants in contemporary social studies of science, are invoked to support the development of alternative points of view. These rhetorical and analytical strategies seem to put feminist science studies at odds with itself. I want to explain the apparent methodological disunity as a function of inadequate philosophical views, i.e., as a function of the inadequacies of the analytical traditions available to feminists.

Neither the normative tradition in philosophy, nor the descriptive tradition in social studies of science, is capable of satisfying the demands of the dual agenda in feminist science studies. One reason for this is that in spite of the vast differences between the traditions, they share a dichotomizing of the social and the cognitive. In this dichotomy, to account for belief by appeal to cognitive processes such as observation and inference is to leave no room for operation of the social (except in the case of false beliefs), and to account for belief in terms of social and other contextual constraints is to displace cognitive processes from their traditional role in the development of knowledge, and especially from the roles assigned them in traditional philosophies of science.[12]

Is it possible to acknowledge the social and ideological dimensions of science with a theory of inquiry that also licenses the comparative assessment of (competing) research programs? This is what I take to be a central challenge of feminist science studies. As long as the dichotomizing of social and cognitive is maintained, this double agenda of feminist and other radical scientists will continue to be frustrated.

What I propose to meet the feminist challenge, then, is a much more thoroughgoing contextualism than the one which urges us to remember that scientific inquiry occurs in a social context, or even that scientists are social actors whose interests drive their scientific work. What I urge is a contextualism which understands the cognitive processes of scientific inquiry not as opposed to the social, but as themselves social. This means that normativity, if it is possible at all, must be imposed on social processes and interactions, that is, that the rules or norms of justification that distinguish knowledge (or justified hypothesis-acceptance) from opinion must operate at the level of social as opposed to individual cognitive processes.

My argument for socializing cognition is not that it meets the feminist challenge, though it does. My argument is that this move is necessitated philosophically and that it is warranted empirically. It is philosophically necessitated by the "problem of underdetermination," the insufficiency of any given body of observational or experimental data to rule out all but one from a set of contesting explanatory hypotheses. It is empirically warranted in that scientific inquiry *is* a social rather than an individual activity. I shall elaborate on these claims in the next two sections.

2. Contextual Empiricism

One of the hallmarks of scientific knowledge is said to be its objectivity. This is a notion that has come in for a great deal of criticism. Feminists have argued both that scientific inquiry is not as objective as it purports to be and that objectivity is a mistaken ideal, reflecting masculinist preoccupations. In these polemics, objectivity itself remains unexamined, a closed box hurled back and forth between rhetorical contestants. By opening the box to illuminate its internal structure, exploring what objectivity might mean, we step aside from global accusations about science and bring feminist critique into closer contact with actual scientific inquiry. As a preliminary move, let me distinguish two senses in which we attribute objectivity to science:

1. Scientific theories provide a veridical representation of the entities and processes to be found in the world and their relations with each other.
2. Scientific inquiry involves reliance on nonarbitrary and nonsubjective (or nonidiosyncratic) criteria for accepting and rejecting hypotheses.

The claim that scientific *theories* are objective is a claim about the outcome(s) of scientific inquiry and traditionally has depended on showing that scientific *inquiry* is objective. Thus, it is the second sense of objectivity that is primary and requires analysis.

What most often counts as a nonarbitrary and nonsubjective criterion is confirmation by experiential evidence. Empiricism is the philosophical elaboration of this notion into a theory of science and, more ambitiously, a theory of knowledge generally. Feminists, in spite of seemingly adopting empiricist forms of argument to condemn masculine bias, have also reviled empiricism as a form of scientism. (This seeming cross-purposiveness is the subject of much of Sandra Harding's work.) I think the feminist rejection of empiricism is a rejection of claims made on behalf of empiricism and of science by some proponents of empiricism. Rather than explore the literature to support this claim, I will focus attention on what is valuable and tenable from the empiricist tradition.

A first step in articulating a form of empiricism that could be useful to feminists is to distinguish the normative from the descriptive functions of empiricism, as well as the two types of empiricist claim. To treat the second task first: Empiricism with respect to meaning holds that all descriptive expressions in a language must be definable in terms of sense experience. Empiricism with respect to knowledge holds that experience or experiential data are the only legitimate bases of knowledge claims. A more modest version holds that experiential or observational data are the only legitimate bases of theory and hypothesis validation in the natural sciences. This latter claim is what I take to be the commonsense core of empiricism. Notice that as I have expressed it, it is a normative claim. Critics of logical positivism gave empiricism a bad name among later thinkers about the sciences. Early critics of positivism, such as Putnam, Scriven, and Achinstein, showed that positivism or empiricism with respect to meaning collapsed upon itself. Their explorations into contemporary scientific practices along with Hanson's and Kuhn's historical investigations showed that the positivist account of scientific inquiry was *descriptively* inaccurate. They did not, however, offer arguments to show that empiricism with respect to knowledge was normatively incorrect (nor is it clear that they intended to). This did not stop many of us (their students) from concluding that empiricism was dead. On a more mature rethinking of these arguments, I think they show: (1) that empiricism with respect to meaning is both incoherent and incapable of illuminating scientific language or linguistic practice in the sciences; and (2) that while empiricism with respect to knowledge may provide constraints on justification in the empirical sciences, it is *not* a description of how inquiry proceeds or theories are developed. [13]

Simply to say that knowledge-empiricism provides constraints on justification in the sciences is not yet to articulate the principle in a way that it could be applied in that context. For example, arguments in the sciences typically go in many directions: that a hypothesis is a consequence of some theory may in certain circumstances be a good reason for accepting the hypothesis. Thus one might express the principle not in terms of exclusivity, but in terms of priority: experiential data are the least defeasible bases of hypothesis and theory validation. While this is the formulation I prefer, there are still important obstacles to articulating the principle in a way that assures its relevance to scientific practice.

The empiricist principle, even expressed in terms of defeasibility, is articulated independently of considerations about scientific practice, logical structure, and the interfacing of these with human cognitive capacities. When empiricism is applied to scientific inquiry, such considerations impose significant constraints on its interpretation and application.

The *prima facie* aims of scientific inquiry, in conjunction with features of elementary logic, introduce a set of problems collectively known as the underdetermination problem. Scientific inquiry consists largely in trying to explain observed regularities in terms of postulated underlying processes. In cases of scientific reasoning serving this aim of inquiry, e.g., that concerning relations among subatomic particles, hypotheses contain expressions ('muon') not occurring in the description of the observations and experimental results (cloud or bubble chamber photographs) serving as evidence for them. We need not draw on so esoteric an arena for an illustration. Hypotheses about causal processes in biology are supported by correlational data isolated from rich and complex arrays of phenomena. Relations between statements articulating hypotheses and statements articulating descriptions of data cannot be described syntactically or formally, because the two categories of statement contain different terms. To make the same point in a different way: data—even as represented in descriptions of observations and experimental results—do not on their own indicate that for which they can serve as evidence. Indeed, phenomena as we encounter them in nature or in the laboratory are complex and susceptible to multiple descriptions. Thus, certain aspects of a phenomenon may be highlighted over other aspects, e.g., the speed of a reaction vs. its intensity, volatility, etc. Data are never naive, but come into contact with theories already selected, structured, and organized. Hypotheses, on the other hand, are, or consist of, statements whose content always exceeds that of the statements describing the observational data.

In general, then, whether proceeding from hypothesis to data or data to hypothesis (or indeed, from experience to data or data to experience), there is a logical gap between them. This gap has been analyzed in various ways by various philosophers. I have argued that evidential relations are not autonomous or eternal truths but are constituted by the context of background assumptions in which evidence is assessed. These assumptions both facilitate inferences between data and hypotheses and make possible the organization of data.

Background assumptions are the vehicles by which social values and ideology are expressed in inquiry and become subtly inscribed in theories, hypotheses, and models defining research programs. If the first step in meeting the feminist challenge is finding an appropriately modest statement of empiricism, the second step is recognizing the role of background assumptions in evidential reasoning and in the analysis and organization of data. The combination of these two steps is the position I am calling contextual empiricism. Clearly, this is a framework that can support the feminist analysis of gender ideology in a given area of inquiry. But hasn't the need for normativity been sacrificed to this descriptive need? Does not the contextualism of contextualist empiricism effectively cancel the empiricism?

An analysis that stops with the invocation of background assumptions, without criteria for ruling out, limiting, or selecting background assumptions, does put normativity and objectivity at risk. As long as the cognitive practices of science are conceived of as in principle the practices of an individual, normativity is beyond our reach, objectivity of inquiry is a delusion, and we cannot account for the stability or the success of scientific inquiry. But my conclusion is not that scientific inquiry is not objective, but that the practices of inquiry are not individual but social. According to positivist empiricism, the relevance of evidence to hypotheses is secured by the formal, i.e., syntactic, relation between a hypothesis and an observation report. Contextual empiricism can neither offer nor require such uncontestable certainty. We can, nevertheless, require that the relevance of data to hypotheses be demonstrable. Satisfaction of this criterion involves broadening the understanding of inquiry. Contextualism demands not relativism, but a fuller account of objectivity and knowledge from which normativity can be generated.

This fuller account, I submit, can be reached by moving from analysis at the individual level to analysis at the social level. I argued in *Science as Social Knowledge* that the objectivity of scientific inquiry is a consequence of that inquiry's being a social and not an individual enterprise. I want here to summarize and supplement those arguments.

3. Social Knowledge

Several sorts of argument are involved in the development of the social knowledge thesis. Empirical arguments support the claim that science just *is* a social practice; conceptual arguments support the claim that the cognitive practices of scientific inquiry are best *understood* as social practices; and logical and philosophical arguments support the claim that if science is to be nonarbitrary and minimize subjectivity, it *must* be a social practice. The empirical arguments have been best articulated by historians, sociologists, and anthropologists of science. Two recent demonstrations of the social production of knowledge that I find particularly illuminating are provided by Sharon Traweek in *Beamtimes and Lifetimes*[14] and by Peter Galison in *How Experiments End*.[15] What studies such as these show is that, in general, what gets to count as scientific knowledge is produced through social interactions. Of course, different theorists make different hay of this conclusion. Articulating the philosophical import of the empirical claim requires additional analysis.

The philosophical claim that objectivity is a function of social interactions depends on making the case that the cognitive practices of science are social. I take those practices to be basically observation and inference. Let me say something about each.

There are several reasons to treat observation in the sciences as social. In the first place, such observation simply does not or can not consist in the perceptual and sensory experiences of a single individual. If the point of scientific inquiry is to explain observed regularities, we want assurance that an alleged regularity *is* one. This means that we treat the descriptions of observations as intersubjectively verifiable, and will not admit as potential data what is not intersubjectively verifiable. It is this requirement of intersubjectivity that grounds the principle of repeatability of observations and experiments, even though this principle may be as much honored in the breach as in the observance. The repetition of experiments often results in the modification of what we take the observed regularities to be. Negotiations among members of an experimental group settle what the results of the experiment are. In both cases, then, what the data are is an outcome of experience (nature) and social interactions. To treat experiential information as constituting data or observations is to presuppose successful intersubjective verification or validation, that is, to treat them as the products of social interactions, whether or not such interactions have actually taken place. Secondly, observational data, as noted earlier, do not consist in reports of any old observations, but in observation reports ordered and organized. This ordering rests on a consensus as to the centrality of certain categories, the boundaries of concepts and classes, the ontological and organizational commitments of a model or theory, etc. These social aspects of observation mean the impossibility of establishing a permanent and immutable (save by expansion) reservoir of data. To say that observational data are the least defeasible bases of hypothesis validation is to assign priority to observation and experience while allowing that the ordering, organization, and importance of their results—data— can change.

How might inference be thought of as social? There are at least two occasions of inference in a context of scientific inquiry: assigning evidential relevance to a set of data and evaluating a hypothesis or theory on the basis of such assignment. On the contextualist view outlined in the previous section, background assumptions are required on both occasions. Just as not any old observations will do, so will not just any old assumptions do, either. The sorts of assumptions upon which it is permissible to rely are also a function of consensus within the scientific community, are learned as part of one's apprenticeship as a scientist, and are largely invisible to practitioners within the community. Assumptions regarding evidential relevance assert some connection between the data assigned relevance and some state of affairs described by the hypothesis to which they are assigned relevance. Assumptions involved in hypothesis acceptance include both substantive assumptions about evidential relevance and methodological assumptions about the strength of evidential support required to legitimate acceptance of a hypothesis. Although invisible, or transparent, to the members of a community holding them, these assumptions are articulable and hence in principle public. This in-principle publicity makes them available to critical examination, as a consequence of which they may be abandoned, modified, or reinforced. As in the case of observation, engaging in inferences that rely on such background assumptions presupposes their adequacy to the task. This adequacy is not (or not only) ascertained by comparison with observations, for obvious reasons. What demonstrable evidential relevance amounts to in practice is a requirement that background assumptions be successfully defended against various sorts of criticism. We can read consensus in a community as signalling belief that certain fundamental assumptions have endured critical scrutiny. [16]

The intersubjective character of observation and the role of a consensual background in both observation and inference mean that critical interchange must be a part of both these cognitive activities. Individuals may be motivated to engage in this interchange by any number of specific interests. What matters from an epistemological point of view is not the interests driving individuals, nor the affective quality of the exchange (competitive, cooperative, hostile, supportive), but that critical interchange occur. It is not the individual's observation and reasoning that matter in scientific inquiry, but the community's. Individual variation is dampened through critical interactions whose aim is to eliminate the idiosyncratic and transform individual opinion and belief into reliable knowledge.

The critical interactions focused on observation are directed at the collection, analysis, and reporting of empirical data, and are relevant to the claim that a given set of observations constitutes data, that is, they transform an individual's observations into data available to and accepted as such by a community. Criticism of background assumptions is included in the more general category of conceptual criticism. Conceptual criticism can be directed at hypotheses, at background assumptions facilitating inferences, and at concepts and assumptions underlying specific classifications and orderings of observational data. It can focus on their internal coherence, their relationships with other hypotheses and theories, and on claims of evidential relevance. Criticism of background assumptions can include the sorts of criticisms directed at hypotheses, as well as observations about the empirical support (or lack of it) for such an assumption, and about untoward consequences of accepting it.

It is just these social features of observation and inference that make it possible to claim some form of objectivity for scientific inquiry in the face of the problems introduced by embracing contextualism. What we are looking for in the account of objectivity is a way to block the influence of subjective preference (read: ideology) at the level of background assumptions involved in observation and inference, and of individual variation in perception at the level of observation. The possibility of criticism does not totally eliminate subjective preference either from an individual's or from a community's practice of science. It does, however, provide a means of checking its influence in the formation of knowledge, for as long as background assumptions can be articulated and subjected to criticism from the scientific community, they can be defended, modified, or abandoned, in response to such criticism. As long as this kind of response is possible, the incorporation of hypotheses into the canon of scientific knowledge can be independent of any single individual's (or homogeneous group's) subjective preferences. Their incorporation is, instead, a function in part of the assessment of evidential support. And while this assessment is in turn a function of background assumptions, the adoption of these assumptions is not arbitrary, but is (or rather, can be) subject to the kinds of controls just discussed. This does not mean that values and interests are entirely eliminated, but that idiosyncratic ones can be.

Objectivity, then, is a characteristic of a community's practice of science, rather than of an individual's, and the practice of science is understood in a much broader sense than most discussions of the logic of scientific method suggest. Those discussions see what is central to scientific method as being the complex of activities which constitute hypothesis testing through comparison with experiential data—in principle, if not always in reality, an activity of individuals. What I have argued here is that scientific method involves as an equally central aspect the subjection of hypotheses, and the background assumptions in light of which they seem to be supported by data, to varieties of conceptual criticism. Because background assumptions can be and frequently are transparent to the members of the scientific community for which they are background, because unreflective acceptance of such assumptions can come to define what it is to be a member of such a community (thus making criticism impossible), effective criticism of background assumptions requires the presence and expression of alternative points of view. We can see why some scientists would be puzzled by the charges that scientific inquiry is not objective. To the extent that members of a scientific community engage in the sorts of interactions described, they are seeking to establish the objectivity of data and inference. But they err in thinking of the individual as the sole locus of variation, idiosyncrasy, or subjectivity. Scientific communities are themselves constituted by adherence to certain values and assumptions, which go unexamined by a critical process involving only members of a community so defined.

The formal requirement of *demonstrable evidential relevance* (of data to hypotheses) constitutes a standard of rationality and acceptability independent of and external to any particular research program or scientific theory. The satisfaction of this standard by any program or theory is secured, as has been argued, by intersubjective criticism. The specification of demonstrability, however, will always be within a particular context. Both observational data and their evidential relevance are constituted in a context of background assumptions. This means that the empiricist principle can be applied within a context, but not independently of contextual considerations. While it is not possible to apply the empiricist principle across contexts, the requirement on demonstrability means that we can generate additional criteria for objectivity by reflecting on the conditions which make for appropriate criticism. These criteria operate on communities, hence on contexts.

Earlier, I invoked the idea of *effective* criticism. Effective criticism produces change. A community's practice of inquiry is objective to the extent it facilitates such transformative criticism. At least four criteria can be identified as necessary to achieve the transformative dimension of critical discourse:

1. there are recognized avenues for the criticism of evidence, of methods, and of assumptions and reasoning;
2. the community as a whole responds to such criticism;
3. there exist shared standards which critics can invoke;
4. intellectual authority is shared equally among qualified practitioners.

Each of these criteria requires at least a brief gloss.

1. Recognized avenues for criticism. The avenues for the presentation of criticism ought to be the same standard and public forums in which "original research" is presented: journals, conferences, and so forth. In addition, critical activities should be given the same or nearly the same weight as is given to "original research": effective criticism that advances understanding being as valued as original research that opens up new domains for understanding; pedestrian, routine criticism being valued comparably to pedestrian and routine "original research." A complex set of processes in the institutions of contemporary science in the industrial and post-industrial world works against this requirement.

2. *Community response.* This criterion requires that the beliefs of the scientific community as a whole and over time change in response to the critical discussion taking place within it. What is required is not that individuals capitulate to criticism, but that community members pay attention to and participate in the critical discussion taking place and that the assumptions that govern their group activities remain logically sensitive to it.

3. *Shared standards.* In order for criticism to be relevant to a position, it must appeal to something accepted by those who hold the position criticized. Participants in a dialogue must share some referring terms, some principles of inference, and some values or aims to be served by the shared activity. Thus, shared elements are necessary for the identification of points of agreement, points of disagreement, and what would count as resolving the latter or destabilizing the former. Similarly, alternative theories must be perceived to have some bearing on the concerns of a scientific community in order to obtain a hearing. This cannot occur at the whim of individuals but must be a function of public standards or criteria to which members of the scientific community are or feel themselves bound. Such standards can include both substantive principles and epistemic, as well as social, values. The point is not so much that individuals spontaneously act out their allegiance to these standards but that they acknowledge their relevance to the evaluation of cognitive practices in their community of inquiry. It may be possible to identify some standards that are shared by all scientific communities. While I doubt this, some are certainly shared by several, so that scientific communities (or the sets of standards that characterize them) stand in a family relation to one another. These sets are local and they may contain elements in some tension with each other. Thus, standards themselves can be criticized by appealing to other standards.

Standards do not provide a deterministic theory of theory choice. [17] Nevertheless, it is the subscription to the existence of standards that makes the individual members of a scientific community responsible to something besides themselves. It is the open-ended and nonconsistent nature of these standards that allows for pluralism in the sciences and for the continued presence, however subdued at times, of minority voices.

4. *Equality of intellectual authority.* This Habermasian criterion is intended to disqualify a community in which a set of assumptions dominates by virtue of the political power of its adherents. What this criterion requires is that the persuasive effects of reasoning and argument be secured by properties internal to them (rather than in properties, such as social power, of those who are propounding them), and that every member of the community be regarded as capable of contributing to its constructive and critical dialogue. The point of satisfying this requirement is to ensure exposure of hypotheses to the broadest range of criticism. Whenever one mentions the intrusion of political power into scientific inquiry, the red flag of Lysenkoism is raised. But the exclusion of women and members of certain racial minorities from scientific education and the scientific professions in the United States also constitutes a violation of this criterion. Assumptions about race and about sex are not imposed on scientists in the United States in the way assumptions about the inheritability of acquired traits were in the Soviet Union. Many scholars have analyzed how assumptions about sex and gender structure a number of research programs in biology, behavioral, and other sciences. Other scholars have documented the role of racial assumptions in the sciences. Yet others have studied the interaction between racial and gender ideologies in the sciences. The long standing devaluation of women's voices and those of members of racial minorities means that such assumptions have been protected from critical scrutiny. Thus a community must not only treat its acknowledged members as equally capable of providing persuasive and decisive reasons, and must do more than be open to the expression of multiple points of view; it must also take active steps to ensure that alternative points of view are developed enough to be a source of criticism. That is, not only must potentially dissenting voices not be discounted, they must be cultivated.

Taking these criteria as measures of objectivity, objectivity is dependent upon the depth and scope of the transformative interrogation which occurs in any given scientific community. Objectivity is therefore a gradational property and as the maximal fulfillment of the above four conditions, exists only as an ideal realized more or less imperfectly in different scientific communities. Knowledge and objectivity, on this view, are identified as the outcomes of social interactions, and hence, located not in individuals but in communities. Individuals must participate in these interactions in order that knowledge be produced but their objectivity consists in such participation, and not in any special cognitive attitude, e.g., impartiality or distance, they bear to proposed objects of knowledge. While the sciences and scientific communities aspire to objectivity, their having aspirations should not be mistaken for satisfaction of the conditions for objectivity. Nevertheless, the community-wide process that tests background assumptions ensures (or can ensure) that the hypotheses ultimately accepted as supported by some set of data do not reflect a single individual's (or a single same-minded group's) idiosyncratic assumptions about the natural world. To say that a theory or hypothesis was accepted on the basis of objective methods does not entitle us to say it is true, but that it reflects the critically achieved consensus of the scientific community. In the absence of some form of privileged access to transempirical (unobservable) phenomena, it is not clear we should hope for anything better.

4. Conclusion

Let me conclude by returning to the problem with which I began: the problem of finding an approach to scientific inquiry that could accommodate apparently conflicting aims of feminist science studies. I claimed that contextual empiricism (supplemented by the social account of scientific knowledge) is a philosophical approach that can meet the challenge presented by feminist science studies. The challenge is to provide an account that can ground both the critical and the constructive projects of feminism. Contextual empiricism in its extended form does so.

The normative dimension of this view mandates at one level an examination of the evidential structure of theories. While this means looking for observational and experimental data at the outset, understanding the relevance of the data requires examining the background assumptions involved in the analysis and organization of data and the background assumptions involved in facilitating reasoning between data and hypotheses. The contextual or descriptive aspect of contextual empiricism means that discovering such assumptions, even discovering that they are laden with social values and ideology, is not grounds for condemning as bad science any work in which they play a role. There are certainly cases of bad science among research programs feminists reject. But if they are bad it cannot simply be because background assumptions (even value-laden ones) play a role in them, but because of methodological mistakes or perhaps because of a dogmatic attitude toward those assumptions. Discovering such assumptions does make them available to critical examination and potentially to transformation or even rejection. As we have seen, the underdetermination of hypotheses by evidence means that there may always be other ways of interpreting and explaining a given set of data. This is not just a point about the multiplicity of logically possible empirically equivalent hypotheses. As theories shift in one domain, background assumptions in another may also shift, requiring modification or reinterpretation of the data in that domain. Or the gratuitousness of some background assumption may become clear when it is confronted with an alternative. This occurred when physical anthropologists and primatologists questioned the universality of male dominance, and the assumption that the behaviors that provided selection pressures for evolutionary change in the hominoid and hominid lines were male behaviors. [18]

The community-level criteria enable us to make comparative judgments across the contexts created by research programs or traditions. Even if two such traditions treat data in incommensurable ways, it is possible to compare the social interactions involved in knowledge construction in the two contexts. It is a requirement (or an application of the requirement to our contemporary social situation) that feminists participate in the social processes that constitute knowledge construction *and* that the relevant research communities respond. The community level criteria make more subtle accounts of the failure of objectivity possible. For example, in some aspects of behavioral neuroendocrinology, researchers have responded to feminist criticism by eliminating value-laden language (sissy and tomboy), and by attempting to develop more rigorous data-gathering procedures. [19] However, for a time the general community (as represented by *Science* magazine, as well as by the propounder of the claim) ignored (data-based) criticism of a claim about differences in size of the male and female corpus callosum. [20] In the first instance the second criterion (of responsiveness) is satisfied; in the second it is violated. The fourth criterion requires that socially significant groups be included in the scientific community to ensure both criticism from all possible points of view and the incorporation into scientific debate of the broadest range of observational data possible. This criterion enables us to condemn the exclusion of women and members of racial minorities from the practice of science as an epistemological shortcoming as well as a political injustice.

That there are standards or values apart from empirical adequacy means that not every hypothesis that can be stretched to fit some set of data is equivalent to every other hypothesis. The multiplicity of standards recognized as relevant to the assessment of theories, hypotheses, and research programs means nevertheless that at least some such other ways may be equally supportable. Indeed, in many cases alternative theoretical approaches are required to reveal the assumptions structuring a current powerful or popular research program. Feminist research programs can involve selection from, recombination of, and introduction of new values and standards into the study of a given bit of nature. Most accounts of objectivity work against the possibility of multiple accounts of some set of natural phenomena. The one offered here, by contrast, supports this possibility. Thus the constructive project is both licensed by and subject to the same normative constraints as license the critical project.

What it does not do is grant to some form of feminism or to any other social or political program an exclusive grant to truth or correctness. The view of inquiry outlined here means that to the extent we speak of knowledge, it is, as I indicated at the outset, partial and fragmentary. The requirement that demonstrability be secured by intersubjective criticism has the consequence that knowledge is constituted by the interaction of opposed styles and/or points of view. While some perspectives may be discredited (for failing to realize any of the partially shared goals of scientific communities), no single one can be privileged over all others. Within any given community, some single perspective may be privileged over others for a time, but exclusive allegiance to this perspective in the face of (inevitable) criticism violates the second criterion of objectivity for communities listed above.

Finally, I think this approach is faithful to a fundamental insight of the feminist analysts of science: that ideological and value issues are interwoven with empirical ones in scientific inquiry. What is important is not that they be banished, but that we have (1) analytic tools that enable us to identify them, and (2) community practices that can (in the long run) regulate their role in the development of knowledge.

NOTES

Reprinted, with minor changes, from *A Mind of Her Own*, edited by Louise Antony and Charlotte Witt (Boulder, Col.: Westview Press, 1991), by permission of the author and Westview Press.

1. Helen E. Longino and Evelynn A. Hammonds, "Conflicts and Tensions in the Feminist Study of Gender and Science" in Marianne Hirsch and Evelyn Fox Keller, eds., *Conflicts in Feminism* (New York, N.Y.: Routledge, 1990), 164–183.

2. Helen E. Longino, *Science as Social Knowledge* (Princeton, N.J.: Princeton University Press, 1990).

3. Londa Schiebinger, *The Mind Has No Sex?* (Cambridge, Mass.: Harvard University Press, 1989).

4. Margaret Rossiter, *Women Scientists in America*, (Baltimore, Md.: The Johns Hopkins University Press, 1982).

5. Evelyn F. Keller, *Reflections on Gender and Science* (New Haven, Conn.: Yale University Press, 1985).

6. Pnina Abir-Am and Dorinda Outram, eds., *Uneasy Careers and Intimate Lives: Women in Science, 1789–1979* (New Brunswick, N.J.: Rutgers University Press, 1987).

7. Ludmilla Jordanova, *Sexual Visions* (Madison, Wis.: University of Wisconsin Press, 1990).

8. Ruth Bleier, *Science and Gender* (Elmsford, N.Y.: Pergamon Press, 1984); Anne Fausto Sterling, *Myths of Gender* (New York, N.Y.: Basic Books, 1985).

9. Gender and Biology Study Group, "The Importance of Feminist Critique for Contemporary Cell Biology," *Hypatia* 3 (1988): 61–76.

10. Keller, *Reflections*.

11. While Kuhn, himself, rejects this interpretation of his work, and while several steps of argumentation are needed to give it this interpretation, he continues to be cited as the intellectual and philosophical legitimator of the sociological approach.

12. Different but typical statements of the sociological approach can be found in Harry Collins, "An Empirical Relativist Programme in the Sociology of Scientific Knowledge" in *Science Observed*, Karin Knorr-Cetina and Michael Mulkay, eds. (London: Sage, 1983), 85–113, and Bruno Latour, *Science in Action* (Cambridge, Mass.: Harvard University Press, 1988). Statements of the philosophical approach include Ernan McMullin, "Values in Science," in *PSA 1982*, vol. 2, P. D. Asquith and T. Nickles, eds. (East Lansing, Mich.: Philosophy of Science Association, 1983), 3–28, and Robert Richardson, "Biology and Ideology: The Interpenetration of Science and Values," *Philosophy of Science*, 51 (1984): 396–421.

13. This "commonsense core" of empiricism is not the view Sandra Harding takes to task in *The Science Question in Feminism* (Ithaca, N.Y.: Cornell University Press, 1986) under the label "feminist empiricism." What she criticizes is the claim that methods currently in use in the natural sciences are sufficient to eliminate masculinist or other bias in the sciences. But this core empiricism says nothing about methods currently in use. Furthermore, either "methods" means methods, e.g., mathematical modeling, current experimental techniques, titration techniques, etc., in which case feminist empiricism is not the same as empiricism; or it means observation and inference (what philosophers mean by method). But empiricism does not claim that observation is sufficient for the validation of scientific claims, but that it is necessary.

14. Sharon Traweek, *Beamtimes and Lifetimes* (Cambridge, Mass.: Harvard University Press, 1988).

15. Peter Galison, *How Experiments End* (Chicago, Ill.: University of Chicago Press, 1987). For a philosophical discussion of the interdependence of researchers,

see John Hardwig, "Epistemic Dependence," *Journal of Philosophy* 82 (1985): 335–349, esp. pp. 345–349.

16. Obviously such consensus can exist without its presupposition being satisfied. Consensus may be produced by processes other than critical discourse, e.g., threat or persuasion.

17. This point was well articulated by Thomas Kuhn in "Objectivity, Value Judgment, and Theory Choice" in *The Essential Tension* (Chicago, Ill.: University of Chicago Press, 1977), 320–339.

18. Cf. Nancy Tanner, *Human Evolution* (Cambridge, Eng.: Cambridge University Press, 1981); and Adrienne Zihlman, "Women in Evolution, Part II," *Signs* 4 (1978): 4–20.

19. Anke Ehrhardt, "Gender Differences: A Biosocial Perspective" in *Nebraska Symposium on Motivation*, vol. 32, ed. Theo Sonderreger, (Lincoln, Neb.: University of Nebraska Press, 1985), 37–58; and David Goldfoot and Deborah Neff, "On Measuring Behavioral Sex Differences in Social Contexts," in *Handbook of Behavioral Neurobiology*, vol. 7, ed. N. Adler, D. Pfaff, and R. W. Goy (New York, N.Y.: Plenum Press, 1985), 767–783.

20. Ruth Bleier, "A Decade of Feminist Criticism in the Natural Sciences" *Signs* 14 (1988): 182–195.

21. I wish to thank Louise Antony, Ernan McMullin, and Charlotte Witt for their comments on an earlier draft, and those who responded to its spoken versions for their helpful criticism and observations. Anne Figert suggested the title.

THE BALLAD OF PONS AND FLEISCHMANN: EXPERIMENT AND NARRATIVE IN THE (UN)MAKING OF COLD FUSION

Thomas F. Gieryn

Cold fusion is rather dead these days, or worse, boring. People scarcely remember Stanley Pons and Martin Fleischmann, and Utah once again means Mormons or good skiing. Most people would rather not hear about those startling claims—Nuclear Fusion in a Bottle! Energy Panacea!—that once made front-page news. These claims, after two years or so, have stabilized not as facts but jokes. Now even the jokes have gone stale.

Death did not come quickly for the claim to cold fusion, even though early returns were far from auspicious. From the moment Pons and Fleischmann first announced their discovery at a Salt Lake City press conference on March 24, 1989, scientists responded everywhere with incredulity. Attempts at replication began immediately, and many yielded disconfirming findings that were instantly transmitted to laboratories around the world via electronic mail and fax machines. Yet controversy continued at fever pitch well into the fall of 1989, and even after months of scrutiny, Pons and Fleischmann are not alone in the belief that cold fusion is real, a fact. But the number of true believers today is small and dwindling, and many scientists still pursuing "cold fusion" research have abandoned essential elements of Pons and Fleischmann's original assumptions and experimental procedures. As 1991 dawned, cold fusion as first described looks so obviously wrong that it seems odd that closure was so long in coming. If cold fusion is such a joke, why did so many for so long view the claims as no laughing matter? My analysis goes back to the first year in the life of an extraordinary claim that says a lot about what is ordinary in the practice of contemporary science.

It may not be so difficult to explain how cold fusion was kept alive for as long as it was; indeed, after what is reported here, the more challenging problem may be to explain how closure on its falsity was *ever* achieved. An expectation that the facticity of Pons and Fleischmann's claim could have been settled *quickly* is grounded in two misperceptions of science: first, that replication is a straightforward and decisive means to adjudicate experimental claims; second, that the fate of some scientific claims rests solely in the hands of scientists. I argue that Pons and Fleischmann were able to extend the life of their claim by contesting the fidelity of replication attempts that yielded disconfirming results. More significantly, while this case of Harry Collins's experimenters' regress (Collins, 1975; 1985) went on, cold fusion moved out from laboratories and e-mail networks to become part of a narrative that got everybody *else* interested and converted many to a belief in its reality. The Ballad of Pons and Fleischmann, a dramatic tale of where cold fusion came from, who Pons and Fleischmann really are, and what cold fusion means to all of us, sustained the viability of the original claim even as experimental evidence (and prominent scientists) overwhelmingly went against it. Broadcasts of this tale in the mass media gave good grounds for accepting Pons and Fleischmann as competent and credible experimenters, and raised hopes for cold fusion so high that contrary experimental results from scientists could not *in themselves* kill it. Death would come, I suggest, only when the Ballad of Pons and Fleischmann itself is shown to be just as much a fiction as the experimental claim.

1. Ambiguous Replications

Here is what Pons and Fleischmann reported at the first cold fusion press conference:

> We've established a sustained nuclear fusion reaction by means which are considerably simpler than existing conventional techniques. Deuterium, which is a component of heavy water, is driven into a metal rod . . . to such an extent that fusion between these components, these deuterons in the heavy water, are fused to form a single new atom. With this process, there is a considerable release of energy. We've demonstrated that this can be sustained on its own. In other words, much more energy is coming out that we are putting in. . . . The heat we measure can only be accounted for by nuclear reactions. The heat is so intense that it cannot be explained by any chemical process that is known. . . . The evidence [for fusion] is that we have direct measurements of neutrons by measuring the gamma radiation which builds up in a tank. . . . In addition, there is a build up of tritium in the cell which we measure with a scintillation counter.

In the weeks and months following this revelation, scientists at Texas A&M, Georgia Tech, University of Washington, Stanford, Minnesota, Brookhaven, Los Alamos, Hungary, Italy, and the Soviet Union all report aspects of cold fusion confirmed, and Hagelstein of MIT begins a theoretical explanation of the findings. But then Brookhaven and Georgia Tech change their minds and report no confirmation, Yale finds no signals of fusion, nor do chemists at Cal Tech, nor do other scientists at British Columbia, Bell Labs, Argonne National Laboratory, Iowa State; a second MIT group denies the existence of the phenomenon their colleagues were beginning to explain, and a Cal Tech physicist shows how cold fusion is theoretically impossible. Which experiments should one believe? The squabbling chemists and physicists behave just as Harry Collins's concept of "experimenters' regress" would have them behave. They negotiate the reality of cold fusion by negotiating the *fidelity* of attempts to replicate Pons and Fleischmann's initial experiment. To an agnostic observer looking at the early weeks of the controversy, it appears that the criterion used to decide the fidelity of a replication are the *results* of those experiments. Reports of successful replication of cold fusion are described by Pons, Fleischmann, and their friends as competent and thus credible, but dismissed by skeptics as incompetent. Reports of failed attempts to detect signs of cold fusion are dismissed by Pons and Fleischmann as "not what *we* did," but critics define them as faithfully following the Utah recipe and the strictures of good scientific practice.

A remarkable display of experimenters' regress signaled the first birthday of Pons and Fleischmann's press conference. A Utah colleague of Pons, physicist Michael H. Salamon, published results in *Nature* (Salamon et al., 1990) of what could be considered the most faithful replication of the original experiment: he used Pons's own experimental apparatus—*his* palladium electrode, *his* deuterium, *his* jar. For this reason, an editor at *Nature* said that "special significance" should be attached to this result (Lindley, 1990). "We did not see a peep. There was not an iota, not a sniff, of conventional fusion occurring. We saw no neutrons or gamma rays that could be attributed to a fusion process" (Salamon in Dagani, 1990). Case closed? Not at all: Fritz G. Will, head of the National Cold Fusion Institute in Utah, opened things up once again by suggesting that "Experimental conditions prevailing in those experiments [the ones monitored by Salamon] were not suitable to finding the phenomenon" (in Johnson, 1990). In particular, Will mentioned humidity as a variable laboratory condition that might affect any replication try—even those using Pons's own apparatus.

One avenue for prolonging experimenters' regress is to expand conceivably forever the "apparatus" *relevant* for an experiment: Salamon *thought* that he was using Pons's own equipment, but (according to Will), he failed to "use" one important feature of the environment that now becomes part of the laboratory conditions for this experiment: humidity. Pons himself, at the first cold fusion birthday party in Salt Lake City, responded to Salamon's putatively negative replication first by reasserting the original claim ("we observe the generation of low levels of nuclear particles and nuclear reaction products from the cells simultaneously") and second by accusing *Nature* of bias against cold fusion (evidenced by their publishing Salamon's findings as if they resulted from a competently performed experiment) and demanding retraction.

At some of these trials of strength (Latour, 1987:78), claims to cold fusion seem to become less real, on the verge of extinction except in cartoons, as the network of enlisted allies gets shorter. Pons and Fleischmann are hooted out of a May 1989 meeting of the American Physical Society in Baltimore, where disconfirming replications are overwhelmingly defined as competent. In November 1989, a panel of chemists, physicists, and engineers brought together by the Department of Energy's Energy Research Advisory Board (ERAB) recommends that no special funding programs be established to further consider Pons and Fleischmann's cold fusion. The Institute for Scientific Information reports that since April 1989, citations to the first Pons and Fleischmann published paper have run 52 percent against the claim, 27 percent in support of the claim and 21 percent neutral; the strictly experimental papers go against cold fusion by a four-to-one ratio (ISI, 1990). On 29 March 1990, *Nature* publishes an editorial titled "Farewell (not fond) to cold fusion" (p. 365), writing "the cold fusion fuss is discreditable to the scientific community as a whole . . . it has licensed magic in . . . that reports of remarkable phenomena—it could next be unicorns again—claim equal credence even when they fly in the face of expectation."

But these trials do not sever *all* associations forged among Pons, Fleischmann, University of Utah administrators, palladium, deuterium, 3He, gamma rays, heat, and lots of other human and nonhuman actants. They merely squeeze the network so that it pushes out in different directions, getting longer by enrolling *other* allies such as humidity levels in laboratories, owners of palladium mines, or electrochemists eager to put their specialty and their careers in the limelight. After a year, stalwart chemists and physicists aligned with the reality of cold fusion remain in place, including Huggins from Stanford. Appleby and Bockris from Texas A&M

modify details of their claims but continue to invest time and money in the experimental pursuit of cold fusion. The Electric Power Research Institute has offered to spend $1 to $2 million that year on cold fusion research, and the State of Utah has pumped in $5 million to set up the National Cold Fusion Institute. New scientific allies have joined earlier converts, all claiming something that extends the reality of the claim: McKubre of Stanford Research Institute International, Wadsworth from Utah, Schoessow from Florida, Yeager from Case Western Reserve ("There is a growing consensus that you can't explain the phenomena by errors"), Oriani from Minnesota, Storms from Los Alamos National Laboratory ("we can safely say the effect is real"; "we can put aside the question of whether it is a real phenomenon or not"), Scott from Oak Ridge National Laboratory and countless others from India, Japan (where forty government-funded groups are doing cold fusion research), Finland, the Soviet Union, Mexico, Spain, Brazil, and Sri Lanka. Nobel laureate Julian Schwinger of UCLA says that "it is no longer possible to dismiss the reality of cold fusion" (see McDonald, 1990; Bishop, 1990).

Neither side can claim absolute victory. Pons and Fleischmann's experiments are too weak to dissociate the long network linking the ERAB Panel, conventional theory in physics, many physicists, *Nature*, disconfirming replications, and the American Physical Society. But disconfirming experiments are too weak as well to dissociate once and for all the network that extends outward from Pons's Utah lab to scattered outposts worldwide. Reality is relative indeed: whether cold fusion is real or not depends upon the heterogenous network you are in and each seems impervious to dissociation by the other's experiments.

2. The Strength of Narrative: Assigning Credibility and Interesting Everybody

Is there escape from experimenters' regress? If *results* are the only criteria for assigning competence and credibility to experiments and to those who do them, then we should indeed give up the wait for closure. But other criteria, outside the experiments themselves, are available. Françqis Lyotard looks to narrative—the discourse of stories, histories, myths, biographies, legends, and tales of the future. The irony is obvious: fiction (long ago relegated by science to the space for non-knowledge) is seen by Lyotard as a vehicle for assigning competence and credibility to some experimental claims but not to others. "Not only the truth of a scientist's statement but also his competence is at stake" in debates like those surrounding cold fusion. "Narratives allow the society in which [legends and tales] are told . . . to define its criteria of competence," and "they thus define what has the right to be said and done in the culture in question" (Lyotard, 1984: 24, 20, 23). Stories provide grounds for people (including scientists) to decide that some experiments are competent and credible while others are not; narratives provide interpretive contexts that give meaning (significance, legitimacy) to neutron counters, laboratory humidity, tritium, experimental claims, physical theory, and human observers.

This point is nicely made in Frank Sulloway's interpretation of the enduring facticity of Freud's psychoanalysis. How do Freudians sustain the reality of their master's claims? In stories told by his epigones, Freud becomes the classic *hero*, who survives isolation in the scientific wilderness, returns with absolutely original truths only to be greeted by rejection and derision by an unprepared society, who persists because of strong conviction that he has the truth, demonstrates unambiguously miraculous cures, single-handedly invents pure psychology by casting out biology, and so revolutionizes the world (Sulloway, 1979: ch. 13). The myth of Freud-as-hero sustains the faithful but also enhances the credibility of his claims among other, bigger audiences. We are offered grounds for believing psychoanalysis and for accepting Freud above all as the most competent explorer of the psyche, not experimental grounds but narrative grounds.

One way out of the impasse of experimenters' regress is not through *experimental* replication but *literary* replication, as James Secord has called it (1989:347). Secord considers the case of Andrew Crosse, the early nineteenth-century geologist who, while using the newly invented voltaic cell to reproduce certain crystalline patterns, began to see mites (acari) emerge apparently quite spontaneously in his apparatus. Were the acari "real," and could life come from electricity itself? Most natural philosophers of the day thought not, and disconfirming experiments were soon reported, but Crosse's acari (like cold fusion) did not die quickly. They survived for a time among some electrical researchers and large segments of a British public increasingly curious about scientific matters. If, as some believed, the voltaic cell was the cause of mites, then the distribution and persistence of that belief itself was caused by a second new technology of the day: the steam press. Widespread literary replication in popular newspapers announcing the discovery of the acari (including a misquotation that seemed to lend Faraday's support to the mite's electrical existence) took Crosse's claim outside the world of experimental natural philosophy, where it could live on relatively immune from disconfirming experiments. For Secord, the case illustrates a contest between experiment (and the scientists who do them) and the popular press (with its huge audiences) for cultural authority in deciding matters of fact. For our consideration of cold fusion, the acari case illustrates how judgments of competence and credibility are not settled through experimental conduct or results, but through (in this case) newspaper stories about the iconoclastic Crosse who, like Freud, is cast as a revered and thoroughly believable scientific hero.

So: out of the laboratory and into the world! Tell, and retell, a story about cold fusion. Give a heart-warming history and a millennial future to associations forged among palladium, deuterium, neutrons, heat, calorimeters, Pons, Fleischmann, and the University of Utah. Write a biography that dresses up Pons and Fleischmann in something more fashionable, more heroic than white lab coats. Cast the moment of discovery as climax to an epic struggle, and replicate the story in newspapers and on television throughout the world. If it worked for Freud and for acari, perhaps it will work for cold fusion as well.

Where would such stories come from? In the case of Freud, Sulloway says that psychoanalytic groupies become the storytellers, replicating the myth of the hero as a means to defend and spread their faith. Pons and Fleischmann have no epigones yet, nor are they skilled in the metier of myth production. Their discourse is scientific, with words like "3He," "calorimetry," and "hydrogenated metals" that bore audiences outside the lab. Fortunately for them, others take up cold fusion and put it in its narrative state. Reporters flock to Salt Lake City for a scoop. Pons and Fleischmann sit back and watch their claim become front-page news, a story so good that millions are suddenly interested, a story that makes us trust them as competent and sincere interpreters of nature, a scenario that would make anybody want—even need—cold fusion. Scientists are not the only ones who make claims into facts, and they never do it alone. Here, maybe, is a force finally capable of dissociating the enemies of cold fusion, accomplishing what their disconfirming experiments could not. Invent narratives so compelling that the *whole world* aligns itself on the side of cold fusion. Nine themes make up the Ballad of Pons and Fleischmann, as I tell the story with help from the journalists:

2.1 ENERGY PANACEA: FREE AT LAST!

So who cares about a little tritium, heat, and a few neutrons in a Utah laboratory? Nobody. Who cares about a source of energy that is

"Nuclear fusion, the power that fuels the sun, is regarded as science's next great frontier in developing new sources of energy" (*Denver Post*,

cheap, limitless, safe, and clean? Everybody. Connect Pons and Fleischmann to the epic struggle to conquer nature. The little glass jar with heavy water, some wire, and a palladium electrode now stands at the climax of an endless human search for an energy source that can power modern life. What do we have now? Fossil fuels like coal, natural gas, and oil evoke acid rain, exhaustion in our grandchildren's generation, and politically unreliable foreigners. Then there is nuclear *fission*, with its memories of Three Mile Island and Chernobyl. But Pons and Fleischmann become Ra, harnessing the power of the sun with the help of deuterium, palladium, and electrochemical skill, where previous attempts to produce usable power have all been dirty or expensive or dangerous. Experiment is translated into energy panacea: no radioactive wastes, no acid rain killing forests and eating statues, no risk of explosion, dependent only upon obviously abundant sea water. Cold fusion is not a finding nor a revision of theory: it is the climax to the greatest story ever told— humans against the elements.

3/24/89). "Many say they believe fusion could replace fossil fuels like coal, gas and oil" (*Int'l Herald Tribune*, 3/24/89). "Scientists have sought a practical application of fusion for about 35 years. Existing nuclear reactors are powered by nuclear fission" (*Denver Post*, 3/24/89). "Fusion is a far 'cleaner' reaction than fission, producing very little radioactive waste. Its raw material, deuterium, is abundant in sea water. And fusion reactors are expected to be inherently safer than fission reactors because the fusion process would shut down automatically if anything went wrong" (*Financial Times*, 3/23/89). "Their discovery could eventually lead to widespread use of nuclear fusion as a major source of electricity, a goal of scientists for decades. It would mean a virtually unlimited supply of cheap, clean fuel" (*Cornell Daily Sun*, 4/7/89).

2.2 WHERE OTHERS HAVE TRIED BUT FAILED

Others have sought to harness the power of the sun and become Ra, and Pons and Fleischmann are not the only ones hoping to bring this energy to earth. But others have failed to deliver the goods with

"[They] have apparently succeeded in doing in a simple chemistry laboratory what has not yet been achieved by gigantic nuclear research projects costing hundreds of millions a year" (*Financial Times*,

their "hot" fusion, despite having all the amenities that Pons and Fleischmann lack. These two are heroes and the rest are goats, and what makes this story so good for selling newspapers is that the goats are rich kids with $2 billion toys (gigantic magnets, lasers). The goats try to capture the sun the hard way, the *hot* way, but it is very expensive to duplicate those high temperatures on earth. Princeton alone wants $445 million to build a Compact Ignition Tokamak machine to do the job, with little assurance that we really will get energy from terrestrial hot fusion. Our heroes do it the simple way, with tabletop toys, no huge magnets or lasers, no sunlike temperatures on earth. Better than the sun, it's cold fusion in Utah. Pons and Fleischmann beat the rich kids at their own game, reducing all their expensive toys and millions of tax dollars to a massive technological headache. We Americans root for underdogs, and it is almost un-American to *like* the rich kids with their expensive toys. Sometimes poor kids from the wrong side of the tracks make good.

3/23/89). "It would circumvent many of the difficulties that have made the world's $2-billion fusion research effort a massive technological headache" (*Toronto Globe & Mail*, 3/24/89). "Scientists for years have been using powerful magnets, lasers and sunlike temperatures in hopes of fusing atoms together and thereby unleashing their energy. Meanwhile in Utah, chemists Pons and Fleischmann claimed Thursday that they could manage the feat in a room-temperature flask containing two metal rods, a derivative of sea water and a bit of electricity" (*San Jose Mercury News*, 3/25/89). "Hopes for achieving 'break-even' fusion by magnetic confinement in the U.S. are being concentrated on a machine called the Compact Ignition Tokamak. This $445 million device is proposed for construction at Princeton University. But the Bush Administration hasn't proposed to finance it at the rate scientists hope for" (*Wall Street Journal*, 3/24/89). "Distinguished professor of chemistry Cheves T. Walling, for instance, says the electrolytic fusion 'looks a helluva lot more promising than the things the physicists have managed to do with magnetically contained plasma or enormous lasers'" (*Chemical and Engineering News*, 4/3/89).

2.3 DISCOVERY LORE 1: DOGGED NORMAL SCIENCE

In the ballad of P&F, narrative themes sometimes come as couplets, juxtaposed stories that hold each other up. Here is half a story about where the discovery of cold fusion came from: it didn't happen overnight. P&F worked hard, patiently, and properly to unlock the secrets of the sun and bring us an energy panacea. Look: they didn't start these experiments yesterday. They have been at it for many years. And they did not start out trying to become Ra. Like any good scientist, they noticed little anomalies in some Kuhnian paradigm and tried to get them to fit into the puzzle, but after testing and fitting, at Pons's lab at night and on weekends, they came up with a whole new puzzle. Nothing fly-by-night about these results: after the first positive signs were in, they tinkered for another five years until they perfected the cells and got them to put out four times the energy they put in, over and over again. Just a couple of hardworking, patient experimentalists doing normal science, convincing their skeptical selves, then submitting findings to a journal for peer review, then seeking grant support via another peer review. Our heroes did all that: science is hard, nature grudgingly reveals her secrets, your peers are demanding. But heroes can overcome these obstacles through

"The simple and inexpensive process, ignored by nuclear physicists was developed more than 15 [misprint: read 5] years ago by Fleischmann and Pons" (*San Francisco Chronicle*, 3/24/89). "The two of them originally tried the experiments because they had seen anomalies in certain processes— Fleischmann in separating hydrogen isotopes and Pons in isotopic isolation in electrodes" (*Science*, 3/31/89). "For years, the two chemists had been intrigued by what they termed inexplicably 'odd' data from separate research efforts. . . . During the next five years, they improved, tested and retested the procedure on weekends and at night in Pons' lab" (*San Jose Mercury News*, 3/24/89). "They have experimented with the process for more than five years and have perfected it to the point that they got out four times as much energy as they put in" (*Los Angeles Times*, 4/5/89). "Two scientists' claim of a breakthrough in fusion energy had been scrutinized by at least two other scientists, who endorsed its publication. . . . But Pons and Fleischmann already had secured publication of their work in the Journal of Electroanalytical Chemistry" (*San Jose Mercury News*, 3/28/89). "When they ran out of money earlier this year, they applied for a grant from the DoE's division of perseverance. They made sure that what they had was real, and waited until others told them it was real.

2.4 DISCOVERY LORE 2: EUREKA!

So how do a couple of normal scientists do something that all the other normal scientists have failed to do? This is the other side of the discovery story: something must make them abnormal, so they could see what nobody else could see. Jack Daniels! How many times, when people tell stories about how they decided to do something crazy, do they use liquor as an interpretive device? The discovery was not made at P's lab bench but at his kitchen table—no electrodes or deuterium in sight—under the influence of good Tennessee bourbon. And the discovery happened again, and again not at the bench, but in Millcreek Canyon, where our heroes went on a hike to clear their minds of Jack Daniels and of normal science. Bourbon and canyon hikes make an energy panacea! But such extraordinary measures were necessary, if our heroes were to go where no scientist had gone before. If they had stayed forever at the lab bench and tinkered with puzzle pieces, they never would have had the courage to become abnormal. With these two tales of discovery, we understand how a persevering pair of patient experimentalists working away for years could *suddenly*, with help from Jack, come up with something revolutionary.

advanced energy projects. . . . The Utah proposal was reviewed favorably" (*Chemical and Engineering News*, 4/3/89).

"[They] suggested that a catalyst prodded the thinking that led to the research: a bottle of Jack Daniels whiskey passed around Pons' kitchen table one night about six years ago. . . . Some might consider a few fortifying shots of Jack Daniels an apt beginning for a project that Pons himself considered so implausibly simple—and so potentially astonishing—that he initially regarded it as 'a joke.' Mr. Fleischmann's term was 'too stupid' to be taken seriously" (*Wall Street Journal*, 3/27/89). "The idea began to take shape five years ago on a hike up Millcreek Canyon on the outskirts of Salt Lake City" (*San Jose Mercury News*, 3/24/89).

2.5 FRESHMAN CHEMISTRY . . .

Here is another narrative couplet: P&F's experiments are as simple as pie to perform, but at the same time, it's weird science! The beauty of the experiment is its simplicity: literally anyone can do it. Even undergraduates doing electrolysis experiments are really doing what P&F did, just separating hydrogen from oxygen, done all the time. And it doesn't take a Tokamak to do that: a ninth-grade chemistry lab has all the ingredients you need to become Ra. P says he'll let his son make the power of the sun on earth. Replication is so easy that any amateur scientist could do it in his or her garage or basement. Why is everybody *else* having trouble finding nuclear fusion?

". . . no more complex than the practical work done by typical chemistry undergraduates. They use electrochemical techniques to achieve fusion of deuterium nuclei trapped inside an electrode made from palladium, a metal similar to platinum" (*Financial Times*, 3/23/89). ". . . the experiment is a simple variant of one done by first-year chemistry students to separate hydrogen from oxygen in water" (*Toronto Globe and Mail*, 3/24/89). "The basic apparatus used by Drs. Pons and Fleischmann would seem familiar to a ninth-grade student of general science" (*New York Times*, 3/28/89). "The reaction took place at room temperatures and was achieved with equipment not much more sophisticated than that of any undergraduate-level chemistry laboratory" (*US News*, 4/3/89). ". . . an electrochemical reaction so simple that others say it could be duplicated in an amateur scientist's home laboratory" (*Toronto Globe and Mail*, 3/24/89). "Because the fusion procedure outlined by Pons and Fleischmann is so simple, it can be repeated in almost any lab" (*Science* 4/7/89).

2.6. . . . BUT WEIRD SCIENCE

But the world press is not beating a path to the door of every ninth-grade chemistry lab, as they did to Utah. That is because *this* under-

"The novelty is that Drs. Pons and Fleischmann's experiment gives off a lot of heat. One experiment burned a 4-inch hole in the labora-

grad experiment with ninth-grade equipment was, just like the movie, weird science. If you try to do a P&F in your garage, watch out! Not every electrolysis experiment burns a four-inch hole in the laboratory floor, and not every freshman chemistry student suddenly boils away 75 ml of water and threatens the lab with a runaway reaction. But these things *happened*: you don't get a hole burned in the lab floor without a lot of heat, and it is weird because no known processes of electrochemistry could explain it. It must be nuclear, or something we haven't thought up yet. This second narrative couplet makes heat, tritium, neutrons, palladium, and deuterium into something that everybody knows (even undergraduates) and at the same time into something nobody knows (unless it really is fusion in a bottle). It is so believable because it is so ordinary: home lab stuff, child's play, replicate it yourself. But it is more believable, too, because of the extraordinary things that happened to the ninth-grade experiment: that four-inch hole in the lab floor is nobody's social construction!

tory floor. This heat could not have come from normal chemical electrolysis, but it may be generated within the atoms themselves—from the fusion of deuterium nuclei" (*Economist*, 4/1/89). "Sometime during the night the palladium cube suddenly heated up to the point where some of it vaporized, blowing the apparatus apart, damaging a laboratory hood and burning the floor. 'It was a nice mess,' Mr. Pons said" (*Wall Street Journal*, 4/3/89). ". . . a device that had been steadily boiling away about two milliliters of heavy water suddenly boiled away 75 milliliters of water overnight and went dry" (*Wall Street Journal*, 4/3/89). ". . . the heat produced by the experiment threatened to 'runaway'—an uncontrollable reaction" (*Toronto Globe and Mail*, 4/5/89). ". . . they've obtained 26 watts per cu cm of palladium. 'No known chemical process' can produce this result, he says" (*Chemical and Engineering News*, 4/3/89). "We can't imagine any chemical process that can explain this, so the only alternative explanation is a nuclear process [that] heretofore has been unrecognized,' Mr. Pons said" (*Wall Street Journal*, (4/3/89).

2.7. JUST LIKE THE LAST BIG BREAKTHROUGH

Besides, what our heroes have done is hardly unprecedented: others have solved the unsolvable, pushed back frontiers of ignorance, taken

"One writer said that if it was true, the effect for humans would be comparable to the discovery of fire" (*Washington Post*, 4/13/89).

crazy risks, worked from the obvious to get initially inexplicable results. Cold fusion has precedents: it is just like those other breakthroughs that have reshaped people, nature, and machines. P&F rank with the unknown cave dweller who gave us fire, and those coming later who gave us hot superconductivity, dense microprocessors, tiny semiconductors, revealing fiber optics. Cold fusion appears as the most recent element in this historical progress. Is it unbelievable? So was television a half-century ago, and maglev trains running on superconductors are just around the corner. If other discoverers and inventors did what no one else had ever done, so our heroes can do what once was unimaginable.

"... the discovery of cold fusion would rank with the biggest of the decade, perhaps even higher than 'hot' superconductivity" (*Dallas Morning News*, 4/3/89). "Avid readers ... are not only ahead of the pack on the cold fusion story, but also would have read of the initial breakthroughs in achieving superconductivity. They would have learned more recently of Intel's and Motorola's ability to place 1.2 million transistors on one microprocessor, of AT&T Bell Labs's ability to make semiconductors so small that their activities must be described in terms of quantum mechanics, ... of fiber optics that will let engineers 'see' the internal workings of an internal-combustion engine. The human enterprise is moving forward" (*Wall Street Journal*, 4/12/89).

2.8. WHO ARE THOSE GUYS?

Our heroes have a past, a life before March 24, 1989, and so do their universities. Where did they come from? We already have clues: P&F are patient persevering experimentalists who needed bourbon to let them take the plunge. But there is more to this biography: they are very careful workers, who use a conservative approach—nothing wild and crazy here except for the hole in the lab floor. These two have weighty reputations, they are highly regarded among electrochemists. They are preceded by their past successes, and they have a

"Both of them are very careful workers who use a conservative approach" (*San Jose Mercury News*, 3/28/89). "If a first-year chemistry student came up with such claims he would be sent home to re-read his elementary physics books. But Drs. Pons and Fleischmann have weighty reputations" (*Economist*, 4/1/89). "Utah's graduate chemistry program is generally ranked among the top 10 U.S. programs, and Southampton is known for its ability to turn basic research into practical industrial science" (*Wall Street Journal*, 3/27/89). "[Pons] said he

"good rep." So do their home institutions: the University of Utah is no backwater Rocky Mountain High. Its graduate program in chemistry is ranked in the top ten, and F's Southampton is where science gets down to business. Deuterium and palladium become tomorrow's dynamo, basic becomes applied, at Southampton. But if these two are *so* good, why did the announcement of cold fusion come like a bolt out the blue? Because their reputations did not carry to those scientists who had previously monopolized the nuclear fusion game, those hot fusioneers. Those physicists with their expensive lasers and huge magnets, working at elite places like Princeton, Rochester, and MIT, did not know about our heroes. They *thought* they knew all about nuclear fusion, but they had the wrong kind! So who are these guys? P&F are the marginal scientists from whom all new ideas are supposed to flow, not constrained by conventional wisdom, free from interference by doubting Thomases in physics, with little stake in the hot fusion status quo. This is the quintessential American myth: the little guy who takes on the powers, rebel cowboys from the Wild West, taking huge risks ($100,000 of their own money, because no one would front them the cash), showing the rich kids and know-it-alls that they could be wrong. Horatio Algers in white lab and Dr. Fleischmann had paid for their work with their private funds, about $100,000, because they had assumed that 'mainstream' scientific financing agencies would not take them seriously" (*New York Times*, 3/28/89). "They and their work were unknown among most fusion researchers" (*San Jose Mercury News*, 3/24/89). "Their work follows a course so different from conventional wisdom on fusion research that many of the leaders in the field were not even familiar with it" (*Los Angeles Times*, 3/24/89). "Electrochemists generally have been more willing than physicists to give Pons and Fleischmann the benefit of the doubt. That's because the two electrochemists . . . are highly regarded in their field" (*Chemical and Engineering News*, 4/3/89).

coats: humble beginnings, wrong side of the tracks, against all odds, ignoring the naysayers, persevering, hard work, up by their own bootstraps with no help from the NSF, poor guys who have made good.

2.9. THE DEVIL MADE THEM DO IT

Our cold fusion narrative is almost complete, except for what happened immediately before the March 24 press conference. Why did our heroes let the *Financial Times* spill the story of their triumph? Is that good science? Why couldn't they wait for the *Journal of Electroanalytical Chemistry* to publish the official peer-reviewed version? The press conference is not our heroes' idea! They are forced to do it, and they go along with it only in the interest of scientific accuracy and to protect the safety of fellow scientists who might do worse than burn holes in floors. P&F really wanted to do more normal science to make sure of what they had; another eighteen months would have been long enough. But the devils were all around them: snoopy reporters in Salt Lake City heard something about weird science and energy panaceas and, coveting Pulitzers, not Nobels, they could not wait for peer review and made plans to blurt it out prematurely. If journalists told the story, details would certainly get mixed up, and other scientists could not

"Pons says he and Fleischmann were under great pressure to publish their findings, although he declines to elaborate on the source of the pressure. 'We would have liked to have another 18 months' to work on the project and tie up loose ends' " (*Chemical and Engineering News*, 4/3/89). "Pons said the decision to publicize the results before submitting a paper to *Nature* was influenced by rumors circulating about the work, patent considerations. . . . The University of Utah has applied for a patent on the fusion process" (*Science*, 3/31/89). "Distorted, inaccurate information about the experiment was leaking out, he says, and 'we decided it would be better to get the story out straight rather than have it come out piecemeal and in error' " (*Chemical and Engineering News*, 4/3/89). "Two chemists say they circumvented normal scientific reporting channels to publicize an apparent breakthrough in nuclear fusion because they were afraid colleagues might blow themselves up by trying to duplicate the experiment" (*Toronto Globe and Mail*, 4/5/89).

possibly replicate, so P&F spill the
beans straight. Our heroes were
forced to that press conference,
kicking and screaming their way to
fame. They could not let their colleagues blow themselves up by following some garbled account in the
local paper, and besides, university
lawyers did not want to miss the
opportunity to stave off future
patent fights. The press conference
had to happen, against the sincere
desires of our heroes, who just
wanted more time to double-check.

Neutrons, palladium, gamma rays, deuterium, heat, and wired-up glass
vessels have become fashionable when dressed up in this narrative. No
longer unconnected and uninteresting bits of naked nature and machines;
they are now the passage to energy nirvana, blazed by two sun-gods. Who
would dare to doubt the competence or sincerity of our heroes? Why
would anyone not follow Pons and Fleischmann in their project to make a
claim real, with its inspiring past and glorious future? Who could *not* be
interested by such a wonderful story as this: Two guys from nowhere—
good track records but unknown outside their own small land—take huge
personal risks and solve a once-intractable problem that has plagued human history from the start. They work long and hard, with only rude
instruments—the kind of stuff ninth graders might use. Weird things
happen, which urge them on, giving them confidence that what they have
is real. Fortified with drink and fresh air, they rebel against conventional
thought, succeed where rich kids and their expensive toys have failed. But
our heroes harbor no malice against their critics, for they go public with
their findings to save life and limb of skeptical peers who might try to
replicate. Pons and Fleischmann become Ra: they harness the Sun, bring
it to earth, so we can drive our word processors and food processors, at
little cost, without pollutants, with no risk of Chernobyl, forever.

Give me the movie rights!

3. From Ballad to Dirge

The Ballad of Pons and Fleischmann has interested almost everybody in
cold fusion. The narrative enhances the competence and credibility of the

discoverers and tells us how our lives would be better if cold fusion were real. We are prepared to march behind Pons and Fleischmann, to abandon coal mines and oil fields, to turn off fission reactors, to ignore the ERAB panel of Luddites. We eagerly support the search for palladium and encourage utility companies to hook their networks into massive cold fusion generators. We salute Pons and Fleischmann with Nobels, and we admire the entrepreneurial spunk of the University of Utah as it exploits patents, negotiates licensing arrangements with General Electric and Westinghouse, and becomes richer than Harvard. We doubt the sincerity and competence of scientists who report disconfirming experimental evidence: they are jealous, or nervous about the renewal of their grants for research now eclipsed by the Utah discovery. A table-top apparatus has moved the world. Narrative keeps cold fusion alive.

"Miss Collwood, I've finished with the cold-fusion file. Bring me the file on oat bran."

NOT SO FAST!

Two years later, cold fusion is, for most of us, a boring joke about a non-discovery. Perhaps narrative is weak after all: just hype to sell newspapers, with no real connection to the adjudication of scientific claims about nature. Not even The Greatest Story Ever Told can stand up, one might conclude, against contrary experimental evidence and widely approved theory. Perhaps experimenters' regress is Harry Collins's private nightmare. In the end, experimental findings really did kill cold fusion, as only momentary ambiguity about who is competent and who is credible disappears in a flurry of failed replications.

Experimental counterevidence (and its supporting physical and chemical theory) surely had a hand in the death of cold fusion, but it did not do the job alone. Skeptical scientists with their disconfirming evidence had help in the killing, the same kind of help that allowed Pons and Fleischmann to keep their claim alive elsewhere when it was essentially dead in the lab early on: a narrative. The Ballad of Pons and Fleischmann took cold fusion out of the lab, enhanced the credibility of the discoverers while making the discovery significant for Everyman. But it was, with time, drowned out by the Dirge of Pons and Fleischmann, a second story that provides an interpretive context for shifting competence and credibility away from Pons and Fleischmann and toward their critics. The evidence against cold fusion took on greater strength when Pons and Fleischmann became not heroes but unscrupulous, incompetent, unethical, greedy, uncooperative, and immodest antiheroes. Here is that sordid tale, in four acts:

3.1. FALSE HOPES AND DASHED DREAMS

P&F are not Ra: there have been so many pretenders to the power of Ra in the past, and there is little reason to get our hopes up over these two. What is the story of cold fusion? Broken hearts, unrequited love. Some Brits in the late fifties measured neutrons, but nothing ever came of it. This is the latest in a long line of pseudo-breakthroughs, meaning lies and jokes. What P&F did *really* is ninth-grade chemistry. Anybody can get "fusion" to work in the lab, but no one has yet scaled it up to a bona fide energy source. Forget the panacea: this is bench science, not even close to application. Little green men are essential

" 'When you teach plasma physics to students, you always cite a lot of examples of processes that lead to fusion. . . . They are all very interesting, but I haven't seen one yet that could lead to a practical fusion reactor' " (*Wall Street Journal*, 3/24/ 89). "In fusion research there are always crackpot claims to produce fusion in a simple way. It always turns out that a little green man from Mars told them to do it" (*Washington Post*, 4/13/89). "False hopes of sustained fusion reactions have been raised in the past. In the late 1950s, a British experiment appeared to have reached the breakeven point as measured by the

actants in the heterogenous network linking palladium and deuterium to neutrons, heat, and gamma rays. It has never panned out before, nor has it this time either.

number of neutrons that came flying out of the experiment. After several weeks of excitement, it was discovered that the neutrons were spurious. Since then, physicists have been extremely skeptical of any claims of sustained nuclear fusion" (*Wall Street Journal*, 3/24/89). "Enthusiasm over the claim has been tempered with a good deal of skepticism, not only due to the lack so far of a detailed account but also because the history of fusion research has been regularly punctuated by 'breakthroughs' " (*Nature*, 3/30/89). "Still, as the recent work on high-temperature superconductivity has shown, there can be much work between scientific discovery and commercial application" (*Science*, 3/31/89).

3.2. PATHOLOGICAL SCIENCE, INCOMPETENT SCIENTISTS

What are the real precedents for this round of cold fusion? Not fire, semiconductors, superconductors, fiber optics, and other inventions that worked. The true precedents are polywater, Benveniste's memory water, antigravity machines. This history of cold fusion puts it outside good science, inside pathological science: our falling heroes deceived themselves into thinking what they had was real. Not even an undergraduate chemistry student would commit the errors P&F committed. And our boys' specialty of electrochemistry is compared to such reliable endeavors as mysticism and alchemy. Nature was

"It is not every week that two chemists go directly to the press with a story that . . . could represent anything from an incredibly important scientific breakthrough . . . to the first step in another polywater fiasco" (*Chemical and Engineering News*, 4/3/89). "French immunologist Jacques Benveniste reported a similar startling discovery about water containing a chemical memory . . ." (*Toronto Globe and Mail*, 4/11/89). "Suppose you were designing jet airplanes and then suddenly you heard on CBS news that somebody had invented an anti-gravity machine" (*International Herald-Tribune*,

butchered: experimental errors or broken instruments are the source of heat, neutrons, or gamma rays. If P&F really did what they said they did, they would be dead from neutron irradiation (unless they wore lead BVDs). They must have done something other than what they said they did: are they hiding something? The coup de grace was to come later, in a September 1989 issue of the *New York Times Magazine*. Our fallen heroes are shown in full color, tinkering with a power cell, under the embarrassing title "COLD FUSION CONFUSION." Here they are compared to Blondlot and his phantom N-rays and accused of self-deception. Their experiments are described as "tricks" 3/24/89). ". . . the researchers' descriptions of their work sound like mysticism" (*San Jose Mercury News*, 3/24/89). "Rafelski pointed out that to generate that much heat from deuterium fusion alone, the fusion cells would also produce so many neutrons that 'they'd all be dead'" (*Science*, 3/31/89). "The crudeness of the approved paper leaves others gasping. 'I wouldn't accept this from one of my undergraduates.' Basic errors were made" (*Toronto Globe and Mail*, 4/11/89). "Experimental errors or broken instruments may be to blame" (*Dallas Morning News*, 4/3/89). "Dr. George Chapline said that the Utah results were a case of self-deception" (*New York Times*, 4/4/89).

© San Francisco *Chronicle*: Reprinted by Permission.

(fusion in a bottle is sort of like the ship in a bottle, or a genie in a bottle—magic tricks, not science). They are described as outsiders to physics and therefore incompetent to do the science they needed to do, and they are stubborn because they refused to back down when others challenged their findings. Pathological science yields only jokes.

3.3. IMPUGNED MOTIVES, QUESTIONABLE MORALS

Horatio Alger would not have told lies! How could our heroes have told everybody something that was not true, unless they are not heroes. Another biography is written, making P&F out to be not just incompetent but slimy laboratory thugs, thoroughly disreputable, untrustworthy. They avoided the scrutiny of their peers by going to the press first, rather than waiting for peer review to run its normal and ethical course. Why did they do such heinous things? They are lustful of fame and gain; their motives are not noble but base. They wanted to stake their claim—to be first, to be famous, to be rich was more important than being right and ethical. Other scientists wait, but these two ballyhooed their claim and, worse, they did not talk modestly and hesitantly about a tentative laboratory finding but allowed them to be attached to epic struggles for an energy panacea—that is grandstanding, a scientific sin. It turns out they were talking through their

"Most Cornell physicists interviewed expressed surprise that the Utah chemists announced their claims before publishing a technical paper. 'It's on the verge of being unethical,' Gottfried said" (*Cornell Daily Sun*, 3/30/89). "Deepening professional skepticism was the unorthodox way in which the claimed achievement was announced. . . . They have not published claims in any scientific journal, a procedure that would have required them to submit convincing experimental results to a panel of their peers" (*New York Times*, 3/28/89). "Some scientists speculate that Utah released its findings early to stake its claim in the field" (*Chemical and Engineering News*, 4/10/89). "Last week's issue contains two examples, concerning the new pulsar in supernova 1987A, in which the researchers concerned were able to keep quiet for the required few weeks. But there are those who feel compelled, either for money or fame, to ballyhoo discoveries before anyone can

hats for the preprint faxed around the world says nothing about scaled up energy sources. They trumped up the findings to get everyone interested *outside* physics, and then hid vital details of the apparatus so that other scientists could not copy. And that was done to protect their lead, so that patents could be filed at a leisurely pace. They hid the recipe (a breach of the norm of communism) so that the glory would continue to be theirs; or did they hide details because not even they know where to find them?

reasonably judge their merits" (*Nature*, 3/30/89). "Although the preprint does not make the dramatic claims about fusion power that were made at the press conference, it is clear that fusion power is the main consideration in the work" (*Science*, 4/7/89). "Replicating the Utah experiment, though, has proved frustrating to many researchers because few had access to technical details. 'We're in a position like trying to cook chicken cordon bleu without a recipe' " (*Chemical and Engineering News*, 4/3/89).

3.4. BAD BOYS (AND THE GOOD GUY)

Our heroes' fall from grace is complete when the real hero is introduced: the fair-haired one from Brigham Young, just down the road from that den of iniquity at Pons's lab. They ripped him off! Poor Steve Jones agreed with our villains that nobody would go public until everybody went public with papers in *Nature*. He trusted them as honest men, but P&F held their press conference and nobody invited Steve Jones. Bad faith, bad science. Jones was there, back in 1986, patiently plodding toward cold fusion; he even went so far as to notarize the page in his lab book where he sketched something that looks remarkably like P&F's cell. Those rats! They stole it all from Steve Jones. Did Jones fight back? Not by slinging more mud, not by grandstanding, not by enrolling

"When Jones heard Pons say at the press conference that his team had already submitted a paper to a journal, he decided that Pons had broken their agreement, and he submitted his paper to *Nature*" (*Science*, 4/7/89). "BYU now interprets the Utah press conference as an attempt to gain precedence for their work in the public mind" (*Toronto Globe and Mail*, 4/1/89). " 'Our log books prove we have been studying this since 1986.' [A] notarized page contained an outline of experiments his team planned to run, including explicit reference to looking for cold fusion in palladium electrodes. . . . A drawing done in May 1986 of a fusion cell looks very similar to what Pons and Fleischmann eventually used" (*Science*, 4/7/89). "Jones had tried to retain a dignified silence after Pons and Fleisch-

patent attorneys, not by making exaggerated claims—everything P&F did! Jones refused to talk until formal release of his findings at the American Physical Society. He maintained a dignified silence and told people not to sell their oil stock because really, cold fusion was no closer to replacing fossil fuels than . . . hot fusion.

mann gave their results to the press before they had been published. . . . When pressed to say whether what he calls 'piezonuclear fusion' could become a practical source of energy, Jones estimated that it would take '20 years to never. If you own an oil well, don't go out and sell it' " (*New Scientist*, 4/8/89). "BYU tried . . . to distance itself from the furor. Jones at first refused to discuss his research results. He planned instead to present them formally at an American Physical Society meeting" (*Chemical and Engineering News*, 4/10/89).

Narrative and experiment, Dirge and failed replications, *together* put cold fusion away.

But where did the Dirge come from? An "interests-based" conspiracy theory is tempting, especially when one considers the *short-term* losers if Pons and Fleischmann succeed in making cold fusion real. The Department of Energy looks bad for backing the wrong horse, having dumped millions into hot fusion, magnets, lasers, windmills, solar collectors— down the drain. If cold fusion is real, anyone and anything hooked into Tokamak stands to lose funding, employment, reputation—nobody loves a loser. Elite scientific institutions like Princeton, MIT, Cal Tech, and DoE national laboratories at Brookhaven and Los Alamos get scooped by *Utah* of all places, raising questions in congressmen's minds about the presently skewed allocation of federal research funds. Physicists must dump sacred theoretical models because a mere electrochemist did them in. Add in all those other organizations, institutions, workers who risk displacement by real cold fusion: coal miners in southern Indiana, utility companies with huge investments in fission . . .

Was the Dirge of Pons and Fleischmann "authored" by these potential losers? Indeed, might powerful interests lined up against the reality of cold fusion be the *cause* of those overwhelmingly disconfirming replication attempts? No: if calorimeters hooked into Pons-Fleischmann cells at Brookhaven, Yale, Bell Labs, and Cal Tech had all registered heat at the levels found in Utah, and if the neutron counters found the quantities expected by Pons and Fleischmann, these counterinterests would have dissolved in a flash. But it is not *just* the confirming evidence that would have translated counterinterests so quickly: the Ballad of Pons and Fleischmann puts so many other powerful forces on the side of cold fusion that not even all the counterinterests listed above could kept the lid on the claim. Confirmatory evidence put in the context of the Ballad of Pons and Fleischmann would have translated those interests opposed to the reality of cold fusion into a figment.

I am not suggesting that interests have no part in the cold fusion episode. Did anyone benefit from the Dirge of Pons and Fleischmann, besides grants officers at DoE who might have breathed a short sigh of relief and smug physicists who were certain all along that their theories could hold against anything an electrochemist might construct? If we all lost an energy nirvana, did anyone *win*? Perhaps scientists as professionals win by protecting the cultural authority we invest in their practices and accomplishments. The cold fusion episode has the potential for making *science* look bad, especially if one draws the conclusion that it is really competitive pressures and the lure for fame and gain that drives scientists, not the disinterested search for truth. The Dirge handles that threat by localizing the trouble in one Utah lab, inhabited by two researchers whose *deviant* misconduct puts them beyond the scientific pale. The Dirge provides an interpretive context in which cold fusion becomes a case of "good science" driving out bad, and with that reading, scientists everywhere take solace.

Experimental evidence, narratives, interests: why should sociologists who investigate the social dimensions of science privilege any one of them, or worse, leave any of them out?

4. Irreduction

To sum up, "cold fusion" is about two scientists who try to make their claim real, and about how difficult it sometimes is to do that. Pons and Fleischmann tried several strategies to keep cold fusion alive, inching it from experimental finding toward fact and even toward an energy machine. They exploited the inherent ambiguity surrounding the fidelity of replication attempts, successfully forestalling a deathly closure by discounting disconfirmations as improperly done. But perhaps many of those replications would not even have been tried had it not been for Pons and Fleischmann's efforts (with journalists' help) to grow their claim outside science. The Ballad of Pons and Fleischmann made cold fusion interesting enough for the U.S. Congress to debate its merits; it made cold fusion relevant for everybody as a solution to whatever ails extant sources of energy; it made Pons and Fleischmann into heroes worthy of our trust in both their skills and their sincerity.

If these are the strategies and weapons for keeping claims alive, they are also the stategies and weapons for killing them off. Cold fusion lived for a *surprisingly* long time only for those who believe that experimental results and their supporting theoretical interpretations are sufficient to bring closure to scientific debate. But neither experimental findings nor theory *were* sufficient because they could not in themselves decide several crucial questions raised by Pons and Fleischmann's claim. Which scientists are competent? Who should we trust? Are the potential payoffs from cold fusion so great that we should back it with grants and research centers even if the evidence for it is shaky and contested? No neutron counter can answer these questions that are central to an understanding of the social dimensions of science. Neutrons need stories, discoverers need biographies, before facts are born, or killed.

REFERENCES

Bishop, Jerry. (1990) " 'Cold fusion' gets cold shoulder from many, a year after findings," *Wall Street Journal* (3 April): B4.

Collins, H. M. (1975) "The seven sexes: A study in the sociology of a phenomenon, or the replication of experiments in physics," *Sociology* 9: 205–224.

————. (1985) *Changing Order: Replication and Induction in Scientific Practice*, London: Sage.

Dagani, Ron. (1990) "Pons demands retraction of cold fusion paper," *Chemical and Engineering News* 16 (April): 5.

Institute for Scientific Information. (1990) "Scientists vote on cold fusion: their verdict? No, not likely," *Science Watch* 1 (March): 7.

Johnson, George. (1990) "Utah monitor of 'cold fusion' casts doubt on its validity," *New York Times* (29 March): A10.

Latour, Bruno. (1987) *Science in Action*, Cambridge: Harvard University Press.

————. (1988) *The Pasteurization of France*, Cambridge: Harvard University Press.

Lindley, David. (1990) "The embarrassment of cold fusion," *Nature* 344: 375–376.

Lyotard, Jean-Francois. (1984) *The Post-Modern Condition: A Report on Knowledge*, Minneapolis: University of Minnesota Press.

McDonald, Kim A. (1990) "Claims of proponents of cold fusion still spark controversy a year later," *The Chronicle of Higher Education* (11 April): A7–A8.

Salamon, M. H. et al. (1990) "Limits on the emission of neutrons, gamma-rays, electrons and protons from Pons/Fleischmann electrolytic cells," *Nature* 344: 401–405.

Secord, James A. (1989) "Extraordinary experiments: Electricity and the creation of life in Victorian England," in *The Uses of Experiment*, ed. D. Gooding, T. Pinch, and S. Schaffer, Cambridge: Cambridge University Press, 337–383.

Sulloway, Frank. (1979) *Freud: Biologist of the Mind*, New York: Basic.

AUTHORITY, DEFERENCE, AND THE ROLE OF INDIVIDUAL REASON[1]

Philip Kitcher

1. Introduction

When Stanley Pons and Martin Fleischmann held their celebrated press conference, laboratory telephones began to ring. Nobody had expected the effects Pons and Fleischmann claimed to have achieved. Among electrochemists, Pons and Fleischmann were well known and well respected. Accordingly, their claims, however incredible, had to be taken seriously. Others, outsiders from physics, had usually never heard of Pons and Fleischmann. Many of the telephone calls they placed posed the same questions: Who are Pons and Fleischmann? Can they be trusted?[2]

Some few hundred miles to the south and west of Utah, there is a group of people who make periodic announcements that are also controversial. They have claimed to have evidence of Noah's Ark, of the copresence of dinosaur and human tracks in the same strata, of human artifacts which, when dated by the standard techniques, yield ages comparable to those of supposedly "ancient" rocks. These pronouncements challenge paleontology just as Pons and Fleischmann challenged our understanding of nuclear fusion. But Duane Gish, Henry Morris, and their colleagues at the Institute for Creation Research do not inspire the same dedicated investigations. They catch the ear of the scientific community only when they are able to threaten, only when they have demonstrated an ability to influence legislators or publishers, making it necessary for scientists to divert time from profitable research to the enterprise of rebutting creationism.[3]

Pons and Fleischmann had considerable authority among electrochemists, and they obtained authority among physicists because they had authority for some people who had authority for some physicists. Gish and Morris have no authority among paleontologists, nor do they have authority with anyone who has authority for paleontologists. But authority is not supposed to matter in science. We are told that science investigates ideas without regard for their origin. This, however, is foolish oversimplification. The individualist dreams of Bacon and Descartes, holding out the epistemic ideal of taking our cognitive lives into our own hands, ignore the fact that not every potential challenge to accepted belief can be considered at once.[4] Scientists expend their cognitive efforts where their contributions to the community enterprise are likely to do some good.

Reliance on authority affects the cognitive lives of scientists in at least three ways. First, there is the general epistemic dependence on the past that permeates everyone's early intellectual ontogeny. We absorb the lore of our predecessors through the teaching of parents and other authorities. Second, at the time of entry into the scientific community, fledgling scientists endorse a community-wide conception of legitimate epistemic authority. Certain people are to be trusted to decide on certain issues and the novice must accept whatever agreements they reach on those issues. Third, during the course of individual research, scientists interact with one another, collaborating and competing, adopting the claims made by *some* of their colleagues, investigating the proposals of others, when the claims and proposals in question go beyond what is agreed upon by the pertinent community. There are differential assignments of authority within the scientific community, and these may shape the course of the members' research.

The concern of this essay is the constitution of epistemic authority, principally with the grounding of the third type of appeal to authority (manifested in the different responses to Pons and Fleischmann vis-à-vis Gish and Morris). Although many of the analyses I shall give might carry over to the more exciting problems of broader kinds of epistemic authority (specifically the constitution of communities as authoritative on particular issues or even the reposing of trust in scientists as a group), I shall not assume that this is so. The goal will be to formulate and tackle manageable problems. Before plunging into the details, I want to relate my project to discussions that have been important in recent historical, sociological, and philosophical studies of science.

2. Explaining Scientific Change

Philosophers, historians, and sociologists who study science are interested in the dynamics of a certain kind of system. At a particular moment in time, t_n, the system is in a state: there is a set of individual scientists S_n, for each member of this set a representative of her claims and commitments C_n^i, a representation of "consensus opinion" C_n, a set of social relations among these scientists relating them both to one another and to entities in the wider society to which they belong, R_n, and a state of nature that the scientists are attempting to describe, W_n. Between t_n and t_{n+1}, the total state changes:

$$\langle S_n, C_n{}^i, \ldots, C_n, R_n, W_n \rangle \rightarrow \langle S_{n+1}, C_{n+1}{}^i, \ldots, C_{n+1}, R_{n+1}, W_{n+1} \rangle.$$

Every component of the system may change. New scientists may enter the population, old ones exit. Everyone's claims and commitments may be modified. Consensus opinion may shift. The social relations may change. Even the world may change—not, I hasten to explain, in the exciting sense people glean from Kuhn, but in the mundane ways in which scientists' interactions with nature alter it.

One central problem in science studies is to understand the dynamics of changes in the state of science. It is surely uncontroversial that such changes of state come about as a result of the activities of scientists, and that, to a first approximation, such activities can be divided into two very broad types. On the one hand, there are what I shall call *conversations with peers*, occasions on which scientists talk to one another, read the work of their colleagues, jointly work through a problem. On the other, there are *encounters with nature*, stereotypically episodes in which a single scientist conducts observations and experiments or reflects privately upon them.[5] In some quarters, encounters with nature are seen as driving scientific change. For many philosophers of science and for some historians, we can drop the representation of the social relations R_n in the description of the state of science and concentrate on the impact of the interactions between W_n and the scientists with their commitments $C_n{}^i$.[6] This extreme view espouses a *principle of social transparency:* For a given initial state of science and a fixed set of interactions between scientists and nature, the succeeding state is independent of the social relations R_n. At the opposite extreme is a position currently popular among many sociologists of science and an increasing number of historians. Advocates of this position give greater weight to conversations among peers, and they emphasize the role of social interactions and background commitments in determining the ways in which encounters with nature are received. When their ideas are most forthrightly expressed, as, for example, by Harry Collins, the suggestion is that consideration of the world and its impact on individual scientists is irrelevant to understanding changes in the state of science.[7] The principle of social transparency is opposed by a *principle of social determination:* For a given initial state of science, the resulting transition is independent of the causal interactions between scientists and nature.

When this opposition is presented as I have formulated it, in terms of the relevance or irrelevance of certain variables, I think it is obvious that there is a spectrum of interesting *plausible* positions between the extremes. The situation is reminiscent of the debates about the causation of human behavior. Genetic determinists insist that behavioral traits are fixed by genotype, so that, given the same genotype, the same trait would result whatever the environment. Social determinists maintain that genotype is irrelevant, that for a given program of social conditioning the same trait would result whatever the underlying genotype. But, as quickly becomes apparent, nobody really believes anything so extreme. Phenotypes, including behavioral phenotypes, are typically the result of an interaction between genotype and environment. The genuine differences about the causation of human behavior thus have to be expressed as questions about the shapes of norms of reaction (graphical representations of the variation of phenotype with environment for a given genotype).[8]

I suggest an analogous response to the debate about scientific change: neither the interactions between scientists and nature nor the social relations among scientists can be dismissed as irrelevant to the transition from one state of science to its successor. Martin Rudwick's pioneering study of the "Great Devonian Controversy" seems to me to show the implausibility of both extremes. If the rocks in Devon had not been folded in the ways that they actually were, both Roderick Murchison and Henry de la Beche would have modified their beliefs in different ways. But, equally, if Murchison and de la Beche had been situated in a different set of social relations, the controversy would have followed another course.[9]

The challenge for students of scientific change is to advance beyond the pallid suggestion that alterations in the state of science are the product of an interaction involving both the social relations among scientists and the character of the world with which they interact. Historians can display the complexities of this interaction in detailed analyses of important changes. Philosophy can contribute by attempting to model simple situations in which the relative contributions of different factors can be easily assessed. So, in this essay, I shall focus on the problem of weighing deference to authority against thinking and observing for oneself.[10] Under what conditions can we expect that attributions of authority will themselves be kept on track by individual scientists' encounters with nature? When should we worry that the effects of authority are so powerful that they will dominate responses to the world, making it impossible for a community to correct its collective misapprehensions? I hope that focusing on special

instances will illuminate the general problem of understanding the interactions that cause scientific change.

3. Costs and Benefits of Deferring to Others

The most obvious advantages of deference to authority are that it enables individual scientists to pursue their epistemic projects more rapidly
and makes feasible investigations that would be impossible for a single
individual. Suppose that a scientist, dedicated to a particular inquiry, has
total resources (time, energy, money) E and needs k items of information.
Let the cost of acquiring each directly be C, the cost of acquiring each
from an authority be c. The scientist's project is individually impossible
but cooperatively feasible just in case

$$kc < E < kC.$$

We can assume that the investigation consists of a period in which the
needed information is acquired followed by a period in which the scientist
attempts to put the information to use. The chances of success in the
project can be written as the product of two probabilities: the probability
that the information acquired is correct and the probability of deploying
correct information at the second stage. The latter can be written as $F(E -$
acquisition costs), where F is nondecreasing and $F(x) = 0$ if $x < 0$.

Consider the simplest case in which $k = 1$. You have two choices: you
can do the work yourself or you can rely on authority. Which decision is
preferable? It depends on two error rates, yours and that of your potential
authority. Assume that borrowing is cheaper than doing the work yourself, $c < C$. Let your error rate be p, the potential authority's error rate q.
Suppose also that your decision is motivated solely by the desire to bring
this project to a correct conclusion. Then you should rely on authority if

$$(1 - p) \cdot F(E - C) < (1 - q) \cdot F(E - c)$$

This inequality is automatically satisfied if the potential authority is more
expert at the relevant task than you are— $p > q$ —for recall that $c < C$
and F is nondecreasing. But even if you are more reliable than the potential authority it may still be worth your while to take the risk of
borrowing.

To see this, imagine that $F(x)$ is: (a) 0 when $x < 0$, (b) mx when $0 <
mx < 1$, (c) 1 when $mx > 1$. Borrowing is epistemically preferable if

$$q < [(C - c) + p(E - c)]/(E - c).$$

Even when you are perfect ($p = 0$), if the costs of borrowing are negligible ($c = 0$), you can tolerate a maximum error rate of C/E in your potential authority, and C/E may be sizeable if you would have to expend a lot of your resources on acquiring the information directly.

Scientists do not engage in such detailed computations of probabilities of success. Their ruminations stand to the algebra much as the impressionistic budgeting of some people does to the more precise calculations of their accountants. The typical scientist judges that a potential authority is sufficiently trustworthy and that acquiring the information directly would be too time-consuming. The point of the exercise so far is simply to note that decisions to borrow from authorities have to involve some estimates of error rates (albeit, perhaps, only qualitative ones). How are such estimates made? How are authorities assessed?

4. Assessing Others: Direct Calibration

Sometimes, like instruments, potential authorities can be calibrated directly. We compare the output of an authority with our own opinions on topics where there is overlap. This is a temptingly simple suggestion, but I propose that, from the beginning, we think about authority in a broader way.

We are interested in a function $a(X, Y)$ that measures Y's authority for X, or, more exactly, X's assessment of the probability that what Y says will be true.[11] Here X is an individual scientist and Y may be another scientist, a research team, a journal, a series of scientific monographs, or some other composite entity on which scientists may potentially depend. (There are often serious questions about the entity whose authority is to be assessed: when an unreliable scientist publishes in a highly prestigious journal, known for its strict refereeing, the authority attributed to the article may be an amalgam of the authority of scientist and journal.) Attributions of authority are rarely uniform across topic. I shall assume in what follows that the assignments of authority are relativized to a range of issues with respect to which the potential authority's deliverances can be assigned the same reliability.

An idealized treatment of authority that includes obvious social factors can proceed by breaking a scientist's credibility into two parts: there is *unearned* authority that stems from the scientist's social position (either within the community of scientists or in the wider society), the type of authority that comes from being associated with a major institution or from having been trained by a prominent figure; this contrasts with *earned* authority, credibility that is assigned by reflection on the scientist's performances or through consideration of others' opinions of those performances. So I propose that we consider communities of scientists in which individuals evaluate one another in accordance with the equation

$$a(X, Y) = w(X, Y) \, a_u (X, Y) + (1 - w(X, Y)) \, a_e (X, Y).$$

In what follows I shall be considering different possibilities for giving weight to unearned authority (different values of w) and different methods of computing earned authority (different measures of a_e).

The best hope for minimizing the effects of the social structure is to suppose that members of the community always set w to be 0 and calculate earned authority through direct calibration. Under these circumstances, $a(X,Y)$ is simply Y's truth-ratio with respect to the sample of statements about which X has an independent opinion: in effect, X uses the straight rule to project the probability that Y's claims will be correct from the frequency with which Y asserts the truth, by X's lights, within the class of Y's statements available for appraisal by X. [12] So, for example, if X believes p_1, p_2, $-p_3$, p_4, and $-p_5$, and Y is recognized by X to assert $-p_3$, $-p_4$, $-p_5$, p_6, and $-p_7$, then $a(X,Y) = 2/3$.

I want to explore the ways in which deference to authorities might affect the development of a scientific field. Intuitively, the worry is that deference might block the spread of new ideas within the community, that proponents of heterodoxy would *ipso facto* lose credibility. A simple, somewhat artificial, way to focus this worry is to consider what I shall call the *alliance splitting problem.*

Imagine that we have three scientists A, B, and C. C advocates a finding that would challenge the accepted ideas of the community to which all three belong. In terms of direct calibration, B and C are natural allies, in the sense that B ascribes to C a higher truth-ratio than B ascribes to A. A is a potential authority who claims that C's alleged finding is bogus. Under what conditions can the presence of A split the alliance between B and C?

If B assigns no weight to unearned authority ($w(B,A) = w(B,C) = 0$), and if B computes earned authority through direct calibration, then, by our assumption about truth-ratios, $a(B,C) > a(B,A)$. Suppose that B is in no position to investigate C's finding directly, that B must arrive at a decision for or against C's finding, that A and C are the only members of the community who express opinions about C's finding (the only potential authorities on whom B can rely). Imagine further that B follows the decision-rule:

(R) If you have to make a decision with respect to p, you are unable to make that decision through independent inquiry, and there are exactly two potential authorities whose opinions about p conflict, then you should follow the judgment of the person to whom you assign higher authority.

Then, plainly, B will endorse C's finding. Under these (admittedly artificial) conditions, we achieve the traditional epistemologist's utopia: social factors play no important role and, in effect, B's individual reasoning underlies her judgments.

Despite its obvious unreality, this is a useful point from which to begin, for it provides a baseline against which the disturbing effects of appeals to authority may be measured. Let us now look at more interesting ways of assessing the authority of others.

5. Assessing Others: Prestige Effects

The most obvious way in which the presence of authorities can break up natural alliances is through prestige effects. Suppose that our community is one in which everyone who has undergone a reputable training program is always assigned a value of unearned authority above some threshold. People who have been associated with privileged institutions are attributed greater unearned authority. Under these conditions, strong natural alliances can be broken.

Consider, once again, our three scientists A, B, and C. As before, C announces a new, controversial finding and A dismisses it as flawed. The public assertions on questions that concern the three are as follows:

A	$-p_1$	p_2	p_3		
B			$-p_3$	p_4	p_5
C	p_1	$-p_2$	$-p_3$	p_4	$p_5.$

This is an extreme situation in which B and C are perfect allies, agreeing on all statements about which each has an independent opinion. B and A, on the other hand, *disagree* with respect to the only statement on which each has an independent opinion. However, because of A's prestigious position, $a_u(B,A) = 1$, and, perhaps because of the limited basis on which B can directly calibrate A, perhaps because of A's prominence, $u(B,A)$ (the weight B assigns to A's unearned authority in assessing A) is some relatively high number r. C is a perfectly respectable member of the community who receives the threshold value for unearned authority k. Let $u(B,C) = s$. Earned authority is calculated through direct calibration.

B's assignments of authority are easily seen to be

$$a(B,A) = r$$
$$a(B,C) = sk + (1 - s).$$

So the natural alliance between *B* and *C* is split if

$$r > sk + (1 - s) \qquad \text{or} \qquad r + s(1 - k) > 1.$$

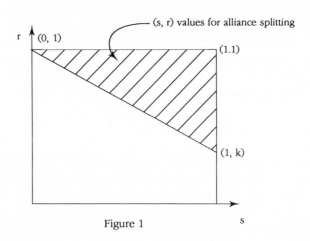

Figure 1

As Figure 1 reveals, (s,r) has to lie in the triangle whose vertices are the points $(0,1)$, $(1,1)$, $(1,k)$. Intuitively, there are many ways in which *A*'s prestige can split even a perfect natural alliance: all that is required is that the weights *B* assigns to unearned authority be sufficiently high and the threshold value of unearned authority for a respectable member of the community sufficiently low. Under these conditions, if *B* is in the predicament of deciding the merits of *C*'s finding subject to the constraints on the artificial decision situation I have described—in particular using rule (R)—then *A*'s prestige will block the acceptance of *C*'s challenge to orthodoxy. As we might have expected, and as Bacon and Descartes feared, appeals to authority can help preserve the *status quo*. [13]

So far there are few surprises. Matters become more intriguing as we add detail.

6. *Assessing Others: Indirect Calibration*

There are numerous people whose advice might be valuable for a scientist but whom the scientist is unable to rate directly. When you need conclusions outside your speciality, direct calibration of potential informants is unreliable, perhaps even impossible, since the sample of statements available for computing a truth-ratio is small, possibly empty. Under such circumstances, attributions of authority must proceed either by using unearned authority or by what I shall call *indirect calibration*— using the judgments of those who have already been assessed in evaluating others.

In general, a social system of authority and deference in a community of N scientists can be represented by an NxN matrix whose entries are the values of $a(S_i, S_j)$ and a set of directed graphs that show how each individual uses colleagues to assess other colleagues. A full formal theory of authority and deference would try to specify the conditions that a coherent system ought to satisfy. I shall simplify the general situation enormously by focusing on cases in which the only type of indirect calibration uses scientists who are directly calibrated to evaluate those who are indirectly calibrated (the maximum length of paths in the direct graphs is 2) and by ignoring possibilities of mutual assessment and iterated adjustments. So we can write the earned authority of Y for X as

$$a_e\,(X,Y) \;=\; \sum_i a(X,Z_i) \cdot t(Z_i,Y)/\sum_i a(X,Z_i)$$

where $a(U,V)$ is the authority *already* assigned to V by U, $t(U,V)$ is the truth-ratio of V as measured by U, and the summation is over all the paths that X uses in evaluating Y. This equation can be extended to include direct calibration as a possible component of total earned authority, if we treat X-X-Y as a degenerate two-step path leading from X to Y. In elaborating this idea I shall *not* assume that $a(U,U)$ is always 1. Indeed, people can sometimes be very unconfident about their direct assessments of their fellows, which is, of course, why indirect calibration is used in the first place.[14]

Let us now consider our earlier example. We have three scientists whose publicly expressed beliefs are as follows:

A	$-p_1$	p_2	p_3		
B			$-p_3$	p_4	p_5
C	p_1	$-p_2$	$-p_3$	p_4	p_5.

Let us suppose that A is a prestigious scientist whom B uses in assessing C. As before, let $w(B,A) = r$, $a_u\,(B,A) = 1$, $w(B,C) = s$, $a_u\,(B,C) = k$. If C's authority is evaluated through indirect calibration, we shall also need to consider B's confidence in her own reliability as a direct assessor of C. Suppose, then, that $a(B,B) = h$. Under these conditions, we have

$$a(B,A) = r$$
$$a_e(B,C) = (r.0 + h.1)/(r + h) = h/(r + h)$$
$$a(B,C) = sk + (1 - s)h/(r + h).$$

Plainly, the value of $a(B,C)$ is reduced from that obtained through direct calibration, $(sk + (1 - s))$, unless B gives no weight to A's unearned authority ($r = 0$).

Under what conditions will the alliance between B and C be split? Suppose first that $h = 1$, the case in which B is confident in her own power to assess C and, in consequence, the situation most favorable for resisting alliance-splitting. The alliance is split if

$$a(B,A) > a(B,C)$$
that is $\quad r^2 + r(1 - sk) > (1 - s) + sk.$

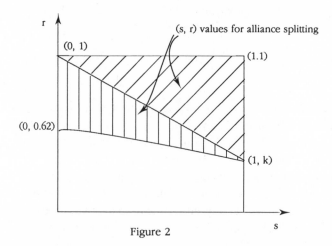

Figure 2

As Figure 2 makes clear, the region of (s,r) points that correspond to alliance splitting is now increased: in particular, even when $s = 0$ (unearned authority is discounted in the evaluation of C), the alliance is split if $r > 0.62$. At the opposite extreme, if B is extremely unconfident about her ability to evaluate C directly ($h = 0$) then the alliance is split if $r > sk$. It follows that if B assigns equal weight to unearned authority in evaluating A and C, and C is a reputable, but not high-ranking, member of the community, then the B-C alliance will be split.

The example I have been discussing reveals complete disagreement between the evaluator B and the putative authority A and perfect harmony between B and the subversive C. Nonetheless, if B is led to give some weight to A's prestigious position the B-C alliance can be split, and it can be split more readily if B calibrates C indirectly. Because of the perfect disagreement between A and B, the alliance cannot be split unless *some* weight is given to A's unearned authority. Let us now consider a more realistic situation, one in which B, who diverges from A in some but not all ways, evaluates a relative newcomer C with whose views B is in sympathy.

Suppose that the public assertions of A, B, and C are as follows

$$
\begin{array}{lcccccccc}
A & p_1 & -p_2 & p_3 & -p_4 & -p_5 & p_6 & p_7 & p_8 \\
B & p_1 & p_2 & p_3 & & p_5 & p_6 & & \\
C & & p_2 & & p_4 & & & -p_7 & -p_8.
\end{array}
$$

Were B to calibrate C directly, ignoring unearned authority, then $a(B,C) = 1$, and B and C would form an unsplittable alliance. But, recognizing that C is relatively unknown and that the truth-ratio is computed on a slender basis, B might choose to calibrate C indirectly by referring to the judgment of the authority A of whom C is severely critical. Imagine that unearned authority is neglected in assessing both A and C ($u(B,C) = u(B,A) = 0$). Let $a(B,B)$, B's confidence in her power to evaluate C directly, be h. Then the attributions of authority are

$$a(B,A) = 0.6$$
$$a(B,C) = [(0.6 \times 0) + (h \times 1)]/[0.6 + h] = h/[0.6 + h].$$

The alliance will thus be split if $h < 0.9$. Unless B is extraordinarily confident of her direct assessments, indirect calibration alone, without invocation of unearned authority, suffices to resist the challenges of the maverick C.

7. Deciding to Replicate: Community Decision

The tendency of the previous discussions is to show that appeals to authority can threaten the fate of heterodox ideas, if the decision-making of the individual scientist is conceived in the simple terms of rule (R). But if we reflect on the type of situation with which I began, exemplified by scientists' reactions to Pons and Fleischmann, Gish and Morris, it is quite clear that (R) fails to represent the scientist's options. Deferring to authority looks more benign if we bring into account some of the forces that oppose epistemic conservatism.

Imagine a community of N scientists, one of whose members announces a challenging new finding. From the viewpoint of orthodoxy it is improbable that that finding is correct. Think of yourself as a philosopher-monarch with power to adjust the labor of the scientific workforce as you see fit. Each scientist can ignore the finding, adopt it, or attempt to replicate it. A community strategy consists of an assignment of each worker to one of these options. As a philosopher-monarch you are interested in which community strategy gives you the best chance of attaining the community ends of science. Let us assume that these have something to do with the consensus opinion of the community including as much true information about nature as possible.

An interesting general problem is to investigate the optimum community strategy under different conditions and to ask what types of social arrangements and distributions of cognitive styles (decision rules and utility structures) lead the community towards or away from the optimum. I am going to pursue a simpler inquiry. Consider three community strategies:

I Everyone ignores the challenging finding.

M Everyone modifies their views to embrace the new finding.

R All but one person ignore the finding; the single exception attempts to replicate it.

The more limited question I shall consider is: Under what conditions is R a better strategy than both I and M?

In advance of the finding, you would have assigned a probability of 0 to the statement asserted by the alleged finder C. Now you use your assessment of C's authority to grant a probability p that the statement is correct.[15] You also assign a probability q that the potential replicator will work reliably, endorsing C's result if it is correct and rejecting it if it is false. The expected utilities of the strategies can be written as

$$U(I) = -pv$$
$$U(M) = pu - (1 - p)w$$
$$U(R) = pqu - p(1 - q)v - (1 - p)(1 - q)w - e$$

where $-v$ is the cost of ignoring the challenge (if true), $-w$ is the cost of building on it (if false), u is the benefit of building on it (if true), and $-e$ is the cost resulting from the loss of work that the replicator would otherwise have done. I shall assume that u, v, and w are all appreciably larger than e, and that $w > u > v$.

I is preferable to M if $p < w/(u + v + w)$. Typically I will be preferable to M because p will be small, $p < 1/3$, and, by the assumption that $w > u > v$, $w/(u + v + w) > 1/3$. Moreover, if the replicator is highly reliable (q close to 1), then R will be preferable to M even when p is relatively high. For R is preferable to M if

$$p < (qw - e)/[qw + (1 - q)(u + v)]$$

and when q is close to 1 and e is small in comparison with w, the right-hand side is close to 1.

The interesting comparison is between R and I. R is preferable to I just in case

$$q > [e + (1 - p)w]/[p(u + v) + (1 - p)w].$$

This sets quite a strong condition on the reliability of the potential replicator. Intuitively, if p is very small and if the costs of building on error are very severe (w is large), the potential replicator had better be extremely reliable. Furthermore, if the right-hand side is greater than 1, the inequality is unsatisfiable however reliable the potential replicator may be. This occurs if

$$p < e/(u + v).$$

How should you, the philosopher-monarch, compute values of p and q? Before C announced his finding you would have attributed to C a certain authority $a(C)$, to be bestowed on any result he asserted, and, on the basis of your prior commitments, you would have assigned this particular result the probability 0. The probability you *now* assign to C's finding should be a weighted average of these, with the weights expressing your relative confidence in your prior judgment about C and in the body of scientific lore that underwrote your dismissal of any such result as that he has now announced. So it is reasonable to write

$$p = z \cdot a(C)$$

where z is between 0 and 1, and is ever closer to 0 the more firmly entrenched the parts of scientific practice that C's claim calls into question. I shall suppose that q is simply your assessment of the authority of the potential replicator.

When well-established parts of science are called into question, it seems reasonable to think that the past track record of those parts of science should be weighted at least twice as heavily as judgments about the authority of a single individual. Thus z should be less than $1/3$, and, even given a perfect potential replicator, I is preferable to M.

Consider now a community that meets the *Pons conditions:* (a) $a(C)$ is close to 1 (the person who announces the finding has high authority), (b) there are potential replicators in the community for whom q is close to 1 and e is negligible (people of high authority who could turn to replication without serious cost to the community), (c) u and v are of the order of $w/2$ (there are serious epistemic gains from incorporating the finding if it is correct). R will be preferable to I if

$$z > e/w,$$

for we require that q, which is approximately 1, be greater than $e + (1 - z)w/zw + (1 - z)w$. Hence, since e is negligible, even a very small weight given to prior judgments about the high authority of the finder will make it profitable for the community to expend some effort in replication rather than simply ignoring the finding.

By contrast, if the community meets the *Gish* conditions, in which $a(C) = 0$ (the authority of the *finder, at least with respect to the kind of statement in question,* is zero), then ignoring the alleged finding is preferable no matter how small the costs of replication or how high the reliability of a potential replicator. For recall that the condition for R to be preferable to I is unsatisfiable if

$$p < e/(u + v).$$

If $a(C) = 0$ then p ($= z.a(C)$) is automatically zero for any choice of z. Since e, u, and v are all positive, the inequality is satisfied.

8. Deciding to Replicate: Individual Decision

Having explored what the community would prefer to see happen in response to a challenging finding, let us now consider whether scientists, attributing authority in various ways and employing various decision rules, could work their way to the type of strategy that the community favors. Imagine yourself in the predicament of a scientific entrepreneur. You have been engaged in a research project when it is announced that one of your colleagues, X, has discovered something that challenges some fundamental ideas of the field in which you both work. I shall suppose that you have two possible responses: you can ignore X and go on with your research project, or you can attempt to replicate X's result, deferring your current project. It is possible that there are conditions under which a third strategy, that of incorporating X's finding into your own research work without any antecedent check, might also become tempting—think of situations in which scientists are in competition on a research project that will lead to an enormous breakthrough and there is consequent pressure to cut corners—but I shall suppose that these do not obtain in the present case.[16]

You make your decision in accordance with the ideas of rational decision theory.[17] The strategy of ignoring X is basically a null option. By pursuing it you do not change your future well-being, so that the extra utility that accrues to you is 0. If you try to replicate, on the other hand, there are potential gains and losses. If you are the first to replicate then there will be some benefit u—possibly epistemic, possibly social, possibly mixed (the attainment of truth, the acquisition of status, the recognition that comes from having discovered something important). If you are the first to show that X is wrong, then you will gain v, the utility accruing to the first refuter (again, this may be epistemic, social, or mixed). But, by diverting your effort from the ongoing research project, there will be costs of delay, d. On the basis of prior assessment of the authority of X and prior reasons for assigning probability 0 to X's challenging finding, you now suppose that there is a probability p that X is right. You are confident that, in any attempt at replication, you will judge correctly. However, to receive the benefits you have to be the *first* replicator or refuter. Your chances depend on the extent of the competition. Suppose that you conceive of all your colleagues as equally likely to win the race to replicate or refute. Then, if $n - 1$ colleagues join you in trying to replicate, the probability of your being the first is $1/n$. The expected extra utility of trying to replicate is therefore

$$pu/n + (1 - p)v/n - d.$$

Trying to replicate X is preferable just in case this quantity is positive, that is

$$p > (nd - v)/(u - v) \qquad \text{if } u > v$$

or

$$p < (v - nd)/(v - u) \qquad \text{if } v > u.$$

Assume that the new finding is sufficiently important that it would bring high credit to the first replicator and epistemic dividends for all researchers in the field, so that $u > v$. If you and all your colleagues decide in the same way, then at least one person will try to replicate X's result if

$$p > (d - v)/(u - v).$$

(This is the condition under which, in a community all of whose members ignore the finding, it becomes preferable for a single person to switch to trying to replicate.) The community can reach this desirable outcome, even when the probability assigned to the finding after the announcement by X is low, provided that $d - v$ is small in comparison with $u - v$. This occurs trivially when the delay costs are smaller than the gains of first refutation: $d < v$. Surely many of the scientists who heard Pons and Fleischmann's claims about cold fusion were engaged in projects that could be delayed without serious cost. For them, there were two significant questions: (1) should a value greater than zero be given to the probability that the claim about cold fusion is correct? (2) would there be significant benefits from refuting Pons and Fleischmann if they were incorrect?

Both questions involve issues of authority. Assuming that the probability assigned to the experimental claim weighs the prior authority of the experimenters against the traditional considerations that underlie the antecedent view that there is zero probability of obtaining fusion on a tabletop at room temperature, then, as before, we may write

$$p = z \cdot a(Y, PF)$$

where Y is the scientist making the probability judgment and PF is the composite entity Pons-Fleischmann. To obtain a nonzero probability, all that is required is that nonzero weight be assigned to the prior authority of the experimenters and that they have nonzero prior authority. All that was needed from the telephone conversations *on this score* was the assurance that Pons and Fleischmann were reputable, not outsiders like Gish and Morris.

The second issue is more subtle. Each scientist could assess for herself the costs of delay in current research. The benefits of refuting a challenge to orthodoxy depend, however, on the authority of the challengers within the community. If nobody is prepared to defer to these challengers on this issue, then, supposing that their challenge is wrong, little or no epistemic damage will be done. Similarly, if the challengers are already seen as having low authority, exposing the flaws in the present challenge will not redound to the credit of the refuter. So v will be a nondecreasing function of the perceived authority of the challengers within the community.[18] Suppose, for the sake of simplicity, that

$$v = V \cdot a^*(X)$$

where V is a constant, X is the challenger, and a^* is some averaging function over $a(Y, X)$ for the scientists Y who belong to the community. V will surely be large, for the benefits of exposing errors made by those to whom everybody assigns an authority of 1 are substantial. The crucial inequality for deciding to replicate is thus

$$d < a^*(PF) \cdot V.$$

When telephone calls reveal that other scientists Y give a sizeable value to $a(Y, PF)$, or when it is found that Pons and Fleischmann have high unearned authority, scientists whose delay costs are small will make the decision to investigate their finding.

I began with the worry that appealing to authority could retard desirable changes in science, making it difficult for correct challenges to orthodoxy to be appreciated. Indeed, as we saw earlier, reliance on authority in assessing the credibility of third parties can lead scientists to take a jaundiced view of novel claims. I have explored a highly idealized model in which the community preference is for some efforts at replication, and I have suggested that a variety of epistemic or social forces could lead scientists to modify their research in ways that satisfy this *generic* preference. Moral: the impact of appeals to authority has to be evaluated by recognizing the other forces that come into play in scientific decision-making— even when a high weight is given to unearned authority, even when calibration is indirect, a community is not doomed to stagnation if there are sufficient rewards (social or epistemic) for entrepreneurs and critics.

9. The Problem of Sociological Skepticism

For more than sixty years, biologists argued about the effectiveness of natural selection as an agent of evolutionary change. The controversies were ended in the 1930s when R. A. Fisher, J. B. S. Haldane, and Sewall Wright devised mathematical models of the genetics of evolutionary change, revealing how natural selection can work at the genetic level and comparing its strength with that of mutation. Their mathematical models are highly artificial, typically too simple for the evolutionary situations that interest us the most. Nonetheless, they are absolutely indispensable. Without them, evolutionary biology would be doomed to continued qualitative claims and counterclaims about the effects of contrary factors, all of which are undeniably present.

The artificial analyses that I have given are intended in the same spirit. Studies of past and present scientific developments and debates serve us admirably in recognizing the joint influences of social and nonsocial factors, of encounters with nature *and* conversations with peers. But we need to understand how such factors might be balanced against one another if the welcome naturalistic turn in studies of science is not to descend into interminable wrangles about whose preferred causal agents are most effective. My own analyses are certainly preliminary and very probably wrong. They need to be deepened and extended by considering far more closely the cognitive capacities and limitations of individual scientists and the kinds of motivations they might be expected to have, by looking at more refined indices of social involvement and more realistic decision situations. But they are, I hope, a beginning, an indication of how social epistemology might aspire to be a serious subject and not just a series of promissory notes.

The stance which I have adopted throughout most of this essay is neutral with respect to large questions about realism, relativism, and truth, the kinds of questions that often divide sociologists and philosophers. My preliminary models could be employed in trying to understand the effects of different systems of authority whether or not one embraced realism, constructivism, or relativism. But, in my judgment, much of the point for investigating the effects of authority comes from the need to respond to a deep problem, raised forcefully in some recent work in the sociology of science, that I shall call the problem of *sociological skepticism*. I want to close with some brief remarks about this problem and the role that a theory of authority and deference should be expected to play in addressing it.

Consider some contemporary part of scientific knowledge, say our present beliefs about the transmission of genes, the replication of DNA, or the structures of the organisms whose fossils are found in the Burgess Shale.[19] Realists contend that natural scientists have discovered objects that exist independently of human cognition, and that the claims we make about these objects are, at least approximately, correct. Thus, independently of us, there are genetic systems that behave in the ways that geneticists describe (homologous regions on chromosomes at which, in the typical case, there are equal chances of segregation to gametes), there are RNA polymerases that interact with DNA molecules in roughly the ways depicted in texts and research reports, and there were once organisms in the Cambrian seas that resembled the current drawings of *Anomalacaris* and *Opabinia*. Sociological skepticism questions our right to confidence about these or similar claims. It begins by asking for an explanation of why we believe what we do. That explanation cannot be that we have direct interactions with nature that imprint us with convictions about what the world contains. For, if we reflect on our encounters with the world, we recognize that they are thoroughly mediated. Others who belong to different cultural traditions conceptualize the world quite differently. Thus our categories of genes, nucleic acid molecules, and extinct marine invertebrates are born of our own cultural heritage. Responding to *something* independent of us, we construct it in our own terms, and the realist claim to discover entities (genes, nucleic acids, *Anomalacaris*) that exist independently of ourselves is mistaken.

In portraying this as a skeptical argument, I intend to provide a clue for addressing it. The direct response to skeptical arguments about a class of beliefs is to appeal to procedures that the skeptic will accept to show that the beliefs called into question are correct and that the standard ways of justifying them are reliable. With respect to some forms of local skepticism, the direct response can succeed: for example, there are versions of skepticism about unobservables to which Grover Maxwell's celebrated "slippery slope" argument is an effective counter.[20] However, given an articulation of the direct response, skeptics have the alternative of broadening their skepticism, retracting concessions about reliable ways of generating beliefs that they were previously prepared to make. In the limit, there may be no procedures whatsoever that they will allow as reliable means of validating the disputed claims. When this occurs, the problem posed is effectively insoluble.

One version of this predicament is completely familiar. Among the targets of Descartes's skeptical scrutiny in the *First Meditation* is the class of perceptual beliefs about ordinary middle-sized objects. Descartes's response to doubt consists in attempting to find propositions that cannot be doubted and modes of reasoning that are guaranteed to be reliable that will jointly vindicate a large class of beliefs about external objects and support our normal ways of arriving at those beliefs. Subsequent epistemologists have found his argument less than compelling, but, from the seventeenth century to the middle of our own century, they have imitated his attempt to discover propositions which can be known *a priori* (known for certain) from which it is possible to derive some kind of guarantee for the soundness of our perceptual beliefs. Within the empiricist tradition, the most prominent version of this strategy has been to analyze the content of our perceptual beliefs, showing how the apparent commitment to external objects can be reformulated in other terms (in a sense-datum language) and how one can provide *a priori* justifications for the veridicality of a class of sense-datum statements.

Today this program for addressing skeptical anxieties about perceptual beliefs is widely judged to be hopeless. The common wisdom reflects the force of arguments about the limits of our *a priori* knowledge. The dependence of our knowledge on experience is so pervasive that, when perceptual experience is called into question, we have no resources for constructing a direct response to the skeptic. In Hilbert's famous phrase, our predicament is that of the boxer who has been deprived of the use of his fists.[21]

Does this mean victory for skepticism? In a sense, yes, for we are forced to admit that there is no transcendental guarantee of the correctness of the beliefs that skeptics call into question. But, in another sense, no, because we can recognize that skepticism simply instantiates a general form of insoluble puzzle: if the task is to deploy reasoning that does not presuppose propositions in a particular class C to validate propositions in that class, then it can always be rendered impossible by taking C to be sufficiently large. We should have recognized in advance that we were being invited to play a mug's game.

Nevertheless, the confrontation with skepticism is valuable because it brings home to us the possibility of engaging in more limited epistemological endeavors. Even if we cannot show that global skepticism is incorrect, we do not have to fall back into complacent dogma. The moral, after all, was that we needed some basis of temporarily unquestioned belief from which to justify, criticize, or revise other parts of our system of belief that are, for the moment, viewed as dubious. Descartes began, let us recall, with the suggestion that our senses *sometimes* deceive us. Using what we think we know about the world and our relation to it, we can try to pursue the more limited question of framing conditions under which perception provides reliable access to external nature. This more limited inquiry will not, of course, settle the *global* issue of the reliability of perception. If the skeptic is right, then it may prove quite valueless in that we simply replace one species of error with another. But if the skeptic is wrong, then the enterprise does have a point, for, using some parts of what we take to be knowledge of the world to appraise others, we may improve our epistemic predicament, both by correcting mistakes and, more importantly, improving our belief-generating procedures.

I may seem to have wandered rather far from my announced theme, but this rehearsal of a familiar story seems to me to illuminate the deep challenge posed by contemporary work in the sociology of science. In emphasizing the dependence of human knowledge on authority, contemporary sociologists identify a pervasive feature of our cognitive lives. The global skeptical challenge is to demonstrate, without relying on the authority of those who have preceded us in our scientific tradition, that the claims we make about nature are, at least roughly, correct: that there are genes,

DNA molecules, extinct marine invertebrates, birds, flowers, and rock strata. If we believe that we believe in these things because we have seen them (or had access to them through extensions of our senses, or manipulated them, or inferred to their existence through excellent arguments), then the sociologist will remind us of how we have been *led* to see them. From birth on, we have been acquainted with ways of responding to the "bloomin' buzzin' confusion" of sensory experience, and our divisions of the flux into objects, kinds, categories, depends on that initial deference to the authorities in our tradition. This can be readily appreciated by understanding how children and fledgling scientists are taught to perceive and talk about the world, as well as by noting the differences in conceptualizations achieved by different traditions. How, then, can one show that one particular tradition (Western science) is privileged, that the objects its members discuss are constituents of an independent nature?

The direct response would be to find some propositions that are accepted without any dependence on the authority of others and some methods of reasoning that are equally socially independent, using them in tandem to vindicate our ontology. But that response has effectively already been tried in the Cartesian epistemological tradition. Descartes's retreat to the stove-heated room was intended to block out not only the deliverances of the senses but also the propositions accepted on the authority of others. Just as the project of founding knowledge on propositions that are independent of and invulnerable to sense experience is impossible, so too there is no way of escaping our dependence on authority. The categories in which we might try to formulate the beginnings of a response to sociological skepticism (an analogue to the Cartesian *cogito*) would be those we draw from our tradition, and it is the reliability of that tradition that is in doubt.

However, it might be thought that there are extra resources in the present case, ways of comparing *different* traditions to validate at least some of our contentions about nature. All cultures may not agree that the cassowary is a bird, but surely there are some stable divisions of the world into objects. Moreover, one might try to settle differences in terms of the relative successes of the categorizations deployed by members of rival cultural traditions. These suggestions are no more helpful than the idea that Cartesian skepticism may be met by comparing the perceptions of different individuals, showing that all agree about some things and that those who agree with us about more things are correspondingly more successful. A thoughtful Cartesian skeptic will point out that common perceptual beliefs may be produced by common perceptual errors. Similarly, sociological skepticism can note that agreement between rival traditions need signal only common elements in the chains of authority and not some apprehension of the way the world is.

In the end, I recommend the same response to sociological skepticism that I outlined for skeptical worries about perception. There are two stories about the Western scientific tradition. On the realist story, we find out more and more about the constituents of an independently existing nature: now we know that the world contains genes, nucleic acid molecules, and the fossils of organisms belonging to a large number of Cambrian phyla that are no longer represented in our fauna. Although our beliefs about these matters involve deference to authority, although what we take to be individual reasoning about nature is shot through with dependence on authority, the world also has a causal impact on us, an impact that can cause us to revise our categories, to change our beliefs, and to escape from the domination of some authorities, replacing them by better ones. On the rival, skeptical, story, this is simply pious hope. The world, as it is, is unfathomable (perhaps it is some intrinsically unstructured noumenal reality), and our experience of it is inevitably structured by the categories of a tradition. We can switch traditions, exchanging one set of categories, one set of authorities, for another, but we can neither break free of traditions nor find a basis for deciding which of the rival traditions is "superior" (if that question has any meaning).

Just as there is no showing that our perceptual experience is reliable without taking for granted a substantial part of the belief system that rests on perceptual experience, so too we cannot find a tradition-free standpoint from which to validate the deference to authorities that permeates our cognitive life. The perceptual skeptic might be right. So, too, might the sociological skeptic. However, once that concession has been made, we can take up an epistemological enterprise that is both important and manageable. Using what we think we know about the world, we can investigate the conditions under which perception is likely to work well. Similarly, we can scrutinize the effects of deference to authorities, using what we take to be our knowledge of nature and of people's relations to it to inquire about the circumstances under which particular systems of authority and deference will advance or retard our cognitive projects. Given what we think we know about human beings and the world, how deep and pervasive are the effects of authority within our cognitive life? How might appeals to authority be uncovered and confining authority-deference systems be replaced by better ones? What social systems maximize the chances that we shall be able to use reliance on authority fruitfully without becoming trapped within a system of authority?

My formal accounts of authority are preliminary ways of approaching some of these issues. They need not only deepening and extending, but also supplementing with historical, sociological, and cognitive investigations of the ways in which deference to authority actually figures in the lives of sciences. Even if the global epistemological questions prove unanswerable, the task of improving our epistemic predicament, of trying to haul ourselves up by our bootstraps, remains. Studying the impact of systems of authority is, I suggest, a significant part of that project.

NOTES

1. I would like to thank Michael DePaul, Richard Foley, Steven Shapin, and Frank Sulloway for helpful discussions of the issues that concern me in this paper.

2. My account of reactions to the Pons-Fleischmann announcement depends on the remarks of my cosymposiasts in a panel on the cold fusion controversy, held at the University of California/San Diego in the spring of 1989. I am particularly indebted to Jan Talbot.

3. For creationist challenges to evolution, see Duane Gish *Evolution? The Fossils Say No!* (San Diego: Creation Life Publishers, 1979), and Henry Morris *Scientific Creationism* (San Diego: Creation Life Publishers, 1974). In the early 1980s this literature prompted a number of prominent scientists to write articles for the general public explaining and defending evolution. Many people also took time from research to debate creationists, and some even wrote full-length books. See, for example, Douglas Futuyma, *Science on Trial* (New York: Pantheon, 1983); Norman Newell, *Creation and Evolution: Myth or Reality?* (New York: Columbia University Press, 1983); and Niles Eldredge, *The Monkey Business* (New York: Pocket Books, 1983).

4. The vision of our epistemic predicament, which I endorse without argument here, has been eloquently presented by W. V. Quine. A passage from his essay "Natural Kinds" sums up my own view both of the program in epistemology that Descartes inspired and of the proper form of skeptical worries: "I see philosophy not as an *a priori* propaedeutic or groundwork for science, but as continuous with science. I see philosophy and science as in the same boat—a boat which, to revert to Neurath's figure as I so often do, we can rebuild only at sea while staying afloat in it." Published in *Ontological Relativity and Other Essays* (New York: Columbia University Press, 1969). Reprinted in Hilary Kornblith (ed.), *Naturalizing Epistemology* (Cambridge Mass.: Bradford Books/MIT Press, 1985). The quoted passage is from p. 39 of the reprinted version. For more detailed discussion of the general epistemological issues, see the final section below.

5. Not only is the boundary between these two types of episodes fuzzy, but I want to emphasize that even the use of "individual reason" involves reliance on authority. Thus the contrast of my title, discussed here, focuses on a difference between two ways in which appeals to authority can enter our cognitive lives. In some instances, we are simply passive recipients of information from others, people who are acknowledged as authoritative. In other cases, we try to work things out for ourselves, interacting with asocial nature or using the reasoning skills that we have acquired. Even in these latter instances we depend on the authority of others, on those who taught us the categories that we bring to our observations or who helped us acquire the reasoning propensities that we put to work. However those authorities are not the *sole* determinants of the resultant beliefs. I have tried to defend the idea that our knowledge is socially dependent even in what might seem to be the hardest case, the case of mathematics. See *The Nature of Mathematical Knowledge* (Oxford: Oxford University Press 1983) especially chapters 2–4.

6. Philosophers as diverse as Karl Popper, Thomas Kuhn, Imre Lakatos, Larry Laudan, and Clark Glymour seem to me to adopt this view. Among historians, the most prominent examples are Alexandre Koyré, Charles Gillispie, and I. Bernard Cohen (and the many scholars whom they have influenced).

7. See *Changing Order,* (London: Sage, 1985). A similar stance on issues about realism can be found in other writers. See, for example, Bruno Latour, *Science in Action* (Cambridge Mass.: Harvard University Press, 1987).

8. I have discussed this debate in more detail in *Vaulting Ambition: Sociobiology and the Quest for Human Nature* (Cambridge Mass.: MIT Press, 1985). See, in particular, chapters 1 and 4.

9. See *The Great Devonian Controversy* (Chicago: University of Chicago Press, 1985), particularly chapters 4–8.

10. Again, I want to underscore the point, made in note 5, that thinking and observing for oneself is not independent of reliance on authority. For further discussion of the omnipresence of authority, see the final section.

11. More exactly, we are concerned with X's assessments of the probability that an arbitrary statement (belonging to a particular class—e.g., reports about a particular kind of topic) will be true, *given simply that Y produced or endorsed it.* As we shall see below in section 7, the probabilities you assign to some statements are computed partly on the basis of the content of those statements and partly by considering the authority of those who produce them. This is most evident in cases where erstwhile trustworthy people announce findings that, given the prevailing body of beliefs, seem highly implausible.

12. This is gross oversimplification of a complex practice. Notice first that if the entire corpus of Y's public pronouncements is considered it is likely to contain so many banalities that the truth-ratio will automatically be very high. By relativizing to a range of issues on which Y's pronouncements are considered, I hope to avoid this difficulty. Intuitively, X looks to Y's original contributions on a par-

ticular topic: so, for example, in assessing Pons and Fleischmann, chemists recalled their particular, original claims within electrochemistry and asked how many of these had been subsequently validated. In practice, the complex assertions that scientists make are often used by their peers in evaluations of authority by effectively *atomizing* their published and circulated work. Whole papers, or even series of papers, are identified with a single, central claim, and track records are judged by considering how many of these claims are right (from the perspective of the assessor).

However, other considerations enter in. Trustworthiness is often appraised by considering the experimental and technical skills of the person in question and, in some sciences, inspecting the visual representations that are produced. Hence, even given the relativization to topic that I introduce in my analysis, the idea of computing truth-ratios oversimplifies the practice of direct assessment. I use it here as a way of contrasting the evaluation of track records with the attribution of authority on the basis of social position (itself an equally complicated business), and, for present purposes, oversimplification enables sharp presentation of the issues arising from the contrast. (I am grateful to Michael DePaul for correspondence in which he raised interesting questions about the actual appeal to track records.)

13. Careful qualification is needed here. As Richard Foley pointed out to me, the algebraic approach that I adopt does not mandate conclusions that authority will inevitably have a cramping, conservative effect. It is possible to apply my basic algebraic approach to *different* problem situations, within which appeals to authority can *aid* the introduction of new ideas into the community: simply suppose that those most likely to make innovations are those with highest authority. I have chosen to apply the algebra within a particular problem-situation, that in which innovations are likely to be produced by mavericks with low authority, because this seems to be a common scenario in the development of at least some sciences and because it highlights the apparent problems with deference to authority. To understand fully the confining or liberating effects of authority one would need both an analysis of the impact of authority in different problem-situations and an account of the relative frequencies with which problem-situations arise.

14. Here again, issues about the *kinds* of statements that are being assessed arise. In using Y to rate Z, $a(X,Y)$ must be computed by considering Y's reliability in judgments about the reliability of others with respect to some particular range of scientific topics. $a(X,X)$ is X's measure of X's ability to rate others on that range of topics. If X believes that her beliefs about this topic are likely to be wrong, then she may assign herself quite a low value for $a(X,X)$.

15. As remarked in note 11 above, the probability is computed by considering two factors: the content of the statement and the trustworthiness of the source. The weighting of the prior probability (based on content, and, in the case at hand, 0) and the probability based on utterance by the source (the reliability of

the source on this range of topics) depends on your assessment of the reliability of the two channels. How likely is it that the traditional wisdom is mistaken? What is the chance that the assessment of the authority of the source is suspect? The ratios of the probabilities assigned in answering these questions give the relative weights assigned to the content-based probability and the authority-based probability. See below.

16. I consider some issues that arise from competition among scientists in "The Division of Cognitive Labor," *Journal of Philosophy* 87 (1990): 5–22, and in "David Hull's Credit Economy" (manuscript). Cooperation, competition, and authority will be treated from a more general perspective in a book, *Nothing Like the Sun: Science Without Legend, Objectivity Without Illusions,* forthcoming from Oxford University Press.

17. This is probably fiction. In general (and in the treatment attempted in *Nothing Like the Sun*), I consider a variety of decision-rules, including some which explicitly allow for use of the kinds of heuristics that recent work in cognitive science has brought to our attention. However, a significant amount of variety can be represented by considering various ways in which people's assignments of utility might differ. Thus it is useful to retain the fiction that rational decision theory is employed and to explore the consequences of the presence of heterogeneous utility structures. For example, people within the community may have different attitudes towards authority, some wanting to ally themselves with the scientific *status quo* and others wanting to rebel against it. I am indebted to Frank Sulloway for numerous conversations on the role of respect for authority in science. His important forthcoming article on "Orthodoxy and Innovation in Science" provides an approach that is complementary to the general attitude and the specific suggestions of the present paper.

18. Michael DePaul pointed out to me the possibility that the utility of a successful refutation might depend not only on the perceived authority of the challengers but also on the number of people engaged in attempts to replicate. Thus, once the challenging finding is taken up, there is a possibility of bandwagon effects, even runaway bandwagons. This can easily be modeled by supposing that

$$v = V \cdot a^*(X)(1 + kn)$$

where v, V, a^* are as in the text, n is the number of scientists attempting to replicate/refute the challenging finding, and k is a constant. Since my principal concern is with the conditions under which *someone* replicates, I am effectively looking at the decision problem for someone when $n = 0$, so that there is no difference between the approach in the text and that which would see utility as an increasing function of the number of other replicator/refuters. However, to model the behavior of communities at a finer grain, considering not only whether *someone* will attempt to replicate but also *how many* will drop their current research and do so, distinguishing these two possibilities would be necessary and important. A more fine-grained analysis is undertaken in *Nothing Like the Sun.*

19. For the reconstruction of the Burgess Shale fauna, see Stephen Jay Gould's wonderful *Wonderful Life* (New York: Norton, 1989).

20. See Grover Maxwell, "The Ontological Status of Theoretical Entities," *Minnesota Studies in the Philosophy of Science*, volume III (Minneapolis: University of Minnesota Press, 1962), 3–27.

21. Hilbert originally suggested that the intuitionist denial of the use of the law of excluded middle in mathematics was like depriving a boxer of the use of his fists. See his "The Foundations of Mathematics" in Jean van Heijenoort, ed., *From Frege to Gödel: A Source Book in Mathematical Logic* (Cambridge Mass.: Harvard University Press, 1967), 476.

ONE MORE TURN AFTER THE SOCIAL TURN . . .

Bruno Latour

Like Antony, I could say to philosophers, uncertain whether to stone or welcome the young domain of social studies of science, "I come to bury those studies, not to praise them." After years of swift progress, social studies of science are at a standstill. Cornered in what appears to be a blind alley, its main scholars are disputing with one another on where to go next.*

Many of them advocate a return to common sense and claim that we should shun extreme radicalism and take on the classic sociology of scientists (not of science), spiced with a speck of constructivism. Through meetings and journals, I sense a reactionary mood: "Let's abandon the crazy schools and turn to serious matters of science policy and the impact of technology on society. The field has suffered enough from extremism; let's go back to the happy medium." The most generous believe that political relevance for our field will be achieved more readily if we stop dabbling with esoteric theories and instead seize traditional concepts off the shelf. A few, who call themselves reflexivists, are delighted at being in a blind alley; for fifteen years they had said that social studies of science could not go anywhere if it did not apply its own tool to itself; now that it goes nowhere and is threatened by sterility, they feel vindicated. A few others, among the most serious, stick to their trade, deny that they are in a blind alley and go on with business as usual, without realizing that the law of diminishing returns is at work here, as elsewhere, and that professional loyalties are no guarantee against obsolescence. But, fortunately, dozens of researchers are looking for ways out of the deadlock: in literary theory, biology, cognitive science, cultural history, ethnology, ethnography of skills, moral economics, interactionism, and networks. That their moves do not appear more principled or straight than those of a disturbed anthill does not mean that they are not going to find the way. Quite the contrary.

Being one of those ants, accused of being not only frantic but also French, I wish to explore in this paper one of the possible ways out of the

272

dead end that would not force us to retrace our steps. Instead of being less extreme, I want to show that by being a little *more* radical we would end up in a productive and commonsensical research program that would allow us to capitalize on the last twenty years' work and resume our swift pace.

1. The Trap We Built for Ourselves

But first we have to survey the path that led the field of social studies of science to its present quandary. Like any summary, it will appear unfair to everyone's work—including my own—but the aim of this paper is the future of our field, not its past.

The name of the domain, "Sociology of Scientific Knowledge," tells it all, as indeed does the name of this volume. So far, it has been the *application* of social sciences—mainly sociology but also anthropology—to the practice of science. The decisive advance occurred when it was realized that, contrary to what traditional sociology of knowledge and Mertonian sociology of science told us, the *content* of science is fully capable of study, and the implementation of this research program is *a single task* for historians, sociologists, philosophers, and economists. I take those two points as being established beyond doubt (Shapin, 1982; Latour, 1987).

Doubts are back, however, as soon as we look at the *explanatory* resources mobilized to account for the practice of science. Our domain is a battlefield littered with interrupted explanations. All the efforts at using macrosociology to account for the microcontent of science are fraught with difficulties; only very broad features like styles, worldviews, and cultures have been explained. The only research programs that have been successful are those which put to use a fine-grained sociology: ethnomethodology, microsociology, symbolic interactionism, cognitive anthropology, cultural history, and history of practices. The problem with those programs is that they, indeed, account nicely for the details of scientific practice but entirely lose track of the main goals of macrosociology—that is, an account of what holds the society together. They have all been accused (and rightly) of cranking out nice case studies without even the beginnings of social theory or political relevance. It seems that either the social science is subtle enough to explain the content of science but the making of a global society is left in the dark, or that macrosociology is back in but the details of science disappear from view. When literary studies are included it is often worse, since we now have fine-grained studies of scientific rhetoric but even the mere idea of a social explanation is given up. When cognitive sciences are brought in, it is worse still, since social scientists have to renounce any interest in noncognitive explanations or be relegated to an appendix. It is as if we cannot have sociology and the content of science under the same gaze at once.

Another way to sum up the diagnosis is to say that most of the so-called social studies of science are largely *internalist* studies. They did not appear so to the English-speaking world because of the very abstract way in which philosophy of science had been carried on in the Anglo-American tradition before we began to work. When, for instance, Harry Collins added to the gravitation waves animals such as replication, negotiation, styles, core-sets, and authority, philosophers of science mistook that zoo for the social (and so did Collins [1985]). Viewed, however from a Continental point of view, most of the "sociological" points could have been made—and indeed had been made—by *internalist* philosophers informed by the history of scientific practice, like Duhem, Mach, Bachelard, or Canguilhem. Social studies of science were not adding society to science but were adding some historical flesh to the often barren English-speaking philosophy of science.

It is now clear that it is as difficult to tie the main concerns of sociology and politics to the microsociological studies of science as it was in the past to tie them to rabid internalism. Most of the good case studies, if we look at them dispassionately, are internalist explanations sandwiched in between macro- or mesosociological explanations without much connection between the two. The reason why this recipe did not appear so clearly at first was that we all had to fight against the dictates of Mertonian sociology, rational reconstruction of science, and history of ideas, each claiming that the study of scientific practice was infeasible *in principle*. The stubbornness of their defenders forced us to a polemical stand. Now that this battle has been more or less won, and we can examine in peace the quality of the explanations given for the social construction of the contents of science, it is fair to say that they are found wanting. Few of them convincingly tie the fabric of macrosociety to the contents of science, and most follow up bits and pieces of networks, the ends of which are left loose. What the best studies achieve is to spread successive levels on top of one another, the first of which is distinctively "macro" while the last one is clearly technical. They fix club sandwiches instead of hamburgers!

This diagnosis is not new. It was, on the contrary, the starting point of the radical brands of "social" (now in quotation marks) studies of science. Reflexivists have argued all along that it was not desirable to provide a social explanation of scientific content since it would mean that sociology was immune to the critical treatment that it applied to chemistry or physics (Woolgar, 1988; Ashmore, 1989). Ethnomethodologists went much further by denying any relevance to sociology and claiming that social explanations should not be provided at all. It is, on the contrary, they claim, the local technical content of the practitioners that should be used to explain their own world. "There is no other metalanguage to use but the language of the sciences themselves" is Garfinkel-Lynch's principle, in which a new brand of internalism and radical sociology have become barely distinguishable (Lynch, 1985).

The same could be said of us, the so-called actor-network theorists. We extend the principle of symmetry to social sciences and we claim that they, too, are part of our problem, not of our solution. Networks of associations replace both the content of science and society. The growth of networks through translations replaces the differences of scale between micro-, meso-, and macrolevels. Exactly as for reflexivists and ethnomethodologists, the question of a social explanation is dissolved (Callon, 1989; Law, 1986; Latour, 1987). But so are also the resources for understanding our own position. Networks may be "seamless webs," but they appear to our colleagues and nevertheless friends to involve a catchall concept, where everything being possible, nothing is clear and distinct anymore. Everything being a network, nothing is (Shapin, 1988; Collins and Yearley, 1990).

Somber diagnosis, indeed! The more conservative schools have failed to provide a continuous tie between the contents of science and the concerns of sociology. And the radical groups who deconstructed the very aim of a social explanation end in sterility, in jargon, or in a maze of entangled networks. The Gordian knot that tied science and society together before Alexander's sword cut them asunder is still there awaiting someone patient enough to tie it again!

Even if I have overdramatized our quandary, it remains true that outsiders to the field see us like that. Whatever we write or say, the field of social studies of science is recast by friends and enemies alike as the "merely social" argument (Star, 1988). Then, it is not difficult for them to argue that to the "merely social" or "sociohistorical" explanation should now be added *another* explanation, a more internalist one. No wonder if many of our critics, feeling vindicated, rejoice and claim that science is indeed thoroughly incapable of analysis in social terms, that they had long ago shown this impossibility from first principles, and that their graduate students should return to the study of scientists (or of science), or delve into the fashionable cognitive sciences or turn to normative philosophy or science policy. Back to common sense! Down with constructivism! Enough of theory! As for many atheoretical historians, unsettled for a moment, they might believe that since boxes of archives are waiting to be ransacked, they no longer need the help of all those crazy sociologists.

Here is the blind alley. Here is the trap that we built for ourselves, from which we should escape and resume our quick progress without accepting those reactionary research programs that represent themselves as commonsense or claim to rest comfortably in the golden mean between internalism and externalism.

2. One-dimensional Science

'Radical', 'progressivist', 'conservative', 'reactionary', 'golden mean'. I used these political adjectives on purpose because they all retrace the same line that is the cause of our deadlock and from which I want to escape. A radical is someone who claims that scientific knowledge is entirely constructed "out of" social relations; a progressivist is someone who would say that it is "partially" constructed out of social relations but that nature somehow "leaks in" at the end. At the other side of this tug-of-war, a reactionary is someone who would claim science becomes really scientific only when it finally sheds any trace of social construction; while a conservative would say that although science escapes from society there are still factors from society that "leak in" and influence its development. In the middle, would be the marsh of wishy-washy scholars who add a little bit of nature to a little bit of society and shun the two extremes. This is the yardstick along which we can log most of our debates. If one goes from left to right then one has to be a social constructivist; if, on the contrary, one goes from right to left, then one has to be a closet realist. As indicated by the two arrows in the diagram below, explanations in this frame of reference are accepted only if they start from one of the two extremities, Nature or Society, and move toward the other. Either one is a "natural realist" and one explains the evolution of society, the establishment of consensus by the state of Nature, or one is a "social realist" and explains by social factors how it is that humans settle on matters of fact, or one alternates between the two (Collins and Yearley, 1990). All the intermediary cases are seen as a mixture of these two pure forms, Nature and Society.

This tug-of-war is played in one dimension. It is fun to play, but after twenty years of it we might shift to other games, especially since it makes incomprehensible the very linkages between Nature and Society we wish to account for. I claim that the only way to go on with our work is to abandon this frame of reference and to set up another standard, all the

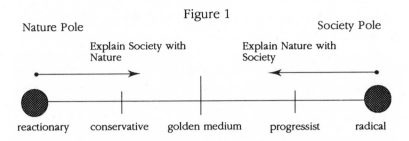

Figure 1

more so if other scholars go on to make it more subtle, more precise by adding finer divisions and other labels to the same one-dimensional yard-stick (Giere, 1988). We do not want finer divisions and new schools of philosophy of science. We want philosophy to do its job and discover the origin of the yardstick in order for us to overcome it.

The yardstick of our debates was set up by Kant for polemical reasons and since then sociologists, as well as philosophers of science, have adopted it without misgiving. Kant rejected at the two poles—Things-in-themselves on the one hand, the Transcendental Ego, on the other— the resources that, when put together, would account for knowledge. This was the foundation of the *Critique* that made us modern, more modern.[1] To be sure, empirical scientific knowledge appeared in the middle, but this middle, the phenomenon, was understood only as the *meeting point* of the two purified sets of resources coming from the subject pole or from the object pole.

There are two reasons why this standard did not appear so bad at first. To begin with, philosophers and sociologists fought so violently to occupy the subject pole designated by Kant—the focus of the Sun in his Coper-nican Revolution—that no one realized that it did not make much difference[2] whether the elected ruler was Kant's Ego, Durkheim's macro-Society, Foucault's *epistemes*, Dewey's praxis, Wittgenstein's language games, collectives of scientists, brains and neurons, minds, or cognitive structures—as long as this one ruler capitalized all the explanatory re-sources and had the object turning around it. Where they came from— transcendence, evolution, practice, innate structures—did not matter too much either, as long as phenomena were shaped, in the end, by the dom-inant authority of this "Sun" pole. The internal rivalry among schools hid the identity of the position to be so strenuously occupied. When compared to the weight of the *Critique* framework, the debates that oppose innate categories to collective *epistemes*, individual minds to groups of scientists, neuronal pathways to social structures, appear minor.

The second reason why this framework had such a great weight is that it was strongly asymmetric. The Sun focus was what counted, not the object circling around it, and thus there were no comparable squabbles about how to modify the status of the object. It really seemed that if one could occupy the right-hand side of the yardstick, much of the left-hand side would be explained. From Kant onwards, the Things-in-themselves were left indeed to themselves, without initiative, without activity, passively shaped and framed by the various models or categories pressed upon them. Their only task was to guarantee the transcendental nonhuman character of our knowledge in order to avoid the dire consequences of idealism. Paradoxically, the beautiful movement of Copernicus's Revolution was used by the *Critique* to describe an anthropocentric (or sociocentric or logocentric) enterprise.

In our small field, Bloor's book (1976) was the high-tide mark of this asymmetrical philosophy. As an obedient child of the *Critique,* Bloor designated Durkheimian social structures to occupy the Sun's focus and gave the name 'symmetry' to the principle that required us to explain successes and failures in the development of science in the same sociological terms. This was, to be sure, a major advance, since until then only good science was explained by appealing to Nature and only bad science by appealing to Society. However, the very success of this principle of symmetry disguised the complete *a*symmetry of Bloor's argument. Society was supposed to explain Nature! We start from one of the poles to account for the other.

If the one-dimensional diagram I have drawn appears simple-minded and sketchy even after Bloor's "strong program," it might very well be that our implicit philosophy is indeed as simple-minded and as sketchy as that. It is certainly as one-dimensional as that, and this is enough to explain our previous deadlock: if any move away from one of the poles is a move toward the other, it means that every new position—whatever its originality, direction, and trajectory—will be logged, obsessively, along this single line as a particular combination of the object pole and the subject/collective pole. The two attractors at the extremity of the line are so strong that no new position is tenable since it will be seen as giving strength to one of the two teams engaged in this tug-of-war. The Wall of Berlin has fallen, ideologies are said to be gone, but realists and constructivists are still positioning one another as if we were in the worst days of the 1960s when our opinions had to be pigeon-holed as Left or Right.

Fortunately, the two factors that rendered the one-dimensional frame of reference inevitable are now gone: from the relative failures of the social studies of science, we learned that the various schools that strive to occupy the subject/society position make no difference to the general structure of the explanation. We also learned the historical origin of this philosophical asymmetry between the two poles, between the representation of things and the representation of humans (Shapin and Schaffer, 1985; Serres, 1987; Latour, 1990b). To this day, Bloor has not realized that his principle cannot be implemented if another much more radical symmetry is not introduced, a symmetry that treats this time the subject/society pole *in the same way* as the object pole (Callon, 1986). This 90° shift is what I call "one more turn after the social turn" (Figure 2). But in order to make this turn and thus free our field from its deadlock, we need to set up another yardstick that will give us another dimension.

Figure 2

Asymmetry before Bloor

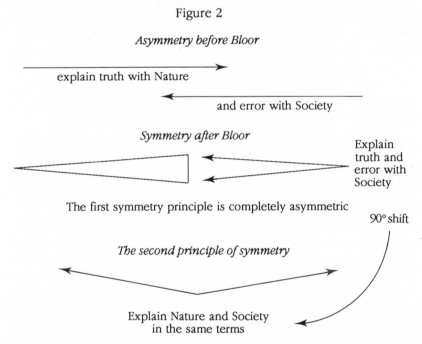

explain truth with Nature

and error with Society

Symmetry after Bloor

Explain truth and error with Society

The first symmetry principle is completely asymmetric

90° shift

The second principle of symmetry

Explain Nature and Society
in the same terms

The second principle absorbs, completes, and makes the first possible
but requires a second dimension to be implemented

3. A Counter-Copernican Revolution

At least the problem is now well-defined. Is it possible to modify the respective position of the two attractors, the object pole and the subject/collective pole? Is it possible to modify their number: one, three, many?

Is it possible to construct another scale that would allow us to evaluate works and arguments in a second dimension not reducible to the single one described above? Is it possible to do all of that without jargon that would add obscurity to obscurity and without leaving the solid ground of empirical case studies of scientific practice, the ground that I said is the only stable certainty of this new field, common to sociologists, philosophers, and historians of science?

A look at the literature of our field shows that these questions are not at the same level of difficulty. Paradoxically, the last two appear more difficult, since no one, to my knowledge, has offered a clear standard for evaluating works and arguments, a standard at least as finely graded as the one we wish to discard, and since the many philosophies which have tried to "overcome the subject/object dichotomy" have been unable to offer us a precise description of scientific practice and are often shrouded in a thick fog.

Let us start at the relatively "easy" part, the ontological one. The first move is a counter-Copernican revolution that forces the two poles, Nature and Society, to shift to the center and to fuse into one another. This fusing, however, is no simple matter, and the properties of the two poles have to be completely redistributed, since it was their separation that defined them. The main property of the object pole was to guarantee that our world of knowledge not be human-made (whatever the definition of 'human' we chose: self, mind, brain, collective); while the main property of the subject pole was, on the contrary, to guarantee that our knowledge be human-made (whichever definition of human activity one sticks to: transcendental Ego, society, subject, mind, brain, *epistemes,* language games, praxis, labor). In addition, the very distinction between the two poles—the distinction which Kant made so sharp—warranted that those two contradictory guarantees would *not* be confused, because the two transcendences—that of the object "out there" and that of the subject/society "up there"—are sources of authority *only if they are as far apart as possible* (Shapin and Schaffer, 1985). They should not mingle with one another any more than the executive branch of government with the judiciary branch.[3]

The word 'fact' sums up this threefold system of guarantees. A fact is at once what is fabricated and what is not fabricated by anyone. But the two meanings of the word are never simultaneously present, so that we always feel it necessary to alternate between two asymmetric explanations for the solidity of reality—constructivisim or realism.

How can we fuse the two poles together and still retain their three main properties?

(a) the nonhuman origin of knowledge;

(b) its human origin;

(c) the complete separation between the two.

If we retain the three at once, it is impossible to move on, since the three together define the *Critique* on which the whole field of science studies is based. If we abandon the first one, we fall into various brands of social constructivism, forced to build our world with social relations. If we abandon the second, we fall into various brands of realism and are led to build Society with Nature. The only one that might be discarded is the third. Is it proven that the first two guarantees are enforced *only* by the *Critique* or the Modern Constitution that imposes their complete separation and classifies all explanations in two asymmetrical repertoires? As soon as the question is raised, the point of view is shifted along a new dimension, orthogonal to the first one, and a striking mirror symmetry appears: the two asymmetrical repertoires of realism and constructivism are mirror images of one another. Their symmetry is so exact that a completely coherent framework may be provided if we retain the first two guarantees and discard the third. To be sure there is a price to pay and that is to abandon the *Critique,* or in other words to rewrite the Modern Constitution.

To be sure, the two remaining guarantees are strongly affected by the abandonment of the third. As with all tight-knit structures, taking away one component alters the position of the others.

First modification: Instead of the two opposite transcendences of Nature[4] and Society—not to mention that of the bracketed-out God—we have only *one* transcendence left. We live in a Society we did not make, individually or collectively, and in a Nature which is not of our fabrication. But Nature "out there" and Society "up there" are no longer ontologically different. We do not make Society, anymore than we do Nature, and their opposition is no longer necessary.

Second modification: Instead of providing the explanatory resources in order to account for empirical phenomena, this common transcendence becomes what is to be explained. Instead of being the opposite *causes* of our knowledge, the two poles are a single consequence of a common practice that is now the single focus of our analysis. Society (or Subject, or Mind, or Brain . . .) cannot be used to explain the practice of science and, of course, Nature cannot either, since both are the results of the practice of science- and technology-making (Latour, 1987, rules 3 and 4). Contrary to the expectation of the "social" students of science—and contrary to the fear of their opponents—the two realisms (social and natural) have to be discarded *together* if either one is to go, since they are one and the same. Or else, both have to be kept.

This new generalized principle of symmetry flows directly from the development of science studies and, in my view, is their most important philosophical discovery. As long as the social sciences did not apply their tools to Nature and to Society at once, the identity of the two transcendences and its common constructed character were left in the dark. Even when established science and stable society were studied together, their common production was still not visible. Only when science in action and society in the making were studied simultaneously did this essential phenomenon become observable. This is why the intermediary solution—social realism alternating with natural relativism—advocated for many years by colleagues like David Bloor or Harry Collins is, in the long run, counterproductive for the field as well as for their own program (Callon and Latour, 1990).

Third modification: This is a direct corollary of the two others. Instead of always being explained by a mixture of the two "pure" transcendences, the activity of nature/society making becomes the *source* from which societies and natures originate. In the Modern Constitution, nothing interesting happened at the meeting-point of the two poles—the phenomenon—since it was just that: at best a meeting point, at worst a confusing boundary. In what I call, for want of a better term, the non-Modern Constitution, everything interesting begins at what is no longer a meeting point but the origin of reality. In the Modern Constitution, one could only say that this production was a hybrid of two pure forms; in the non-Modern one, it is an understatement to talk of hybrids or of monsters. Collins's gravity waves, Shapin's and Schaffer's air-pump, Callon's scallops, Geison's microbes, to take just a few examples, are not to be defined as being half natural, half social. They are neither objects, nor subjects, nor a mixture of the two. This is why, after Serres (1987), I call them *quasi-objects*. It is out of their production and circulation that something originates that looks somewhat like Nature "out there," as well as somewhat like Society "up there." What metaphor could express this reversal? Pure Nature and pure Society may exist but they would be like two solid tectonic plates cooling from the hot liquid magma emerging at the seams. Our work aims at exploring this seam and at taking into account the temperature and the direction of the flow.

Fourth modification: History, which was locked away, according to the Modern Constitution, is back in the center. Since whatever happened had to be either the discovery of nature "out there" or the construction by society "up there," history had to be a zero-sum game to be explained by two lists of ingredients, one coming from nature, the other from society. Now, on the contrary, it is the experimental scene that produces and shapes new actants[5] that then increase the long list of ingredients that make up our world. Historicity is back, and it flows from the experiments, from the trials of force (Latour, 1990a). We do not have, on the one hand, a history of contingent human events and, on the other, a science of necessary laws, but a common history of societies and of things. Pasteur's microbes are neither timeless entities discovered by Pasteur, nor the effect of political domination imposed on the laboratory by the social structure of the Second Empire, nor are they a careful mixture of "purely" social elements and "strictly" natural forces. They are a new social link that redefines at once what nature is made of and what society is made of.

Fifth and final (?) modification: The ontological activity that is no longer capitalized at the two extremities may be redistributed among all the actants. It was the necessity of the dual system of appeal either to nature or to society that in the Kantian framework caused all the agencies to be assigned to two and only two lists. Now that we are freed from this necessity, we are allowed to have *as many poles as there are actors*. This irreductionist principle is probably the most counterintuitive consequence of science studies but it is a necessary and a coherent one (Latour, 1988, part II). Monsters that the Modern Constitution wished to cleave into two pure forms (entelechies, monads, field, forces, networks) are back, claiming an ontological status that does not resemble either that of the forlorn and passive things-in-themselves, or that of humans-among-themselves. Too social to look like the former, they remain too nonhuman to resemble the latter. Dignity, activity, and world-making ability are reclaimed by those actants that are, nevertheless, fully nonhuman, and fully real. Mere intermediaries in the Modern Constitution, they become full-blown mediators in the non-Modern, more democratic, one. Yes, the Gordian knot is tied once again and tightly so.[6]

The problem with this counter-Copernican revolution is that it seems absurd if logged onto the realist-constructivist frame of reference, since every reading of the new object-subject production will appear as yet another "golden-mean" solution. Worse, since the new frame does not make reference to the two extremes, Nature and Society, that previously allowed a coherent interpretation to be drawn, it seems as if common sense were abandoned and a completely obscure field of studies of science were to replace a narrow-minded but at least well-defined one. If I begin, for instance, granting activity to the nonhumans once again, sociologists of science (Collins and Yearley, 1990) begin to protest that outmoded realist positions are back, even though the new active nonhumans are utterly different from the boring inactive things-in-themselves of the realists' plot.

Conversely, if I speak of a history of things, realist philosophers immediately start accusing me of denying the nonhuman reality of Nature, as if I were asking actors to play the equally tedious role of humans-among-themselves so common in the stories of the sociologists. On the other hand, their joint indignation is understandable since they have no other frame of reference than the Modern one and thus they cannot locate our position on their instruments. After having written three books to show the impossibility of a social explanation of science and having been praised (and more often castigated) for providing a social explanation, I am now convinced that no further progress will be made if we do not change our touchstone.

4. Adding a Second Dimension

Now that the ontology of a viable substitute for the Modern Constitution has been sketched, the next goal is to set up a clearcut standard to locate the various positions and to differentiate nuances of argument at least as finely as with the old instrument—and more finely, if possible. If I sketch the new yardstick, I obtain a diagram that is admittedly crude, but let us remember that the philosophy implicit in science studies might be as crude as that. The one-dimensional yardstick allowed one to position any entity along the object-subject line. I showed that although this was useful, it did not do justice to most of the discoveries of science studies: objects and subjects are belated consequences of an experimental and historical activity that does not clearly differentiate if an entity is "out there" in nature or "up there" in society. This means that any entity should also be logged according to its degree of stabilization.

Figure 3 is an attempt to define any entity by two sets of coordinates instead of one. One line is the distance to P, the locus of the phenomenon in Kant's scenario, and goes either to the subject/collective pole or to the object pole. The other is the degree of stabilization going from O to P', from instability to stability. It is clear from the diagram that the one-dimensional yardstick I criticized above corresponds to only *one* value of the stabilization gradient. When everything is settled, there is indeed a clear-cut difference between A "out there," and B "up there." Pasteur's microbes are clearly discovered or constructed out of natural and material

Figure 3
Stabilization gradient

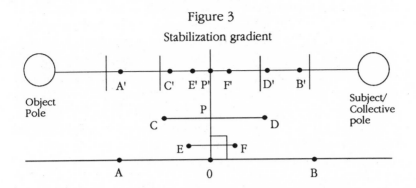

Object
Pole

Subject/
Collective
pole

actants that lie outside the control of our human wishes; hygienic ideas about asepsy and antisepsy are sure means of settling the dispute between Health and Wealth during the Second Empire. For this value of OP′, science students are torn between those two alternative transcendences: a nature that is not of our social making; a society that is not of natural origin. They then have to explain Pasteur's achievements by what nature is like, or to account for his discoveries by what society is made of, or to choose any intermediate mixture of pure nature and pure society, or to alternate at will between extreme naturalism and (should I say?) extreme socialism.

But suppose that I now wish to write a book on Pasteur's microbes where I change the value of this whole debate along the "stabilization gradient" (Latour, 1988). Let us say that I now explore the line CD instead of the line A′B′, or even the line EF. The complete gamut of positions is now squeezed in the middle and a different account of the entities Pasteur is struggling with becomes possible. Is the microbe a living entity, a chemical one, a physical one, a social one? This is still uncertain. Is nature large enough to accommodate invisible powerful microbes? We will learn the answer from Pasteur's experiments. Are the Second Empire and the Third Republic able to absorb new social links that will add the multitude of microbes to the normal social relations? We are learning the response from Pasteur's laboratories. Whereas, for a higher value of the "stabilization gradient," it is important to decide whether or not something is social or natural, it is meaningless for lower values since this is where what natures and societies are is defined.

Naturally, as the diagram nicely indicates, if I now project the state of the nature/society building I am studying onto the one-dimensional yardstick, my analysis will be completely misunderstood. C′ will be taken to mean the emergence of a stabilized natural actant—the nonhuman microbe plays a big role in my story—and D′ will be taken to mean that I give too much activity to stabilized social groups (or too little, depending on who is reviewing the book). Worse still, if EF is projected on the same line, E′ and F′ are now seen as wishy-washy solutions to the problem of realism versus constructivism! I am now seen as attempting to escape the internalist/externalist quandary by squeezing my entities around P′, the safe and golden mean, the meeting point of nature and society. But I am not interested just in P′; I am interested in all the values taken along the orthogonal dimension. Instead of having endless discussions on social constructivism, is it asking too much to focus our debates on a few other values of the stabilization gradient?

There is another major advantage in unfolding our debates on two dimensions instead of one: points become lines. As soon as we consider two sets of coordinates for every single entity—its degree of naturalness or socialness on the one hand, and its degree of stabilization on the other—we become able to do justice to the variable ontology of the entities we all studied in our case studies. Boyle's air pump, Pasteur's microbes, Millikan's electrons, do not have to be defined as points in the one-dimensional diagram, but as *trajectories* in the two-dimensional one. The "same" microbe may be close to E, then to F, then to B′, then to A′, then to C, depending on its history. The "same" entity may occupy many states, being impurely social, then purely social, then purely natural, then impurely natural. The "same" actant will be immanent and then transcendent, made and nonmade, human made and discovered, freely decided and imposed upon us as a *Fatum*. To use still other words, essences become existences and then essences again. Quasi-objects may alternate and become objects, or subjects, or quasi-objects again, or disappear altogether. The main philosophical interest of science studies, I contend, is in habituating us to consider those variable ontologies. Every actant has an original signature in the diagram above, and there will be as many "microbes" as there are points along the trajectory.

Many words have been offered recently to define such a trajectory. Serres (1987) used the word 'quasi-object' to designate what circulates in the collective and shapes it by its very circulation. Callon (1986) has offered the term 'actor-network' to convey the same double function of nature-building and society-building. In a more restricted way, Shapin and Schaffer (1985) have proposed 'forms of life' and Lynch (1985) 'experimental practice' to designate this activity that turns on the silent laboratory-made or society-making experiment. I have played with the words 'allies', 'collective things', 'entelechies', 'actants', 'networks', and 'modalities'. All

these words, since they designate either state, or process, or actions, however, may be misunderstood when they are seen as one pole in the one-
dimensional frame or as the mere combination of the two. In order to be
adequate, they themselves have to be adjusted to this new two-dimensional
yardstick. As soon as they are meant to designate points, they become
meaningless. Their meaning comes only when they are used to stretch the
ontological variations of those bizarre monsters we have uncovered.

'Monsters', 'imbroglios', and 'mixtures' are themselves ambiguous
terms. The paradox is that with the one-dimensional yardstick science students are unable to account for their own discoveries. The reason why we
all went studying laboratories, active controversies, skills, instrument-
making, and emerging entities was to encounter unstable states of nature/
society and to document what happens in those extreme and novel
situations. Most philosophies of science and all of the social sciences were,
on the contrary, considering either stabilized sets of natures facing stabilized sets of societies, or letting only one of them be unstable at once. The
misunderstanding was complete since what is the rule for us was the exception for them. We see only emerging society/nature, they consider only
purely social or strictly natural entities. What is the rule for them, purity,
is the exception for us. Whereas they are obsessed by the debates between
"out there" and "up there," we focus on a region hitherto unknown which
might be called "down there." Had we possessed the one-dimensional
yardstick only, considered the two sides apart, inspected the lines from the
two extremities, and tried to explain an agent by using Nature and Society as causes, we could have been unable even to suspect the existence of
the basic phenomenon discovered by science studies, that is the coproduction of collective things. All the entities from the bottom half of Figure 3
would be squeezed around P, the place for wishy-washy interpretations.
Thus the framework that the whole field employs to calibrate its evaluations of case studies is totally unable to do justice to what the case studies
reveal. The only thing it can convey about entities is that they are a tangle
of science and society or a little bit of both . . . No wonder that the domain is in a blind alley; it is not even able to define the instrument that
would allow us to read its results!

5. A Non-Modern World for Science Studies

Science students all too often either believe they should shun philosophy or that they should borrow whatever philosophy there is off the shelf.
It is my contention that in order to make sense of quasi-objects, science
students will have to take philosophy much more seriously; they even

might have to redefine their own metaphysics in order to deal with the bizarre ontological puzzles revealed by their discoveries of the collective-things. The originality of this discovery cannot, in my view, be over-stated. To use again the terms I have defined above, science studies ease us into the *non-Modern* (or a-modern) world. Until now, we have been shaped by the idea that we were modern. What we are witnessing, and what explains the present interest in science studies, is the end of this belief, the end of the two Enlightenments. The first Enlightenment used the nature pole in order to debunk the false pretenses of the social one. Natural sciences were at last unveiling nature and destroying obscurantism, domination, and bigotry. The second Enlightenment used the social pole in order to debunk the false pretenses of the natural one. The social sciences—economics, psychoanalysis, sociology, semiotics—were at last debunking the false claims of naturalism and scientism. Marxism, of course, made so strong an appeal because it appeared to join the two Enlightenments together: the natural sciences helped us to criticize powers and dominations; the social sciences allowed us to criticize the natural sciences, and their naturalized powers and dominations. When the painful realization dawned that Marxism was untenable, we then moved to what is called "post modernism." We were still modern, we still wished to debunk, and criticize, and unveil, but the solid grounds that guaranteed the strength of our attack had vanished. It seemed that without a belief in a solid state of society, or a solid state of science, there could only be despair and cynicism.

It was at this historical moment that science studies entered the field. For it, an unstable state of society *and* nature is a normal state of affairs. What explains, in my view, the present limitations of our field is that we have not yet reconciled our discoveries with our philosophical framework. We still believe it necessary to be modern or postmodern, when our own field studies point to another historical moment: we have become non-modern, that is, we have never *been* modern. Suddenly, we look at our sciences, our technologies, our societies, and they are on a par with what anthropology has taught us of other cultures.

With such a realization, the Modern framework that made unthinkable the discoveries of science studies is now entirely dissolved. The two poles on the horizontal line in the Modern yardstick were used to differentiate between the few collectives which had access to Nature because they could break away from the constraints of Society, and others—the primitives, the ancients, the poor—which were forever inhabiting the prison of their symbols or their social categories. Such was the great divide between Us and Them, a divide that is nothing but the anthropological rendering of the divide between the object pole and the subject/collective pole, the exportation abroad, so to speak, of our civil strife. It was the two divides taken together that made us modern. Not only did we completely separate the representation of things from the representation of humans—not to mention the bracketing out of God—but this separation set us apart from any other society of the past and any non-Western society, since we were the only ones doing so. The nonmodern representation is that neither of those two divides is necessary. There is no separation between the object and the society; we Westerners go on doing what everyone has always been doing, that is, growing "down there" collective-things that may end up being nature "out there" and society "up there." There has never been any modern world (Latour, 1988). Still, there are many differences between various productions of collective-things, but they are probably no more than differences of scale like so many loops of a spiral (Serres, 1987); to "bigger" collectives more "objective" natures; to "smaller" collectives, more "subjective" natures. Comparative anthropology may start at last to be symmetric.

Once we enter the nonmodern world (and again this is not a new era but only the retrospective discovery that we never entered the modern era, that no Copernican revolution has ever taken place), we are able to understand why the main philosophical schools are so inadequate to help us in our empirical field studies of science-society-making. Everything hinges upon what to do with the point P′ in Figure 3. What was in the seventeenth century the settlement of a dispute over the authority of humans and nonhumans, a mere *distinction* between two regimes of representation (Shapin and Schaffer, 1985), became a *separation* with Kant's Copernican Revolution. Kant had not finished writing up his Modern Constitution when dialectical philosophers tried to overcome the radical distinction between the object pole and the subject pole he had proposed. Instead of retracing his steps, however, they pushed the *Critique* further. Not only did they maintain the ternary structure Kant had offered, they elevated the distinction between object/subject to the rank of a *contradiction*. This contradiction was then "solved" by letting the object and the subject overcome each other in turn, making a synthesis out of the two. The strength of the spring, the strength that made the whole dialectical machine tick, was directly related to the distance between the pure object and the pure subject. Far from dissolving the two opposing positions, dialectics made good use of absolute contradiction to produce history out of it. The worst thing that could have happened to a dialectician would have been to dissolve for good the dichotomy that made us modern. While, with Kant, a trace was left clearly visible of the radical move that built up the separation between object and subject, no such trace remained in dialectics. "Overcoming" the distinction made it invisible and forever impossible to overcome. The power of denial became a fantastic denegation of the quandary.

Dialectics at least tried to span all the ontological states and to embrace nature and society in a single narrative. Not so later, with the many schools of phenomenology and with existentialism. Although intentionality was supposed to do away with the object-subject dichotomy, it was more like someone whose legs are stretched between two boats that are pulling apart. The tension was so extreme that, in effect, intentionality was allotted to humans. As to things out there, emptied of any meaning, will, intentionality, or even being, they had to fend for themselves. They had to wait for meaning to be granted to them by an intentional consciousness. Of course, in a well-balanced minuet, the other side was taken over by the many schools of thought who naturalized the whole question and transformed collectives, cultures, languages, and ideas into parts of the material world of mindless things. Materialism, biologism, evolutionary theory, behaviorism, evolutionary epistemology, neurosciences, all these attempts, no matter how interesting, are nothing more, according to the geometry of our diagram, than a folding along the vertical plane of symmetry. The distance to P' remains the same. For science students, not much is gained by merging the subject/collective pole into the Nature pole. The practice of science, its historical production, remains as invisible as it does with phenomenology (Bradie, 1986).

Still, phenomenology and evolutionary theory remained remarkably useful for science studies compared to what was to come later. Modernist philosophers are now trying to save us from the perils of post-modernism by widening still further the gap that Kant already made so large. Habermas, for instance, strives to render as *incommensurable* as possible the free speech situation of human actors, on the one hand, and the technical efficacy of mindless nonhuman agents on the other. Like Kant, he makes it impossible to focus on what is in the middle, to study empirically the fabric of science-society tangles, but what was a tragedy in Kant becomes a farce with the modernists, since the number of quasi-objects thus ignored has become gigantic. Every issue of our world is tying science, society, and technology together, but those ties are said to be unlawful. They should not exist. The entire enterprise of the modernists eventually collapses and it is only by carefully abstaining from any sort of empirical work on science and technology that Habermas and his followers have been able to maintain the incommensurability of humans and nonhumans.

Every minute in laboratories scientists and engineers make them commensurable, but to see this, one has to move closer to the center, closer from "down there," one, that is, has to become nonmodern!

I have not found a word to describe what the relation has become in the hands of the honest Habermas's critics: the ugly term 'hyperincommensurability' might be fitting for the ugliest philosophical movement of the post-moderns who cannot any longer even take their own Critical stand seriously. Disappointed rationalists, they share all the features of rationalism, except hope; children of the *Critique,* they maintain the will to denounce and debunk, but have no longer any grounds to do so, and turn the Critical stand against themselves. What all the other schools had desperately striven to maintain that is, some kind of possible, even nostalgic, relation with the "other side," is now broken. Scientism and technicism now freely alternate with extravagant claims about societies and language-games, and self-destructive and self-deprecating jokes. Science and technology production, the making of natures and societies, are so far off-camera now that these critics cannot even understand what the field of science studies is about.

The only nice thing about postmodernism is that there is nowhere else to go after it, and that it brings to a close the whole modern enterprise. With postmodernism, we have finally reached the breaking point of the whole *Critique.* Everything happens as if the main schools of philosophy had tried to avoid the consequences of the growth of science and technology. The more intermediary cases there are, the more distant from one another the two poles of nature and of society become. A distinction becomes a separation, then a contradiction, then an unreconcilable tension, then an incommensurability, and ends up in complete estrangement. Let the tangles of sciences and societies grow and the philosophers will tell you that they should not exist. Enough is enough! One cannot indefinitely keep at bay the growing numbers of quasi-objects. One cannot indefinitely naturalize the whole collective building of society. One cannot forever ignore the practice of science- and society-making. The *Critique* was a parenthesis and it is now closing. The year 1989 might not be a bad date for its demise since it is the very same year that witnessed, on the one hand, the dissolution of socialism and, on the other, the dissolution of naturalism. The two poles of our one-dimensional yardstick have been under attack the same year! The fall of the Berlin Wall and the first conferences on global warming all point to the same transformation as the one I have outlined here: it is impossible to dominate nature and to dominate society separately. The modern *Critique* was a nice try but it makes less and less sense, and now that we have realized that neither Nature nor

Society can be put at the two opposing poles, it is better to recognize that we have never really been modern, that we have never ceased to do in practice what major schools of philosophy forbade us to do, that is to mix objects and subjects, grant intentionality to things, socialize matter, redefine humans. We, the Westerners, have never been all that different from the Others who were unjustly accused of confusing the representation of nature with Nature as it really is. It is about time to take up again the threads of the many philosophers squeezed out by the *Critique* in order to create a makeshift philosophy specifically adjusted to the need of our empirical science studies.

6. Conclusion

I hope to have clarified why it is impossible to escape from our blind alley without doing some philosophical work. The idea that science studies may ignore philosophy altogether, or be content with philosophy *of science,* or not build up its own metaphysics and ontology is foreign to me. Now that we have a touchstone to evaluate science studies, not only by their longitude, so to speak—along the realist/relativist axis—but also by their latitude—along the stabilization gradient—and now that we have freed our interpretations from the prejudices of the *Critique,* the whole task appears straightforward. We can go on doing what the best scholars among us have tried to do for years, but now we know why and when such efforts are at their best. We do not have to retrace our steps, to recant constructivism, and to become "reasonable" again, falling back on a "golden mean" wishy-washy position.

Like Antony, "I have neither wit, nor words, nor worth, action, nor utterance, nor the power of speech," but I hope to have convinced the philosophical reader that the whole domain of science studies, once its "social" attire has been set aside, becomes an exciting domain, not only for understanding science/society but also for easing philosophy out of its modern (and postmodern) predicament.

NOTES

*Laurent Bibard, Jim Griesemer, Tom Gieryn, Lisa Lloyd, Philip Kitcher, Mike Lynch, Ernan McMullin, Leigh Star, and Isabelle Stengers were all kind enough to try to make this argument a little less unreasonable. The editor of this volume tried in vain to mend my broken English as well as my broken arguments.

1. In the remainder of this essay, I use 'modern' in a technical sense: it means the political philosophy that separates entirely the *representation* of things (science) from the *representation* of humans (politics). Although both are representations, their common origin is hidden. I also use the word '*Critique*' not to refer only to Kant's works but to the whole idea of a critical stand starting from one or from the two opposite poles defined by Kant.

2. There are differences, indeed, to which I cannot pay justice in such a short space but my point is that they will become much more clearly visible when we shift from the one-dimensional yardstick to the other more complex measure to be defined below.

3. This is why I called this partition the "Modern Constitution of truth" (Latour, 1990a), 'Modernity' being defined as the complete separation of the representation of things—science and technology—from the representation of humans—politics and justice—not to mention the bracketing out of God. A Constitution is the written or unwritten document that settles the organization of power.

4. The use of the word 'transcendence' to describe Nature might seem unusual. But once the symmetry is built, the use of the term is inescapable: the content of scientific knowledge radically escapes from the making of social ties; it is transcendent to society, it is "out there." Symmetrically, society is not of our own making, as Durkheim has shown long ago, it is transcendent to our own individual construction, it is "up there." So we live—or rather, we used to live—in between those two transcendences, Nature and Society, none of them of our making, each of them providing its own explanatory resources.

5. 'Actant' is a bit of jargon borrowed from semiotics to make clear that we do not have to choose beforehand "mere things" and "human actors." The attribution to actants of volition and action (anthropomorphism) is as important to document as the attribution to them of "thingness" and "passivity" (phusimorphism). Natural forces are no more immediately given than are human agents (Latour, 1988, part II).

6. It is on purpose that I turn the metaphor upside down. I am against Alexander and his swift but deadly sword, and I want to rehabilitate the patient work of weaving back together science and society, the cart and the horse.

REFERENCES

Ashmore, Malcolm. 1989. *The Reflexive Thesis: Wrighting Sociology of Scientific Knowledge,* Chicago: University of Chicago Press.

Bloor, David. 1976. *Knowledge and Social Imagery,* London: Routledge.

Bradie, Michael. 1986. "Assessing evolutionary epistemology," *Biology and Philosophy,* 1, 401–459.

Callon, Michel. 1986. "Some elements of a sociology of translation: Domestication of the scallops and the fishermen of St. Brieux Bay," in Law (editor), 196–229.

————. 1989. *La science et ses réseaux. Genèse et circulation des faits scientifiques*, Paris: La Déecouverte.

Callon, Michel and Latour, Bruno. 1990. "Do not throw out the baby with the Bath School: A reply to Collins and Yearley," in Pickering (editor).

Collins, Harry. 1985. *Changing Order: Replication and Induction in Scientific Practice*, London: Sage.

Collins, Harry and Yearley, Steven. 1990. "Epistemological Chicken," in Andy Pickering (editor).

Giere, Ronald N. 1988. *Explaining Science: A Cognitive Approach*, Chicago: University of Chicago Press.

Latour, Bruno. 1987. *Science and Action*, Cambridge, Mass.: Harvard University Press.

————. 1988. *The Pasteurization of France*, with Appendix: *Irreductions: A Politico-scientific Essay*, Cambridge Mass.: Harvard University Press.

————. 1990a. "The leverage point of experiments," in H. Le Grand (editor), *Experimental Enquiries*, Dordrecht: Reidel, 49–80.

————. 1990b. "Postmodern? No simply Amodern. Steps towards an anthropology of science. An essay review," *Studies in the History and Philosophy of Science*, 21, 145–171.

————. 1991. *Nous n'avons jamais été modernes. Essai d'anthropologie symétrique.* Paris: La Découverte.

Law, John. 1986. "On the methods of long-distance control: Vessels, navigation, and the Portuguese route to India," in Law (editor), 234–263.

Law, John, editor. 1986. *Power, Action and Belief*, Keele: Sociological Review Monograph No. 32.

Lynch, Michael. 1985. *Art and Artifact in Laboratory Science: A Study of Shop Work and Shop Talk in a Research Laboratory*, London: Routledge.

Pickering, Andy, editor. forthcoming. *Science as Practice and Culture*, Chicago: University of Chicago Press.

Serres, Michel. 1987. *Statues*, Paris: François Bourin.

Shapin, Steve. 1982. "History of science and its sociological reconstruction," *History of Science*, 20, 157–211.

Shapin, Steven. 1988. "Following scientists around" (review of Latour's *Science in Action*), *Social Studies of Science*, 18, 533–550.

Shapin, Steven and Shaffer, Simon. 1985. *Leviathan and the Air-Pump*, Princeton: Princeton University Press.

Star, Leigh. 1988. "Introduction," Special Issue on Sociology of Science and Technology, *Social Problems*, 35, 197–205.

Woolgar, Steve. 1988. *Science: The Very Idea*, London: Tavistock.

INDEX